Chromatic beauty in the late medieval chanson

This book focuses on the analysis of late medieval chansons that use chromaticism in provocative ways. Covering the period of the trouvères through the mid-fifteenth century, Thomas Brothers examines the way in which accidentals function as an expressive tool, both at the level of local detail and at the level of overall design. The book is based on a comprehensive survey of accidentals in surviving sources for the period. From the perspective of this survey, Professor Brothers brings recent advances in analysis of late medieval music to the well-known textual problems surrounding musica ficta.

Chromatic beauty in the late medieval chanson

An interpretation of manuscript accidentals

Thomas Brothers · *Duke University*

CAMBRIDGE
UNIVERSITY PRESS

PUBLISHED BY THE PRESS SYNDICATE OF THE UNIVERSITY OF CAMBRIDGE
The Pitt Building, Trumpington Street, Cambridge CB2 1RP, United Kingdom

CAMBRIDGE UNIVERSITY PRESS
The Edinburgh Building, Cambridge CB2 2RU, United Kingdom
40 West 20th Street, New York, NY 10011–4211, USA
10 Stamford Road, Oakleigh, Melbourne 3166, Australia

First published 1997

Printed in the United Kingdom at the University Press, Cambridge

Typeset in Adobe Minion 10.5/14pt, in QuarkXpress™ [SE]

A catalogue record for this book is available from the British Library

Library of Congress cataloguing in publication data

Brothers, Thomas David.
Chromatic beauty in the late medieval chanson: an interpretation
of manuscript accidentals / Thomas Brothers.
    p.   cm.
Includes bibliographical references and index.
ISBN 0 521 55051 3 (hardback)
1. Monophonic chansons – 500–1400 – History and criticism.
2. Polyphonic chansons – 500–1400 – History and criticism.
3. Polyphonic chansons – 15th century – History and criticism.
4. Chromatic alteration (Music)   I. Title.
ML2502.B76   1997
782.4'3–dc21   96-50936 CIP MN

ISBN 0 521 55051 3 hardback

Contents

To my parents

This book offers a selective survey of accidentals in late medieval chansons. It emphasizes interpretation of how the accidentals function, not only at the level of local detail but also as part of an overall design. The chanson tradition from Gace Brulé through Guillaume Du Fay hardly needs an advocate today; it has long been a central area of research, and the music-loving public responds to it with more and more enthusiasm, year after year. But what is needed for this tradition is sustained critical attention. There are probably many reasons why late medieval music has not inspired a tradition of analysis and interpretation comparable to that which we take for granted with more recent music. The leading obstacle may be conceptual difficulties surrounding the control of pitch relations. This is the general problem to which the present study responds in a particular way: how inflections are used by the composer as an expressive tool. A trace of support for this approach comes from the defense of chromatic writing "for the sake of beauty" (*causa pulchritudinis*), first encountered at the beginning of the fourteenth century. Anonymous 2 implies that the "beautiful use" of accidentals occurs mainly in chansons. This book follows his lead by attempting to trace and interpret a tradition of using accidentals for expressive purpose in lyric song.

The foundation for my work has been a study of manuscript evidence for accidentals during the period *c.* 1275–1475. Thousands of chansons from this period survive. I have examined most of them, through microfilm copies (a handicap, but a necessary one) of the surviving sources and, when they exist, through modern editions. My goal has been to gain an overview of what the manuscripts report, an overview that is both chronologically broad and complete in concordances. Based on this survey, I have chosen songs that feature accidentals one might wish to highlight, for one reason or another, in musical analysis. The selected songs do not necessarily represent common practice; rather, they illustrate the beautiful use of inflections. Details differ from period to period, place to place, composer to composer, song to song. Thus, the broad basis of selection, *causa pulchritudinis*, yields a varied sampling of compositional practice. Indeed, diversity emerges as one theme of the study. I argue against overly systematic methods of analysis and in favor of the view that composers enjoyed a great deal of freedom around the point of how they might shape melodic and harmonic design.

On the other hand, patterns of use, when they emerge, have also guided the selection. Chapter 1 focuses more than the others on a single source; the chapter is mainly a report on accidentals in *Trouvère MS O (Paris, Bibliothèque Nationale, MS f. fr. 846)*. Unusual patterns of inflecting imply the possibility of common origins; we may be able to detect a coherent redactional style. Chapter 2 is a report on accidentals in polyphonic songs by Machaut, who is well known for bold and inventive chromaticism. Chapter 3 surveys the late fourteenth and early fifteenth centuries; since this repertory is hard to locate by time and place and even composer, any patterns of use that emerge are potentially helpful. And for Chapter 4, the main pattern of use may be the eventual absence of use. I argue that the emergence of a more seriously considered modal theory of polyphony in a treatise by Tinctoris should be related to a marked dropping off of expressively charged accidentals in songs by Okeghem, Busnoys and their contemporaries. Du Fay, on the other hand, carries on the tradition that is well represented in earlier music. Du Fay's death in 1474 occurs, coincidentally, at the very time Tinctoris has begun work on his modal treatise, dedicated to Okeghem and Busnoys. Thus, the chronological boundaries of the book loosely define a large-scale pattern of use. Not only that: patterns of use serve to legitimize musical analysis whenever it becomes possible to integrate the two. In these ways, details of the source (notated accidentals) are related first to analysis of individual works and second to analysis of style. These are the primary concerns.

Another obstacle to analysis of late medieval music is the routine problem of establishing musical texts, and in this regard music ficta is especially famous. The problem involves, first of all, variants, for the transmission of accidentals is often unstable from source to source. The beautiful accidentals drift through the written record like butterflies moving from flower to flower. But the larger and more provocative textual issue comes from the idea that conventional inflections were not notated, since educated performers understood from context how they should be applied. It is probably no exaggeration to say that this issue stands as one of the defining topics for twentieth-century musicology. This has been so at least since the time of Hugo Riemann, and it has continued to be so through the work of Edward Lowinsky, Margaret Bent, Lewis Lockwood, Karol Berger, Peter Urquhart and many others. One cannot write on accidentals today without addressing this problem, and it is touched upon in every chapter of the book.

Yet the problem of implied but unnotated inflections is not the main topic of this study, which is directed primarily towards uncovering and

interpreting compositional practice. As the first step in a working methodology, I put aside this contentious issue. My interest is in how we might best
make sense of what the manuscripts say in terms of compositional practice
rather than performance practice. Obviously, it is impossible to completely
separate the two, and it is necessary to address this linkage. My procedure
has been to comment on issues surrounding implied but unnotated
inflections whenever the results of the main orientation – survey of notated
evidence and analysis of beautiful use – seem to offer some benefit. Others
before me have insisted that what is needed for work on textual problems
surrounding musica ficta is comprehensive study of manuscript evidence.
Partly, I began this study with that in mind. My initial expectations,
however, gradually yielded to a different way of thinking about implied but
unnotated inflections. My commentary on this famously intractable
problem tends towards a position of arguing against the idea that performance practices for inflecting were universally understood on the basis of
musical context – this is the direction in which a survey of manuscript evidence has led. In my opinion, the theorists do nothing to dispel that point
of view, for, to the contrary, they present the topic of musica ficta as much
more a matter for *organizing* music than it is for performing music.
Performance is straightforward, they imply, once the singer understands
how to read accidentals. It is possible, I think, that they tell us little or
nothing directly about unnotated traditions.

I did not begin this book with the belief that unnotated inflections are a
myth, and I do not finish it with this belief. But I do conclude that the likelihood of a universally understood performance practice has been greatly
overestimated for the period *c.* 1275–1450. I do not aim to impose the view
that inflections are notated literally and completely on the entire repertory
of this period. Rather, my purpose is to draw attention to lines of analysis
that follow from it, while critiquing the bias towards a universal code for
performing unnotated inflections when that bias gets in the way. I offer no
general "solutions" as they are commonly conceived, to the great problem
of unnotated inflections, and the reader who is looking for those still-
elusive solutions will be disappointed (or will misread what I say). My
purpose, instead, is to highlight idiosyncratic use, to identify patterns of
use that indicate shared traditions, and to analyze how these function. As I
argue in the Introduction, it is reasonable to assume that practice was
diverse rather than uniform. Taking that point of view, one realizes that the
search for general solutions to performance practice is more complicated
than ever. The only general response to the problem of unnotated
inflections that I pursue throughout the text is this: if one assumes that

there is room for doubting the universal nature of the implied but unnotated tradition for inflecting, then here are various ways of making sense of a diverse written record.

Inevitably, one's point of view determines how one reads the evidence and pursues analysis, both at the level of textual criticism and higher-level interpretation. Since musica ficta is commonly thought of as a topic belonging more to textual criticism than to musical analysis, it is important to note the shift in emphasis that comes from viewing it as primarily a notated phenomenon. There is more to this point than simply weighing in on a controversial topic. For tensions arising over textual problems are inseparable from tensions arising between competing interpretations of pitch relations; I should like to expose this inseparability more fully than has been done before. In reviewing the possibility that the notated evidence for inflections is to be taken literally, I make some effort to draw the reader into alternative points of view, but my purpose has not been to give a balanced discussion of every controversy; the space for that is simply not available. Virtually any point of view under represented herein will be immediately accessible through Karol Berger's important survey of the theoretical discourse. What I wish to avoid is any impression of certainty, for I am less interested in arguing away the idea of unnotated inflections than I am in taking the present perspective as far as it can be taken. The researcher pursuing the intractable problems surrounding musica ficta may humbly take comfort in Darwin's encouragement: "How can anyone not see that all observation must be for or against some view if it is to be of any service?"

Thus, the book is shaped first by emphasis on the expressive potential of accidentals rather than musica ficta as a topic for performance practice; second, by emphasis on manuscript evidence rather than on imagined performance practices or on the testimony of music theorists. The survey of manuscript evidence is restricted to a single genre, the chanson. This restriction is more than a practical matter: I argue that there is something to be gained by viewing accidentals in the chanson as a distinct phenomenon. The survey highlights continuity within this genre (with polytextual chansons excluded). It stretches across two traditional historiographic boundaries – that between trouvère monophony and ars nova polyphony, and that between ars nova (or, as a late development within ars nova, ars subtilior) and the early fifteenth century. It is a point of interest to discover continuities as well as discontinuities in the contributions made by inflections to lyric expression over this broad span of time.

I have tried to take advantage of recent gains in analysis of the late medieval chansons, especially from the work of John Stevens, Hendrik van der Werf, Richard Crocker, Carl Dahlhaus, Sarah Fuller, Daniel Leech-Wilkinson, Alejandro Enrique Planchart, David Fallows, Reinhard Strohm, Howard Mayer Brown, and Leeman Perkins. One goal of the book is to integrate observations about manuscript evidence for accidentals with these recent analytical advances. A great debt is owed to Karol Berger's well-known survey of music theory pertaining to musica ficta. The work of Margaret Bent, Andrew Hughes, Klaus-Jürgen Sachs, Jan Herlinger, and Oliver Ellsworth on music theory has also been indispensable. Likewise, the book benefits from the great harvests of insights that have accrued through many close codicological studies (too few of them cited in my text). And the book would not have been possible without the advantage of the many fine editions that fill our library shelves; it is the lack of broad accessibility to the repertory that causes problems again and again in earlier studies, I believe.

The conventions for making the music examples were selected partly out of an interest in diplomatically representing accidentals as they occur in the late medieval sources and partly with the intention of making the music accessible to the general reader. Only accidentals signed in the cited sources are represented. Each accidental is transcribed according to my sense of which pitch it is first meant to inflect; in the example, it is placed directly in front of that pitch. Thus, the problem of duration is left open, as are all other editorial problems related to inflections. Accidentals are translated into the modern system, so that the two different medieval signs (square *b* and round *b*) are represented as sharps, naturals, and flats; I also make these translations verbally when I refer to inflections in the text. (For example, the square *b* placed on *c* is referred to as *c*-sharp and the square *b* placed on *b* is referred to as *b*-natural.) Asterisks above the staff indicate a transition to a new staff in the manuscript or a clef change when these are potentially relevant to the duration of an accidental. (For example, the cantus of Machaut's *Biauté qui toutes autres pere*, m. 36, experiences a clef change, then, in m. 37, a staff break.) Signature accidentals are carried according to the source, even if they appear to be pre-empted by another accidental during the course of the line. (For example, the tenor of *Biauté qui toutes autres pere*, part 2, carries *b*-flat in the signature throughout, even though *b*-natural is signed internally.) Voice parts are indicated even if there is no indication in the original source (as there never is for "cantus"). *Mensurstriche* are used for the purpose of avoiding the modern eye's impulse to associate an accidental with the measure in which it appears. Generally, the reduction of note values is 2:1, but this follows the varied practices of modern editions that I have relied upon; spelling of Old French also follows modern editions I have used. The trouvère examples follow standard procedures (standing for van der Werf, for example) of indicating syllable counts at the top of the example and numbering the lines of the stanza; a rhythmically neutral style of transcription is used. Bracketed words and pitches indicate editorial suggestions for lacunae from the original source. The polyphonic examples do not indicate ligatures or coloration; since almost all of the examples are available in other modern editions, the reader can easily retrieve that sort of information for further inquiry. Letter notation for pitch follows the medieval system (see the Introduction) except when reference is made to a pitch without implying any specific octave location, in which case capital letters are used.

Many songs are mentioned and analyzed in this book, and it has not been possible (nor would it have been profitable) to explain every textual decision upon which analysis is based. Similarly, the examples may bring to mind various textual problems that have been left unmentioned. To the reader who looks at a musical example, considers the analysis of it that I offer, and still has questions about this or that particular inflection – or, more likely, absence of an inflection – I can only say that there is much work left to be done on musica ficta, and that I would be pleased if the present critique eventually makes even a small contribution to answering those questions. Textual matters come to the foreground of the discussion occasionally. In Chapter 1, there are some comments to make about collation between *MS O* and other, less inflected trouvère sources. In Chapter 2, *De toutes flours* serves as a case study for analysis of variants; in Chapter 3, *Medée fu* does the same. The "good examples" in which one can integrate textual criticism with musical analysis turn out to be discouragingly few. Most of the time, one has to rely on intuition, which one hopes to educate as thoroughly as possible. If there are better textual grounds for analysis in the future, that will probably be due to expected gains in *Quellenverständnis*.

It is a pleasure to acknowledge some of the many debts that I have incurred in writing this book. While working on it, I often thought of my main teachers in the field of early music – Lawrence Bernstein, Joseph Kerman, Richard Crocker, and Richard Taruskin. It would please me if each were able to find a little bit of himself in this book. I first developed several of the main themes – the importance of the *difficilior lectio potior* argument and the manipulation of harmonic syntax — in a paper that was read at a meeting of the Southeast Chapter of the American Musicological Society in February of 1993; a revised version was then read at a national meeting of the Society in November of the same year. Two articles were prepared in 1994 and 1995 for *Studi Musicali* and the *Journal of Musicology*. I thank Alejandro Planchart and Anthony Newcomb for timely comments during the early stages of my work; likewise, Alexander Silbiger and Timothy McGee each commented extensively on the Introduction and early chapters. I owe much to the deep knowledge and kind generosity of these scholars. Part of Chapter 3 was read at the First International Conference on Gilles de Bins, dit Binchois, October 1995, in New York City; I am grateful for comments from several participants, particularly Edward Nowicki. At Duke University, Anna Harwell and Andrea Johnson provided reliable research assistance. Patrick Macey, Daniel Leech-Wilkinson, Hendrik van der Werf, and David Fallows each helped me to think through various parts of the book. David Fallows, Alejandro Planchart, and John Nádas made materials available to me without which this study would not have been possible. For Chapter 3, John Nádas shared with me the benefit of his expertise, and James Haar wrote an extensive response to an overview of the entire book; I am extremely grateful for the generous assistance of my North Carolinian neighbors. The music library at Duke, under the direction of John Druesedow, has been a steady and friendly resource. Larry Todd helped to move my work forward at a number of turns. Julie Cumming read the penultimate draft, and her extensive commentary improved the final draft immensely. Peter Williams discussed the book with me from my first thoughts about it through the final draft; for his advice I am particularly grateful. Brad Maiani provided expert service in setting the musical examples, which Duke University kindly paid for through one of several research grants that supported my work.

My children, Joseph Leo and John Roger, don't quite know what musica ficta is, but they still helped. My wife, Tekla Jachimiak, knows more than she probably had planned on knowing, and she helped in many ways. My parents, Don and Phyllis Brothers, have supported all of my ambitions for a very long time, and the dedication of this book to them is a very small token of my gratitude.

Introduction: musica ficta, *causa pulchritudinis*

Also, false music has been invented for two reasons, namely, because of necessity and because of beauty in melody itself. The reason of necessity arises because we could not have a fifth, a fourth or an octave, as in the places examined in the chapter on proportions. The reason of beauty is manifest in the *cantus coronatus*.[1]

Anonymous 2,
Tractatus de Discantu (*c.* 1300)

Musica ficta goes by many names during the period covered in this book. In the passage translated above, from the theorist known (after Coussemaker) as Anonymous 2, falsa musica designates precisely the same phenomenon that musica ficta, *synemmenon, coniuncta,* and musica colorata designate in other treatises. These are terms for pitches not included in the traditional Guidonian gamut, the core of which may have been conceived by Guido himself, and the fully developed late medieval codification of which was established by the thirteenth century.[2] Example I.1 contains the pitch field of the codified gamut, along with the late medieval letter notation that is used in this book.

Pitches outside of these borders and, especially, pitches within the borders but located elsewhere on the intervallic continuum are classified as "false," "invented," "hooked on," etc.[3] The sense of invention carried by the

[1] "Fuit autem inventa falsa musica propter duas causas, scilicet, causa necessitatis et causa pulchritudinis cantus per se. Causa necessitatis, quia non poteramus habere diapente, diatessaron, diapason, ut in locis visis in capitulo de proportionibus. Causa pulchritudinis, ut patet in cantilenis coronatis." *Anonymous II: Tractatus de Discantu (Treatise Concerning Discant),* ed. and trans. (passage quoted above with my slight modifications) by Albert Seay, Colorado College Music Press Texts/Translations, 1 (Colorado Springs: Colorado College Music Press, 1978), 32–3. See Jan Herlinger, *The Lucidarium of Marchetto of Padua: a Critical Edition, Translation, and Commentary* (Chicago: University of Chicago Press, 1985), 38–40, for discussion of the earliest source for this treatise. The treatise seems to have been formed as a combination of two previously independent works, as discussed by Seay, *Tractatus de Discantu,* i–iii.

[2] Karol Berger, *Musica ficta: Theories of Accidental Inflections in Vocal Polyphony from Marchetto da Padova to Gioseffo Zarlino* (Cambridge: Cambridge University Press, 1987), 5. See the hexachordal sorting of the gamut given by Berger on p. 9.

[3] To a degree, the outer boundaries of the gamut were in flux. Since these expansions were supported by analogy – that is, they were viewed as octave transpositions of pitches already belonging to the gamut – theorists show some hesitation in classifying them as belonging to the realm of musica ficta. For example, the Parisian Anonymous of 1375 (Goscalcus?) acknowledges that there are seven hexachords "by custom" (*secundum usum*). He then describes ten "hooked on" hexachords (*coniunctae*), beginning with *F gravis.* But he then immediately qualifies this lower hexachord as the eighth deduction "by art" (*secundum artem*). See Oliver B. Ellsworth, *The Berkeley Manuscript: University of California Music Library, MS. 744 (olim Philipps 4450),* Greek and Latin Music Theory 2 (Lincoln, Nebr.: University of Nebraska Press, 1984), 54–7. In the fifteenth century, on the other hand, high *ff* is sometimes signed with a flat to indicate that this pitch is indeed beyond the conventional gamut; some theorists regarded that practice as unnecessary and pedantic. For identification of the Parisian Anonymous of 1375 with the composer Goscalcus, see Klaus-Jürgen Sachs, *Der*

Example I.1 The gamut with medieval letter notation (after *MS Ghent, Universiteitsbibliotheek, 70/(71)*, facsimile in Karol Berger, *Musica ficta*, 9)

term "musica ficta," therefore, has nothing to do with the modern-day notion of incompletely notated accidentals. Rather, the pitch has to be invented because it does not belong to the codified gamut. The phenomenon has a precise definition, since it is conceived in relation to a closed theoretical system.[4]

Not uncommonly, late medieval descriptions of the phenomenon move a step beyond abstract pitch sets when they refer to practical manifestations of the gamut, either through staff notation or on the monochord.

Petrus Frater dictus Palma Ociosa (1336):

> False music is that which cannot be found in the gamut of the hand, according to the theory of plain chant. . . . Furthermore, it should be noted, generally, that false music is properly defined as the placement of soft *b* or square *b* at unusual locations.[5]

Walter of Odington (*fl.* 1298–1316):

> These two changeable tones, *b* and *bb*, are called proper degrees of the monochord; however, the rest of the changeable tones are called false music, not because they

Contrapunctus im 14. und 15. Jahrhundert, Beihefte zum Archiv für Musikwissenschaft 13 (Wiesbaden: Franz Steiner, 1974), 184; Sachs's suggestion is supported by Anna Maria Busse Berger, *Mensuration and Proportion Signs: Origins and Evolution* (Oxford: Oxford University Press, 1993), 175.

[4] Karol Berger would expand this definition so that it includes not only pitches that are external to the Guidonian gamut but also any irregular solmization: "a feigned step does not have to differ in pitch from the true one found in the same place. All that is necessary in order for a step to be feigned is that its syllable be feigned"; *Musica ficta*, 13. This puts an emphasis on solmization that I would resist. At the very least, it should be observed that this point of view does not ring true for the thirteenth and fourteenth centuries. Berger invokes Jacques de Liège in support. But when this

theorist speaks of false music, it seems clear that his interest is in the irregular placement of tones and semitones – that is, the inflections. Jacques refers to hexachordal syllables more extensively than other theorists because he is writing mainly about plainchant. But his understanding of false music is the same as his thirteenth-century predecessors and his fourteenth-century followers. The matter is clear during this period and clouded only later by theoretical overlay.

[5] "Falsa musica est quae non potest inveniri in Gamma manus secundum artem plani cantus . . . Praeterea notandum est in generali, quod falsa musica dicitur proprie, quando locabitur *b* molle vel *b* quadratum in locis non usitatis." *Compendium de discantu mensurabili*, edition by Johannes Wolf, "Ein Beitrag zur Diskantlehre des 14. Jahrhunderts," *Sammelbände der Internationalen Musikgesellschaft* 15 (1913–14), 513 and 515.

are dissonant, but because they are outside [of the regular disposition of the monochord] and were not used by the ancients.[6]

And, from the end of our period, Johannes Tinctoris, in his dictionary of musical terms (1475):

A *coniuncta* is the placement of round *b* or square *b* in an irregular location.[7]

During the twentieth century, musica ficta has often been presented as a topic of great mystery. But it is useful to begin our survey by recognizing the relatively simple and straightforward way that the topic is presented during the period *c.* 1275–1450.

*

The value of the brief passage from Anonymous 2 quoted above is its reference to a "beautiful use" of musica ficta; this signals the potential significance of chromaticism for musical analysis. Subjective judgments from this period are so rare that we need to make the most of every word.

The theorist gives two reasons for using musica ficta. The first, the "reason of necessity," is frequently mentioned in treatises from the thirteenth century through the sixteenth. As its title implies, *Tractatus de Discantu* is mainly about basic techniques for making polyphony, and it is routine to invoke the necessity rule in this context. Musica ficta is needed to adjust fifths, fourths and octaves, to make these intervals perfect when they would not be otherwise. For example, in order to get a perfect fifth above *b*-natural (which belongs to the gamut) one must inflect with *f*-sharp (which does not). Or, in order to get a perfect fifth below *b*-flat one must inflect with *E*-flat. As the theorists often say, one would not be able to form vertical sonorities properly if one were limited to the traditional pitches of the Guidonian gamut.

Anonymous 2's report on the necessity rule is as routine as the other reason he gives for using musica ficta is rare, and for this reason the statement is precious, even though it is also brief and vague. One could argue that the necessity rule itself has something to do with beauty, for properly ordered polyphony is indeed a beautiful thing. But by introducing *cantus coronatus* at this point, the theorist seems to be directing his thought away from polyphony. At the least, the pairing implies a complementary rela-

---

[6] "Due autem voces mobiles, scilicet *b* acuta et *bb* superacuta sunt proprie voces monocordi; reliquas vero vocant falsas musici, non quod dissone sint, sed extranee, et apud antiquos inusitate." *De speculatione musice*, in *Scriptorum de Musica Medii Aevi: Nova Series a Gerbertina Altera*, ed. E. Coussemaker (Paris: Durand, 1864), I: 216.

[7] "Coniuncta est appositio *b* rotundi aut *b* quadri in loco irregulari." *Terminorum Musicae Diffinitorium*, edited and translated by Carl Parrish as *Dictionary of Musical Terms* (London: Collier-Macmillan, 1963), 14.

tionship, and it may even carry a sense of opposition. Now, "beauty" can be a simple word, signaling personal, subjective reaction, or it can be a complicated word, signaling rigorous involvement with a philosophical system.[8] We may find ourselves, even in the late twentieth century, unwilling to recognize a simple usage in a medieval treatise on music theory. But the larger context of this passage suggests that the theorist uses the word not in the sense of systematic regard for rational order but, rather, just the opposite – as a way of valuing departure from such systematic ordering.

That speculation is aided by the fortunate fact that *pulchritudo* is used several times in close succession and with reference to three compositional devices.[9] First it is presented as a justification for parallel motion. The text explains that even though contrary motion is one of the foundations of discant, it is beautiful to use occasional and brief parallel motion. Second, "beauty" is used to justify dissonance. The logic is exactly the same: discant must be composed mainly of consonances, which provide the foundation of the polyphonic fabric, but deviation from this foundation is possible and it may be beautiful, since it makes the consonances more delightful. These two references shed light on the third, the beautiful use of pitches that do not belong to the Guidonian gamut. The theorist must be thinking in terms of optional and limited deviation from a systematic foundation; in the case of false music, that foundation is the traditional gamut. When the theorist allows deviations from contrary motion and consonance, he implies, in each case, a functional analysis: parallel motion provides variety, dissonance makes consonance sound fresh. For false music, there is only the tantalizing reference to "cantus coronatus." If, in his distinction between necessity and beauty, the theorist is thinking about two different ways of using musica ficta, then he may also be setting polyphony against monophony, the latter indicated by "cantus coronatus." It is easy to ground the necessity rule in the codifications of music theory, which pays close attention to the measurement of vertical intervals. For monophony, that grounding is not so easy; to the contrary, with monophony, musica ficta more obviously violates modality and hexachordal organization, the basic theoretical constructions that touch upon linear organization of pitch. If the application of musica ficta in monophony cannot be easily integrated

---

[8] In the exegetical criticism of D. W. Robertson, Jr., "the key principle of medieval aesthetics is the Augustinian definition of beauty as *convenientia*, which means the harmony that obtains when individual elements are organized according to symmetry and hierarchy in order to form a whole." The characterization of Robertson is by Lee Patterson, *Negotiating the Past: the Historical* *Understanding of Medieval Literature* (Madison: University of Wisconsin Press, 1987), 33.

[9] Seay, *Anonymous II: Tractatus de Discantu* (*Treatise Concerning Discant*), 30–3. As noted already, the treatise seems to have been created through the bringing together of two separate works. These three references to beauty come at the beginning of the second treatise.

with theory, what better way to justify it than by simply acknowledging the potential for beauty?

"Cantus coronatus" had several meanings during the late Middle Ages, so it is difficult to pin down Anonymous 2. Sometimes the term means a prize-winning song. But this usage hardly seems to fit: if prizes were awarded to songs because of musica ficta, then we would find a lot more accidentals than we do find. In another usage, "cantus coronatus" may have carried connotations of royalty, but it is unlikely that Anonymous 2 is saying that aristocratic composers were particularly inclined towards chromaticism.[10] A reference that is both contemporary and compatible with Anonymous 2 offers the best help of understanding him. Johannes de Grocheio discusses "cantus coronatus" much more extensively, and there would seem to be no doubt but that Grocheio uses the term to designate a genre.[11] John Stevens and Christopher Page have independently identified this genre as that sometimes known today as the *grand chanson courtois*, the high-style song of the trouvères.[12] If we put Grocheio and Anonymous 2 together, the latter seems to say that optional deviations from the gamut are sometimes used in this repertory. This interpretation makes sense in light of the distinction between necessity and beauty: it would be natural to set sophisticated polyphony alongside a sophisticated monophonic genre in order to draw attention to different styles of using musica ficta.

To our benefit, the theorist steps out of a mode of discourse centered on a quantifiable phenomenon in order to make a more casual observation

[10] A more plausible interpretation has to do with a technique for ornamenting melody in improvisation, though I find that this interpretation, too, fits less well. Charles W. Warren translates *cantus coronatus* according to the more general sense of *coronare* ("to encircle") in light of Grocheio's reference to the melody being "crowned around the tones" (*circa sonos coronatur*). Warren imagines an improvisatory practice of ornamentation; in this light, one could read Anonymous 2 as referring to an improvisatory practice involving chromaticism. See Warren, "Punctus Organi and Cantus Coronatus in the Music of Dufay," in *Papers Read at the Dufay Quincentenary Conference, Brooklyn College, December 6–7, 1974*, ed. Allan Atlas (Brooklyn: Brooklyn College, 1976), 128–43; this possibility is discussed further in Chapter 1. On the range of meanings for "cantus coronatus," see Hendrik van der Werf and Wolf Frobenius, "Cantus coronatus," *Handwörterbuch der musikalischen Terminologie*, ed. H. Eggebrecht (Wiesbaden: Fritz Steiner, 1983).

[11] Johannes de Grocheio, *De musica*, facsimile edition, transcription and German translation in Ernst Rohloff, ed., *Die Quellenhandschriften zum Musiktraktat des Johannes de Grocheio* (Leipzig: Deutscher Verlag für Musik, 1972); English translation by Albert Seay as *Johannes de Grocheo: Concerning Music (De Musica)*, Colorado College Music Press Translations 1 (Colorado Springs: Colorado College Music Press, 1967; 2nd edn, 1973). See, however, the important discussion of Grocheio's text in Christopher Page, "Johannes de Grocheio on Secular Music: a Corrected Text and New Translation," *Plainsong and Medieval Music* 2 (1993), 17–42.

[12] See John Stevens, *Words and Music in the Middle Ages: Song, Narrative, Dance and Drama, 1050–1350* (Cambridge: Cambridge University Press, 1986), 431–2, 495, and 505; Christopher Page, *Voices and Instruments of the Middle Ages: Instrumental Practice and Songs in France, 1100–1300* (Berkeley and Los Angeles: University of California Press, 1986), 196 ff; and Page, *Discarding Images* (Oxford: Oxford University Press, 1993), 71 ff.

about practice. We may regard the passage as thirteenth-century recognition of a phenomenon that endured for a long time in the French chanson, both monophonic and polyphonic – the optional use of inflections according to no theoretically quantifiable purpose. We are invited to regard non-systematic or even strange applications as legitimate, as authorial or editorial, rather than as the bedeviling corruption of careless copyists. We are invited to focus on the expressive potential of accidentals, and to assess the contribution they make to the tradition of lyric song.

Au renovel

Au renovel (Ex. I.2), attributed to the celebrated trouvère Gace Brulé, will serve to focus our thoughts about how beautiful inflections might work in high-style songs. The version of this song of interest, in this regard, comes from *Trouvère MS O*, a manuscript distinguished by its substantial number of songs that have optional inflections. Chapter 1 is largely given to songs from this manuscript, and we shall see there how this collection provides a stylistic context for *Au renovel*; the weight of consistent practice inspires confidence both in *MS O's* readings, idiosyncratic though they may appear in isolation, and in the possibility of advancing interpretation of them. Since the manuscript was probably compiled around 1300, somewhere in the region north of Paris, it is relatively near in time and place to Anonymous 2. Gace Brulé, long dead by 1300, may well have composed a melody that is still represented in surviving sources, to one degree or another, but, almost certainly, he did not have anything to do with the inflections transmitted by *MS O* (the only manuscript to transmit the song with any inflections at all). Example I.2 compares *MS O's* redaction with that from *MS K*, which represents a mainstream of transmission; it is possible that the former was based on the latter. The following interpretation of *MS O's* melody does not depend on the view that we have before us a revised version of the melody transmitted by *MS K* and other sources, but that is one way to look at the situation.[13]

13 All surviving versions of the song are presented by Hendrik van der Werf, ed., *Trouvères-Melodien*, Monumenta Monodica Medii Aevi (Kassel: Bärenreiter, 1977), I: 358. Facsimile editions of the two sources cited in Example 1.2 by Pierre Aubry and A. Jeanroy, *Le Chansonnier de l'Arsenal (Trouvères du XIIe-XIIIe Siècle)* (Paris: Geuthner, 1909), 54; and Jean Beck, *Le Chansonnier Cangé: Manuscrit français no. 846 de la Bibliothèque Nationale de Paris*, Corpus Cantilenarum Medii Aevi, ser. 1, 2 vols. (Paris: University of Pennsylvania Press, 1927), f. 3. The surviving sources date from long after Gace Brulé died, so there is no way of knowing whether he was responsible for any of the known versions of the melody (the poem, as usual, being transmitted more stably, causing less suspicion about authority). This is a typical situation for trouvère songs. Yet, and this is also typical, most of the melodies resemble each other closely enough to encourage the

Example I.2 *Au renovel* by Gace Brulé, according to *Trouvère MSS O*, f. 3, and *K*, f. 54 (poem after *The Lyrics and Melodies of Gace Brulé*, ed. and trans. Samuel N. Rosenberg and Samuel Danon [New York: Garland, 1985], 100, which is based on *MS O*)

Example I.2 (*cont.*)

6. Ire   et   es - maiz   qui   m'est   au   cuer   pro - chain - ne;

7. Car   fins   a - mis,   a   tort   a - choi - so - nez,

8. Est   mout   so - vent   de   le - gier   es   fra - ez.

During the *frons* (phrases 1–4), *MS O* conforms to the reading transmitted by *MS K*. Moving into the *cauda*, phrase 5 likewise holds no surprises. But with phrase 6, *F*-sharp is introduced. *F*-sharp leads to a cadence on *G*, and it is surely significant that this cadence, too, is unique to this manuscript; the agreeing manuscripts all move to *F* at the end of this phrase. The digression indicates an interest in cadential diversity. The agreeing manuscripts feature cadences on *D*, *C*, and *F*, and to this plan the reviser whose work is preserved by *MS O* adds *G*. Clearly, *F*-sharp has been introduced to highlight the wayward cadence.

assumption that Gace did compose a melody that formed the basis for later revisions. Among the eleven copies of the song that survive with musical notation, six (*Trouvère MSS K, L, N, P* and two copies in *X*) agree with one another down to details of no consequence; two others (*MSS U* and *M*) concur in most important details. Hence, version A in the example, taken from *MS K*, is confirmed by seven additional readings. Important variants transmitted by *MS O* are not repeated in any other source. The suggestion that the more widely circulating version was known to the person responsible for the redaction preserved in *MS O* follows from general trends in the repertory (see Chapter 1).

With phrase 7 *MS O* is back in agreement with the main group. But the final phrase of the stanza is marked by another important revision. *F*-sharp returns, and it does so not in connection with a wayward cadence on *G* but as part of a neumatic ornament on the penultimate syllable. The inflection recalls, in a slightly coy way, the wayward cadence from the end of phrase 6; read in this way, it suggests a slight pull toward *G* at the conclusion of the stanza. In this version of the melody, as in all the others, *D* emerges as the primary pitch in a hierarchy that the listener projects upon the song. But the unsuspected late drift through *F*-sharp undermines this hierarchy. *F* natural is still an important pitch in *MS O*'s redaction, for it is emphasized in phrases 1–5, and it returns between the *F*-sharps of phrases 6 and 8. The cross relation gives added force to *F*-sharp, and it heightens the sense of an unstable melodic flow.

The first *F*-sharp has cadential logic to recommend it. Judging it in isolation, one can easily invent a theoretical precept to justify it: "raise leading tones at cadences." No such statement from the period exists, but then Anonymous 2's reference to *cantus coronatus*, slender as it is, may be the only reference to musica ficta in trouvère songs that we have. The only way to arrive at such a precept is by inference from practical evidence. But, as we shall see, the repertory is hardly consistent on this point of practice. What emerges, in many cases, is that only *some* cadences on *some* pitches are inflected. Hence, even if the precept "raise leading tones at cadences" were mentioned by a theorist from the period, manuscript evidence speaks against uniformity and in favor of selective application. The first *F*-sharp in *MS O* does indeed highlight the cadence on *G*, but it seems important that this cadence is inflected while others are not.

The second *F*-sharp is completely optional; there is no rule one could invent to justify it. And, as I have argued, it makes an unsettling contribution to the design. We do not find applications like this in thirteenth-century motets, but we find enough of them in high-style songs preserved by *MS O* to suggest a consistent style of redaction. Thus, manuscript evidence supports the interpretation of Anonymous 2 that we have already advanced: that the theorist is comparing a polyphonic application to a monophonic one, and a theoretically codified application to one whose only justification is beauty, subjectively determined.

The attraction of variety may be the most basic way to understand Anonymous 2's regard for beauty. And the principle of variety accommodates a great deal; to analyze it more deeply, we will be on our own, without a contemporary witness. It is nice to have Anonymous 2's generalization, vague though it is, since so much emphasis in modern-day research on musica ficta has followed a path different from that which he seems to open up. Emphasis is usually placed on re-creating lost and foreign conceptual systems for controlling pitch relations. Understandably enough, musicology has tended to look for rules ("raise leading tones at cadences"); in contrast, we have read Anonymous 2 as praising applications for which there are no rules. He may even be sanctioning applications that contradict the rules; that is certainly what he does when he allows dissonances and parallel motion. This may seem like a lot to make out of a small comment, but much has been made in different directions, out of even less. There have been two main orientations towards musica ficta in modern musicology: the topic is viewed as a branch of performance practice, and it is viewed in terms of music theory. Both orientations lead to emphasis on systematic rules, yet from manuscript evidence – which, in my opinion, must be regarded as the *primary* evidence – one often gains the impression of inconsistent and at times unsystematic practice. Consequently, doubt surrounds the entire topic. From such a great distance, there can be no certainty, and the simple phenomenon may be read in contradictory ways. One must explore the potential of a well-defined point of view, which becomes an anchor in a sea of floating signs. To establish that the theorist is not talking about systematically codified applications but is, instead, praising applications that have no basis in theory, turns out to be no small matter.

In this book, the focus is on the quirky inflections, the ones that in one way or another call into question the hegemony of uniform, theoretically codified rules. Treatises from the late Middle Ages were written for specific purposes, and they may be of only limited use for higher-level interpretation. They may have been written for the education of beginners; or they may demonstrate how to abstractly organize discrete quantities of sound. The emphasis, in each case, is on codification; in neither case will there be much occasion to discuss idiosyncratic inflections. But these may be just the kinds of inflections that we should attend to in our efforts to get closer to the musical legacy of the late Middle Ages. It has often been observed that interpretation must not be limited by the basic concepts and terms of the period.[14] Marie de France insisted that the ancient authors did not necessarily shy away from obscure meanings in their work. Instead, they offered future readers the opportunity to gloss the text and discover meaning. The act of glossing, in Marie's opinion, may bring to the reader the benefit of increased subtlety of mind.[15] We would do well to hold to

[14] For a clear statement of this position, see Daniel Leech-Wilkinson, "Machaut's *Rose, lis* and the Problem of Early Music Analysis," *Music Analysis* 3 (1984), 9.
[15] The passages are quoted and discussed in David Hult, *Self-fulfilling Prophecies: Readership and Authority in the First Roman de la Rose* (Cambridge: Cambridge University Press, 1986), 96.

such a lofty purpose in our study of this ancient music, whose beauty one
can sense even if its firm grasp remains beyond reach.

Chromaticism as digression

Musica ficta begs to be treated as a central issue for musical analysis. This is
true, first, because the phenomenon brings us into direct confrontation
with basic problems of interpreting pitch relations. As we have seen, musica
ficta, by definition, stands outside of basic hexachordal theory; by extension, it stands outside of modal theory as well. It is possible to integrate
musica ficta with these theoretical sets through the concept of transposition, but that line of analysis turns out to be less than straightforward, as we
shall see. Musica ficta also needs to be placed at the center of analysis
because it plays an important role in harmonic syntax of fourteenth- and
fifteenth-century polyphony. Interest in pitch relations stems from the bias
– admittedly, a modern bias – that therein lies the key to musical expression. If every age brings its own concerns to the study of history, this analytical interest in pitch is surely one of ours. Did some composers care about
the details of melodic and harmonic design while others did not? Did
composers think about chansons in terms of modality, or was that irrelevant? If it was irrelevant, what was relevant? There will never be firm
answers to these questions, but they are questions we cannot avoid.

Anonymous 2 may be read, most neutrally, as recognizing variety as the
justification for using inflections that have no theoretically quantifiable
purpose. We may push him slightly, in the direction of a more decisive
interpretive strategy. The definition of musica ficta, as we have seen, is
precise: it is a matter of all pitches that do not belong to the Guidonian
hexachordal gamut (which I shall also describe as the "diatonic pitch
field"). Therefore, an inflection may be regarded as a digression or deviation from this diatonic pitch field. And if we think of the gamut as a rational
construction, one complementary to and interdependent with modality,
then musica ficta stands as an irrational phenomenon. We need to consider
the possible ramifications of this point of view, to sift out qualifications of
it and shades of understanding that lead from it. Throughout the Middle
Ages, music was the envy of other arts because of the theoretical rigor that
came from its association with number and order. That same theoretical
rigor provides us with a way to open up interpretive strategies based upon
the notion of digression.

It is true that theorists were not happy with the idea of defining musica ficta as a phenomenon that existed outside of basic theory. A substantial discourse (reviewed below) shows them striving to bring the phenomenon into theory by redefining the gamut; they want to abolish the dichotomy between the diatonic pitch field and the false or invented pitches. Judged from one point of view, this discourse was not successful: the Renaissance inherited the concept of musica ficta, defined precisely as it had always been defined. And at the practical level, too, it may be doubted that the discourse was ever successful. For in many of the songs featured in this book, musica ficta is used as something special; this will be the case particularly when cross relations are prominent. Thus, compositional practice supports, to a degree, the notion derived from theory: that musica ficta stands theoretically as a disruption of the diatonic order. To be sure, that is not always the case; we are not dealing with a monolithic phenomenon. For example, accidentals may be used to transpose the diatonic order. It is not uncommon to find a trouvère song notated at two different pitch levels, in precisely the same intervallic pattern, with musica ficta used in one version for the purpose of preserving that pattern. And there are, of course, other kinds of applications by which an inflection represents not the stroke of irrational disruption but, rather, that of rational ordering. But the more basic point is that even though musica ficta was readily available to composers of vernacular song, it never became a "normal" feature of the pitch field. The majority of chansons from this period make sparing use of it. Many use it not at all. Typical use of the diatonic pitch field forms a context in which atypical use of a chromatic pitch field stands out.

Moreover, the special status of musica ficta was confirmed by its routine absence from plainchant, which had a universal presence and which featured the diatonic gamut mainly if not exclusively.[16] This practical situation was solidified by the pedagogical role of the hexachordal gamut. Learned musicians knew the diatonic pitch field as the main part of early training, internalizing it to the degree that the singer could respond to the mere pointing to a knuckle with the appropriate intervallic negotiation. A dichotomy of pitches, a distinction between those belonging to the Guidonian gamut and those outside of it, was deeply embedded in the culture.

One way to relate this notion of musica ficta as digression to contemporary thought is by analogy with rhetoric, where digression was one of the standard devices, or "colors" (*colores*). Geoffrey of Vinsauf lists digression as the sixth means of expanding verbal discourse:

[16] I am aware that there is some evidence for performance of plainchant with deviations from the gamut (see Chapter 1). One may assume, however, that those would have been relatively rare; they would have been no less special than inflections in vernacular song.

If the line of discourse needs to be stretched further, step outside of the bounds of the matter, recede a bit, and devote your pen to other things; but do not digress so widely that it will become burdensome to regain your place. This manner of Amplification requires a restrained talent, lest the course of the Digression be longer than is proper.[17]

Analogies between rhetoric and music were commonplace during the thirteenth century, so it is not inappropriate to relate this passage to Anonymous 2's "beautiful use," which we have defined as optional deviation from the diatonic pitch field.[18] "Digress, but not so far as to lose the way back" – that dictum is easy to follow in music, easier than in rhetoric, perhaps. I shall use the word "discursive" to describe songs that have many digressions or make prominent use of digression. ("Discursive" has several meanings; it is used here in the sense of the *Oxford English Dictionary*'s "running hither and thither.") *MS O*'s redaction of *Au renovel*, in which accidentals lead the piece through varied and unexpected areas, stands as a good illustration.

Johannes de Grocheio suggests that vernacular songs and polyphony (*cantum civilem et mensuratum*) are not governed by the modal system; this position is important for our understanding of the beautiful use of musica ficta.[19] We have already noted the similar use, by both Grocheio and

---

[17] "Si velit ulterius tractatus linea tendi,/Materiae fines exi paulumque recede/Et diverte stylum; sed nec divertere longe/Unde gravet revocare gradum: modus iste modesto/Indiget ingenio, ne sit via longior aequo." Edition and translation by Ernest Gallo, *The Poetria Nova and its Sources in Early Rhetorical Doctrine* (Paris: Mouton, 1971), 42–3.

[18] The term "musica ficta" seems to come from *verba ficta*, the term for a neologism. See F. Alberto Gallo, "Beziehungen zwischen grammatischer, rhetorischer und musikalischer Terminologie im Mittelalter," in *International Musicological Society, Report of the Twelfth Congress Berkeley 1977*, D. Heartz and B. Wade (Kassel: Bärenreiter, 1981), 789.

[19] Grocheio, ed. Rohloff, *Die Quellenhandschriften zum Musiktraktat des Johannes de Grocheio*, passages on 124 and 152; the first passage is given also by Page, "Johannes de Grocheio on Secular Music," 19–20; it is cited also by Harold Powers, "Mode," in *The New Grove Dictionary of Music and Musicians*, ed. Stanley Sadie (London: Macmillan, 1980), XII: 397. In support of Grocheio one might tentatively cite an anonymous fourteenth-century treatise which speaks of: "irregular music [which] is called rustic or layman's music . . . in

that it observes neither modes nor rules" ("Irregularis autem dicitur cantus rusticanus sive laycalis . . . eo quod neque modis neque regulis constat"). And one might also cite Jerome de Moravia, who describes alternate tunings for the viella, saying that they are needed because it "is necessary for secular and all other kinds of songs, especially irregular ones, which frequently wish to run through the whole hand" ("necessarius est propter laycos et omnes alios cantus, maxime irregulares, qui frequenter per totam manum discurrere volunt"). Both quotations and translations from Shai Burstyn, "The 'Arabian Influence' Thesis Revisited," *Current Musicology* 45–7 (1990), 135–6. For further discussion of this point on the irrelevance of modes for trouvère music, see the literature cited by Burstyn, and see especially van der Werf, *The Chansons of the Troubadours and Trouvères* (Utrecht: A. Oosthoek's Uitgeversmaatschappij, 1972), 46–59. More sympathetic to modal analysis of troubadour (and, by implication, trouvère) melodies is William Mahrt, "Grammatical and Rhetorical Aspects of Troubadour Melodies," in *The Cultural Milieu of the Troubadours and Trouvères*, ed. Nancy van Deusen (Ottawa: Institute of Mediaeval Music, 1994), 116–24.

Anonymous 2, of the term "cantus coronatus," and here would appear to be an opportunity to extend this connection: by recognizing the importance of musica ficta in polyphony and in the *cantus coronatus,* Anonymous 2 may be read as also acknowledging lack of modal control; the two go hand in hand. If we accept that modality does not provide a syntactic ordering of pitch in the chanson – and, to anticipate the argument that will be laid out in the last chapter of this book, I find that position to be valid until the generations of Okeghem and Busnoys – then we are in a position to recognize an idiom for which the *flexibility* of melodic discourse is a value. In the absence of a universal, *a priori* syntax for controlling pitch relations there are many possibilities. It is easy for composers to manipulate pitch idiosyncratically, and that is just what the notated record for accidentals in chansons suggests they did. Ease of manipulation also makes it much more difficult for us to interpret the results. The musical situation finds a linguistic parallel. Medieval writers of Latin do not always show the strict and consistent regard for vocabulary, grammar and usage that is characteristic of their classical forerunners. Their lack of rigor makes it difficult to work with variants in medieval Latin texts.[20] The same problems, flexibility of syntax and difficulty in assessing variants, characterize late medieval music, and to an even greater degree. Furthermore, they are both signalled by musica ficta. Syntactic flexibility may be one key to analysis of how musica ficta functions, and it may also be one key to understanding the unstable transmission of accidentals. Thinking of the phenomenon in this way, it is a mistake to force the irregularities of practice into the uniform molds that theorists inevitably recommend.

Emphasis on syntactic flexibility puts the spotlight on subtlety and idiosyncrasy. That subtlety is an important value for late medieval music comes as no surprise. The challenge is how to uncover it, in the face of rough transmission, and then how to interpret it, in the absence of substantial guidelines to higher-level interpretation from the period. How the analyst conceives of modality, for example, and its relationship or non-relationship to vernacular songs represents a fundamental step that moves interpretation of accidentals in one direction or another. There are (at least) three ways to think about the relationship between musica ficta and mode:

---

[20] "The linguistic and stylistic canons of classical Greek and Latin are relatively strict and well defined, whereas the vocabulary, grammar, and usage of many medieval authors (especially when an oral prehistory is in question) is often not certain enough to allow reliable discrimination between variant and error." Edward J. Kenney, "Textual Criticism," in *New Encyclopaedia Britannica: Macropaedia,* 15th edn (Chicago: Benton, 1981), xviii: 194.

(1) musica ficta causes transposition of the mode; (2) it stands at a secondary level and has no effect on mode; (3) it represents a departure from mode. There are obvious examples of the first case, but it is probably a limited phenomenon; how far one takes this approach in musical analysis is a contentious problem that demands careful attention. The view that accidentals stand in a secondary position has been persuasively rejected, in my opinion.[21] I would prefer to see how far analysis can be taken in the third direction, for which purpose we may claim the tentative support of Grocheio and Anonymous 2 when they imply that modality does not govern polyphony and secular songs and that chromaticism is a source of beauty. From this position, analysis is led into a view of accidentals as tools for achieving variety, subtlety, digression and even irrationality.

Once may object that it is, perhaps, all too easy for the modern mind to leap into the exotic beauties of irrationality. Yet "irrational" is a suitable way to describe a piece that *cannot be reduced* to a single, hegemonic category. This may happen on two levels: the pitch field may be erratic and unstable, due to emphasis on a cross relation; and there may be no single pitch that dominates hierarchically, due to discursive design. *F*-sharp in *Au renovel* both disrupts the pitch field and undermines the strength of the final cadence. The concept of mode is customarily used to assert rational control of both levels – dominance of a unified pitch field and of a single pitch. And if mode is a rational construction, then undermining mode is an irrational activity.

Binchois' celebrated *De plus en plus* will serve to extend this point, and it will also bring our inquiry round to the polyphonic chanson.

De plus en plus

From the period of the polyphonic chanson, there survives only a single, distant echo of Anonymous 2's "beautiful use" of musica ficta. It comes approximately a century later, in a treatise attributed to the composer Philippotus de Caserta (*c.* 1400):

> Boethius invented musica ficta for two reasons, namely, because of necessity and because of beauty in melody. We have the reason of necessity because we cannot

---

[21] For this view, see Carl Dahlhaus, "Tonsystem und Kontrapunkt um 1500," *Jahrbuch des Staatlichen Instituts für Musikforschung Preussischer Kulturbesitz 2* (1969), 7–18; and also Dahlhaus, "Relationes Harmonicae," *Archiv für Musikwissenschaft* 32 (1975), 208–27. See Karol Berger's convincing critique of Dahlhaus's position: *Musica ficta,* 166–70.

have consonances in all locations, as stated above. The reason of beauty, however, is manifest in the *cantilena*.[22]

Anonymous 2's "cantus coronatus" (which would not have carried generic connotations by 1400) yields to the neutral "cantilena"; the substitution does nothing to weaken our assumption that the reference pertains to a genre. The simplest analysis of this passage is that it recognizes the tradition of using musica ficta optionally in chansons.

De plus en plus (Ex. I.3) is lightly inflected, and I use it here only partly to illustrate the chromatic tradition; just as importantly, there is a point to make about how "irrational" might be a useful word for describing certain approaches to organizing pitch. A single sharp in the cantus (m. 11) stands at the midpoint of the song, where it is given a certain prominence. When the song is performed through the complete repetitions of rondeau form, there will be returns to the beginning from this midpoint as well as continuations into the second part. If we regard the cantus in a polyphonic chanson – the only voice that receives text underlay, as a rule – as a melody that dominates the texture, then its inflections take on greater importance, potentially, than those in the tenor or contratenor. The cantus bears the main burden of projecting the poem with melodic elegance; in this sense, it may be regarded as having descended from the trouvère tradition of lyric melody. The gracefulness of the cantus in *De plus en plus* suitably fits the poem, a statement of desire for a distant lady. But Binchois wrote many graceful melodies; the success of this famous song cannot be accounted for on that basis alone. Parallel to melodic elegance is the enigmatic design, to which *f*-sharp makes a small but important contribution.

The cantus unfolds by outlining what we recognize today as an arpeggiated *C*-major triad (mm. 1–2). The clarity of this gesture is an important component in the design of the entire piece. The arpeggiation functions as a motto, one that immediately establishes a musical identity for the song; the standing of it is analogous, perhaps, to the poetic motto, "de plus en plus," which provides a verbal identity.[23] There can be no question, I think,

[22] "Boecius autem invenit fictam musicam propter duas causas, scilicet causa necessitatis et causa pulchritudinis cantus. Causa necessitatis est quia non poteramus habere consonantias in omnibus locis ut supra dictum est. Causa vero pulchritudinis ut patet in cantilenis." The entire treatise is edited by Nigel Wilkins, "Some Notes on Philipoctus de Caserta (*c.* 1360?–*c.* 1435)," *Nottingham Mediaeval Studies* 8 (1964), 95–9. On the attribution to Philippotus, see, most recently, Reinhard Strohm, "Filipotto da Caserta, ovvero i Francesi in Lombardia," in *In cantu et in sermone: For Nino Pirrotta on his 80th Birthday* ed. F. Della Seta and F. Piperno (Florence: L. S. Olschki, 1989), 65–74; as cited in Strohm, *The Rise of European Music, 1380–1500* (Cambridge: Cambridge University Press, 1993), 59.

[23] As Walter Kemp has noted, isolation of an opening gesture is something Binchois does more than a few times; see *Burgundian Court Song in the Time of Binchois: the Anonymous Chansons of El Escorial, MS V. III. 24* (Oxford: Oxford University Press, 1990), 18–32.

Example I.3 Binchois's *De plus en plus* (after W. Rehm, ed., *Die Chansons von Gilles Binchois*, Musikalische Denkmaler 2 [Mainz: Schott, 1957], 10–11, with adjustments according to *MS Escorial A*, f. 39v and 46v; emendation by Rehm at m. 11 in the contratenor follows *MS Oxford 213*, f. 67v)

Example I.3 (*cont.*)

but that *C* is the most important pitch in the first phrase, which is then given an "open" ending on *g* (m. 4). Phrase 2 immediately returns to the main pitch – not in the cantus, but in the supporting tenor and contratenor (m. 5). And when Binchois ends phrase 2 on *c* (m. 8), we can see how he has used basic principles of closure to make a single unit out of the first two phrases. Other songs from the early fifteenth century begin with similar arpeggiations. That is how Nicholas Grenon begins his charming *Je suy defait*, for example, and how Arnold de Lantins begins *Ne me vueilliés*. In each of those rondeaux, the final cadence is located precisely where the arpeggiated opening predicts it should be located; in each case, the endings bring full closure.[24] Binchois, on the other hand, uses the initial clarity of *De plus en plus* in the service of a very different strategy for organizing the

[24] *Ne me vueilliés* in *MS Oxford 213*, f. 44; ed. Charles van den Borren, *Pièces Polyphoniques Profanes de Provenance Liégoises (XVe siècle)*, Flores Musicales Belgicae (Brussels: *Éditions de la Librairie Encyclopédique*, 1950), 12. *Je suy defait* in *Oxford 213*, f. 32v; ed. Gilbert Reaney, *Early Fifteenth-Century Music*, Corpus Mensurabilis Musicae II (Rome and Stuttgart: American Institute of Musicology, 1955–83), VII: 3.

piece as a whole, and the case can be made that this strategy is what distinguishes the song from its more ordinary companions.

For what is most striking about *De plus en plus* is that it strongly emphasizes one pitch at the beginning, only to end on another. If the second half of Binchois' refrain were to move conventionally back to *C*, the piece would be straightforward; it would resemble Arnold's *Ne me vueilliés*. Instead, *De plus en plus* finishes surprisingly on *D*. *G* is emphasized in phrases 3 and 4; it is possible to think of it as a pitch of transition between *C* and *D*. It is true that the final cadence is prepared, ever so slightly, by the cadence on *D* in measure 15; nevertheless, it is hardly predicted in a way that makes it sound secure. And since *D* has already occupied *ouvert* position at the midpoint cadence (in the tenor), the final cadence is all the more ambiguous. One step above the main pitch is a traditional location for *ouvert* endings, and there is indeed something open-ended about this song. It is as if the ending is located one step up in the air. The song cannot be analytically reduced to a single pitch.

The song would be much less interesting if it routinely ended on *C*, and it would also be less interesting without *f*-sharp at the midpoint. As always, inflections represent details that may be more or less important, depending on the larger context. *De plus en plus* is transmitted by two fifteenth-century sources. *MS Escorial A* carries all of the accidentals given in Example I.3; they are all missing from the other source, *MS Oxford 213*. It is easy to imagine why *f*-sharp might have been dropped from the cantus. When, according to prescribed rondeau form, there is a return from this midpoint back to the beginning of the song, the *f*-sharp does resolve, with only a slight delay, on *g*, at the peak of the triadic motto. Harmonically, the resolution is irregular, but that is not too unusual for Binchois. When the cantus moves from *f*-sharp into the second part of the musical refrain, however, the inflection does not resolve at all. Modern-day editors have assumed (and I would agree) that the cantus sings *f*-natural in measures 13 and 14. As a result, *f*-sharp from the midpoint is left dangling, as if suspended in mid-air – now a tritone up in the air.

The inflection effectively causes a dislocation between the two halves of the musical refrain, and we may relate this dislocation to the unusual design. The first part of the refrain is stable and predictable while the second part is unstable and unpredicted.[25] To take away the sharp at the

---

[25] To comment further on the design, I would note the emphasis on *G* in both phrases 3 (mm. 9–12) and 4 (mm. 13–17), and how this emphasis lends coherence to the song. Also, the repeated minim figure in the cantus, the drop down to *G* and the leap up to *g* all connect the two phrases. These similarities bridge part 1 of the rondeau refrain with part 2, in spite of the intervening *f*-sharp. It is interesting to consider *bb*-flat in the cantus at measure 18 as a gesture that turns the line away from *cc*, the top peak of the melody and, as we have seen, the main pitch (by octave equivalence) of the first part.

midpoint is to smooth over the transition between the two halves. The deletion is a brief though significant trivialization of Binchois' "difficult" reading. Music theory from the period offers no help in understanding these events. Modal theory does not help us understand details like the triadic motto at the beginning, and it does nothing to elucidate the process of moving from stability to instability.[26] Theories of transposed hexachords do not help us understand the midpoint *f*-sharp. In this case, these conventional theories generate only hollow labels; they do not open up interpretive strategies for understanding the piece. We are challenged to abandon the conventional theories and to recognize a loose and flexible musical syntax, one that accommodates idiosyncratic inflections and idiosyncratic design. Indeed, this may be the general point to make about melodic and harmonic design in late medieval songs: there is a great deal of freedom in areas where we tend to look for systematic syntax.

The written records for both *Au renovel* and *De plus en plus* indicate instability in the transmission of accidentals, though the likely explanations for these cases differ. For *Au renovel*, there is no reason to believe that Gace Brulé had anything to do with accidentals notated in a late redaction. One is encouraged to imagine an editorial hand for whom accidentals represent one tool for melodic revision; they enhance the discursive qualities of line. With *De plus en plus*, Binchois was probably responsible for the accidentals, which were then stripped at some point, as the piece moved along its path towards the moment of copying into *Oxford 213*.[27] There is

---

[26] The song is analyzed modally by Bernhard Meier, "Die Handschrift Porto 714 als Quelle zur Tonartenlehre des 15. Jahrhunderts," *Musica Disciplina* 7 (1953), 195, n. 57. Meier suggests that textual phrases 1 and 2 are in mode 5, phrase 3 mode 6, and phrases 4 and 5 mode 2. To think of the piece as moving through three modes is to make artificial divisions in the cantus melody, divisions that do not advance analysis of the total design; it is also to gloss over the important sense that *C* is strong at the beginning while *D* is weak and capricious at the end.

[27] *MS Escorial A* is a Burgundian source (most likely) and Binchois may have been very close to it, so it is automatically assumed to be superior to *Oxford 213*. However, as Dennis Slavin has observed, *De plus en plus* and several other songs by Binchois copied into *Escorial A* by scribe A show signs of revision, perhaps made by the composer himself; hence, we should consider the possibility that the uninflected reading in *Oxford 213* documents an earlier version. See Slavin, "Questions of

Authority in Some Songs by Binchois," *Journal of the Royal Musical Association* 117 (1992), 22–61. A song associated with Binchois that resembles *De plus en plus* is the anonymous *Belle, esse dont vostre plaisir*, MS Escorial A f. 32v, ed. by Walter Kemp, *Anonymous Pieces in the Chansonnier El Escorial, Biblioteca del Monasterio, cod. V. III. 24*, Corpus Mensurabilis Musicae 77 (Neuhausen-Stuttgart: American Institute of Musicology, 1980), 21. It is a *C*-piece, with *f*-sharp in the cantus at the midpoint cadence. Kemp argues that Binchois wrote this and many other anonymous songs in *Escorial A*; see *Burgundian Court Song in the Time of Binchois*. I should mention the four sharps in the contratenor of *De plus en plus*. The first one, in measure 6, sounds a diminished fourth against the cantus. The second one, in measure 7, sounds, for a brief moment, a diminished fifth against the cantus. The third sharp in measure 11 sounds another diminished fifth against the cantus. And the last one, in measure 14, sounds yet another brief diminished fifth. Clearly, none of these dissonances should be

no way to know why that happened; certainly the manuscript shows no pattern of this. Yet it is not a unique occasion, and one can discover similar cases of accidentals having been removed completely. The phenomenon may be analogous to the removal of a song's verbal text, or to the deletion of "supplemental" voices like contratenors and triplums. In neither *Au renovel* nor *De plus en plus* is there any reason to believe that unnotated traditions for performing inflections accounted for the variants. What we have are not cases of the same piece being more or less explicitly notated; rather, we have less interesting and more interesting versions. Important details – beautiful details – are gained and lost. It has been claimed that the "apparently casual attitude to written accidentals only makes sense in the context of performing reminders to the performer," but that claim does not ring true for these two cases. And these cases are hardly isolated within the chanson tradition, *c.* 1275–1450.[28]

Unnotated conventions?

In the shop-talk of modern musicians who perform late medieval music, the term "musica ficta" means something slightly different from pitches not included in the Guidonian gamut. The sense of invention carried by the word "ficta" is associated not with the theoretical problem of pitches that stand outside the boundaries of the conventional gamut but, rather, with the notational problem of inflections that are implied but not notated on the page. Nowhere during the period covered in this book is the term defined in this way.[29] Falsa musica, musica colorata, *synemmenon, coniuncta* – each term has its own logic, and in every case that logic has nothing to do with the issue of unnotated conventions. "Musica ficta" became the dominant term because (one may assume) it was less offensive

"corrected" by a modern editorial hand that moves in the spirit of *causa necessitatis,* the theoretical precept of the period that recommends adjusting vertical intervals when they can be made perfect. We should regard the contratenor as designed to contribute a degree of harmonic tension. As I shall argue in Chapter 3, this is the way contratenors often function: they move in and out of agreement with cantus and tenor. No theorist qualifies his discussion of *causa necessitatis* with the aside that contratenors are exceptions to the rule. It is, rather, a matter of compositional practice going beyond the fundamental precepts of music theory.

[28] Quotation from Margaret Bent, "Musica Recta and Musica Ficta," *Musica Disciplina* 27 (1972), 88.

[29] Incorrect usage of "musica ficta" weaves in and out of the secondary literature, even in some relatively recent studies. The correct definition has been advanced by (among others) Joseph Levitan, "Adrian Willaert's Famous Duo *Quidnam ebrietas*: a Composition which Closes Apparently with the Interval of a Seventh," *Tijdschrift van de Vereniging voor Nederlandse Muziekgeschiedenis* 15 (1939), especially 182–90; Carl Dahlhaus, "Tonsystem und Kontrapunkt um 1500," 7–18; Margaret Bent, "Musica Recta and Musica Ficta"; and Karol Berger, *Musica ficta.*

than "falsa musica", less technical than *synemmenon* and *coniuncta*. Certainly, it did not become the dominant term because its meaning could be bent to include the idea of implied but unnotated inflections. The unnotated phenomenon is more explicitly covered in the High Renaissance (or, rather, it is more explicitly exposed).[30] Obviously, it is not a simple matter to project the High Renaissance view backwards over several centuries, so the whole matter is open to question.

The idea that unnotated inflections were a central part of the late medieval tradition has been heavily promoted in modern musicology, and it is not too much to say, perhaps, that this emphasis has made musica ficta one of the defining topics for the discipline. This was true by at least the beginning of this century, with the work of Hugo Riemann, who charged the musicologist with the project of recovering a lost practice that was self-evident during the period (*Verlorenselbstverständlichkeit*).[31] Riemann came to the topic through a focus on music theory, but it was, for him, far more than a theoretical matter. It was a theoretical matter that, on the one hand, showed the editor how to complete the musical text; on the other hand, it helped the scholar to locate that text in the historical evolution of tonality. Recovery of the lost and formerly self-evident practice makes the musical text comprehensible to the tonality-educated ear.[32] Enjoying the improved perspective of the present day, it is all too easy to see the anachronism in Riemann's work. We are more likely to tolerate cross relations and less likely to sweep away contradictions between practice and theory by invoking the vague workings of an unnotated practice. We are more sensitive to the genuine differences in melodic and harmonic design that distinguish this period from later periods. Through a century of musicology, we have indeed become closer to late medieval music.

Yet the belief that unnotated inflections were obvious is still very much alive, and many scholars have come to accept it as a given fact of late medieval music, in spite of the poor support for it by writings from the period. As I have already explained, the main purpose of this book is not to dispel this idea; yet it is necessary to critique some of the basic premises that come along with it, in order to advance on the main line of inquiry –

---

[30] For the sixteenth-century evidence, see Lewis Lockwood, "A Sample Problem of *Musica Ficta:* Willaert's *Pater Noster,*" in *Studies in Music History: Essays for Oliver Strunk,* ed. H. S. Powers (Princeton: Princeton University Press, 1968), 161–82.

[31] Hugo Riemann, *Verloren gegangene Selbstverständlichkeiten in der Musik des 15.-16. Jahrhunderts: Die Musica Ficta; eine Ehrettung,*

Musikalisches Magazin 17 (Langensalza: H. Bayer, 1907).

[32] As Raymond Haggh observes, Riemann must be "read in the light of his desire as an editor to make earlier music conform as much as possible to a major or a minor tonality"; commentary to his translated edition of Hugo Riemann, *History of Music Theory, Books I and II: Polyphonic Theory to the Sixteenth Century* (Lincoln, Nebr.: University of Nebraska Press, 1962), 396–7.

interpretation of beautiful accidentals. My main interest is to account for notated inflections, as they come and go. The music highlighted in this book was chosen because it lends itself to this project; certainly, one could argue in a different direction and, in doing so, end up highlighting a completely different set of pieces. My intention, in critiquing the matter of unnotated inflections as a conventional performance practice, is neither to dismiss the entire project nor to offer general guidelines ("solutions," as they are commonly conceived) that hold throughout a given repertory or period. It is very difficult, given the present stage of research, to generalize very far about practice; the approach taken here is to work at the local level, building out carefully from there, as the evidence allows. My main purpose in debating against the universality of unnotated conventions for inflecting is simply to advance the *possibility* that the manuscript evidence can be taken at face value. This literal approach to inflections may seem radical, but it is hardly new, and many scholars have come to it. Hendrik van der Werf, for one, takes this position with respect to trouvère songs, and several scholars have taken it in their study of Machaut's songs.[33] Other scholars have taken this position with respect to repertories that are transmitted with less cohesion and more variety.

Riemann understood that musica ficta is of central importance not only for recovering but also interpreting the musical text. With this I agree, though my orientation turns out to be nearly the opposite of his: it is to give priority to manuscript evidence over theoretical precepts, and it is to emphasize, in interpretation, a conception of pitch relations that differs in fundamental ways from the familiar tonal paradigm – or, better, it is to emphasize a *variety* of conceptions. Manuscript evidence implies that the situation was diverse rather than uniform. Perhaps this is the point upon which differently situated scholars can most easily agree: the period must have known diversity in practice. We must assume, I think, that diversity was the normal condition for virtually every aspect of the phenomenon. The theoretical discourse tends towards consistency and at times universality, but that should not lead us to believe that there were universally followed performance practices, not even that there was universality about the degree to which the musical flow is controlled by an *a priori* system of syntactic rules. Consider the diversity of scribal practice. This we have no trouble identifying, since we see the scribe's work (but not, necessarily, the

[33] Hendrik van der Werf, *The Extant Troubadour Melodies: Transcriptions and Essays for Performers and Scholars* (Rochester: Van der Werf, 1984), 41. On Machaut, see Johannes Wolf, *Geschichte der Mensural-* *Notation von 1250–1460* (rept. Hildesheim: Breitkopf und Härtel, 1965), 174–5; Bettie Jean Harden, "Sharps, Flats and Scribes: 'Musica Ficta' in the Machaut Manuscripts" (Ph.D. diss., Cornell University, 1983), *passim.*

composer's or the performer's) directly, on surviving pieces of parchment or paper. Some scribes put the signs above notes, some put them behind notes, some put them immediately in front, and some put them much further in front. And, as anyone who has worked in the period knows, more than a few scribes place accidentals in a way that can only be described, with barely concealed frustration, as very casually. Should we not assume that performance practice was also diverse, and that compositional conception may have been too? Manuscripts differ from one another, causing anxiety about textual authority and textual instability. Certainly we should imagine a variety of explanations for variants. Certainly conventions of performance, made explicit here but not there, do not account for all variants. I find it likely that they do not even account for most.

To support the possibility that manuscript accidentals are complete and should be read literally, I would summarize four main points:

(1) Theorists do not directly indicate that they are describing the workings of an unnotated tradition, or even that such a tradition existed.

From the sixteenth century, there are scattered indications that unnotated conventions for using inflections were an important part of polyphonic music. We lack this kind of evidence for the thirteenth, fourteenth and much of the fifteenth centuries. Theorists describe the conventions, but they never say to follow them routinely, in the absence of signed accidentals. More often than not, it seems, theorists state plainly that the signs square *b* and soft *b* should be used. To cite a few examples:

Johannes de Grocheio (*c.* 1300):

> The Moderns, moreover, in order to produce a notated record of consonances, of *stantipedes* and of *ductiae*, have added another [means of notating diverse songs] which they call "false music" because they extend the two signs ♭ and ♮, which they use to indicate a tone and semitone step in ♭ fa ♮ mi, to all other places with the same meaning, so that, where there was a semitone, they make it into a tone with ♮, so that there may be good line and good harmony, and in the same way, where there was a tone to be found, they compress it into a semitone by means of ♭.[34]

Prosdocimo de' Beldomandi (1412):

> It must be known, too, that the signs of musica ficta are two, round or soft *b* and square or hard ♭. These two signs show us the feigning of syllables in a location

---

[34] "Moderni vero propter descriptionem consonantiarum et stantipedum et ductiarum aliud addiderunt, quod *falsam musicam* vocaverunt, quia illa duo signa, scilicet ♭ et ♮, quae in ♭-*fa*-♮-*mi* tonum et semitonum designabant, in omnibus aliis faciunt hoc designare, ita quod, ubi erat semitonus, per ♮ illud ad tonum ampliant, ut bona concordantia vel consonantia fiat, et similiter, ubi tonus inveniebatur, illud per *b* ad semitonum restringunt." Ed. and trans. (with my slight adjustment) by Page, "Johannes de Grocheio on Secular Music," 21.

> where such syllables cannot be; wherever round or soft *b* is applied, we ought to sing the syllable "fa," and wherever square or hard ♮ is applied we ought to sing the syllable "mi," whether or not these syllables are in those places.[35]

Quotations from Petrus Frater dictus Palma Ociosa and Tinctoris given at the beginning of this Introduction also signal the importance of notating accidentals. Theorists had plenty of opportunities for discussing unnotated conventions. That they did not take them raises doubts that such conventions existed.[36]

On the other hand, musicologists have highlighted two remarks from our period that do signal unnotated conventions. Nevertheless, there are reasons for caution in each case; it seems likely that the intended applications are specific and restricted. The most famous passage is from Tinctoris, who states his case with characteristic force:

[35] "Item sciendum quod signa huius ficte musice sunt duo, scilicet b rotundum sive molle et b quadrum sive durum, que duo signa nobis demonstrant vocum fictionem in loco ubi tales voces esse non possunt, unde ubicumque ponitur b rotundum sive molle dicere debemus hanc vocem fa, et ubicumque ponitur ♮ quadrum sive durum dicere debemus hanc vocem mi, sive tales voces ibidem sint sive non. . ."; *Contrapunctus,* ed. and trans. Jan W. Herlinger, Greek and Latin Music Theory 1 (Lincoln, Nebr., and London: University of Nebraska Press, 1984), 74–7. Also, consider Anonymous 11 (before 1490): "One should recognize this: Writers of mensural music usually place a sign like this ## in places where *coniunctae* appear; but *organistae* usually join to these notes a sign in the form of a cross: +." "Et sciendum: mensuristae in locis in quibus committuntur coniunctae solent ponere tale signum ##; sed organistae ipsis notis solent adiungere quamdam virgulam per modum crucis +." Ed. and trans. Richard Wingell, "Anonymous XI (CS III): an Edition, Translation, and Commentary" (Ph.D. diss., University of Southern California, 1973), 37 and 210. Wingell translates *organistae* as "writers of polyphony." But surely the reference here is to organists (or, perhaps more generally, "instrumentalists"), for + is used in keyboard notation to designate the hard *b.*

[36] For the suggestion that Prosdocimo, in a different passage from the treatise I have quoted, alludes to unnotated conventions, see Margaret Bent, "Musica Recta and Musica Ficta," 77. Bent also cites (p. 89) Jean de Murs on transforming lower-neighbor whole steps into half steps; but this part of the treatise (*Quot sunt*

concordationes) has been placed in the third quarter of the fifteenth century by Klaus-Jürgen Sachs, *Der Contrapunctus im 14. und 15. Jahrhundert,* 180. A general comment that has been used to support the idea of unnotated conventions, *causa necessitatis,* comes from *c.* 1400: "Who will not marvel to see with what expertise in performance some musical relationship, dissonant at first hearing, sweetens by means of their skilful performance and is brought back to the pleasantness of consonance?" "Quis enim non mirare poterit quo proferendi magisterio proportio musicalis artis, primaria traditione dissona, eorum super artificiali docescat et ad consonantie gratiam reducatur?" Ed. and trans. Christopher Page, "A Treatise on Musicians from *c.* 1400: the *Tractatulus de differentiis et gradibus cantorum* by Arnulf de St. Ghislain," *Journal of the Royal Musical Association* 117 (1992), 20. Finally, it should also be acknowledged that several late medieval treatises refer to a tradition of applying unnotated inflections in performance of plainchant; see, for example, the *Quatuor principalia,* quoted and discussed by Margaret Bent, "Musica Recta and Musica Ficta," 89–90. Bent interprets this passage as an objection to improper solmization and to failure to sharpen melodic leading tones. Yet the passage is not unproblematic, and it is possible to read it differently. Without the qualifier *vix* in the second sentence, it is possible to read the entire passage as opposed to any unnotated inflections in plainchant. As a result, the objection which Bent takes as one made against improper use of solmization syllables would be taken, instead, as an objection against the inflections themselves.

> In order to avoid the hardness of the tritone, however, by necessity these two tones
> are formed from the fourth type of fifth. Nor then is it necessary that the sign of
> soft *b* be added; rather, if it is seen to have been added, it is said to be asinine. . .[37]

This claim has been used to support the twofold notion that the notation of musica ficta in polyphony is incomplete and that the way of completion was obvious.[38] Tinctoris's scorn is taken to signal the depth and breadth of the unnotated tradition. But it must be acknowledged that Tinctoris is not writing about the notation of musica ficta; rather, he is describing the notation of *b* (and *bb*), the only place in the traditional gamut that requires a choice between two steps on the same space or line of the staff. No one ever says that it is asinine to notate musica ficta, since the context will make it clear when it should be applied, and this suggests that it was not at all asinine to use the signs. Tinctoris is anticipated by the Parisian Anonymous of 1375:

> two signs are found in song – the sign *B* mollis and the sign *B* quadratum – which
> show where "fa" and "mi" ought to be sung; they can be placed in different
> locations in the hand – as I shall explain later concerning *coniunctae*, but they are
> frequently on *B-fa-B-mi*. In general, it is not necessary to notate them. For that
> reason, note that whenever one ascends from (or from below) *F-fa-ut* to *b-fa-#-mi*,
> indirectly or directly, or when one descends to *F-fa-ut* before ascending to *C-sol-fa-
> ut*, he ought to sing *fa* on *b-fa-#-mi* (by *b*), unless the song should end on *G*
> bassus.[39]

Reading "In general, it is not necessary to notate them" is less than straightforward. The context is precisely the same as that invoked by Tinctoris: avoid (what we call) indirect tritones. The clause in question directly follows acknowledgment that the signs are frequently used on *b*, so it is not unreasonable to suggest that it qualifies that acknowledgment. It may not have been intended to also qualify the inflections of musica ficta (*coniunctae*). For later, when the theorist turns more explicitly to musica

[37] "Ut autem evitetur tritoni durities, necessario ex quarta specie diapente isti duo toni formantur. Neque tunc *b* mollis signum apponi est necessarium, immo si appositum videatur, asininum esse dicitur . . ." *Liber de natura et proprietate tonorum*, ed. Albert Seay, Corpus Scriptorum de Musica 22/I (n.p.: American Institute of Musicology, 1975), 74; translated edition by Seay as *Johannes Tinctoris: Concerning the Nature and Propriety of Tones*, Colorado College Music Press Translations 2 (Colorado Springs: Colorado College Music Press, 1976), 11.

[38] For example, Edward E. Lowinsky, "Foreword" to *Musica Nova*, ed. H. Colin Slim, Monuments of

Renaissance Music 1 (Chicago: The University of Chicago Press, 1964), viii–ix.

[39] "in cantu inveniuntur duo signa, scilicet signum B mollis et signum B quadrati, demonstrancia ubi fa et mi debeant cantari, et possunt poni in diversis locis manus, ut patebit inferius de coniunctis, sed ipsa frequenter sunt in B-fa-B-mi, virtualiter licet semper non signentur. Pro quo nota quod quandocumque ab vel de sub F-fa-ut ascenditur usque ad b-fa-#-mi mediate vel immediate, et iterum descenditur usque ad F-fa-ut priusquam ascendatur ad C-sol-fa-ut, debet cantari fa in b-fa-#-mi per b, nisi cantus finiat in G basso." Ellsworth, ed. and trans., *The Berkeley Manuscript*, 44–5.

ficta, he says very plainly: "every *coniuncta* is signed by *b* or #, placed in an unusual location."[40] This casts doubt on universal claims one might want to make for "In general, it is not necessary to notate them." And since the theorist follows "In general, it is not necessary to notate them" by describing the convention of avoiding indirect tritones, we may assume that his words pertain to that restricted context – the same context Tinctoris has described. It is quite a leap to assume that he is alluding to a coded practice for all fourteenth-century music. This is a restricted remark, not a sweeping generalization about the obviousness of all inflections to all informed musicians.[41]

One may doubt the universal validity of these two statements not only because they are formed in such a restricted way but also because the specific convention that is being described – avoid indirect tritones – does not, itself, appear to have been universally observed. The evidence of practical sources, as we shall see, documents violations of this convention. Indirect and even direct tritones were sometimes valuable in the chanson tradition. Theorists may have liked the rule to avoid them, and most composers in most pieces may have liked that rule. But if we accept that there is at least a degree of clearly documented interest in using them, then our confidence about an unnotated convention for avoiding them must recede.

When theorists recommend how to notate musica ficta, they would seem to be speaking mainly to the composer and, by extension, to the scribe.[42] They do not tell us that they are documenting conventions of performance practice for realizing implied but unnotated accidentals, so, at the least, the possibility is left open that more than a few readings should be taken literally, as precise descriptions of the pitch content.

(2) Surviving manuscripts routinely show a troubling array of variants for accidentals, but there must have been various causes of this phenomenon. Taken by itself, the phenomenon does not strongly support the idea of unnotated conventions.

Two conditions drive the notion that accidentals were implied through conventions of performance practice that were understood by composer,

[40] "omnis coniuncta aut signatur per b aut # in locis inusitatis positum." Ellsworth, ed. and trans., *The Berkeley Manuscript*, 52–3.
[41] This interpretation runs contrary to the position taken by Karol Berger, "Musica ficta," in *Performance Practice: Music Before 1600*, ed. Howard Mayer Brown and Stanley Sadie (New York: Norton, 1989), 107.
[42] Peter Urquhart argues convincingly that Tinctoris is speaking to composers when he discusses how to use musica ficta when correcting vertical harmony; Urquhart argues that this particular statement cannot be used to support the idea that singers would have automatically corrected the problem. See "Cross-Relations by Franco-Flemish Composers after Josquin," *Tijdschrift van de Vereiniging voor Nederlandse Musikgeschiedenis* 43 (1993), 27–8.

scribe, and performer. First is the fact that manuscripts often disagree with one another in notating accidentals. Musical texts can be so unstable, giving rise to profiles for variants that are so troubling, that it becomes attractive to look for a blanket explanation, such as imagined conventions of performance practice seem to supply. The second condition is that the situations described by practical sources are often at odds with precepts prescribed by theorists. Since the precepts are laid out with some consistency, and with a tone that implies universal coverage, they may seem to take priority over the transmitted musical text – especially since troubling variants make it difficult to have confidence in the sources. Both conditions tell us something about the period, but they do not necessarily tell us anything about unnotated conventions for applying accidentals. There must be various causes for each of them. Recognizing this lessens the drive behind the belief that unnotated conventions were an active and universal force.

It has often been assumed that one explanation for variants is that conventions of performance practice are sometimes made explicit and sometimes not. I do not find this to be a convincing explanation for most cases of manuscript variants in chansons. We have already seen how this analysis accounts for neither Gace Brulé's *Au renovel*, where one thinks mainly of an actively edited text, nor Binchois' *De plus en plus*, where one thinks mainly of a deteriorating text. There must have been opportunities for intervention at many turns on the rough paths of transmission, about which we know practically nothing, as the music made its way into the large anthologies that we are forced to rely upon so heavily. As I have suggested, the situation may be analogous to text underlay. It is not uncommon to find a song carrying a substitute text or no text at all; similarly, it is not uncommon to find some or even all accidentals removed. Machaut's *De toutes flours*, for example, was almost certainly notated by the composer as a highly inflected piece (as we shall see in Chapter 2). It survives stripped of idiosyncratic chromaticism in one late source. Cesaris's *Bonté bialté*, a song that demonstrates extreme chromaticism, survives in only a single source, where it is stripped of the verbal text that the composer certainly had in mind. Du Fay's *Navré je sui* lacks both important inflections and its verbal text in a peripheral source. These are cases of wholesale distortion; minor distortions of both text underlay and accidentals are more common. The composer may have cared very much about these details, while the scribe of a large anthology may not have cared about them at all. The composer was interested in subtlety and nuance, or, as the case may be, in system and convention, and his interests may not have been shared.[43] The composer's idiosyncratic chromaticism may have been "corrected" by an editor, calling to mind the well-known editorial principle *difficilior lectio potior* – by which we are advised to "take the more difficult reading," under the assumption that idiosyncratic readings will be conventionalized or trivialized. It is rarely easy to gather together a strong array of evidence supporting this kind of analysis. But it may turn out that there are enough good cases to encourage the suspicion that corruption often determined the record of variants. Losses range in importance from surface details that make the design sparkle to details that signal and shape the design of the piece as a whole.

Musicologists have paid close attention to the possibility of unnotated conventions for inflecting because the matter is one of completing the musical text. Ironically, the effect of heavy emphasis on unnotated conventions is to devalue inflections. The feature of the musical text that the scholar works so hard to uncover becomes relatively unimportant. The same is true when emphasis is placed on viewing the phenomenon primarily as a matter of music theory. This will tend to be the case: when musica ficta is conceived mainly as a topic of universal conventions of performance practice or of universal precepts of music theory, normative usage will be emphasized and idiosyncratic usage will be marginalized or explained away. Taking manuscript evidence as a point of departure, this study moves in the opposite direction. As a result, there is more room for *lectio difficilior,* a standard approach to editing that has been largely absent from musica ficta studies due to heavy emphasis on normative practice. Making room for this principle means that it is more difficult to make generalizations. The only way to proceed is to isolate local tendencies through analysis which synthesizes as much evidence as possible – evidence of sources, style (assessed chronologically, by region and by composer), theory, and especially the design of a particular piece.

(3) There must be various causes for apparent discrepancies between the rules prescribed by theorists and the notated situations described in practical sources, including the likelihood that composers enjoyed the freedom to violate the conventions of their day.

Of course, it is possible that unnotated conventions for using inflections account for some discrepancies between theory and notated practice. But

---

[43] Graeme Boone observes systematic text underlay in Du Fay's songs; see "Dufay's Early Chansons: Chronology and Style in the Manuscript Oxford, Bodleian Library, Canonici misc. 213" (Ph.D. diss., Harvard University, 1987).

there must have been other causes, too. Surely there is corruption. It is also possible that, in some cases, the notation is coded in a way that is not completely clear to us.[44] It is just as likely that composers simply did things their own way, sometimes, in contradiction to conventional theory. The temptation to make too much out of music theory from the Middle Ages arises from the sheer distance separating us from the period, a distance that manifests both in conceptual alienation (the thinking is so foreign) and dimness of view (the picture is so incomplete). And there is a more subtle problem. One may detect, here and there, with various degrees of candor, the attitude that this music is more rooted in theoretical abstraction than later music is. Edward Lowinsky, for example, asserted candidly that "drawing a line between theory and practical music . . . conforms with the situation obtaining in the 19th and 20th centuries rather than with that of the 15th and 16th."[45] Lowinsky's bias is bound up with the complementary notion that the credit for breaking medieval shackles goes to Renaissance Man. This obsolete historiography, rooted as it is in nineteenth-century thought, did not benefit from the extensive knowledge of late medieval music that we enjoy today.

Without wishing to diminish the importance of studying music theory, one may suggest that too much weight has been put on theoretical conventions at the expense of manuscript evidence. Based on a survey of manuscript evidence, I find it impossible to avoid the impression that composers were willing to both selectively apply and deliberately contradict the paradigms described by theorists. It should come as no surprise that music theory is "regular" and conventional while compositional practice is "irregular" and unconventional. We cannot easily follow the universal mode of discourse that theorists are locked into. They may be locked into it either because they are writing for beginners, or because they are advocating a practice that is not widely followed – or simply because that is the way theorists think.

As always, one's point of view conditions how one reads the evidence. Ironically, it has been possible to think about the phrase "causa pulchritudinis" in a way that is, at heart, the opposite of how I have read it. Here is one of the best-known statements on musica ficta from modern musicology, again from Edward Lowinsky:

---

[44] For example, there may be conventions by which a sign is used only at the first appearance of a particular note but remains valid for all subsequent appearances of that note. This was a favored notion of Riemann's that he surely pushed too far; see Willi Apel, "The Partial Signatures in the Sources up to 1450," *Acta Musicologica* 10 (1938), 6.

[45] "The Function of Conflicting Signatures in Early Polyphonic Music," *The Musical Quarterly* 31 (1945), 229.

> The old teachings distinguish two reasons for *musica ficta*: *causa necessitatis* and *causa pulchritudinis*. Necessity and beauty are the parents of *musica ficta*. Necessity deals with rules pertaining to perfect consonances, beauty with rules pertaining to imperfect consonances. To the musicians of the time, they were of equal importance.[46]

This is not the place to try to reconstruct how Lowinsky arrived at this crisp and sweeping generalization.[47] For our purposes, it is sufficient to recognize how different this view is from that which we have drawn from Anonymous 2. The reference to imperfect consonances means, of course, that Lowinsky is not thinking about monophony, but there is an additional and more revealing difference. "Causa pulchritudinis" would seem to be more highly charged for Anonymous 2 than it is for Lowinsky, who uses it to describe systematic application at cadences. This systematic application is designed to contribute a reliable cadential formula that can be easily implemented by performers and easily recognized by listeners. Emphasis is placed on a rigid paradigm; in contrast, we have emphasized the idea of non-systematic use, of stepping outside of paradigms. The same evidence looks very different from different points of view.[48] The kind of inflection that Lowinsky is describing is one that we shall spend some time with – to avoid confusion, I shall refer to it as the "propinquity" application. There is evidence that during our period the propinquity application was manipulated in various ways; it was not simply a uniform and rigid practice. Lowinsky's systematic orientation is appealing in its simplicity, its presumed universality, and the solutions to textual problems that it offers. But for the period of *c.* 1275–1450, I think, it is misleading for just these reasons.

Consider an example of manipulated propinquity (Ex. I.4). According to theoretical convention, when a sixth expands out, in resolution to an octave, the sixth should be inflected so that it comes as close to the octave as possible – meaning that it should be a major sixth. Yet in *Le Basile*, Solage signs *b*-flat in the cantus before a cadence on *C/c* (tenor/cantus), thereby contradicting the propinquity rule. Based on the design of this song, we may project some good reasons onto Solage's decision to use this event and

[46] "Foreword" to *Musica Nova*, viii.

[47] Lowinsky was probably working mainly with Gaffurius. See Berger, *Musica ficta*, 122–3, for discussion of the relevant passage from Gaffurius.

[48] To continue this point, the passage from Philippotus, *c.* 1400, quoted above as a late echo of Anonymous 2, cannot be read as having anything to do with the paradigm Lowinsky sketches. Yet that is how Karol Berger reads it, and he does so, I suggest, as a result of his tendency towards reading the theorists for what they might report on performance practice, regardless of whether or not that connection is suggested by the text; for Berger's reference, see *Musica ficta*, 94 and 122–3.

Example I.4 Mm. 23–6 of Solage's *Le Basile* (after Gordon Greene, ed., *French Secular Music: Manuscript Chantilly, Musée Condé 564*, Polyphonic Music of the Fourteenth Century 19 [Monaco: L'Oiseau-Lyre, 1982], 97; adjusted according to *MS Chantilly 564*, f. 49v)

manipulate the convention (see Chapter 2). The broader point to make is this: if we accept the possibility that composers enjoyed the freedom to manipulate the basic precepts of music theory, then we must doubt the universal validity of these precepts as automatic guides to performers in the imagined tradition of imaginary accidentals.

At this point, it no longer seems radical to take the position that the notation of accidentals may be complete and precise. Modern-day work on musica ficta is conditioned by awareness of a range of possible positions. On one side of the spectrum stand extreme speculations like Riemann's (or another well-known project of Edward Lowinsky's: it is a short step from Riemann's "lost self-evidency" to Lowinsky's "secret chromatic art"). Then, at the other side, stands the position that musica ficta is primarily a notated phenomenon. From this sense of two extreme positions, opposed to one another, a reasonable middle ground appears to form. That middle ground would be the commitment to unnotated inflections, but on a rigorously restricted basis: one regards the unnotated practice as dependent upon the precepts described by theorists. But this is a false middle, since it disappears once we dismiss the extreme speculations. Without them, we are left with manuscript evidence and theoretical evidence, and the puzzlement about how to make sense of discrepancies between the two. In the face of a chaotic situation, with so much intractable evidence, it is tempting but ultimately unsatisfactory to rely on the certainty of theoretical postulates. The notated record, with its puzzling and diverse variants, implies not only lack of consistency but some delight in inconsistency. When manuscript evidence contradicts theoretical postulates, my response has been to place greater weight on the source and to try and detect a reason for the discrepancy. One is left with the stark possibility that the theoretical precepts, universally and consistently prescribed though they may be, have no prima facie validity as guidelines for discovering conventions of unnotated performance practices. If composers are free to contradict them, then the many cases in which they seem to ignore them appear in a different light. We may explain those cases by imagining a separation between theory and practice – or, a separation between the first stages of a pedagogical program and the final stages of high art. And in the end, it may turn out to be not a matter of holding fast to one approach or the other but, rather, of recognizing a pluralistic situation that is difficult to sift through.

(4) Theories of hexachordal solmization do not provide the missing link for uncovering unnotated conventions.

It is obvious that late medieval composers knew nothing of systems for organizing melody and harmony that are familiar to us, such as the system of common-practice tonality. But it is not so obvious how they used their own familiar systems, or, indeed, if they used them at all. Much has been made of theoretical discourse concerning the *coniunctae,* or "hooked on" hexachords. The topic is valued as one that may open up the lost performance practice for inflecting pitch, the self-evident practice that never occurred to Riemann – indeed, heavy emphasis on hexachords is a relatively recent development, having received a boost in several studies from around 1970.[49] The basic question is whether *coniuncta*-theory was designed for practical purposes or whether it was something less practical and more abstract. In chansons, I see only isolated examples of possible

[49] Bent, "Musica Ficta and Musica Recta"; Hughes, *Manuscript Accidentals: Ficta in Focus 1350–1450,* Musicological Studies and Documents 27 (Rome: American Institute of Musicology, 1972); Gaston Allaire, *The Theory of Hexachords, Solmization and the Modal System: a Practical Application,* Musicological Studies and Documents 24 (n.p.: American Institute of Musicology, 1972); Jehoash Hirshberg, "Hexachordal and Modal Structure in Machaut's Polyphonic Chansons," in *Studies in Musicology in Honor of Otto E. Albrecht* ed. John Hill (Kassel: Bärenreiter, 1980), 19–42. Building upon some of this work is Peter Lefferts, "Signature-Systems and Tonal Types in the Fourteenth-Century French Chanson," *Plainsong and Medieval Music* 4 (1995), 117–48. And so is Yolanda Plumley, *The Grammar of 14th Century Melody: Tonal Organization* and *Compositional Process in the Chansons of Guillaume de Machaut and the Ars Subtilior* (New York: Garland, 1996). These two studies came to my attention only as the present study neared completion. Also not considered here is Christian Berger, *Hexachord, Mensur und Textstruktur: Studien zum Französischen Lied des 14. Jahrhunderts,* Beihefte zum Archiv für Musikwissenschaft 35 (Stuttgart: Franz Steiner, 1992); on this see the persuasive critique by Sarah Fuller, "Modal Discourse and Fourteenth-Century French Song," paper read at the 1995 National Meeting of the American Musicological Society, New York City. One feels that the potential benefits from this hexachordal line of inquiry have hardly been exhausted, even while one questions the overly systematic reach of most of the studies just named.

applications. In general, the situation appears to stand as a classic illustration of theory following practice and providing an abstract gloss on practice.

The matter extends beyond the problem of uncovering unnotated conventions, for hexachordal theory has been invoked as the basis for systematic frameworks for analyzing pitch, especially in fourteenth-century music but in earlier and later music as well. Just as Riemann was inclined to use imagined traditions of performance practice in the service of reconstructing a lost harmonic system, so are scholars interested in hexachordal theory interested in using differently imagined traditions to reconstruct alternative systems. So, to argue that these theories have little practical value is no small matter. My approach in this book is to try to make sense out of the text as notated through one or more sources, and it is to welcome idiosyncratic efforts. Hence, I gain some benefit (I admit) from de-emphasizing hexachordally based theory, which is used to generate unnotated inflections and to support rigid systems of analysis. It is hardly possible to give due consideration here to the full range of hexachordally based interpretations, though there will be a few more opportunities to comment on specific details of recent scholarship in Chapters 2 and 3.

The earliest full description of *coniuncta*-theory comes from the Parisian Anonymous of 1375.[50] The basis for the theory is simple. In response to any inflection, signed with hard-*b* or soft-*b*, one may construct a hexachord, according to which the inflection represents *mi* or *fa*, respectively. *C*-sharp, for example, is taken as *mi*, generating a hexachord that begins with *ut* on *A*; and *E*-flat, taken as *fa*, generates a hexachord with *ut* on *B*-flat. In this way, the Parisian Anonymous describes ten "hooked on" hexachords. It is true that this full description of *coniuncta*-theory in 1375 is anticipated by several earlier references to non-traditional hexachords; nevertheless, a more telling antecedent is located elsewhere. It is located in *synemmenon*-theory of the mid- to late thirteenth century. *Synemmenon*-theory features tetrachords rather than hexachords, yet it clearly provides the proper context for the later *coniuncta*-theory. The connection between the two theories, one tetrachordally based and the other hexachordally based, suggests how

---

[50] The Anonymous of 1375 presents the earliest reference to *coniuncta*-theory; see Oliver Ellsworth, "The Origin of the Coniuncta: a Reappraisal," *Journal of Music Theory* 17 (1973), 86–109. An earlier reference to hexachords built on *D* and *B*-flat occurs in Petrus Frater dictus Palma Ociosa, *Compendium de discantu mensurabili* (1336); modern edition Johannes Wolf, "Ein Beitrag zur Diskantlehre des 14. Jahrhunderts," 515–16. There is also a peripheral reference from Theinred of Dover, a twelfth-century English theorist; see "Theinred of Dover," by Andrew Hughes, in *New Grove Dictionary of Music and Musicians*, XVIII: 731.

theoretical speculation can have a life of its own. It is easy to believe that this life had little to do with the workings of practice. For tetrachords certainly did not have a practical application related to the phenomenon of musica ficta, and this casts doubt on the practical application of later hexachordal theory, into which tetrachordal theory evolved.

Since composers needed falsa musica, the label "false" was troubling – "not false, but true and necessary," the theorists say.[51] Not enough has been made of the terminological struggle, lasting all through our period and into the sixteenth century, that signals the theoretical problem. "Falsa musica" yielded to "musica ficta," but the newer term still described a practice that remains outside of the systematic workings of music theory. Since the pitches are true and necessary, there should be a place for them in theory, and the direct way to accomplish this was by redefining the gamut. Italian theorists were less bothered than the French by the problem of reorganizing the gamut, but they did respond to the problem at least on the surface level of terminology. Marchetto of Padua found "musica colorata" a much better term than "falsa musica." Just as colors (*colores*, meaning any rhetorical device) are used in rhetoric to beautify sentences, so are musical "colors" used to beautify consonances, says Marchetto. In this way, he justifies the phenomenon even while keeping it as something apart from the rigors of music theory.[52] Prosdocimo follows Marchetto's approach. (Ugolino, who follows Prosdocimo in many things, is a significant exception to the Italian pattern, as we shall see.) The French theorists, on the other hand, are committed to the venerable tradition of spinning out abstract and rigorously ordered pitch fields, following the model from Antiquity that Boethius provided for them. The French theorists do this in

[51] Philippe de Vitry, *Ars nova*, ed. G. Reaney, A. Gilles, and J. Maillard, Corpus Scriptorum de Musica 8 (n.p.: American Institute of Musicology, 1964), 23; in "A Phantom Treatise of the Fourteenth Century? The *Ars Nova*," *Journal of Musicology* 4 (1985–6), 23–50, Sarah Fuller argues that Philippe's authorship of the treatise should be doubted. The earliest references to falsa musica are now placed *c.* 1200; see Christopher Page, *Summa musice: a Thirteenth-Century Manual for Singers* (Cambridge: Cambridge University Press, 1991), 96 and 177; further references cited on p. 96. An important discussion of terminology is in Levitan, "Adrian Willaert's Famous Duo *Quidnam ebrietas*," 182–90.
[52] *Marchettus of Padua: Pomerium*, ed. G. Vecchi, Corpus Scriptorum de Musica 6 (n.p.: American Institute of Musicology, 1961), 71. Thus, in Marchetto's use of

"musica colorata", the connection to Boethian discourse on the chromatic genera would seem to be secondary and almost coincidental (or, the theorist is combining the two meanings). Mainly, Marchetto thinks of "musica colorata" as a device for ornamenting a basic structure, just as the rhetorical colors are devices for ornamenting a speech. There is widespread usage of "color" in this way in music theory of the thirteenth and fourteenth centuries. It has not always been recognized that the basic definition is simply any identifiable technique that is used to beautify music, just as the basic definition in rhetoric is any discrete device. To make music with *colore ficticio* (invented color) is simply one technique among many. In addition to this passage from *Pomerium*, see also Marchetto's *Lucidarium in arte musice plane*, ed. Herlinger, especially pp. 148 ff.

the thirteenth century by working with tetrachords, and they do it in the fourteenth century by working with hexachords.

"*Synemmenon*" literally means "something hooked on"; "*coniuncta*" is the Latin translation, made by Boethius.[53] Since "*synemmenon*" had a Greek pedigree, it is easy to understand why thirteenth-century theorists turned to it in their efforts to legitimize false music. Undoubtedly, they also had access to more recent discourse in which "*synemmenon*" designated not only a hooked on tetrachord but also a fresh pitch, the soft *b*, generated by that tetrachord; the discourse runs through Hucbald (*c.* 900), Hermannus (*c.* 1050), William of Hirsau (1069), and John (*c.* 1100).[54] The *synemmenon*-tetrachord had been used to generate *b*-flat, so it seemed logical to use it in connection with the other altered degrees. Four mid- to late thirteenth-century treatises emanating from an intellectual milieu that found its center in Paris use "*synemmenon*" as a theoretically sanctioned substitute for "falsa musica." Two of these treatises, one presented as a continuation of Johannes de Garlandia's *De mensurabili musica*[55] and the

[53] For the passage from Boethius, see Anicius Manlius Severinus Boethius, *Fundamentals of Music*, trans. and with introduction by Calvin M. Bower, ed. Claude Palisca (New York: Yale University Press, 1989), 46. The connection between "*synemmenon*" and "*coniuncta*" is laid out clearly by Oliver Ellsworth, "The Origin of the Coniuncta: A Reappraisal."

[54] See Dolores Pesce, *The Affinities and Medieval Transposition* (Bloomington: Indiana University Press, 1987), for useful summaries: Hucbald, pp. 5–8, Hermannus, pp. 25–8, William of Hirsau, pp. 28–30, and John, pp. 44–7. John's *De musica*, of *c.* 1100, uses "*synemmenon*" to refer to *B*-flat above Gamma *G*; the treatise is translated in *Hucbald, Guido, and John on Music: Three Medieval Treatises*, trans. Warren Babb (New Haven: Yale University Press, 1978), reference on p. 128. Jerome de Moravia's (after 1272) incorporation of material from John demonstrates the availability of the earlier theories during the late thirteenth century; see Pesce (p. 57), and also Ellsworth, ed. and trans., *The Berkeley Manuscript*, 37.

[55] The reference comes in Chapter 15, transmitted, along with revised versions of Chapters 1 and 2 and several other additional and later chapters, only in the copy of *De mensurabili musica* compiled by Jerome de Moravia. Here there is a description of how to use the *synemmenon* to change the sequence of tones and semitones in discant; there seems also to be the implication of adjusting a minor third to make it major;

see *Johannes de Garlandia: De mensurabili musica: Kritische Edition mit Kommentar und Interpretation der Notationslehre*, ed. Erich Reimer, Beihefte zum Archiv für Musikwissenschaft 10–11 (Wiesbaden: Franz Steiner, 1972), I: 94–6. In his translation of the treatise, Stanley H. Birnbaum discusses the corruptions in the text, and the fact that the rules given must refer to polyphony rather than plainchant; *Concerning Measured Music*, Colorado College Music Press Translations 9 (Colorado Springs: Colorado College Music Press, 1978), 52, nn. 66 and 67, and 53 n. 69. It is not clear from the discussion whether "*synemmenon*" refers to simply an altered note or to an entire tetrachord; that ambiguity is intrinsic to the concept (see below). Reimer argues that Jerome was responsible for the additions to Garlandia's text. The important point for our discussion would seem to be that both Jerome, in compiling his supplement to *De mensurabili musica* (if, indeed, this is a valid analysis of the situation), and Anonymous 4, in the sections of his treatise which are likewise independent of Garlandia, work with the same material, though independently of one another. Reimer observes this general situation – that the respective passages show similarity in content but no direct dependence upon one another. Hence, these references to the practical application of *synemmena* probably stem from a third party, though perhaps not from Johannes de Garlandia. See Reimer, ed., *Johannes de Garlandia* II: 1–7 and 39–42, and I: 30–1.

other by Anonymous 4,[56] include practical discussion of how to apply *synemmena* in discant. The most complete explication comes from Jerome de Moravia, who describes a reorganized gamut.[57] The fourth treatise tells how to locate *synemmena* on the monochord.[58] These references are both diverse and complementary; we can assume that the glance towards tetrachordal structures was not merely the conservative whim of a single theorist but was, rather, a familiar topic. If that assumption seems risky, note that these references outnumber fourteenth-century references to *coniuncta*-theory. The purpose of this discourse is obvious: it is an attempt to reorganize theory so that it accommodates current practice.

With respect to musica ficta, *coniuncta*-theory is better known today, but it followed *synemmenon*-theory as a way to reckon with the phenomenon. It is a matter of a double translation, from one language to another and from one type of theoretical abstraction to another, since, for the late medieval theorists, "*synemmenon*" refers only to tetrachords, "*coniuncta*" only to hexachords. *Coniuncta*-theory comes late in the day, as an afterthought in the theoretical overlay to the phenomenon of musica ficta, and this chronological and conceptual sequence weakens its importance. It is possible that French musicians took a fundamentally different attitude towards inflections than Italian musicians took, and that they rigorously applied *coniuncta*-theory through an intricate system of solmization. But it seems easier to believe that both groups of musicians usually thought about the signs for musica ficta in a way that is not terribly different from the way in which we think about them today: a sign serves to identify, simply and directly, a location on a continuum of half steps. According to this way of thinking, tetrachordal and hexachordal theories represent little more than abstract glosses on this continuum.

---

[56] *De mensuris et discantu* is by the English theorist Anonymous 4 (after 1280); modern edition by Fritz Reckow, *Der Musiktraktat des Anonymus 4*, 2 vols., Beihefte zum Archiv für Musikwissenschaft 4–5 (Wiesbaden: Franz Steiner, 1967), I: 71–3. Recent suggestions for dating these treatises are given by Jeremy Yudkin: Garlandia, *c.* 1260; Anonymous 4, after 1280; Jerome de Moravia, between 1280 and 1304. See *De Musica Mensurata: The Anonymous of St. Emmeram*, ed., trans. and with commentary by Jeremy Yudkin (Bloomington: Indiana University Press, 1990), 33, n. 64.

[57] Jerome de Moravia (between 1280 and 1304) designates ten *synemmena* tetrachords, beginning on, respectively, *Gamma, A, C, D, F, c, d, f,* and *g,* in order to generate the *synemmena* pitches *A*-flat, *B*-flat, *D*-flat, *E*-

flat, *G*-flat, *d*-flat, *g*-flat, and *a*-flat; the tetrachord is defined as upward movement through semitone–tone–tone. The relevant passage is presented by Ellsworth, "The Origin of the Coniuncta: a Reappraisal," 97.

[58] The anonymous *Sequitur de synemenis* is edited and translated by Jan Herlinger in *Prosdocimo de' Beldomandi: Brevis Summula Proportionum Quantum ad Musicam Pertinet* (Lincoln, Nebr.: University of Nebraska Press, 1987), 123–35. *Sequitur de synemenis* and Anonymous 4's *De mensuris et discantu* are transmitted together in two English manuscripts. The treatises date from the late thirteenth century, and they report Parisian practice; for descriptions of the manuscripts, see Reckow, *Der Musiktraktat,* I: 1–16.

Theorists signal that there is both a practical side and a theoretical side to their discourse. The signal comes in both the early discussions of *synemmenon* and the later discussions of *coniuncta*. For each word has two definitions. The primary meaning, in each case, is the pitch generated by an irregularly placed semitone; it is this definition that allows the words to serve as synonyms for "musica ficta" (or "falsa musica"). Secondarily, "*synemmenon*" and "*coniuncta*" define tetrachordal and hexachordal patterns, respectively, and this secondary definition may be read as a theoretical gloss on practice, a tetrachordal or hexachordal gloss on the irregularly placed semitone. The purpose of the two-sided definition is that it serves to integrate theory and practice. The Anonymous of 1375 lays this out clearly:

> everyone can distinguish the syllables of any song and judge them as bound by reason, unless by chance some unusual song should turn up, which some call – but wrongly – musica falsa, others musica ficta; still others name it – and rightly – *coniuncta*. . . . For a *coniuncta* is the attribute, realized in actual singing, of permitting one to make a semitone out of a tone and conversely. Or rather, a *coniuncta* is the mental transposition of any property or hexachord from its own location to another location above or below.[59]

Falsa musica, called by whatever name and indicated by the signs soft-*b* and hard-*b*, is the practical reality – "not false, but true and necessary." It is the transposed hexachord that must be imagined.

Hence, "*synemmenon*" and "*coniuncta*" are better terms than "falsa musica" and "musica ficta" because they signal theoretical justification for a phenomenon that otherwise sits awkwardly outside of the rigors of music theory. If, as argued here, *coniuncta*-theory had little importance for either compositional practice or performance practice, then the significance of the theoretical discourse lies precisely here: the theoretical achievement is the *elimination of the concept* of "invented music" (or "false music"). There is no such thing, anymore, as a false or invented pitch; instead, there is an expanded and more accommodating gamut. Theorists abolish the dichotomy between pitches that are sanctioned theoretically and those that

---

[59] "potest uniusquisque voces cuiuscumque cantus discernere easque secundum racionem debite iudicare, nisi forsitan intervenerit aliquis inusitatus cantus, quem aliqui sed male falsam musicam appellant, alii fictam musicam, alii vero coniunctas eum nominant et bene . . . Est enim coniuncta quedam acquisita canendi actualis attribucio in qua licet facere de tono semitonum, et e converso. Vel aliter: coniuncta est alicuius proprietatis seu deduccionis de loco proprio ad alienum locum secundum sub vel supra intellectualis transposicio."

Ellsworth, ed. and trans., *The Berkeley Manuscript*, 50–3. *Sequitur de synemenis* explains that in common usage unusual divisions on the monochord are called "falsa musica," but "*synemmenon*," the designation used by philosophers, is preferable; see the edition by Herlinger, 128–9. The implication that "*synemmenon*" designates primarily the individual pitches themselves is also clear in Jerome de Moravia; see the passage quoted by Ellsworth, "The Origin of the Coniuncta: a Reappraisal," 97.

are not. The subtlety of this matter would seem to have been lost on a peripheral theorist like Ugolino, who explains both the invented pitches and the alternative hexachordal gamut completely in terms of a dichotomy between musica recta – a term usually avoided by the French theorists – and musica ficta. The whole point of the alternative hexachordal gamut had been to eliminate the dichotomy that Ugolino preserves. And Ugolino's treatise has been an important source for scholars who advocate the use of *coniuncta*-theory in the exegesis of polyphony.[60]

Still, Ugolino's lack of rigor, which leads to the incompatible use of the concepts of both musica ficta and *coniuncta*-hexachords, is revealing. We may take it as a manifestation of the fact that *coniuncta*-theory remained, for the most part, an abstraction. In practice, the concept of musica ficta held on; hence, my argument that the inflections hold their special status. They never – at least in the Middle Ages – become completely "normal" in the sense that theorists aim for by redefining the gamut. As I have argued already, this is so partly because of the status of the diatonic pitch field as the usual one for plainchant, partly because of the pedagogical standing of this pitch field, and partly because of the way in which composers use inflections. By slipping from the rigor of the French theorists, Ugolino's muddled presentation points up the discrepancy between theory and practice.

*

Scholars who see *coniuncta*-theory as the key that unlocks performance practice think of the music as hexachordally coded. The signs are read mainly as identifiers of hexachords. A single sign may generate a series of inflections or it may generate no inflection at all. This stands against the view that the main purpose of the signs is to inflect pitch, to locate a place on a continuum of half steps. The two views yield different orientations towards textual problems. For example, what appears to be a *b*-flat placed low may actually be a flat on *G* that signals *fa*, thereby generating not what we call *G*-flat but what we call *F*-sharp. In this example, the flat indicates

---

[60] *Declaratio musicae disciplinae*, edited and translated in Andrew Hughes, *Manuscript Accidentals: Ficta in Focus 1350–1450*, 21–37. Bartolomeo Ramis de Pareia scorns the Guidonian system, and he also ridicules Ugolino's casual use of solmization syllables, as well as his marginal status: "For the universal faith of modern writers in the Guidonian syllables has grown to such a degree because of the long duration of the custom, as when Ugolino of Orvieto, a recluse in the cathedral of Ferrara, begins to treat syllables he calls them Greek terms and adds: 'The Greeks had only five, namely, *re, mi, fa, sol, la*, lacking *ut*.' He makes this acceptable because their art starts from proslambanomenos, which is *a re*; from this point he completes his series. This indeed would not be brought to light and public view except as deserving to be considered laughable and ridiculous." *Musica practica*, trans. and ed. by Clement A. Miller (Neuhausen-Stuttgart: American Institute of Musicology, 1993), 95.

Example I.5a Mm. 1–14 of Franchois Lebertoul's *O mortalis homo/O pastores/O vos multi* (after G. Reaney, ed., *Early Fifteenth-Century Music*, Corpus Mensurabilis Musicae 11 [n.p.: American Institute of Musicology, 1959], II: 47; adjusted according to *MS Oxford 213*, f. 41v)

Example I.5b   *O mortalis homo*, mm. 20–1 (beginning of part 2)

the position of the half step, but it does not directly inflect the pitch with which it is associated. The flat makes sense only when one thinks of it as marking *fa* in a hexachord that starts on *D*.

This technique is used, but so rarely that we may speak of "irregular signing." My impression is that the usage is so isolated that it is difficult to accept it as an indication that *all* accidentals have hexachordal implications. Franchois Lebertoul's *O mortalis homo/O pastores/O vos multi* will serve to illustrate the particular example I have just explained.

A G-flat signature occurs in the cantus throughout and in the contratenor for the ballade's second part. Since the signature occurs several times in two voices, it cannot be explained away as a copying error. It makes sense to read it in the way I have just described: the flat indicates *fa* on *g* (and *G*), thereby inflecting *f* to produce what we call *f*-sharp. There are several internally signed *f*-sharps (one *f*-sharp in the cantus and one *F*-sharp in the contratenor) in this piece, and if one reads the signatures as I have suggested then these sharps are redundant. It is not hard to imagine how the redundancy could have arisen.[61] In the chanson tradition, irregular signing

---

[61] *f*-sharps make good sense in this song, both contrapuntally and melodically. Used in the *ouvert* ending, *f*-sharp is left dangling. The gesture is an idiomatic one for this period (see the discussion in Chapter 3 of Ex. 3.10a); it is often associated with the 4–3 appoggiatura figure that occurs here, which figure is used also with *c*-sharp in this piece. And for the contratenor at measure 21, *F*-sharp is a more likely inflection than *B*-flat in the tenor (suggested by Reaney as an editorial emendation; *Early Fifteenth-Century Music*, Corpus Mensurabilis Musicae 11 [Rome and Stuttgart: American Institute of Musicology, 1955–83], II: 47) to make a good vertical fifth, according to *causa necessitatis*. Similar

notation is used in the anonymous *Aylas! Quant je pans* from *MS Lucca, Archivio di Stato, 184*; modern edition by Gordon Greene, *French Secular Music: Rondeaux and Miscellaneous Pieces*, Polyphonic Music of the Fourteenth Century 22 (Monaco: L'Oiseau-Lyre, 1989), 42. According to Greene (pp. 172–3), the signatures contain redundant flats and sharps: the cantus has a signature of *d*-flat, *c*-sharp, *G*-flat and *F*-sharp, while tenor and contratenor both have *G*-flat and *F*-sharp. The sharp inflections serve harmonically, both for necessity and propinquity. The conventional format for conflicting signatures, with "extra" flats in the tenor and contratenor, is inverted. Karol Berger has stressed the harmonic logic behind this

like this may not go far beyond signatures, where it is used only exceptionally. It is easy to see why, since it is much more confusing than the simpler
practice of having sharps raise pitch and flats lower pitch.[62]

*

Theorists routinely refer to accidentals in terms of solmization syllables,
and this may seem to confirm the hexachordal significance of the signs. Yet
it is clear that solmization syllables could serve merely as a shorthand way
of identifying intervals and not necessarily as markers of hexachords. The
Anonymous of 1375, for example, solmizes the whole step *b*-flat to *G*-sharp
as *sol-fa*; the solmization syllables, obviously, represent nothing more than
an abstract whole step.[63] Since the main purpose of both accidentals and
solmization syllables was to identify the location of half steps, the two easily
mixed; they did not necessarily mix in a theoretically rigorous way.
Universally, theorists who write about musica ficta and vertical consonances are not interested in hexachords but in how the signs change pitch.
Furthermore (and contrary to earlier claims), it is important to emphasize
the fact that three fourteenth-century theorists say explicitly that this is
exactly what the signs do. Again, the Parisian Anonymous of 1375: "wher-
ever the sign *b* is placed, the true sound of that joint ought to be lowered by
a major semitone and called fa. And where the sign # is placed, the sound of
that joint ought to be raised by a major semitone and called mi."[64] The ten-

conventional format, and Edward Lowinsky has tied it to
cadential formulas; I attempt to expand upon this way of
thinking in Chapter 3. This hexachordal reading of *O
mortalis homo* was recognized by Charles van den Borren;
see *Polyphonia Sacra: a Continental Miscellany of the
Fifteenth Century* (London, 1932; rev. 2nd edn. 1962), lii.
Borren did not, however, follow through on the
implication of *F*-sharp in his transcription, p. 273. For a
reading that follows – incorrectly, I think – the
implications of a systematic approach to solmization, see
Gaston Allaire, "Debunking the Myth of Musica Ficta,"
*Tijdschrift van de Koninklijke Vereniging voor Nederlandse
Muziekgeschiedenis* 45 (1995), 110–26. Allaire's position
leads him to mistrust *c*-sharp, signed in the cantus at
measure 4; see p. 114 and p. 125, n. 17.
[62] Karol Berger observes how what I have called
"irregular signing" is rare, both in practice and theory;
Musica ficta, 17–18. The other main hexachordal use of
accidentals would seem to be notation of an *E*-flat
signature without a *B*-flat signature. The absence of the
B-flat may be accounted for by solmizing *E*-flat as *fa*,
thereby generating implied *B*-flat as *ut*. (For example, see
Fuions de ci by Senleches, discussed in Chapter 3.) The

phenomenon of signatures is multidimensional and still
poorly understood. Irregular signing may be part of the
practice, though, as I argue in Chapter 3, it does not seem
that hexachords play anything but an exceptional role.
[63] Ellsworth, ed. and trans., *The Berkeley Manuscript*,
242–3.
[64] "Item ubicumque ponitur signum *b* debet deprimi
sonus verus illius articuli per unum maius semitonum, et
dici fa. Et ubi signum # ponitur, sonus illius articuli debet
per maius semitonum elevari, et dici ibidem mi."
Ellsworth, ed. and trans., *The Berkeley Manuscript*, 52–3.
As I have said, three fourteenth-century theorists state
that the purpose of the signs is to change the pitches with
which they are associated, contradicting earlier claims
from hexachordally oriented scholars. Dolores Pesce,
noting the Parisian Anonymous of 1375, draws attention
to misstatements in Margaret Bent, "Musica Ficta," in
New Grove Dictionary of Music and Musicians XII:
802–11; see Pesce, *The Affinities and Medieval
Transposition*, 81 and n. 12. Karol Berger observes
associations between the signs and the lowering or raising
of pitch made by Petrus Frater dictus Palma Ociosa
(1336) and by Johannes Boen (1357); *Musica ficta*, 18.

dency in the theoretical discourse to discuss the signs in terms of solmization syllables is less important than it once seemed.

It is plausible, I think, that solmization was an active tool for beginners,
and that it had no strong role in negotiating complicated melodies, especially inflected melodies. It seems unlikely that advanced singers depended
upon the cumbersome array of *coniunctae*-hexachords to negotiate sophisticated polyphony, which, so often, does not lend itself to hexachordal
parsing. It is simpler to believe that they internalized the sizes of intervals
and sang free of solmization; this is what Gaffurius claims they did.[65]
Perhaps the single most important factor arguing against the importance
of solmization for musica ficta is that in polyphony most inflections have a
harmonic basis. Purely melodic applications are uncommon in the French
song tradition. Du Fay's celebrated use of flexible thirds (*Terzfreiheit*) is
one strong example of melodically based inflections; but Du Fay's
constructions hardly suggest hexachords. One can call any sharp "mi" and
any flat "fa," but if the inflection has a harmonic basis, the label will have no
purpose, as a rule.

*

It may not be at all anachronistic to take the position that the main purpose
of the signs is to identify a place on a continuum of half steps – that is, to
inflect pitch. In this view, the signs have a simple and direct purpose; in the
hexachordally based view, they are tied to an elaborate and somewhat
imprecise mechanism. I do not wish to hide my own agenda, which should
be clear enough: I emphasize musica ficta as a tool available to the composer (and his editor) for expressive purpose, more than as an issue that is
clarified by performance practice. I gain, with this point of view on the
simpler meaning of an accidental, a degree of confidence in a secure
musical text, and I can proceed with the task of identifying the function of
the inflection as a discrete event having some potential place in a larger
design. To assume that the music has been precisely and completely notated
facilitates musical analysis. The view that the performer was required to
complete the musical text by various conventions of performance practice
easily undermines musical analysis. The conception and dissemination of
polyphonic music becomes more complicated and haphazard. Margaret
Bent, for example, imagines this scenario:

> If the singer was responsible for applying accidentals, he must have done so in the
> first instance to the single part in front of him, and according to melodic criteria.

---

[65] The passage is quoted by Berger, *Musica ficta*, 7.
Bartolomeo Ramis de Pareia describes how to sing an
augmented second by thinking of it as the equivalent
of a minor third; see *Musica practica*, 89.

Cadences and structural harmonic points can normally, in any case, be anticipated by identifying the characteristic cadential figures appropriate to each single line of the polyphony. The simultaneous result, the superimposition of each part upon the others, could then be adjusted in rehearsal to meet any overriding harmonic considerations which individual singers had been unable to anticipate. The fact that many of these additions and adjustments were not added to the manuscripts but retained in the memory need not tax our credulity: medieval singers were subjected to disciplines which must have equipped them for life with enviable musical memories.[66]

Rehearsal, adjustment, memorization – repeated in different places with different musicians, this procedure would routinely lead to variants. Contrast this with the simpler assumption that since composers had at their disposal a precise means of communicating inflections – and since theorists recommended that composers use the signs, without commenting on the imagined procedure of rehearsals, adjustments and memorization, without indicating that the text demands any of this for its completion – the procedure imagined by Bent was not a normal part of how polyphony was conceived and disseminated. Of course, it may have happened (as there are some indications that it happened in the sixteenth century). And Bent may have given us an analytical model that accounts for variants in some cases. But based on my survey of manuscript evidence in the chanson, I see the need to pursue alternative points of view.

The cantus in a polyphonic chanson

Other problems, in addition to the well-known textual ones, block our efforts to analyze the contribution of accidentals to lyric beauty. If one were to write a history of chromaticism over the course of a later period, fewer tangential issues would get in the way. In order to interpret accidentals in late medieval chansons, it is necessary to take positions on topics that deserve full-length treatment of their own. Analysis of texture is one of these. Is the polyphonic chanson conceived in a hierarchical way, with the top voice as leading voice and all other voices subservient, to one degree or another? Or are the voices more or less equal, especially cantus and tenor? Subtle ramifications for analysis flow from how one responds to these questions, which will never be confidently resolved but which may be debated with some benefit.

[66] Bent, "Musica Recta and Musica Ficta." 74–5. Peter Urquhart imagines differently: "inflections probably had to be added at sight, the first time through the piece. To expect that Renaissance musicians extensively rehearsed problematic passages without signs of congruence, that is, without rehearsal numbers or points to re-enter, is simply unrealistic." "Cross-Relations by Franco-Flemish Composers after Josquin," 22.

The decision to begin this book with trouvère monophony signals my own response. By juxtaposing trouvère melodies with Machaut's polyphony, I imagine a bridge over what may be the most imposing break in the long history of the chanson. It is not a bridge about which too much can be said, since the early history of the polyphonic chanson is poorly documented. This is not the place to dwell on the various possibilities; yet there is a conceptual point to make. For our purposes, the main connection between the two repertories involves the role of the leading melody voice in the polyphonic chanson. This is the voice (usually the only voice) that receives text underlay. In this book it is referred to as the "cantus."

The point to make is that, to a degree, the cantus carries on principles of melodic design that were cultivated in trouvère songs. This is not to say that the polyphonic chanson is a musical creation of pure melody plus accompaniment, for it is more than that; one may stress the role of the cantus as leading melody at the same time that one recognizes the impact of contrapuntal and harmonic considerations on its design. My interest is in the contribution of inflections to lyric expression, and I assume, by viewing polyphonic texture as I do, that the cantus carries the burden of this expression. From this point of view, polyphonic chansons differ from motets, where, as a rule, no single voice dominates; the voices are conceived much more as equal partners in a contrapuntal project. In contrast, we may view the cantus in a chanson as having been designed with the idea that it will command attention. To stress its dominance is to regard inflections in that voice as causing a stronger sense of intervention, potentially, than those in the other voices. A single *f*-sharp in the cantus of *De plus en plus* may be more important than six sharps in the contratenor. This view of texture in the polyphonic chanson is one justification for restricting the present survey to accidentals in chansons. Since there is greater emphasis on an integrated texture in motets, there is less reason to highlight one voice and its inflections in that genre.

There can be no proof of this, and others may see things differently; yet one must take a position, and from that position analysis may proceed. Issues surrounding textural hierarchy involve more than the *res facta* that we see on the page. They involve notions about compositional methods that preceded the piece and performance practices that were brought to it. If there are only two voices, the second voice is labeled "tenor." As a rule, it does not get text underlay, and, for the most part, it moves beneath the cantus, just as a tenor in a motet moves beneath texted upper voices. Beyond this basic format the idiom is flexible. Contratenors and triplums come and go as supplements to the main pair. Sometimes, the supplemental voices are well integrated with the two main voices, implying that they may not have been added to a pre-existent duet but, instead, were part of the original conception. Often, they are not so well integrated. Always, they can be put aside, leaving the main pair to stand alone as a self-sufficient duet. From these basic facts of the tradition I draw the conclusion that the cantus is the leading melody. Tenor, contratenor and triplum support it, comment on its design, make it more interesting, and perhaps even reinterpret it, but they do not challenge its dominance. A relatively short time ago, say as little as twenty years ago, this way of thinking seemed obvious.

That is not the case today, however, and the challenge has come partly from a critique of compositional method and, more imposingly, from new ideas about how chansons were performed. Debate about compositional method has moved around notions of successive versus simultaneous composition. Did composers really need to build a song successively, from cantus to tenor and then to supplemental voices, or were they able to think in terms of a two-, three-, or four-voiced texture from the start? The theorists suggest a sequential approach, beginning with the cantus. Machaut himself describes this sequence.[67] Yet it is clear that composers must have been able to work with more than one voice at a time or they would not have produced the results that they did; it is also clear that not all chansons may be read hierarchically.[68] And one can argue that the whole question of compositional sequence is secondary, anyway; it is the result that must be judged. How the songs were performed would have had a big impact on

[67] Machaut's description comes in a letter from *Le Voir dit*, where he says that he has added a tenor and contratenor to a poem and melody that he had made earlier; excerpt given by Friedrich Ludwig, ed., *Guillaume de Machaut: Musikalische Werke* (Leipzig: Breitkopf und Härtel, 1926–9), II: 56b. The passage is discussed, most recently, by Daniel Leech-Wilkinson, "*Le Voir Dit* and *La Messe de Nostre Dame:* Aspects of Genre and Style in Late Works of Machaut," *Plainsong and Medieval Music* 2 (1993), 48–9. This point about the dominance of the cantus – dominance, at least, for issues of musical analysis – in ars nova chansons is made more forcefully than ever before in Peter Lefferts's "Signature-systems and Tonal Types in the Fourteenth-Century French Chanson," 117–48. In Lefferts's view, the cantus signals the composer's participation in conventional practice, even while the tenor may obscure that participation. For example, Machaut's ballade *Riches d'amour* cadences on *c* in the cantus. The tenor harmonizes the final cadence with *F*, but that is a secondary matter, according to

Lefferts's analytical focus on "tonal type."

[68] For a current list of references, with commentary, to literature on this problem, see Lawrence Earp, *Guillaume de Machaut: a Guide to Research* (New York: Garland, 1995), 285. The recommendation to begin with the cantus is repeated as late as Nicolaus Burtius in 1487; quotation given by Harold Powers, "Mode," 400. Leech-Wilkinson, "*Le Voir Dit* and *La Messe de Nostre Dame*" (54–6), gives a persuasive analysis of *Dix et sept, cinq*, arguing for its simultaneous rather than successive composition. I would agree with him that "Clearly the relationship between material and form was far from fixed" (p. 61). Yet I would question how widely applicable within the chanson repertory is his assertion (p. 64) that "matters of part-writing come near to the end of the reconstructable process of composition," since this assertion must stand, first, against the evidence of treatises ("begin with the cantus"), second against the evident attention to melodic design routinely bestowed upon the cantus.

those results. Recent years have seen a critique of performance practice that includes the argument that the regular texting practice of underlay in one voice only is less important than it may seem, and that all-vocal scoring was the favored practice, regardless of where the words have been inscribed.

In support of all-vocal performance is a small amount of documentary evidence from the period and a very large presence of lovely, persuasive performances from the past few decades.[69] All-vocal scoring puts equal weight on all voices, and it yields a firm emphasis on harmony. Since harmony in late medieval polyphony has been misunderstood and under-valued, this is a good thing. The results appeal directly to the modern ear, so heavily trained in a different though related kind of harmony. The price paid is reduced emphasis on the cantus, which is now challenged by all voices, especially the triplum, which often rises above. The cantus becomes less a leading melody and more a single component of a polyphonic whole. A recent modification of all-vocal scoring is telling, for it would seem to represent a concern about this price paid: only the cantus sings text, while the other voices sing wordless vocalization. Whether or not one is inclined to accept the authenticity of this solution, it is important to recognize how it serves as a compromise that returns the cantus to its prominent position. In the old way of doing things, that position is conveyed automatically when the cantus is sung and accompanied by instruments.

The view that the polyphonic chanson is like a motet in that all voices play a more or less equal role leads to interpretive results different from those developed in this study. It may lead, for example, to an interest in iso-lating a kind of migrating main line that moves through the ensemble, such as one might discover, say, in a string quartet by Haydn.[70] Even though

---

[69] For a thoughtful and brief review of performance practice trends, see Christopher Page, "The English *A Cappella* Heresy," in *Companion to Medieval and Renaissance Music,* ed. Tess Knighton and David Fallows (London: Dent, 1992), 23–9.

[70] Without wishing to simplify or misrepresent what is a very nuanced and sensitive interpretation, I would suggest that this is close to the direction pursued by Daniel Leech-Wilkinson in "Machaut's *Rose, lis* and the Problem of Early Music Analysis," *Music Analysis* 3 (1984), 9–28. For example (p. 21): "the generally low tessitura of the Cantus, and in particular its tendency to make a voice-leading complex rather than an intact part in those passages of extended prolongation (where Machaut has taken such care in the Triplum to confirm and not to weaken the implications inherent in the

Cantus), all suggest that the two upper voices were conceived together, and together with the Tenor and Contratenor, taking mutual account of one another's needs." Leech-Wilkinson says (p. 26, n. 16) that he chose *Rose, lis* for analysis in this article because of the fine recorded performance by Gothic Voices, directed by Christopher Page: *The Mirror of Narcissus: Songs by Guillaume de Machaut,* Hyperion A 66087. It is, indeed, a fine performance, and it is one that could do no better in representing the ideal of complete integration of the voices. The results of this are that cantus regularly yields to triplum at the top of the texture and to the fore of the listener's attention. At all of the important returns of the cantus to *c,* the triplum rings out on *g* above, obscuring the moment as one of linear completion.

these performance-practice issues may be so poorly documented that the modern-day musician must simply make a choice, based on personal preference, they are also inseparable from issues of higher-level interpretation. At some point, the latter issue may take over from the former, and proceed on its own terms, independently of the handicap of poor documentation for practices of the period. I believe the "migrating line" approach to be misguided; instead, as I have argued, one may place special emphasis on inflections in the cantus. These issues will come to the foreground at several turns in this study, particularly in Chapter 3, where editorial decisions about conflicts between voices and how they relate to the presumed hierarchy of texture are considered, and where patterns of inflections in the cantus are reviewed.[71]

[71] I also take up issues of how we regard accidentals in supplemental contratenors and triplums when those inflections conflict with a reading for cantus and tenor that makes good contrapuntal sense, on its own. As I shall argue in Chapter 3, I find it unlikely that such a situation demands that we adjust the cantus and tenor. The related issue is to what extent supplemental contratenors and triplums may be designed to be out of synchrony with the cantus and tenor pair.

This chapter is devoted mainly to the late thirteenth-century trouvère manuscript *Paris, Bibliothèque Nationale MS fr. no. 846* (known by standard abbreviation as *MS O* and known also as the "Cangé Chansonnier"), which is unusual for the large quantity of accidentals it contains.[1] Among the 351 songs in this source, 51 have *F*-sharp signed, and 21 have either *C*-sharp or *E*-flat; it is uncommon to find these accidentals in other trouvère sources.[2] The manuscript is distinguished not only by quantity of accidentals but also by the idiosyncratic uses to which they are put. It is unusual in several other respects, including, for one, the arrangement of its contents. Unlike most trouvère anthologies, which feature arrangement by author, *MS O* is ordered according to alphabetical groups determined by the first letter of the first word of each poem. Within these groups, there is no rigorous order of any kind, though various patterns emerge; for example, songs by Thibaut de Navarre, who is often given pride of place in trouvère anthologies, tend to lead off the alphabetical groups.[3] Therefore it is not

---

[1] Abbreviations for trouvère manuscripts follow *G. Raynauds Bibliographie des altfranzösischen Liedes*, rev. edn by Hans Spanke (Leiden: E. J. Brill, 1955; repr. 1980). *MS O* has been dated to the late thirteenth century; see David Fallows, "Sources, MS, section III, 4: Secular Monophony," in *New Grove Dictionary of Music and Musicians*, XVII: 641; and also Gilbert Reaney, ed., *Manuscripts of Polyphonic Music: 11th-Early 14th Century*, Répertoire international des Sources Musicales, ser. B vol. IV (Munich: Henle, 1966), 379. See also Mark Everist, *Polyphonic Music in Thirteenth-Century France: Aspects of Sources and Distribution* (New York: Garland, 1989), 201 ff., for the suggestions (acknowledging François Avril) that the manuscript may have been decorated in Paris or under Parisian influence, *c.* 1280–90, or that it may date as late as *c.* 1300. For inventory, facsimile edition, introductory essay, and transcriptions see Jean Beck, *Le Chansonnier Cangé: Manuscrit français no. 846 de la Bibliothèque Nationale de Paris*, Corpus Cantilenarum Medii Aevi 1, 2 vols. (Paris: University of Pennsylvania Press, 1927). In his transcriptions, Beck freely omits and adds accidentals. I identify songs from *MS O* (for example, "Beck 1" for *Ausi cum l'unicorne sui*) according to Beck's inventory in I, xxii–xxvii of *Le Chansonnier Cangé*. "R numbers" (for

example, R 2075 for *Ausi cum l'unicorne sui*) refer to the catalogue of trouvère songs by Gaston Raynaud, revised by Hans Spanke as *Raynauds Bibliographie des altfranzösischen Liedes*.

[2] My presentation proceeds as if the inflected songs form a coherent layer of the manuscript. Though this may well not be the case (see below), it encourages dealing with the songs collectively, thereby focusing attention on the inflections. One hopes that future studies will provide more control over the vast repertory of trouvère songs and the complicated patterns of transmission that they suggest; it will probably turn out that the situation is more complicated than my references to a single coherent layer suggest. Just as it is difficult to advance the argument that the inflected songs in *MS O* form a coherent layer of transmission, so is it difficult to make the case that these songs came about by revising uninflected versions that happen to have been preserved in other surviving manuscripts, though some observations and speculations are offered below.

[3] Alphabetical organization is used more often in motet manuscripts (one sign among several that the compiler of the manuscript was familiar with motets). On the ordering within *MS O*'s alphabetical groups, see Beck's commentary, *Le Chansonnier Cangé*, II: especially 13–14.

surprising that Thibaut's celebrated *Ausi cum l'unicorne sui* (Ex. 1.1; Beck 1; R 2075; *Trouvères-Melodien* II: 290) was chosen to be the very first song in the book. Illuminations signal each new alphabetical group in the manuscript, and the illumination that decorates *Ausi cum l'unicorne sui* strikingly depicts an image from the first stanza of Thibaut's poem, where the narrator proclaims himself to be "like the unicorn, struck with awe when he gazes upon the maiden . . . so joyful in his torment that, fainting, he falls into her lap; then he is murdered in betrayal."[4] To this scene, the illuminator has added a mirror, placed in the lady's hand.

Thematic illuminations directly tied to poems are just as unusual for trouvère anthologies as alphabetical organization. As if to assure the user of *MS O* that the melodies, too, will go beyond ordinary, the first phrase of *Ausi cum l'unicorne sui* features a distinctive gesture that is unique in the transmission of this song. Eight other chansonniers carry the song with musical notation, but none documents the cross relation, *b*-flat versus *b*-natural, that we find in the first phrase of *MS O*'s redaction.[5] Not only the cross relation, but also the striking drop away from *b*-natural stands out. It is possible to project on this line – tentatively, from the distance of so many centuries – a sense of poignancy as it falls away from implied movement

[4] Translation by Kathleen J. Brahney, ed., *The Lyrics of Thibaut de Champagne*, Garland Library of Medieval Literature, ser. A, 41 (New York and London: Garland, 1989),103. It is not uncommon in other manuscripts for illuminations to depict authors; this manuscript is again different, for it does not even provide author attributions. For more on the organization of the manuscript, interpretations of its illuminations, and the unique shift in emphasis that results from the format and style of the book, see Sylvia Huot, *From Song to Book: the Poetics of Writing in Old French Lyric and Lyrical Narrative Poetry* (Ithaca: Cornell University Press, 1987).

[5] The surviving versions of the song can easily be compared by consulting Hendrik van der Werf's important edition *Trouvères-Melodien* (hereinafter, *T-M*), II: 290. *MS R* (*Paris, Bibliothèque Nationale, MS f. fr. 1591*) does have the falling third motif at the end of the phrase, making it the manuscript closest to *MS O* in the transmission of this song; but *MS R* lacks accidentals. For my transcriptions of trouvère songs, I follow van der Werf, John Stevens and others in presenting the songs in a neutral rhythmic notation. I assume, like Stevens (and van der Werf is not far from this assumption), the superiority of an isosyllabic rendition: one note or note-

group per syllable, with syllables sung at a steady pace. The argument is succinctly presented in John Stevens, "Medieval Song," in *The New Oxford History of Music: the Early Middle Ages to 1300*, ed. Richard Crocker (Oxford: Oxford University Press, 1990), 360–3. By presenting the songs in a consistent style of transcription one gains the additional benefit of easy comparison. I present the melodies in a rhythmically neutral manner even though *MS O* shows, here and there, what has been termed a "semi-mensural" overlay. It was this notational feature that led Beck to choose the manuscript for the first volume in his facsimile series. The redaction seemed to him to provide the key to interpreting the whole repertory of trouvère songs. On this, Mark Everist comments: "The most likely interpretation of the [rhythmic] notation in this manuscript is that it is nothing more than an affectation to give the book, rather than the music, a semblance of being up-to-date with the most recent Parisian trends." *Polyphonic Music in Thirteenth-Century France*, 203. More sympathetic to the rhythmic notation of *MS O* is Vincent Corrigan, "Modal Rhythm and the Interpretation of *Trouvère Song*," in *The Cultural Milieu of the Troubadours and Trouvères*, ed. Nancy van Deusen Musicological Studies 62/1 (Ottawa: Institute of Mediaeval Music, 1994), 125–32.

Example 1.1 *Ausi cum l'unicorne sui* by Thibaut de Navarre, according to *Trouvère MS O*, f. 1 (poem after Kathleen Brahney, ed., *The Lyrics of Thibaut de Champagne*, Garland Library of Medieval Literature, ser. A, vol. 41 (New York and London: Garland, 1989), 102, with spelling adjusted to *MS O*).

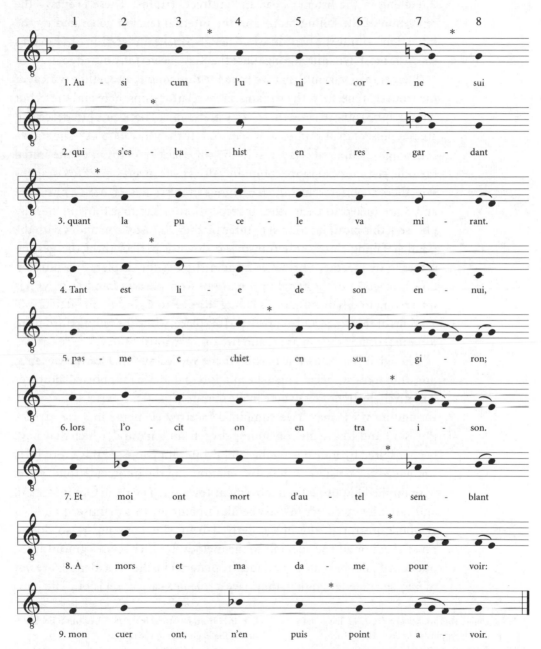

1. Au - si cum l'u - ni - cor - ne sui

2. qui s'es - ba - hist en res - gar - dant

3. quant la pu - ce - le va mi - rant.

4. Tant est li - e de son en - nui,

5. pas - me e chiet en son gi - ron;

6. lors l'o - cit on en tra - i - son.

7. Et moi ont mort d'au - tel sem - blant

8. A - mors et ma da - me pour voir:

9. mon cuer ont, n'en puis point a - voir.

towards *c*, a goal that will not be attained for some time. The lift to and fall away from *b*-natural is repeated at the end of phrase 2. And this is followed by more melodic tension, for now *b*-natural is heard in close proximity to *F*, etching in the listener's ear an "indirect" tritone. These events – the repetition of the falling motif and the internal tension generated by the inflections – unite the two phrases. They also make this version of Thibaut's song the most dynamic among those that have been transmitted to us.

The array of variants that we have for this song is altogether typical of the trouvère repertory: the variants show relationships, here and there, but it is rarely possible to construct a vertical stemma. The events just described are not present in any other source in exactly the way of *MS O*.[6] The stanza is through-composed;[7] as a result, the song lacks repetition of the initial melodic *pes*, a formal move commonly used by trouvères. As if to compensate, there are briefer melodic repetitions in the stanza. In *MS O*, phrases 2 and 3 are linked to each other by repetition of the first four pitches. By phrase 4, this motif is reduced to three pitches. Phrase 4 concludes with the familiar falling third, now transposed down a perfect fifth; the gesture serves to tie together phrases 1, 2 and 4 (here is the displaced resolution, down an octave, of the dangling *b*-naturals from phrases 1 and 2). Now, it is interesting to discover that *this* falling third, *E* to *C*, occurs in virtually all versions of this song, and at precisely this place, while the falling third from *b*-natural occurs only in *MS O* and two other manuscripts.

Though it is not possible to construct a vertical stemma for the variants, one cannot resist speculating (speculation that may be supported, however tentatively, by trends elsewhere in the manuscript). The reviser whose work we find in *MS O* may have combined received elements in a clever way. Phrases 1 and 2 have the concluding drop from *b*-natural, which may have been inspired by transposing the later drop from *E* to *C*; to this motivic tie was added the tension of the cross relation and the indirect tritone, along with implied but unrealized movement toward *c*. The redaction is forceful and carefully executed. Just as the illuminator for this manuscript adds a symbolic mirror to the image derived from Thibaut's poem, so does a musical editor add accidentals to the melody. Neither revises gratuitously, but both do not hesitate to develop the material further. Accidentals are not merely sprinkled in; rather, they have a role in a careful revision. The idio-

---

[6] *MS a* (*Rome, Vatican, MS Reg. lat. 1490*) has *b*-flat signed for the first phrase, as does *MS V* (*Paris, Bibliothèque Nationale, MS f. fr. 24406*), but neither has *b*-natural at the end of the phrase. *MS R* (*Paris, Bibliothèque Nationale, MS f. fr. 1591*) has precisely the same drop from *b*-natural that *MS O* has, but it has no *b*-flat at the beginning of the phrase.

[7] *Oda continua* is Dante's term for this form; on the term, see Stevens, "Medieval Song," especially 373.

syncratic design includes elements of continuity and discontinuity, and that is a pattern that we shall discover in a number of songs from this manuscript.

For all of these reasons, *MS O* is a good starting point for our survey of beautiful accidentals in chansons. Since this manuscript is, above all, an anthology dedicated to lyric songs in the tradition of *fin' amors*, it may be the closest surviving record of the practice observed by Anonymous 2 – musica ficta used for the sake of beauty in the *cantus coronatus*, which we may take as a synonym for *grand chant courtois*, the genre to which this chansonnier is mainly dedicated.[8]

*

Before going further, it will be useful to reflect upon three textual problems that must be dealt with time and again. These intractable problems frustrate analysis, not only for trouvère songs but for virtually every area covered in this book. It is necessary to have some working assumptions in order to proceed with analysis, and it is in this spirit that I will briefly sketch the issues and, for each case, a reasonable way to respond.

The first problem is the central one in modern-day research on musica ficta: whether the musical text has been incompletely notated with the expectation that implied inflections will be understood by educated performers. Hendrik van der Werf, one of the foremost scholars of trouvère songs in our time, remarks on

> the idea that, during the Middle Ages and the Renaissance, scribes did not need to notate all of the required chromatic alterations because the performers knew when to make them. This theory not only has never been proven but it also is in no way supported by the sharp and flat signs which actually appear in the troubadour and trouvère manuscripts. If the persons for whom the written collections were intended were experts on chromatic alterations, the scribes would not have had much reason to write any sharp or flat signs; at most, they might have given them for specifically dubious passages. To the best of my knowledge, this is nowhere the case. Thus, the most prudent approach to our evaluation is to begin with assuming that a scribe marked all the alterations which he considered appropriate.[9]

[8] On *MS O* as a lyric anthology with an unusual emphasis on the courtly love song, see Beck, *Le Chansonnier Cangé*, I: xx; and also Huot, *From Song to Book*, 74–80. In this study, I do not cover accidentals used in other genres (for example, the *lai* copied onto f. 103, *Puis qu'en chantant*). Johannes de Grocheio identifies *Ausi cum l'unicorne sui* as a *cantus coronatus*. Edition of Grocheio's treatise by Rohloff, *Die*

Quellenhandschriften zum Musiktraktat des Johannes de Grocheio, reference on p. 130; the same passage is given in a revised edition with translation by Christopher Page, "Johannes de Grocheio on Secular Music," 23 ff. Grocheio also cites *Quant li rossignoz*, by Chastelain de Coucy, as a *cantus coronatus*; this song is entered twice in *MS O* (Beck 272 and 288).

[9] *The Extant Troubadour Melodies*, 41.

I find much in *MS O* to recommend van der Werf's prudent approach
and little to undermine it. For present purposes, I would adjust his last
thought slightly: rather than imagining a scribe who contributes
"appropriate" alterations, I imagine a reviser who takes advantage of
expanded notational possibilities to produce a fresh redactional style. In
the study of trouvère songs, especially, it is difficult to lift thinking about
unnotated practices out of the realm of speculation. The tools for study of
later repertories are not available: gains from collation are extremely
limited, since *MS O*'s readings are usually isolated, and there is virtually no
information from music theory that we can use with confidence. My
approach here, as elsewhere, is mainly to try and make sense of the evidence
as it is notated. In contrast to Beck, who often eliminated idiosyncratic
accidentals, I find the notated inflections in this manuscript, on the whole,
to be persuasive.

The two other textual problems that come up again and again are (1) the
difficulty of identifying precisely which note or notes the signs inflect and
(2) the question of whether unsigned *b*'s indicate what we call *b*-natural.

The problem of identifying which note a sign inflects is a problem of
duration (how long the sign governs), and it is also one of placement
(whether the sign is located before, after, above or below the pitch or
pitches it is meant to inflect). The normal practice is to place the sign before
the pitch it inflects. We should expect this for the entire period covered in
this book. Occasionally, signs are located immediately after the pitch they
inflect;[10] and occasionally (usually when a plica is involved) they are
located between two notes on the same pitch, presumably to inflect both.[11]
It is true that the scribe of *MS O*, like many scribes, can be casual about vertical placement. Difficulties sometimes arise when it is not clear whether a
square-*b* (or even a soft *b*) inflects *b* or *c*. [12] Usually, context clarifies the
matter.

More troubling is the question of how long accidentals govern.
"Signature" accidentals, placed at the beginning of the staff in order to
inflect all pitches on that staff, appear not to have been used in *MS O*. Yet it

---

[10] For example, *Tant ai amors servie longuement* (Beck
342; R 711), where *f*-sharp is post-placed on staff 2 and
c-sharp is post-placed on staff 8; see also staff 7 of *Li
plusor ont d'amors chanté* (Beck 178; R 413) and staff 6 of
Or voi je bien (Beck 232; R 1247). These cases could be
thought of, alternatively, in terms of mid-placement
rather than post-placement, since the lines turn
downwards through the same inflected pitch. That is, it is
possible that the accidental is placed in the middle of two
pitches as a way to inflect both, one in ascent and the

other in descent. Mid-placement is discussed further in
Chapter 3.

[11] For example, staff 1 of *Comment que d'amours me
dueille* (Beck 67; R 1007); also, staff 2 of *J'oasse bien jurer*
(Beck 167; R 285).

[12] Signs in this manuscript are often placed a little high.
For example, all hard-*b*'s in *Quant l'erbe muert* (Beck
305; R 1795) are most likely *b*-naturals rather than *c*-
sharps, even though they are placed high on the staff.

is doubtlessly true that many accidentals govern more than a single pitch; the "once only" rule for accidentals, which tends to be the rule given by theorists, is inadequate. The generalization that makes sense most often in this manuscript is that signs govern for the duration of the staff but not over staff breaks.[13] This generalization is implied by patterns of reiteration: it is rare to find the same accidental notated more than once on the same staff, and it is common to find an accidental restated at the beginning of the next staff when the flow of the line seems to call for continuing the inflection. "Cancellations" would shed light on this problem, but they are rare.[14] Perhaps the scribe simply followed what he found in his exemplars, which could have been laid out with different staff lengths and which may have even followed different conventions. Did the shape of the melody make it obvious to the singer when to hold an inflection for the duration of an entire staff and when to cancel it? In a good number of songs sharps are signed only in a descending line, and without any eventual resolution – the inflected pitch is left dangling, so to speak.[15] So it will hardly do to assume that ascending sharps were routinely canceled in descent. Nevertheless, it could still be valuable to mix analysis of melodic shape with textual analysis of accidentals, here and everywhere in late medieval songs. Even though there will always be limitations to this kind of analysis, with its circular pattern of speculation, it may open up perspectives that are otherwise unavailable.[16]

The problem of reading unsigned *b* is equally intractable, though pat-

[13] Hendrik van der Werf suggests the possibilities that accidentals may hold their force for the duration of the verse or the duration of the staff, whichever comes first; see *The Lyrics and Melodies of Gace Brulé*, Garland Library of Medieval Literature, ser. A, 39 (New York and London: Garland, 1985), 345 and n. 12. There are a few good examples in which accidentals appear to hold only through the phrase ending and not into the next phrase; for example, see *N'est pas a soi qui eimme coraument* (Gace Brulé: Beck 213; R 653; *Trouvères-Melodien*, I: 391). But it is my impression that these good examples are far fewer than those that appear to follow the rule of automatic cancellation at the end of the staff. Another alternative is that a single sign placed at the beginning of the piece governs for the entire stanza. For example, see *Pluie ne venz* (Beck 246; R 2105): *MS O* has only a single *b*-flat, placed at the beginning, while *MS M* signs all three *b*'s in the song with flats. For further discussion of placement problems in troubadour and trouvère songs, see van der Werf, *The Extant Troubadour Melodies*, 39 ff.

[14] There is a good example in *Quant je plus sui en paour* (Beck 277; R 1227): a figure featuring ascent through *F*-sharp to *G* and immediate downward turn is notated twice. Only in the second statement does the scribe cancel *F*-sharp by placing a flat on *F* in the descent; presumably, this is because the two *F*'s are on the same staff in this second statement but not in the first, where the staff break serves to cancel the inflection. But similar turns occur in many other songs without cancellations.

[15] See *Aÿmanz fins et verais* (Beck 18; R 199), *En douce dolour* (Beck 122; R 1972), and *Neant plus que* (Beck 218; R 1892).

[16] To take one example of how analysis and text criticism intermix: the assumption that accidentals are in force for the duration of the staff makes good sense when it renders a reading in which a line that is literally repeated carries precisely the same inflection each time. But for a substantial group (25) of songs it seems likely that the intention is, rather, *not* to make the inflections consistent in repeated phrases. A variation technique seems to be at work (examples given below). I am comfortable with the idea that both possibilities, precise and imprecise repetitions, stand alongside one another.

terns of notation again provide a slight advantage. Some theorists declare that unsigned *b* is to be read as "hard *b*" and that *b*-flat requires the flat sign, while others say that an unsigned *b* may be read one way or the other, depending on the context.[17] (Significantly, theorists who say that the singer should be able to make the choice, guided by context, do so in reference to indirect tritones. As we shall see, there are reasons to doubt the relevance of this precept for *MS O*.) Patterns of notation in this manuscript imply that unsigned *b* should be read as *b*-natural. 163 songs are notated with *b*-flat, compared to only 41 notated with *b*-natural. The imbalance implies that *b*-natural is notated mainly in special cases. In most songs where *b*-natural is signed, *b*-flat is signed as well, suggesting that the natural sign is there for clarification. Only thirteen songs show *b*-natural but not *b*-flat. In four of them, the accidental may have come about through transposition, for in each case the song is notated at a different pitch level in another manuscript.[18] Because of these patterns of notation, I assume that unsigned *b* is to be read as *b*-natural.

In spite of the theoretical distinction between musica recta and musica ficta, according to which inflections of *b* belong in a different category from inflections on all other degrees, it would be artificial to exclude from this discussion (and from this book) inflections of *b*, which may be used in the same ways that the other inflections are used. For example, several songs in *MS O* use the dropping-third gesture at the end of a phrase (as in *Ausi cum l'unicorne sui*), with the third notated sometimes *b* to *G* and sometimes *F*-sharp to *D*. It appears that at this analytical level the boundary between musica recta and musica ficta is irrelevant.[19] The example also suggests the possibility of uncovering a consistent redactional style preserved by this manuscript, a possibility that will emerge at several turns in our survey.

---

[17] For an overview of the problem of whether *b*-flat needs to be signed, with citations of theorists who land on each side of the issue, see Bettie Jean Harden, "Sharps, Flats and Scribes: 'Musica Ficta' in the Machaut Manuscripts" (Ph.D. dissertation, Cornell University, 1983), 40–5. Karol Berger: "As we learn from many theorists, mi is assumed in the places of b and bb unless the round b is implied or expressly indicated." See *Musica ficta*, 4, n. 10.

[18] The clearest illustration of this is *Bien font amors* (Beck 43; R 738): *MS O* carries a stray bb-natural that corresponds with *f*-sharp notated in *MS M*, where the melody is notated a fourth lower. For *Dous est li maus* (Adam de la Halle: Beck 112; R 1771; *T-M*, II: 636), *MS O* presents the song a fourth lower than all other

manuscripts, and *F*-sharp and *b*-natural follow accordingly. Transpositions are also evident in collation of *Tuit mi desir* (Thibaut de Navarre: Beck 201; R 741; *T-M*, II: 106) and *A vous* (Beck 9; R 679; *T-M*, I: 224).

[19] On the other hand, the fact that many anthologies of troubadour and trouvère songs use accidentals almost exclusively in connection with *b* indicates that the theoretical distinction between musica recta and musica ficta is relevant. Hendrik van der Werf observes that flats are routinely placed on *b* but never on *B*. As an explanation, he suggests that *B*-flat is avoided because it does not belong to the Guidonian gamut, while *b*-flat does; see *The Extant Troubadour Melodies*, 41. Yet, it is rare for trouvère songs to descend below *B*, making it less surprising that *B*-flats are rare.

Syntactic flexibility

In our efforts to comprehend accidentals, textual problems present one kind of obstacle; from a different direction come conceptual problems surrounding the interpretation of pitch relations. When studying much later music, we parse accidentals on the basis of a secure knowledge of musical syntax. For late medieval music, that kind of security will always stay beyond reach; yet there is still hope for advance. One hopes for some advantage by mixing more deeply and more extensively analysis of accidentals with analysis of musical syntax. By beginning with trouvère monophony, we are in a position to clarify a perspective on melodic syntax that will be useful for study of later polyphony; and, of course, one also hopes to advance appreciation of this elusive body of monophonic music.

With virtually any kind of music it is difficult to analyze melody, but for trouvère songs there is a real need to move forward, since the music resists analysis. The problem manifests in the traditional undervaluing of the repertory in modern musicology. There has been a tendency to regard the melodies as either improvisationally formulaic or as having been transmitted so casually that one imagines (so the argument goes) the users of the songs caring more about the poems, which tend to be stably transmitted, than they care about the melodies. Neither claim rings true for the songs that will occupy our attention in this chapter. The phenomenon of building upon received musical material is part of the musical culture. With thirteenth-century motets, too, the musical material is routinely in flux, though it is a different style of flux: in the motet, new lines are added to received polyphony according to the rules of discant; in *grands chants courtoises*, melodic revision is carried out within formal restrictions. Most likely, the thirteenth-century *compositeur* did not recognize a firm line between composition and revision. Mark Everist observes that, for the motet, "the 'renewing' of pre-existent materials becomes just as varied, and just as imaginative, as the creation of new works" – this characterization would seem to hold in equal measure for the *grand chant courtois*. Potentially, each received version lays claim to being a *res facta*, as a carefully made melody that reflects someone's choices and preferences.[20]

That the melodies resist analysis presents a more difficult barrier. The

[20] Quotation from Mark Everist, *French Motets in the Thirteenth Century* (Cambridge: Cambridge University Press, 1994), 7. The alternative view is that the written record documents a process of embellishment and variation within a tradition that was mainly oral rather than written. The two views are not mutually exclusive, of course; but they may lead to very different kinds of interpretation. Hendrik van der Werf explores the tradition in terms of oral transmission in *The Chansons of the Troubadours and Trouvères*.

problem centers on the mystery of what syntactic rules operate in this music. As we have seen, Johannes de Grocheio suggests that modal theory does not govern vernacular music and polyphony. Yet there have been some modern-day attempts to use modal theory as a basis for analysis, and it is easy to understand why. Modal theory (or, more accurately, "modal theories") constitutes the foremost body of contemporary writings about linear organization of pitch, so it would seem like a promising way to bridge the large conceptual gap that we face. But many troubadours and trouvères must have worked independently of theory and notation. The impact of learned music on their tradition is suggested here and there and in various ways, though the details of how this happened are almost completely obscure. Were learned scribes responsible for notating most of the melodies within the pitch field of the Guidonian gamut, or did the trouvères routinely compose and sing them that way? Even when the melodies move within the traditional gamut (which means most melodies), there are reasons for doubting the relevance of modal theory – and reasons for taking Grocheio seriously. For it is not a simple matter to use modal theory to satisfy the concerns of modern-day analysis, as many scholars have observed. The theories change, and there is a tendency to absorb escape hatches designed to accommodate exceptions in compositional practice. This process weakens the rigor we would like to draw out of the theories. Furthermore, it often seems that the basic postulates of modal theory represent loose tools for classification rather than rigorous rules for explaining syntax, such as one might imagine controlling the organization of pitch.

And that is a basic issue: one goal for using modal theory or for working with any kind of melodic syntax would be to draw generalized syntactic rules, and, following this, to apply the rules in cases where there is some complexity or some manipulation of them. The issue is not forced by a simple trouvère song that clearly establishes *D* as its main pitch, has internal cadences on *a*, and moves through its phrases in a way that neatly follows the species of fifths, fourths and octaves that some theorists associate with *protus* mode. The difficulties come when we try to generalize on the basis of such an example. Can we legitimately conclude that the fifth degree above the final is a point of high tension in every melody? Or, alternatively, is that pitch linked to the final as a secondary point of rest, and in such a way that it carries no tension at all? Or is neither quality intrinsic to the fifth relationship? "Tension" and "rest" – these are the active words for analysis when the discussion turns away from a melodic manner (pitches and patterns of pitches loosely associated with one another and, through these changing associations, collectively identifying mode) and toward syntax (rules governing how pitches are functionally bound to one another).

Alternatively, one may try to adjust modern-day expectations of a systematic melodic syntax. Except for obvious copying errors, it is almost impossible to identify melodic mistakes in this repertory; this alone suggests a lack of syntactical rigor. Furthermore, the melodies are pliable as they move from manuscript to manuscript, even to the degree that different final pitches may be supplied for a melody that is otherwise transmitted stably. That condition would suggest that the revisers of the melody did not perceive a strong syntactic relationship between melodic flow and final. The same freedom may manifest in selection of cadential pitches, which, throughout the repertory, tend not to be as closely coordinated with the final pitch as expectations of a rigorously operating modal syntax would lead one to hope for. And when we discover songs that feature one pitch yielding to another as hierarchically predominant during the course of a stanza, we should again suspect lack of syntactic rigor. These phenomena undermine analysis based on the final, the universal precept of modal theory. The idiom appears to be flexible in areas where we are conditioned to look for system.

Lan que li jor sunt lonc en mai, by the troubadour Jaufre Rudel, has been analyzed by Leo Treitler,[21] mainly from the point of view of text–music relations; we may profitably build on his efforts in order to ponder three issues involving melodic syntax: (1) The song does not end on the melody's main pitch; as a result, modal analysis by final is undermined. (2) Treitler proposes (though I doubt) that a syntax based on third-chains conditions the melody. (3) The version notated by troubadour *MS W* (Ex. 1.2) carries a unique and telling variant of an accidental in the final phrase, and we may speculate about its syntactic significance.

The three surviving sources agree with one another in many details, even though one version (our Ex. 1.2, from *MS W*) is notated a fifth higher than

---

[21] Treitler presents these views in two overlapping essays: "Medieval Lyric," in *Models of Musical Analysis: Music Before 1600*, ed. Mark Everist (Oxford: Blackwell, 1992), 1–19; and "Music and Language in Medieval Song," in *The Medieval Lyric*, ed. Howell Chickering and Margaret Switten (Mount Holyoke College, 1988), 12–27. The earlier essay was adapted from a talk given at the Medieval Lyric Institute in 1987. The two essays are not identical, but they overlap considerably; in the earlier essay Treitler's assumptions about melodic syntax are more explicitly stated than in the later one. Treitler apparently follows van der Werf's edition of the song (though without acknowledgment); he accepts van der Werf's reconstruction of the missing sections, and he follows van der Werf's procedure of notating all three versions at the same pitch level for comparative purposes, using *b*-flat signatures in the transcription of *MS W* to accommodate the transposition. Treitler does not report the fact that *MS W*'s version is notated at a different pitch level, leaving the reader with the impression that the manuscript carries both a *b*-flat signature and an *E*-flat inflection.

Example 1.2 *Lan que li jor sunt lonc en mai* by Jaufre Rudel, according to *Troubadour MS W*, f. 189v (following suggestions for filling lacunae offered by Hendrik van der Werf, *The Extant Troubadour Melodies: Transcriptions and Essays for Performers and Scholars* [Rochester: van der Werf, 1984], 215–19)

the other two. Treitler interprets – correctly, I think – the melody as having a tentative ending, and I think that he makes a good point. The melody ends on *G* (*C* in the other manuscripts), but *a* (*D*) is established more firmly throughout the stanza. In this interpretation, phrases 2 and 4, each ending on *G*, bring an *ouvert* quality to the first part of the stanza; the arrival on *G* at the end then conditions the entire stanza in this way. Treitler's interest in text–music relations leads him to describe the unexpected ending in terms of enigma or longing, moods compatible with sentiments of the poem.

More difficult to accept is the suggestion that the entire melody is controlled by a syntax of third-chains. Treitler hears *G* as being linked to a
third-chain *G-b-d-f,* which alternates with the chain *a-c-e-g.* He character-
izes third-chains as "tonal sonorities" and "established structures," and his
position is that they have such a strong presence in this idiom that the entire
chain is invoked by only a few notes or even a single note – just as, say, a
dominant-seventh chord may be so invoked.[22] This is the unlikely premise
that yields the untenable gloss of alternating third-chains.[23] At this point,
Treitler's analysis imposes more syntactic rigor on the melody than it is able
to support. It is much simpler to say that *G* has an *ouvert* quality because it is
a step away from the pitch that gets greater emphasis. That is an assertion
that one finds vast support for in the routine practices of the period.

We may also draw attention to the accidental (which Treitler does not
comment on) introduced in the last two phrases of *MS W.* The inflection
may be taken as an editorial response to the song's tentative ending. *MS W*'s
b-flat would have been *E*-flat in the transposed version, but this inflection is
nowhere to be found in the other two manuscripts.[24] Clearly, *MS W*'s *b*-flat
has nothing to do with either modality or third-chains. Its function would
seem to be one of destabilizing *a.* In later (and polyphonic) repertories one
can see clearly that "*mi*" cadences carry an *ouvert* quality; since endings on
mi are virtually non-existent in the troubadour-trouvère repertory, we may

[22] The analogy is suggested in "Medieval Lyric," 5: "The
idea behind the third-chain principle is embodied in
modern theories of tonal voice-leading. It is the idea that
the tonal quality of a note is prolonged by the third and
fifth above it and displaced by a tone above or below it."
[23] For example (*ibid.,* 8): "the melody [in phrase 1] takes
the *e*' [at the transposed pitch level given in our
Example, read, in medieval letter notation: '*b*'] that had
been skipped on the way up and associates it with the
low *c*' (by way of *d*') [read: '*G* (by way of *a*)'] as a
contrasting module to the third *d*'-*f*''' [read: '*a-d*']." It is
hard for me to discover any basis for associating *e*' with *c*'
[that is, *b* with *G*], since the line moves in conjunct
motion. Further: "The melody of the second line
sharpens this contrast extending to the third-chains *d*'-
f'-*a*' [read: *a-c-e*] and *g*'-*e*'-*c*' [read: *d-b-G*]. . ." But, again,
the line is marked by almost uniform conjunct motion.
In two of the three main manuscripts, there is only a
single leap (*MS X* carries one additional leap), except for
the opening leap of a third, so it is hard to see how the
contrasting third-chains have become "sharpened." Van
der Werf works with third-chains in his analysis of this
song, but more cautiously; see *The Chansons of the*

Troubadours and Trouvères, 85–9. The more general
problem I am identifying here, of imposing upon these
melodies an analysis that claims more systematic
organization than they can bear, also turns up elsewhere
in van der Werf's work. For example, consider this
remark (*The Chansons of the Troubadours and Trouvères,*
104) regarding *MS O*'s version of *Ne me song pas
achoison de chanter* (Beck 214; R 787): "Of more
relevance, however, is the question of whether in the first
line in the O and K versions the *C* or the *D* is the
structural tone." I see no basis for favoring either pitch in
this way. The fact that it is not clear which pitch is more
important is not necessarily a problem that needs to be
resolved by choosing one or the other; rather, ambiguity
like this would seem to be a basic feature of the melodic
idiom.
[24] The sign is repeated after the staff break (supporting
our working assumption that signs govern for the
duration of the staff), and it seems likely that all *b*'s after
the first inflection are to be sung as *b*-flat. In his
comparative edition of the three versions, van der Werf
reports that *MS X* introduces *b*-flat in phrases 5 and 6.
The inflection is relatively insignificant.

assume that they carry this same quality here.[25] In this way, the inflection of
b-flat in *MS W* helps push the line towards *G*, where the stanza will end; and
from this point of view we may read the inflection as a response to the
song's "weak" ending. From this emerges a possible explanation for *MS W*'s
transposition up a fifth. Imagine that the reviser of the song had this
inflection in mind, and that he was free to notate at any level. Since *b*-flat is
a more familiar accidental than *E*-flat, which would have been required at
the other pitch level, the inflection may have determined the transposition.
If, for whatever reason, he was interested in notating within the confines of
the traditional gamut, this was the way to accomplish that.

A focus on how accidentals function yields a lateral point of entry into
the difficult topic of melodic syntax. Accidentals – even *b*-flat, in a case like
this – encourage us to construct a methodology for analysis that is independent of modal theory. It is the lack of syntactic rigor that makes
inflections possible; and in this case, the inflection may be taken as a reaction to the ambiguous nature of the syntax. Emphasis on modal syntax or
any other rigidly defined syntax (such as third-chains) moves analysis in
the other direction, away from flexibility and towards system. One may
assume that the late medieval period knew a range of possibilities – even on
this fundamental point of melodic syntax – and that different repertories
will demand different ways of thinking. Any gain in understanding of how
accidentals function will be a gain for understanding syntax.

One simple premise to work with is that accidentals signal movement in a
general direction (sharps up and flats down) and towards or away from a
specific pitch (most obviously the neighboring pitch). Here is a syntactic
rule that is easy to manipulate – for example, when the implied resolution of
the inflection arrives after a delay or not at all. That is how I have read *F*-
sharps in *MS O*'s redaction of Gace Brulé's *Au renovel* (see the Introduction):
the first *F*-sharp directs the line towards a wayward cadence on *G*; then, at the
end of the song, *F*-sharp returns as an allusion to the previous digression and
as a way of making the conclusion more interesting. In *MS O*'s redaction of
Ausi cum l'unicorne sui, sharps are also left dangling and unresolved. As it
happens, the specific melodic gestures in both cases – the falling third of *Ausi
cum l'unicorne sui* and the four-note neume of *Au renovel* – are used else-

---

[25] Only one song in *MS O*, *Chascuns qui de bien amer*
(Beck 77; R 759), ends on *mi*. It seems likely that the
song originated as a duplum for a motet; hence, the
ending on *a*, arrived at through *b*-flat, was originally
supported by *D* underneath, in the tenor. On the
chanson and the motet, see van der Werf, *The Chansons
of the Troubadours and Trouvères*, 134–6, with an edition
of the motet. This point about *mi-clausulae* is taken up
in more detail in Chapter 2, where it is observed that
they never occur in *clos* position in Machaut's songs; they
occur in *ouvert* position fairly often, however. It is harder
to establish this point for trouvère melodies, since both
practice and transmission are inconsistent. But the fact
that *mi*-endings are so rare must be significant.

where in this manuscript, hinting at common origins and a consistent style of redaction.[26] Comparative analysis is one way to approach the problem of how accidentals function. The typical conditions of transmission for trouvère songs block the attempt: it is always difficult to identify a coherent repertory, to isolate what has been shaped or reshaped by whom. *MS O*, with its relatively large layer of inflected songs, offers an advantage.

In *MS O*'s version of *Quare eusse* (Ex. 1.3; Beck 310; R 641), delayed resolution binds *frons* to *cauda*. Each *pes* ends with a drop from *F*-sharp to *D*, recalling *Ausi cum l'unicorne sui*. *F*-sharp at the end of the first *pes* is left dangling; the only time it resolves directly is at the beginning of the *cauda*, on *G*. The effect of both the cross relation between *F*-natural and *F*-sharp and the delayed resolution is to make the *frons* more dynamic. *F*-sharp first contributes an element of discontinuity (within each *pes* and between the two *pedes*) and then an element of continuity (between *frons* and *cauda*). The accidental is employed with a sense of how it interacts with stanzaic form, and this same interest manifests elsewhere in the manuscript, in a variety of ways, which we may now consider.[27]

[26] Four songs featuring the four-note neume are attributed to Gace Brulé, suggesting the possibility of a common origin for the redactions. In addition to *Au renovel*, see *Je ne puis pas si long fuir* (Beck 150; R 1414; T-M, I: 470), *Oëz por quoir* (alternative incipit *Savez, pour coi plaing et souspir*, Beck 222; R 1465; T-M, I: 474), and *N'est pas a soi qui eimme coraument* (Beck 213; R 653; T-M, I: 391). Like *Au renovel*, *MS O*'s redaction of *Oëz por quoi* has the four-note neume (expanded to five notes) with *F*-sharp on the penultimate syllable, before the ending on *D*. *N'est pas a soi qui eimme coraument* uses the neume at the ends of phrases 1 and 3, establishing a crisp cross relation between *F* and *F*-sharp. The same neume is used twice, again with *F*-sharp, in *S'onques nuls* (Beck 326; R 1126). In *Je ne puis pas si long fuir*, the four-note neume is used just as it is in *Au renovel*, to add an unsettling dimension to the final phrase of the stanza by pointing away from the final. The neume turns through *b*-natural, pointing towards *c*, and in the final phrase this implication is left dangling as the line descends to the main and final pitch, *F*. This version of *Je ne puis pas si long fuir* features systematic alternation between *b*-natural and *b*-flat, with phrases 1, 3, 5, and 8 colored by *b*-natural, phrases 2, 4, 6, and 7 by *b*-flat. The four-note neume links phrases 1, 3 and 8. Here is an example of additional accidentals being tied to a more frequent thematic repetition, making the redaction both more unsettling and more coherent than other versions. For examples of raised thirds dropping away at phrase endings (resembling *Ausi cum l'unicorne sui*) see *Li douz pensers* (Thibaut de Navarre: Beck 174; R 1469; T M, II: 204), *Li rosignox chante tant* (Thibaut de Navarre: Beck 175; R 360; T-M, II: 64), *Conment que longue demeure* (Chastelain de Coucy: Beck 64; R 1010; T-M, I: 260), *Li nouvauz temps et maiz et violete* (Chastelain de Coucy: Beck 182; R 986; T-M, I: 243), *Leaus desirs et pensée jolie* (Martin le Beguin?: Beck 191; R 1172). I should note that these figures are not at all unique to this manuscript.

[27] For another example of delayed resolution in the manuscript, consider *A la saison* (Beck 14; R 2086; also copied into this manuscript as *Quant la saison*, Beck 303). The song is notated with accidentals only in *MS O*, which shows six *F*-sharps and one *c*-sharp; if we assume that each sign governs for the duration of the staff, then all *F*s are inflected. Leaps from *F*-sharp to *a* occur regularly, in six of seven phrases, between syllables 4 and 5. In three phrases (2, 4, and 7), *F*-sharp "resolves" to *G* only at the end of the phrase, with a delay of seven syllables, and tension is stretched out over the course of the phrase. The *F*-sharp points more clearly towards *G* than do the uninflected *F*s of other manuscripts. It is telling that *MS O* uniquely carries not only *F*-sharps but also greater repetition of the gesture, compared with other manuscripts: no other manuscript has the precise return of material from phrases 2 and 4 in phrase 7, as *MS O* does. We shall see this pattern of coordinating added accidentals with more frequent thematic repetition often in the manuscript.

Example 1.3 *Quare eusse*, lines 1–5, by Pistoleta, according to *Trouvère MS O*, f. 125 (poem after van der Werf, *Extant Troubadour Melodies*, 280*)

Form

Musical form in trouvère songs is easier to understand than melodic syntax is; to the extent that the two intersect, we may use one to try and unravel the mysteries of the other. Very common is a stanza built with a *frons* consisting of two identical two-line *pedes*, followed by *cauda* of variable length. If we are able to coordinate observations about accidentals with their placement according to stanzaic form, we should be able to analyze more securely how the inflections function.

MS O's version of the celebrated *Biaus m'est estez*[28](Ex. 1.4) is not heavily inflected, but it will serve well to demonstrate this possibility of a coordinated analysis. Most obvious in this song is a stylistic marker of the *grand chant courtois* far more typical than accidentals: this is the use of ligatures, usually in a range from two to five notes per syllable. Heavy neumatic ornamentation is responsible in no small way for imparting to trouvère

---

[28] Gace Brulé (Beck 39; R 1006; *T-M*, I: 438). As van der Werf suggests (*T-M*, I: 438) in his transcription of *MS M*, for phrases 1 and 3 the syllable count stretches by one extra syllable, and "*bruil-le*" becomes "*bru-eil-le*," while "*muil-le*" becomes "*mu-eil-le*."

Example 1.4 *Biaus m'est estez* by Gace Brulé, according to *Trouvère MSS O*, f. 15v, and *M*, f. 25v (poem after Rosenberg and Danon, eds., *The Lyrics and Melodies of Gace Brulé*, 80, which is based on *MS O*)

Example 1.4 (*cont.*)

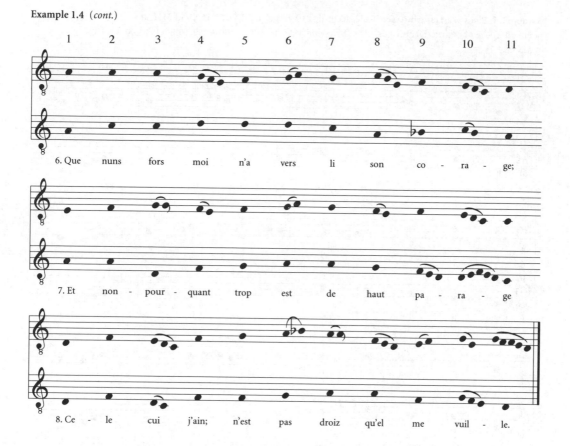

6. Que nuns fors moi n'a vers li son co - ra - ge;

7. Et non - pour - quant trop est de haut pa - ra - ge

8. Ce - le cui j'ain; n'est pas droiz qu'el me vuil - le.

songs a stately manner, wonderfully realized in isosyllabic rendition (a steady pulse of one note or note-group per syllable). The twists and turns of a florid line may serve to delay progress towards cadential goals. Neumes may serve to undermine the stability of a neatly ordered cadential plan. Thinking in this way, neumatic ornamentation and chromatic inflections become analogous when each demonstrates melodic intervention. In the version of *Biaus m'est estez* transmitted by *MS O*, both kinds of intervention are coordinated with stanzaic form.

The song survives with melody in only two sources. The relatively heavy neumatic inflection of *MS O* (32 neumes), compared with *MS M* (eleven neumes), is evident at a glance. The expansive quality of *MS O*'s version is established right away, in the first *pes*. Phrase 1 rises to its peak in a more leisurely manner than does the analogous phrase of *MS M*, which ascends quickly and without ornament until the penultimate syllable – a traditional place for neumes. In *MS O*, the location of neumes varies from phrase to phrase: phrase 1 has neumes on syllables 3, 7 and 10, phrase 2 on syllables 4, 6, 8, and 10. This is significant, for surely the sense of intervention will be stronger when neumatic placement is unpredictable. The trend continues into the *cauda*: neumes occur on syllables 3, 4, 6, 8, and 10 in phrase 7, and for phrase 8 a neume on syllable 3 anticipates the extraordinary placement of neumes on every one of the last six syllables. Here is the full, leisurely blossom of the high-style idiom.

Details in the organization of pitches contribute to the expansive atmosphere. Again, this is evident from the first *pes*. By moving from *D* to *C* over the course of phrase 1 and then back from *C* to *D* over the course of phrase 2, *MS M*'s first *pes* is indeed logically ordered. The logic is loosened in *MS O*: phrase 1 begins on *D* and moves to *F*, and phrase 2 starts on *G* and moves back to *D*. Phrase 5 of *MS O* features a cross relation, *b*-natural followed by *b*-flat. *b*-natural serves to set off the *cauda* from the *frons* (a technique that is used often in this manuscript), and *b*-natural is also a gesture of expansion, for it pulls the line up to *c*, the first peak in a double arch. *b*-flat then marks the phrase as internally unstable, by virtue of both the cross relation and the conclusion on *mi*.

We discover, in this redaction, evidence of a mind willing to experiment with formal design when phrase 6 sounds as a nearly literal repetition of phrases 2 and 4. This is an unlikely formal move in the traditional bar form, which is used straightforwardly in *MS M*. The unusual extra repetition, which the poetic form accommodates, recasts the stanza as a series of four couplets, with the peak occurring in couplet 3 (in phrase 5). Repeated endings on *D* for phrases 2, 4, 6, and 8 reinforce the sense of a four-couplet form. The reviser thinks first about the combined linear shape of two phrases to form a couplet, then about how the couplets combine to form the stanza. His plan moves from the repeated *pedes* through the digression and peak of phrase 5 and the return of phrase 6, then through a balancing focus on the melody's lower range (together with heavy neumatic inflection) in phrases 7 and 8. Discursive gestures are coordinated with cohering ones: the stanza is ordered by thematic repetition and by the regular returns to *D*, while it is made more discursive by the irregularly placed neumes and by expansive movement through a more varied pitch field. Ordering repetitions draw the listener in; expansive and discursive features yield a lovely, airy quality. Gace Brulé's modern-day reputation has benefited from this anonymous reviser's efforts, certainly long after the trouvère's death and perhaps near the end of the trouvère tradition.

*

Table 1.1 lists songs from *MS O* in which accidentals are introduced at phrase 5, causing a digression from the pitch field mapped out in the *frons* and setting off the first phrase of the *cauda*. Several songs resemble *Biaus*

Table 1.1

Song (with Beck no. and Raynaud/Spanke no.)	*accidental in phrase 5*
Dame, ensi est q'il m'en couvient aler (Beck 84, R 757)	b-flat[a]
De chanter ne me puis tenir (Beck 93, R 1475)	b-flat
Ennuiz et desesperance (Beck 123, R 213)	b-flat
Je n'oi pieca nul talent de chanter (Beck 148, R 801)	b-flat
Par grant franchise me covient chanter (Beck 247, R 782)	b-flat
Quant fine amor me prie que je chant (Beck 264, R 306)	b-flat
Quant noif et giel et froidure (Beck 270, R 2099)	b-flat[b]
Sire, loez moi a choisir (Beck 319, R 1393)	b-flat[c]
Se par force de merci (Beck 324, R 1059)	b-flat
Amours qui m'a doné (Beck 29, R 1062)	e-flat
Bien doi chanter (Beck 52, R 116)	e-flat
Encor n'est raisons (Beck 129, R 1911)	e-flat
Enz ou cuer m'est entrée finement (Beck 126, R 675)	b-natural
Au commencier de ma novele amour (Beck 25, R 1960)	f-sharp
Quant je plus sui en pa our de ma vie (Beck 277, R 1227)	f-sharp[d]
Trop m'abelit (Beck 347, R 1993)	f-sharp
Chanter me fait ce donc je crien morir (Beck 59, R 1429)	c-sharp
Desoremais est raisons (Beck 111, R 1885)	c-sharp

Notes:
[a] Thibaut de Navarre, ed. in *T-M*, II: 120–3.
[b] Gace Brulé, ed. in *T-M*, I: 548–51.
[c] Thibaut de Navarre, ed. in *T-M*, II: 169–89.
[d] Blondel de Nesle, ed. in *T-M*, I: 60–85.

m'est estez in having a cross relation within phrase 5.[29] Now, the technique of setting off phrase 5 from the material of the *frons* is hardly unusual in trouvère songs recorded by other manuscripts, but the typical means for this is to have some contrast in range or melodic contour. The reviser at work in *MS O* readily turns to accidentals for this purpose. The technique spills over into revision of the through-composed stanza of *A enviz sent mal*; even though the stanza is through-composed, the digression in phrase 6 so closely resembles phrase 5 of *Biaus m'est estez* that there can be little doubt but that the two revisions came from the same hand.[30]

In other songs, accidentals are introduced only at the very end of the

[29] Moniot de Paris, *Ne me done pas talent* (Beck 216; R 739; *T-M*, II: 350–64) has *b*-flat followed by *b*-natural in phrase 5. *Qui bien vuet amors descrivre* (Beck 283; R 1655) has *e*-natural followed by *e*-flat.

[30] *A enviz sent mal* is attributed to Thibaut de Navarre (Beck 3; R 1521, *T-M*, II: 234). Phrase 6 of *A enviz sent mal* features a digression through *f*-sharp and a return to *f*-natural, and as a result it is internally unstable, like

phrase 5 of *Biaus m'est estez*. My assertion that *f*-natural follows *f*-sharp is based on the assumption that the accidental governs only on the staff where it is placed. Here again we discover discursive accidentals balanced with tighter organization, which manifests through slightly greater emphasis on *d* (indicated by the fact that all versions of this song begin on *d*, but only *MS O*'s version ends there).

stanza, in either the penultimate phrase (six songs)[31] or final phrase (four-teen songs).[32] A fresh inflection brings a sense of conclusion. That similar techniques will come to be used in polyphonic chansons from later centuries represents a meaningful coincidence. Setting off the *frons* from the *cauda* anticipates the very common practice in polyphonic ballades of a division between the two main parts; and we shall see Machaut using accidentals for precisely this purpose. In the early fifteenth century, we shall see the technique of introducing flats towards the end of a piece. Several *G*-pieces in *MS O* show alternation between *h*-flat and *b*-natural above a stable pitch of reference, anticipating Du Fay's celebrated use of *Terzfreiheit*.[33] Similar techniques arise independently, out of the same field of possibilities. Syntactic flexibility encourages experiments with accidentals, and it is important to recognize that some composers were interested in controlling their experiments through formal design.

"Difficult" intervals and contours

Writing around 1475, Johannes Tinctoris says that the melodic tritone is difficult or impossible for singers to execute.[34] Of course, he is right. The tritone was difficult for singers in 1475, it is difficult today, and we may assume that it was difficult around 1300. It is significant, therefore, that *MS O* notates a few direct tritones, along with other difficult intervals, such as diminished fifths and augmented fifths. The same tritone leap, *C* to *F*-

[31] *Amours qui mout mi guerroie* (Beck 23; R 1722); *Chanter m'estuet* (Thibaut de Navarre: Beck 56; R 1476; *T-M*, II: 212); *On voit sovent en chantant amenrir* (Beck 230; R 1391); *Onques ne me poi parcevoir* (Beck 233; R 1803); *Quant voi renverdir l'arbroie* (Gace Brulé: Beck 306; R 1690; *T-M*, I: 516); *Une dolour enossée* (Thibaut de Navarre: Beck 349; R 510; *T-M*, II: 80–3).

[32] *A la doucor de la belle seson* (Gace Brulé: Beck 8; R 1893; *T-M*, I: 538–40); *Au douz mois de mai joli* (Beck 27; R 1050); *Bien me deusse targier* (Chastelain de Coucy: Beck 45; R 1314; *T-M*, I: 295–8); *Bien est obliez chanters* (Beck 49; R 905); *Costume est bien* (Thibaut de Navarre: Beck 71; R 1880; *T-M*, II: 273); *Chascuns qui de bien amer* (Beck 77; R 759); *Desconforter, plains de doleur et d'ire* (Gace Brulé: Beck 95; R 1498; *T-M*, I: 480); *Fine amour* (Beck 132; R 221); *Grant piece que ne chantai* (Beck 138; R 65); *Je chantaisse volentiers liement* (Chastelain de Coucy: Beck 151; R 700; *T-M*, I: 232–40); *J'ai oublié poinne et travauz* (Beck 166; R 389); *Merci clamans de mon fol errement* (Chastelain de Coucy: Beck 204; R 671; *T-M*, I: 208–23); *Quant la saisons* (Beck 303;

R 2086); *Se valors vient de mener bone vie* (Beck 329; R 1218).

[33] See *Tout autresi con dou soloil li rai* (Beck 345; R 99), *Mout ai esté longuement esbahiz* (Gace Brulé: Beck 203; R 1536; *T-M*, I: 494), and *L'an que rose ne fueille* (Chastelain de Coucy: entered twice in *MS O*, as Beck 183 and 195; R 1009; *T-M*, I: 251), for example. *On voit sovent* (Beck 230; R 1391) has *b*-flat toward the end of the penultimate phrase in several manuscripts (MSS *K*, *X*, and *N*). MSS *O*, *a*, and *Z* also have the *b*-flat, but they add a turn in the last phrase through *b*-natural, as if to elaborate upon the chromatic event by adding a cross relation. *MS O* takes the chromaticism one step further, still, by adding *F*-sharp in close juxtaposition to the *b*-flat.

[34] *Liber de natura et proprietate tonorum*, in Johannes Tinctoris, *Opera Theoretica*, ed. A. Seay, Corpus Scriptorum de Musica 22/1 (n.p.: American Institute of Musicology, 1975), 76; translated edition by A. Seay as *Concerning the Nature and Propriety of Tones* (Colorado Springs: Colorado College Music Press, 1976), 14.

sharp, is notated twice in *Puis que je sui de l'amourouse lois* (Adam de la Halle: Beck 255; R 1661; *T-M*, XII: 615).[35] Even without the accidental (which is how other manuscripts read), the phrase divides naturally at this place. The accidental causes a striking dislocation; one cannot help feeling that it also establishes *G* more firmly as an important pitch, second in a hierarchy led by *C*.

The first *pes* of *Lanque voi l'erbe resplandre* (Gace Brulé: Beck 180; R 633; *T-M*, XI: 379) seems to feature a leap from *F* to *b*-natural – "seems to," since the *b* is unsigned. A bald tritone like this makes it difficult to have confidence in the assumption that unsigned *b* should be taken as *b*-natural. More than a few scholars would assume without hesitation that the leap implies *b*-flat. Yet the context of this song may lead us to resist this assumption. *Lanque voi l'erbe resplandre* has two more leaps from *F* to *b* (in the second *pes* and in phrase 9), and in each case *b*-flat is signed. If singers understood that the unsigned *b* in the first *pes* needs to be sung as soft *b* rather than hard *b*, then why was it necessary to notate flats for the other two *b*'s? Furthermore, consider this: phrases 5 and 7 are nearly identical except that *b*-flat is signed in phrase 7, during an ascent from *a* to *c*, while the accidental is absent from the same ascent in phrase 5. Taken together, the two sets of inconsistently notated *b*'s lead one to believe that the reviser enjoys the possibility of using accidentals to distinguish similar phrases from one another. Accidentals provide a subtle (or not-so-subtle) tool for variation. In this view, the tritone of phrase 1 becomes transformed into a perfect fourth in phrases 3 and 9.

We have already seen how accidentals may be coordinated with stanzaic form; this is the general context in which to place the inconsistently notated *b*'s of *Lanque voi l'erbe resplandre*. More specifically, it belongs to a group of songs from this manuscript that show accidentals used in one *pes* but not the other. These are the possibilities:

> An accidental is absent from phrase 1 and added to phrase 3 (like
> *Lanque voi l'erbe resplandre*).[36]
> An accidental is absent from phrase 2 and added to phrase 4.[37]

---

[35] Two *unica* placed next to each other near the end of the "S" group both use the same leap of an augmented fifth, *F* to *c*-sharp: see *Se j'ay chanté* (Beck 327; R 2061) and *Sovent m'ont demandé* (Beck 328; R 682). Both are *D*-pieces, and in each case the leap comes towards the end of the stanza.

[36] *Amour qui* (Beck 20; R 1110); *J'avoie lessié* (Beck 157; R 822); *La douce voiz* (Chastelain de Coucy: Beck 184; R

40; *T-M*, I: 186–93); *Une chanson* (Thibaut de Navarre: Beck 348; R 1002; *T-M*, II: 142–5).

[37] *Lons desirs et longue atente* (Beck 190; R 746); *Oëz pour quoi plaing et souspir* (Beck 222; R 1465); *Puis que li maux* (Beck 256; R 1457); *Quant foillissent li boschaige* (Beck 265; R 14) – on this song, see note 41, below; *A la saison* (Beck 14; R 2086).

Both phrases of the second *pes* are distinguished from both phrases of the first *pes* by use of accidentals.[38]

The corresponding phrases have the same accidental but at slightly different places.[39]

An accidental is present in the first *pes* but dropped in the second *pes*.[40]

If this last pattern stood alone, it would be tempting to explain it away: the notational inconsistency may be nothing more than a scribal convention, according to which the singer knows to carry the first inflection over to the second statement of the same material. But since the pattern often occurs the other way around, with the accidental absent from the first *pes* and present in the second, it is reasonable to think of the evidence as collectively manifesting an interest in variety. Sometimes there is additional variation through melodic ornament.[41] There are too many cases (I have cited twenty-five) to dismiss the pattern as scribal carelessness.

Tinctoris made his now-famous remark that the flat sign may be omitted when the context makes clear the need for it with reference to what we call indirect tritones (see the Introduction). I have argued already that this precept cannot be taken as prima-facie evidence that singers knew when to inflect trouvère songs with musica ficta in the absence of signs; especially important to this point is the fact that *MS O* notates explicitly a good number of indirect tritones and indirect diminished fifths, as well as indirect diminished fourths.[42] *Pour conforter ma pesance* (Thibaut de Navarre:

---

[38] *Pour demorer* (Beck 257; R185); *Tant ai en chantant proié* (Blondel de Nesle: Beck 335; R 1095; *T-M*, I. 52).

[39] Compare phrases 1 and 3 of *Li tres douz temps* (Beck 188; R604); also, phrases 1 and 3 of *Tres fine Amors* (Beck 344; R 1065).

[40] *Bone amors* (Beck 48; R 1569); *Comment que d'amors me dueille* (Blondel de Nesle: Beck 67; R 1007; *T-M*, I: 42); *Dame, merci* (Thibaut de Navarre: Beck 90; R 335; *T-M*, II: 43); *Desoremais est raisons* (Beck 111; R 1885); *Ire d'amors* (Gace Brulé: Beck 149; R 171; *T-M*, I: 327); *Nuns hons ne seit* (Beck 215; R 1821); *Onques d'amors* (Beck 226; R 138); *Pluis ne venz* (Beck 246; R 2105); *Se j'ai chanté* (Beck 327; R 2061); *Se valors vient* (Beck 329; R 1218).

[41] *MS O*'s version of *Quant foillissent li boschaige* (Beck 265; R 14) transforms phrase 4 so that it exists in an *ouvert–clos* relationship with phrase 2 (in contrast to *MSS P, N, K,* and *X,* each of which has an exact repeat of phrase 2 in phrase 4); the transformation includes the addition of the *b*-flat. See also *Amour qui* (Beck 20; R

1110) and *Ire d'amors* (Gace Brulé: Beck 149; R 171; *T-M*, I: 327). Hendrik van der Werf discusses inconsistently notated *pedes* in songs by Gace Brulé in *The Lyrics and Melodies of Gace Brulé*, 345 and n. 11.

[42] See *Amours qui mout me guerroie* (Beck 23; R 1722: leaps from *E* to *G* to *b*-flat in most sources, and motion from *B* through *F* in several sources), *Amours qui m'a doné* (Beck 29; R 1062: *b*-natural through *e*-flat, then *b*-flat through *E*-natural), *De cuer dolant* (Beck 106; R 1500), *Fine amour et bone esperance* (Beck 132; R 221), *Mout ai esté longuement esbahiz* (Gace Brulé: Beck 203: R 1536; *T-M*, I: 494), *On voit sovent en chantant amenrir* (Beck 230; R 1391), *Pour demorer* (Beck 257; R 185: indirect diminished fifth, *a* through *e*-flat, followed by descent to *b*-natural to form an indirect diminished fourth), *Quant je plus sui en paour* (Blondel de Nesle: Beck 277; R 1227; *T-M*, I: 60: entered again in *MS O*, with contrafact text, as Beck 58), *Trop m'abelit* (Beck 347; R 1993).

Example 1.5 *Pour conforter ma pesance*, by Thibaut de Navarre, according to *Trouvère MS O*, f. 95 (poem after Brahney, ed., *The Lyrics of Thibaut de Champagne*, 26, with spelling adjusted to *MS O*)

Beck 236; R 237; *T-M*, XII: 11) provides a lovely example (see Ex. 1.5). In a different context, Tinctoris describes how a vertical diminished fifth is permitted if it resolves properly, by contracting; that is how we may parse the indirect diminished fifth in *Pour conforter ma pesance*: c "resolves" to b and F-sharp to G.[43] There is room in this idiom for rough, irregular contours – or, following Tinctoris, "difficult" contours. And this is why I doubt the rel-

---

[43] Passages by Tinctoris from the second book of *Liber de arte contrapuncti* discussed by Karol Berger, *Musica ficta*, 95–100; on indirect tritones, see pp. 70–84. John Stevens discusses *Pour conforter ma pesance* in *Words and Music in the Middle Ages*, 42–3 and 469–70; inexplicably, Stevens drops the *F*-sharp from his transcription of the song as Example 3, p. 42, which is based on *MS O*.

evance in this repertory of the precept against indirect tritones. The reviser's ear is not necessarily guided by standards of melodic decorum associated with plainchant. Prominent cross relations may be thought of in the same way. At times, the tension of the cross relation seems to be the main point of a phrase[44] or even an entire stanza.[45] The rules for plainchant do not automatically apply to secular song. Yet if the rules do not automatically cross genres, we can be sure that every singer and virtually every listener of secular song *knew* plainchant. So, one may argue, it is by violating those melodic norms that difficult leaps and contours derive expressive power.

Two phrases of *Fine Amor claimme a moi* (Beck 133; R 26) will serve to conclude this discussion of cross relations in *MS O*, and it will also bring us around to issues involving transmission (see Ex. 1.6). From both the *f*-natural in phrase 7 and the *f*-sharp of phrase 8, the melody moves away logically, so this cross relation is not particularly obtrusive. More assertive is the set of cross relations on *c* that follows: *c*-sharp brings a special poignancy, since the line turns away from the implied resolution to *d*, leaping up abruptly to a sudden *c*-natural.

MS O's version of this melody has much in common with that transmitted by *MS M*. It is plausible, I think, that the version recorded by *MS M* (or something very similar to it) served as the basis for the revision that we have in *MS O*. Three sources, *MSS O, M*, and *a*, have the melody with a G final, while at least three others have it a step lower. (Patterns of collation like this suggest that more can be made out of the phenomenon of transposition than has been attempted so far.[46]) *MSS O* and *M* (but not *a*) share *f*-sharp in the *frons*, and this inflection surely came about through an inter-

---

[44] For example, *Lors que rose ne fuille* (Chastelain de Coucy: Beck 195; R 1009; *T-M*, I: 251) and *A la doucour dou tens qui reverdoie* (Beck 5; R 1754; *T-M*, I: 269).

[45] *Pour longue atente de merci* (Bernart de Ventadorn: Beck 260; R 1057; *Extant Troubadour Melodies*, 36*), an *oda continua* transmitted with a contrafact text in *MS O*, shows some of the most chromatic writing in the manuscript. There are textual problems in interpreting some of the hard-*b*'s as *c*-sharp or *b*-natural. My reading of the accidentals would be as follows (and, at several places, in contradiction to Beck, *Le Chansonnier Cangé*, II: 245). Phrase 2: *c*-sharp followed by *c*-natural followed by *b*-flat. Phrase 4: *b*-flat followed by *b*-natural. Phrase 5: *b*-natural. Phrase 6: *f*-sharp followed by *b*-flat. Phrase 7: *b*-flat followed by *c*-sharp followed by *c*-natural.

[46] It is unlikely that most transpositions can be understood as simply the more or less haphazard notation of songs at varying pitch levels – that is, as a phenomenon explained by the fact of oral transmission followed by written redaction at pitch levels that were more or less randomly selected. If that were true, then transpositions would be more erratically distributed and with more variety. Beck's explanation, that transpositions accommodated different vocal ranges, is unlikely, especially in a case like this, with differences of a whole step. At the least, it may be possible to use transposition patterns in forming a written stemma, as I suggest tentatively in this analysis of *Fine Amor claimme a moi*. *MS O*'s version of *Biaus m'est estez* may also represent a transformation of the melody that is represented by *MS M* (see Ex. 1.4, above; compare especially, for this point, the final line of the stanza). The relationship between *MSS O* and *M* is taken up again, below.

Example 1.6 *Fine Amor claimme a moi par heritage*, lines 7 and 8, according to *Trouvère MS O*, f. 54

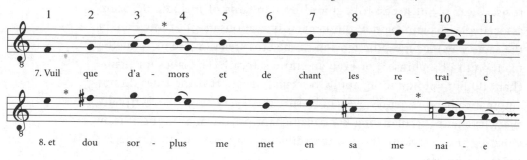

est in duplicating the intervals notated diatonically at the alternative transposition (i.e., the half step *f*-sharp to *g* in *MSS O* and *M* corresponds with *e* to *f* in the alternative). In the *cauda*, *MS O* moves uniquely and assertively through two sets of cross relations, as we have seen. The first cross relation would seem to have been prepared by the earlier use of *f*-sharp, which is recorded by both *O* and *M* and which seems to have been produced by the transposition. The second betrays the idiosyncratic style of redaction that distinguishes *MS O*. As we have seen before, there is an interest in both discursive elements and cohering ones, for the audacity of the chromatic writing is balanced by stricter thematic repetition: the most daring phrase, with *c*-sharp and *c*-natural in close juxtaposition, is repeated literally in *MS O*, while no other manuscript carries a melodic repetition at this point in the stanza.

Transmission

At several turns we have touched upon issues related to transmission, and even though it is difficult to go very far beyond speculation with this topic, speculation seems warranted, if for no other reason than the need to make gains in sorting through a very large body of poorly understood music. This is the great hope for future study of the trouvères: with so many melodies, and with a good number of sources for many of them, it should be possible to gain greater control of variants and, thereby, gain insight into how the melodies were created, revised, transmitted and, perhaps, performed. More specifically, one may attempt to imagine the circumstances surrounding the style of redaction we are interested in. Important for us are a few faint bits of evidence that indicate relationships between the inflected songs in *MS O* and other versions in other manuscripts.

It has been argued, reasonably enough, that the lines of transmission for trouvère songs were alternately oral and written. Oral transmission, especially, would seem to account for the marked instability of the melodies, and one cannot help wondering whether oral transmission had something to do with notated accidentals in *MS O*. I have already outlined my opinion (following van der Werf) that there is no good reason to imagine that performance practice relieved the scribe of the burden of notating inflections. The topic should now be turned around to ask if there is any reason to believe whether accidentals that *have* been notated in this manuscript had their origins in unnotated practice. Perhaps the manuscript reports inflections that were routinely sung but rarely reported elsewhere. Arguing against this is the likelihood that some accidentals arose as integral parts of melodic revision. If an accidental is tied to a unique melodic revision, and if it serves an important function in the design of that revision, then it would seem to be a product of the revision rather than an explicit record of some widely known but seldom recorded performance practice. In this view, the reviser at work in *MS O* proceeds in the traditional way of making something new out of a received melody. The difference is that he commands a new notational tool with which to do his work.

Yet if we set aside the idea of coded conventions, it is possible to imagine, still, an oblique connection between *MS O*'s accidentals and an unnotated practice involving digression from the diatonic pitch field. Scattered remarks from the late Middle Ages mention a performance practice of applying various types of semitones. Apparently, this practice embraced virtually all kinds of song. Recent work by Timothy McGee, especially, draws attention to the references. Reporting (presumably) Parisian practice and writing between 1272 and 1304, Jerome of Moravia describes various vocal ornaments. He says that the French "intermingle enharmonic half steps and chromatic trihemitones with the diatonic type. They interchange a semitone for a tone and the reverse, and as a result, to all other people they [appear to] sing out of tune."[47] Writing slightly later, and from Italy, Marchetto of Padua also refers to what we would call microtonal

[47] "Nam diesim enharmonicam et trihemitonium chromaticum generi diatonico associant. Semitonium loco toni et e converso commutant, in quo quidem a cunctis nationibus in cantu discordant." Quotation and translation from Timothy McGee, *The Sound of Medieval Song: Ornamentation and Vocal Style According to the Treatises* (forthcoming). Jerome's treatise is edited by Simon Cserba, *Hieronymus de Moravia, O.P.: Tractatus de Musica*, Freiburger Studien zur Musikwissenschaft 2 (Regensburg: Verlag Friedrich Pustet, 1935); passage quoted here on p. 187. I thank Professor McGee for generously sharing his forthcoming book with me before its publication. McGee works with treatises by Regino of Prum, Guido, Theinred of Dover, Anonymous 1 (Coussemaker), Marchetto of Padua, Walter of Odington, Arnulf of St. Ghislain, and Bonaventura of Brescia, among others.

inflections, and he finds a place for them in harmonic theory of the period. At the end of the fourteenth century, Arnulf of St. Ghislain says that the effect of microtonal inflections is both sensuous and angelic.[48]

If singers sometimes sprinkled microtonal inflections into the performance of songs that were diatonically notated, then the practice could have indirectly inspired the reviser who uses notated inflections in *MS O*. The performance practice may have inspired the general idea of working with a notatable discursive style, the details of which were arrived at independently. The two practices would represent independent manifestations of a similar aesthetic ideal. I would emphasize my opinion that discursively motivated accidentals in *MS O* do not need to be explained as a phenomenon related to performance practice. Nevertheless, it is interesting to consider the idea that the underlying conception was inspired by such a practice.

*

Jean Beck thought that the idiosyncratic accidentals in *MS O* were added by the scribe himself, as he copied. It is unlikely that the situation was that simple. Through collation emerges a range of relationships between this manuscript and others. Many songs in *MS O* are completely uninflected,

---

[48] On Marchetto, see especially Jan Herlinger, "Marchetto's Division of the Whole Tone," *Journal of the American Musicological Society* 24 (1981), 193–216. On Arnulf of St. Ghislain, see Christopher Page, "A Treatise on Musicians from ?c. 1400: the *Tractatulus de differentiis et gradibus cantorum* by Arnulf de St Ghislain," *Journal of the Royal Musical Association* 117 (1992), 1–21, relevant passage on pp. 16 and 20. Charles Warren interprets the enigmatic term "*cantus coronatus*" along related lines. Following John Stevens and Christopher Page, I have suggested (in the Introduction) that Anonymous 2 and Johannes de Grocheio both use the phrase to identify a subgenre of vernacular song, the "high style" or *grand chant courtois*. Warren, on the other hand, sees in Grocheio's description "*circa sonos coronatur*" – "crowned around the tones" – a reference to improvisatory ornamentation. Warren reads Anonymous 2 as alluding to an improvisatory practice in which musica ficta is used to beautify a song. It is a short step to relate this to the ornamenting microtones described by Jerome, Marchetto, and Arnulf. I find the interpretation unlikely, however, for the complete context of Grocheio's remarks seems more clearly in the direction of identifying attributes of genre. If he uses this term to mean either a genre or a performance practice – and sometimes both, it would seem, according to Warren's interpretation – that is a confusing feature of a text that otherwise appears to have been quite rigorously conceived. For Warren's views, see "Punctus Organi and Cantus Coronatus in the Music of Dufay," *Dufay Quincentenary Conference*, ed. Allan W. Atlas (Brooklyn: Brooklyn College, 1976), 128–43, especially 136–7. Shai Burstyn has stressed the likelihood of microtonal inflections in trouvère performance, suggesting (as does McGee) that a performance practice that had its origins in Mediterranean and Middle Eastern cultures shaped Western European vocal styles; see "The 'Arabian Influence' Thesis Revisited," *Current Musicology* 45–7 (1990), 119–46. Burstyn makes this intriguing suggestion: "Numerous discrepancies between concordant troubadour and trouvère melodies involve *B* versus *B*-flat, *F* versus *F*-sharp and *C* versus *C*-sharp. Could these possibly be the only notational solutions the diatonic system afforded the scribes who, in fact, attempted to record tones located *between* these intervals?" At the least, I would say that it is rare to have different signs given for the same place in different sources.

and they closely match concordant sources. For this group of songs, the manuscript stands in the mainstream of transmission. Other songs recorded by *MS O* match the versions recorded by other manuscripts except for inflections, which therefore appear to have been added, perhaps in the spontaneous manner imagined by Beck. Still others diverge significantly but without inflections, suggesting a unique but not unusual redaction. And many of the songs emphasized in this chapter appear to have been redesigned with inflections in mind, implying an idiosyncratic style of redaction. *MS O*'s version of *Ne me done pas talent* (Moniot d'Arras: Beck 216, R 739; *T-M*, XII: 350) shows, in phrase 5, *b*-natural followed by *b*-flat, which leads to a cadence on *a*. Six surviving manuscripts carry this melody, but only *MS O* has these inflections and this cadential pitch. Most likely, the same person reworked both this song and *Biaus m'est estez* (and related examples, discussed above), which has exactly the same cross relation leading to the same cadential degree, again in phrase 5. Now, the melody for *Ne me done pas talent* has been copied into *MS O* twice (the second time with a contrafact text, *Phelipe, je vous demant*; Beck 238; R 334). But the events just described are lacking in the other entry, and the melody agrees more with those transmitted by other manuscripts than it does with *MS O*'s own alternative version. Most likely, the scribe took songs as they came to him, some with accidentals and some without.

A future goal will be to identify connections between patterns of transmission and style of redaction. Such a connection would imply common origins, the voice of a single musical milieu. It is possible to propose tentative hypotheses along two lines of inquiry: we may expect some gains by working with songs that appear in similar sequences from source to source; also, the manuscript's *unica* may indicate a redactional style located close to the source.

The alphabetical organization used in putting together *MS O* obscures groupings of songs that can be easily identified in related sources. As we know, the alphabetization extends no further than the first letter of each incipit; beyond this, there are patterns such as placement of Thibaut's songs at the beginning of each group, often followed by Gace Brulé's songs. *Unica* tend to be placed towards the ends of the alphabetical groups. Alongside these calculated patterns emerge a few uncalculated ones. It is common to discover in trouvère anthologies small clusters of songs that appear in the same order, from source to source, suggesting that they moved along together. Through Beck's inventory of *MS O*, the eye is easily led to these clusters when concordant sources show consecutive folio numbers. In some manuscripts this phenomenon is much more extensive, and these cases may be useful in working with *MS O*, where, one assumes, larger clusters have been scattered because of the alphabetization. The main connections are with the closely related anthologies *K*, *N*, *P*, and *X*, four manuscripts that may have emerged from the same workshop – in the case of *K* and *N*, even from the same scribe. In his study of anonymous songs, Hans Spanke relates coherent patterns of transmission in the closely related group of sources to those in other manuscripts, including *MS O*.[49]

In *MSS K*, *N*, *P*, and *X*, anonymous songs are gathered together in similar sequences at the end of each anthology. Spanke numbers the anonymous songs according to their order in *MS K*, and he divides the resulting list into three groups: 1–86, 87–119, and 120–40.[50] One basis for these groups is the fact that 31 of 33 songs in the second group are also found in *MS O*; in contrast, only eleven from the first group are also found in *MS O*. Significantly, perhaps, there is a slight correlation between Spanke's division and the notation of accidentals in *MS O*. Of the eleven songs from Spanke's first group that appear in *MS O*, none has discursive accidentals.[51] But in the second group, three songs (87, 90, and 92) out of the first six show discursive accidentals in *MS O*. *Chanter me fait* (Beck 59; R 1429) has *c*-sharp in phrase 5, as part of a distinctive move to *d* and as a means to set apart the *cauda*. Similarly, *f*-sharp is introduced in phrase 5 of *Conment que longe demeure* (Chastelain de Coucy: Beck 64; R 1010; *T-M*, I: 260); the phrase ends (uniquely in *MS O*) with the inflected falling third we have seen before. *Desconfortez, plains de doleur et d'ire* (Gace Brulé: Beck 95; R 1498; *T-M*, I: 480) is built very stably around *G*, with *b*-flat introduced at the penultimate syllable of the stanza, a technique also evident elsewhere. Spanke singles out these three songs (together with a fourth) as marked by a few other distinguishing features in their distribution through the surviv-

[49] *Eine Altfranzösische Liedersammlung: der Anonyme Teil der Liederhandschriften KNPX*, Romanische Bibliothek 22 (Halle: Max Niemeyer, 1925), especially 263–90. *MS L* should be added to the *KNPX* group, as a closely related manuscript; see van der Werf, *The Chansons of the Troubadours and Trouvères*, 30–3. On *MSS K* and *N* as having been entered by the same hand, see Mark Everist, "Song Manuscripts of the Middle Ages," unpublished paper; see also Spanke, *ibid.*, 267. I am grateful to Professor Everist for sharing his work with me before its publication.

[50] *Eine Altfranzösische Liedersammlung*, 285–9, division of the two parts at no. 87, top of p. 288. The separation between groups one and two is marked partly by the fact that the first group shows only scattered distribution in

other manuscripts while the second shows much heavier and more consistent distribution, with nearly all songs occurring in *MS O*. Furthermore, "peripheral" manuscripts give attributions often for this second group, rarely for the first. The third group is dominated by songs that are transmitted only in *MS K*. Spanke suggests that, for songs from the second group, *MSS K* and *O* go back to a common source.

[51] Using Beck's inventory for *MS O* (*Le Chansonnier Cangé*, I: xxii), the songs are nos. 16, 24, 79, 134, 146, 179, 245, 295, 296, 298, and 341. In this group, *b*-flat is the only accidental that occurs in *MS O*, and in only three songs. In songs 179 and 341 all *b*'s are flatted, and there is a single, stray *b*-flat in song 16.

ing sources: they are not included in the anonymous section of *MS N*, for example, but, instead, they are placed at the very end of *N*'s collection of songs by Gace Brulé; they also occur within a few folios of one another in *MSS V* and *X*. In *M* they are scattered, not by alphabetical distribution but by assignment to different composers (Pierre de Molins: R 1429; Chastelain de Coucy: R 1010; and Gace Brulé: R 1498). In spite of this scattering, with *MS M* we must pause for a moment and consider a few important connections between this manuscript and *MS O*.

It would seem important that two of the three songs just cited are also recorded by *MS M* with discursive inflections. The applications are similar, though not identical, to those recorded by *MS O*. Both manuscripts show *f*-sharp in phrase 7 of *Conment que longe demeure*. In *MS M*, the inflection is associated with the four-note neume that we have already associated with *MS O* (though the neume is absent from *MS O*'s redaction of this song). And both manuscripts show *Terzfreiheit* in their redactions of *Desconfortez, plains de doleur et d'ire*. As just noted, *MS O* introduces *b*-flat at the end of a melody that emphasizes *G. MS M* follows a different design at a different pitch level, but it still shows *Terzfreiheit*: the final is *D*, and *F*-natural (phrases 1 and 3) alternates with *F*-sharp (phrases 2 and 4). These are the only two manuscripts to carry inflections for this song. Furthermore, *O* and *M* are close to each other in cadential pattern, both featuring the same pitch at the end of each of the first four phrases. Another song shared by the two manuscripts, *Fine amour et bone esperance* (Beck 132; R 221), may also show *Terzfreiheit* over a stable reference to *G* in both redactions.[52]

MS O shows various connections to various manuscripts. Since there are

---

[52] That is, if we accept the suggestion that there is a copying error in *MS M*. The two manuscripts agree up to the column break in *MS M*, after which *MS M* presents the melody a fourth lower relative to *MS O*. The result is that *MS O*'s *b*-natural in the last phrase of the stanza is preserved in *MS M* as *F*-sharp. Hendrik van der Werf's edition of the song follows *MS M* without noting the copying error; see *The Lyrics and Melodies of Gace Brulé*, 387. There are a few other vague but perhaps significant connections between the two sources, some involving transpositions. For *Li nouvauz tanz et mais et violete* (Beck 182; R 985; *T-M*, I: 243), *MS O* has a "dangling third" at the end of phrase 6, with the third, *f*-sharp, contrasting with *f*-natural, used in every other phrase. In *MS M*, the same degree is inflected, though, again, with a different design and at a different pitch level. The raised seventh (*b*-natural) is used for most of the song, and *b*-

flat is introduced for contrast at the end of the first phrase. *Fine Amor claimme a moi* (Beck 133; R 26) has already been discussed. Two songs, *Fine amours en esperance* (Beck 132; R 221) and *Bien font Amors* (Beck 43; R 738), show *f*-sharp in *MS M* and *b*-natural in *MS O* during passages that are notated a fourth apart. For *Par grant franchise* (R 782), *MS O* introduces *b*-flat in the *cauda*; and, at precisely this place, *MS M* shifts up a fifth, avoiding the inflection. Cases like these are not so easily placed in the category of copying errors, and they beg for systematic study of transpositions throughout the repertory. Theodore Karp discusses the possible existence of a lost source that would explain some connections between *MSS O* and *M* in "Borrowed Material in Trouvère Music," *Acta Musicologica* 34 (1962), 87–101, especially 93.

a few traces of discursive accidentals in concordant sources, this style of
redaction may have originated outside of the immediate milieu represented by MS O.[53] One would expect the degree of revision or stability
characteristic of a melody through its surviving sources to be at least par-
tially dependent on how long it circulated, with longer periods of circulation yielding more variants. Adam de la Halle's songs, for example, were
relatively recent compositions that rarely receive inflections in MS O.
When they are inflected, the inflection is usually of the "tacked on" type,
with the melody recast only slightly or not at all. For older songs, the versions had time to branch out and depart from one another through a series
of redactions, and this process sometimes included the addition of accidentals, probably late in the history of the tradition.

*

Traditionally, a manuscript's *unica* are regarded as having the potential to
reveal the musical environment surrounding the manuscript most directly,
since they may be local items. It is of interest that six of MS O's 74 *unica* are
copied without music (in Beck's inventory, nos. 7, 66, 223, 242, 244, 330).
Poem and staves are entered in the normal way, indicating that music was
expected. Could the poems have circulated without music? That is an
obvious possibility, though it goes against the commonly held assumption
that the poems were universally conceived and performed as songs. It is not
uncommon to find incompletely copied songs among trouvère sources. But
the distribution of these songs in MS O may be significant. Since the total
number of songs in the manuscript lacking music comes to sixteen, there is
some significance to the fact that six belong to the *unica* group. If the
unique songs were local, they may have been generated for this manuscript.[54] Perhaps these six poems were entered with the expectation that
someone was going to supply them with melodies that never did get made.
This hypothesis is supported by the fact that of the ten remaining songs
that lack music in this manuscript, three have concordant sources that

---

[53] *MS O* and *MS Z* agree on *c*-sharps and *F*-sharps for
Desoremais ets raisons (Beck 11; R 1885). The song is
placed next to two other songs in *MS Z* that have *F*-
sharps – *Li miens chanters ne puet mais remanoir* (R
1813) and *Loiaus amours et desiriers de ioie* (R 1730).
This is significant, since there is only one other song in
MS Z with musica ficta (*Gadifer par courtoisie*, R 1121).
Theodore Karp notes connections between *MS O* and *MS
V* and also connections between *MS O* and *MS T* in "The
Trouvère MS Tradition," *Twenty-fifth Anniversary*

*Festschrift (1937–1962): The Department of Music,
Queens College of the City University of New York*, ed.
Albert Mell (U.S.A: Q. C. Press, 1964), 25–52.

[54] The sixteen songs lacking music are listed by Beck, *Le
Chansonnier Cangé*, I: XV, n. 5. Hendrik van der Werf
suggests that "it is tempting to surmise that the person
who did so much editorial work on a number of
melodies in [*MS O*] was the composer of these
anonymous songs"; *The Chansons of the Troubadours
and Trouvères*, 33.

either lack music or presumably lacked it at the time of initial copying. Then, for two of the remaining six from this music-less group, there are slightly fainter indications that the poem circulated without a melody, since the songs survive in *MS M* in the same way.[55] A systematic study of "songs without music" throughout the entire repertory may someday show this pattern to be merely coincidental, but for the time being it stands as one way to make sense of shadowy evidence. Twelve of sixteen songs is a very high percentage.[56]

Among the 74 *unica* in *MS O*, there are a few examples of accidentals used for discursive purpose. Two songs use the same augmented fifth, *F* to *c*-sharp; it cannot be coincidental that they sit next to each other in the manuscript. And the song that follows uses the four-note neume with dangling sharp that we have seen a number of times.[57] Another pair copied together show an identical use of raised thirds, from which the line falls away at phrase endings.[58] *De cuer dolant* (Beck 106; R 1500) has *Terzfreiheit*. *Li joliz temps d'estey* (Beck 189; R 452) has two *c*-sharps, which distinctively intervene in descents from *d* to *G*, the main pitch of the

<hr />

[55] *Bien cuidai* (Beck 41; R 1965) lacks music in *MS C*, the only other source. *Chanson de plains et de sopirs* (Beck 65; R 1463) survives in only one other source, *MS R*, and in a section to which the scribe added melodies; see Johann Schubert, *Die Handschrift Paris, Bibl. Nat. Fr. 1591: Kritische Untersuchung der Trouvèrehandschrift R* (Frankfurt, 1963). *Des or me vuil esjoir* (Beck 94; R 1408) lacks music in *MS M*, its only other source. *Baudoyn, il sunt dui amant* (Beck 38; R 294) lacks music in *MS O* and in *MS M*, one of the four additional sources. *Une chose* (Beck 350; R 332) lacks music in *MS O* and in *MS M*; the third source, *MS T*, is not available to me.

[56] A few other songs in *MS O* show evidence of having circulated without music, even though a melody is recorded in *MS O*. *Amis, quelx est li mieuz vaillanz* (Beck 34; R 365) is found in only three manuscripts: it has a melody in *MS O*, but not in *MSS C* and *I*. In *MS O* it is placed at the end of the first alphabetical group, in the midst of many *unica*; furthermore, since *MS O* is the only manuscript to transmit the poem with a melody, it is indeed interesting that the melody has been lifted from the celebrated *Can vei la lauzeta mover* (edition in van der Werf, *The Extant Troubadour Melodies*, 62). For *Joie d'amors* (Beck 158; R 506), *Quant li noveaus* (Beck 313; R 454), and *Se par force de merci* (Beck 324; R 1059), *MS O* is the only manuscript to transmit melodies; again, the songs are placed amidst or near the *unica* groups in *MS O*. *Quant la saison desirrée* (Beck 309; R 505), *Tant ai*

d'Amors (Beck 346; R 2054), and *En chantant* (Beck 127; R 1464) show similar patterns: they are each transmitted in one or two other manuscripts without music, and, again, the songs have been placed in *MS O* near the *unica*. *Chancon de plains* (Beck 65; R 1463) is left with no music in *MS O*; it is also transmitted by *MS R*, which carries unique melodies. *Pour verdure ne pour prée* (Beck 245; R 549) has no music in *MS O*, while *MSS K, N, P,* and *X* agree (which is not unusual, since they may be dependent upon one another) and *MS M* has a different melody (with a few and likely coincidental similarities to the other melody). For *Quant voi venir le beau tens et la flour* (Chastelain de Coucy: Beck 276; R 1982; *T-M*, I: 279), *MSS U* and *T* have the same melody, *MSS R* and *M* have different melodies, and *MS O* has no melody. Further research may find deeper ways of coordinating evidence of style and transmission among songs that show this pattern of circulating without melodies, at least through part of the repertory.

[57] The augmented fifths occur in *Se j'ai chanté* (Beck 327; R 2061) and *Sovent m'ont* (Beck 328; R 682). The four-note neume occurs in *Se valors vient* (Beck 329; R 1218).

[58] *Tres fine Amors* (Beck 344; R 1065) and *Tout autresi* (Beck 345; R 99). Additional examples of raised thirds dropping away at phrase endings include *Li joliz temps d'estey* (Beck 189; R 452) and *Quar eüsse* (Beck 310; R 641).

melody. *Bien doi chanter* (Beck 52: R 116) uses a variety of cross relations to shape a highly discursive stanza.

The question of how close the style of redaction was to the musical milieu of the manuscript has no clear answer. Some songs preserved uniquely in *MS O* do show precisely the same applications that turn up in the manuscript's redactions of widely circulating songs. At the same time, there is evidence to suggest that some songs came to the manuscript with inflections already made. Hendrik van der Werf has suggested that, since *MS O* is unusual in its notation of both accidentals and its semi-mensural rhythmic notation, the redaction may have been influenced by the learned world of the motet.[59] With respect to accidentals, it is hard to see where a stylistic model might lie. As I have argued in the Introduction, Anonymous 2 presents *causa necessitatis* and *causa pulchritudinis* as two different justifications for *falsa musica*. He implies that they belong to different spheres of musical activity, *causa necessitatis* to polyphony and *causa pulchritudinis* to the *cantus coronatus*. This reading of the theorist is supported by the notational evidence of practical sources: motets rarely show inflections beyond those demanded by *causa necessitatis*, and the special style of redaction for trouvère songs preserved mainly by *MS O* may be regarded as the leading manifestation that we have of musica ficta, *causa pulchritudinis*. It is certainly possible that the technical means of notating musica ficta came, directly or indirectly, from the motet tradition (and one would want to observe the fact that all techniques for notating trouvère songs came from outside of the tradition). But the inspiration for the style of redaction featuring discursive inflections probably emerged as an internal development within the trouvère tradition itself.

An elevated style

We began this chapter with Thibaut de Navarre's *Ausi cum l'unicorne sui*, the song that holds pride of place in *MS O*, having been chosen to lead off the book. For the illumination that graces the capital "A," a mirror has been added to the scene described in Thibaut's poem. Paul Zumthor's views on the interchangeability of central concepts in this poetic tradition make it

[59] *The Chansons of the Troubadours and Trouvères*, 43, and *The Extant Troubadour Melodies*, 46. Alphabetical organization and illuminations tied to poetic themes recall motet books, too (though not exclusively); on these, see Huot, *From Song to Book*, 74 ff. In this regard, it should be observed that *MS O's Bien m'ont Amors entrepris* (Beck 53; R 1532) is virtually a motet – or, if you like, a polyphonic chanson with rhythmically ordered tenor.

easy to understand this addition of a mirror, which has symbolic value in the tradition of *fin' amors*.[60] How, then, should we interpret the addition of accidentals to Thibaut's melody?

It would be easier to answer this question if text–music relations in this repertory were more straightforward than they appear to be. Interpretation cannot be based on the simple proposition that the musical side of a song takes its meaning from the poem – in spite of Beck's unlikely claim that *MS O*'s accidentals often highlight specific words or phrases. I have emphasized how the inflections function in musically autonomous ways.[61] This approach follows from the assumption that there is a degree of independence between words and music. No one from the period describes such independence, and it would be extraordinary if they did. But several practices suggest it. Melodic revision is commonplace, and it usually proceeds independently of the words, except for limitations imposed by the need for formal congruence. The period routinely welcomes new melodies for old poems and new poems for old melodies. The use of the same melodic stanza for multiple poetic stanzas is a basic feature of the idiom. Time and again, important words receive no musical emphasis, while insignificant words do receive musical emphasis. How different the attitude is from that of the High Renaissance, when it becomes conceivable to "correct" melismatic plainchant, making sure that melismas occur on the main syllable, the main word, and so forth. This attitude is completely foreign to that which seems to animate *grands chants courtoises*, where it is

---

[60] Zumthor comments on the symbolism of mirrors in the world of *fin' amors*, and on the interchangeability of the central concepts in this tradition, in "De la circularité du chant," in *Poétique* 2 (Paris: Seuil, 1970), 129–40; translated by R. Carter as "On the Circularity of Song," in *French Literary Theory Today: a Reader*, ed. Tzvetan Todorov (Cambridge: Cambridge University Press, 1982), 179–91. See Huot, *From Song to Book*, 74–80, for further comment on this illumination, related illuminations featuring mirrors and unicorns, other illuminations in *MS O*, and additional literature on medieval symbolism involving mirrors (a very large topic). More prosaically, Beck suggests that the illuminator for *MS O* misreads the poem, and thinks of the maiden in the phrase "quant la pucele va mirant" as subject with reflexive verb (*quant la pucelle se mire*) rather than as object of the unicorn's gaze: in order for the maiden to gaze at herself, she needs a mirror; see *Le Chansonnier Cangé*, I: xiv, n. 2.

[61] Reference in Beck, *Le Chansonnier Cangé*, II: 70. As a rule, literary scholars write about the poems as poems, even if they do so reluctantly. Zumthor ("On the Circularity of song," 179–80), for example: "The most important feature, but also the hardest to deal with, is the musical aspect of this 'song.' Words and melody are the product of a single impulse, they generate each other in a relationship which is so intimate that any analysis has to treat both simultaneously. Unfortunately, no more than a tenth of the texts have come down to us along with their melodies, and deciphering of the latter raises problems which are still more arduous than the establishing of the former. We thus have no choice, except in a few untypical cases, but to focus our observations – like an archaeologist studying potsherds – on the linguistic half of the *chanson*, in the hope of restoring the original harmonious design from the few surviving fragments." One can only sympathize with the assertion that music is hard to deal with. But the 1500 surviving melodies must represent more than potsherds.

appropriate to have a degree of independence between poem and melody.

The view of text–music relations in the *grand chant courtois* that I have just sketched is compatible with that developed by John Stevens.[62] Stevens emphasizes formal congruence between poem and melody, and he advocates isosyllabic rendition as a practical way to attain this. Neumatic inflection up to five notes per syllable does not obscure audibility of the syllable count in performance (explaining, perhaps, why longer melismas are rare). But beyond these limitations of formal congruence there is room for a degree of independence between words and music. Stevens cites Guido d'Arezzo's notion of a "double melody" – a melody of words and one of pitches. He finds that direct and semantic relationships between words and music are rare, and he stresses the possibility that there may be some value in having a degree of independence between the two. As so often happens with medieval music, the task is to describe, in a positive way, techniques that initially appear to lack something when compared with later developments in music history.

Comparing the *cantus coronatus* to melismatic plainchant, Grocheio provides a useful reference:

> These three chants, that is, the Responsory, Alleluia and Sequence, are sung immediately after the Epistle and before the Evangel in mystery and reverence for the Trinity. The Responsory and Alleluia are sung in the manner of an estampie or cantus coronatus, so that they may impose devotion and humility in the hearts of the audience. But the Sequence is sung in the manner of a carol, so that it may make them joyful and lead them to receive correctly the words of the New Testament, that is, the Holy Evangel which is sung immediately thereafter.[63]

If Grocheio is talking about how the melody conveys the words, then he is saying what we already know by common sense: syllabic melody draws attention to the message of the words, melismatic melody adds a special element of mystery. It is only a short step to say that melismatic melody elevates the words, and, from there, to suggest that the artifice of melismatic song, both liturgical and secular, is to create a delivery that is distinctly *not*

---

[62] *Words and Music in the Middle Ages*, especially the first and last chapters.

[63] "Isti autem tres cantus, puta responsorium, alleluia et sequentia, cantantur immediate post epistolam et ante evangelium in mysterio et reverentia trinitatis. Responsorium autem et alleluia decantantur ad modum stantipedis vel cantus coronati, ut devotionem et humilitatem in cordibus auditorum imponant. Sed sequentia cantatur ad modum ductiae, ut ea ducat et laetificet, ut recte recipiant verba novi testamenti, puta

sacrum evangelium, quod statim postea decantatur." Rohloff, *Die Quellenhandschriften zum Musiktraktat des Johannes de Grocheio*, 164; translation from Seay, *Johannes de Grocheo: Concerning Music (De Musica)*, 40, with "estampie" and "carol" as emendations from McGee, *The Sound of Medieval Song: Ornamentation and Vocal Style According to the Treatises*. McGee has a different interpretation of Grocheio, according to which the theorist describes a performance practice.

like speech. Melody in the *grand chant courtois* projects the poem into a psychological space that is not the day-to-day space of corporeal love, but, rather, the imaginary space of a higher, idealized love. The songs are ennobling – according to Grocheio, they "move the souls of kings and princes to audacity and bravery, to magnanimity and liberality" – because they move on a higher, less personal emotional plane. A melismatic setting makes it clear that the poem's world is ideal rather than literal. The stylistic antipode to the *grand chant courtois* is the dance-based refrain song with syllabic delivery. This is not to say that there is no possibility of a closer connection between text and music, just that we should recognize the value in keeping a degree of detachment between the two. One may find, here and there, a stray accidental that seems to have been motivated by the words, but it is hard to remove the suspicion of coincidence from such examples. For the majority of cases, it seems clear that verbal texts do not give rise to accidentals.[64]

*

The culture of *fin' amors*, of lyric song and romance, seems to have evolved through a complicated relationship with the more firmly established culture of the Church. For music, we know little about contextual details of this relationship, but we know enough to imagine that it included a pattern of emulation and rejection – embrace of the model and deliberate veering away from it.[65] Does musica ficta in the *grand chant courtois* represent a move towards independence from plainchant? This would be one way to regard discursive accidentals. One could think in the same way about the semi-mensural overlay that surfaces here and there in *MS O*: it marks a step towards the motet and, at the same time, a step away from plainchant. Even though this manuscript shows a fairly casual attitude towards the semi-mensural overlay, this turned out to be a direction from which there was no turning back; with the ascendance of the polyphonic chanson, mensural

[64] For Machaut, for example, the role of music is to bring *joie*, even to dour poems; see Douglas Kelly, *Medieval Imagination: Rhetoric and the Poetry of Courtly Love* (Madison: University of Wisconsin Press; 1978), 7–9. Kelly gives (pp. 239–56) an important survey of word–music relations in the chanson tradition, and he concludes: "Music is an independent aspect of composition in most cases. . ." For Machaut, see also Daniel Leech-Wilkinson, "Machaut's *Rose, lis* and the Problem of Early Music Analysis," 9–28 and especially 13. For arguments in favor of a stronger bond between words and music in Machaut, see the literature cited by Lawrence Earp, review of two books by Daniel Leech-Wilkinson, *Machaut's Mass: an Introduction* and *Compositional Techniques in the Four-Part Isorhythmic Motets of Philippe de Vitry and His Contemporaries*, in *Journal of the American Musicological Society* 46 (1993), 303, n. 18.

[65] On the emulating side of the equation, see Jacques Chailley, "Les premiers troubadours et les *versus* de l'école d'Aquitaine," *Romania* 76 (1955); 212–39.

melody came to stay. The introduction of musica ficta into *grands chants courtoises* may have represented a breaking away from plainchant nearly as radical as the introduction of measured rhythms.[66]

Yet the point should not be overstated, since inflections of *b* in plainchant may well have provided the historical model for using musica ficta in trouvère songs. The author of *Summa musice* (*c.* 1200) acknowledges the expressive force of the cross relation:

> However, if the text treats of some matter which is arduous in either its deep meaning or its surface meaning, then the music should be grave and should cross from soft *b* to hard *b* and vice versa.[67]

The cross relation is justified as a musical response to the words. To pursue the idea that text illustration in a very general way (rather than a specific, word-painting way) justified inflections in *grands chants courtoises* leads inevitably to thoughts of chromatic sensuality. The late musical development of chromaticism would find its context in the male-dominated cult of idealized feminine beauty. The possibilities of a view towards discursively employed musica ficta as an irrational element that is tied to an idealized vision of femininity need only be alluded to, as a potential line of future interpretation.

The alternative is to emphasize how the inflections function in a musically autonomous way, with no explicit reference (but with a limitless range of potential references) that restricts meaning. As I have argued, what makes digressions from the diatonic pitch field possible is the loose and easily manipulated nature of the melodic syntax. The two orientations – one stressing musical meaning as dependent on the text, the other stressing

---

[66] Though one must immediately acknowledge the possibility that plainchant was performed less diatonically and more chromatically than notated sources would imply. On this, see John Snyder, "Non-Diatonic Tones in Plainsong: Theinred of Dover Versus Guido d'Arezzo," in *La Musique et le Rite Sacre et Profane*, ed. Marc Honegger and Paul Prevost (Strasbourg: Assn. des publications près les Universités de Strasbourg, 1986), II: 49–67. Further discussion of this point in McGee, *The Sound of Medieval Song: Ornamentation and Vocal Style According to the Treatises.* Both the Parisian Anonymous of 1375 and Anonymous II, for example, discuss *coniunctae* in plainchant. See also above, note 36 from the Introduction.

[67] "Si vero dictamen rem laboriosam vel secundum virtutem vel secundum apparentiam significat, nota debet esse gravis et transire de b molli in ♮ durum et e

contrario." Christopher Page, ed. and trans., *The Summa Music: A Thirteenth-Century Manual for Singers* (Cambridge: Cambridge University Press, 1991), 116 and 194. The path experienced by *On voit sovent* (Beck 230; R 1391) may illustrate the sequence of development I am suggesting: cross relations between *b*-natural and *b*-flat may have inspired further inflections in later redactions. In *MSS N, K,* and *X, b*-flat is introduced toward the end of the stanza, in phrases 7 and 8, forming a cross relation with *b*-natural elsewhere in the stanza. In *MSS Z* and *a, b*-flat is introduced in phrase 7, and the cross relation is then reinforced by restatement of *b*-natural in phrase 8. *MS O* has both of these inflections and still another: *b*-flat in phrase 7 is made even more pungent by the ensuing descent to *F*-sharp, which produces an indirect diminished fourth that resolves fully only with the arrival on the final *G.*

musical autonomy that is more difficult to conceptualize – are not incompatible. It may turn out that a complete understanding of this style of redaction will demand a synthesis of the two. It is always difficult to project higher-level interpretation onto music that comes to us with so much of its context lost. Still, the historical moment of these inflections in this manuscript is one to treasure. Discursive organization of pitch, irregular and difficult contours, melodic tension from cross relations, the achievement of a complicated hierarchy of pitches that is ambiguous and self-contradictory, an unstable and unpredictable pitch field – these qualities surface here as they have nowhere else before in the notated record of European music. In the late stages of the evolution of trouvère song, it became attractive to experiment with accidentals as a tool for revising received melodies.

*

With Chapter 2, we turn to the polyphonic chanson, and that is where we shall stay for the rest of this book. Lyric monophony in French courtly culture did not disappear, but for the fourteenth and fifteenth centuries it is no longer central. At the time, the shift towards polyphony must have seemed like progress. But, as always in music history, every gain also involves a loss. One trade-off is located in the relationship between words and music: the tight formal congruence of the isosyllabic model yields to an interest in measured melisma, which leaves no room for the former unity of musical and poetic phrase lengths. Gained with polyphony are the well-developed techniques of counterpoint, conveying power and depth; lost is a kind of subtlety and ambiguity that is easily exploited in unaccompanied monophony. The polyphonic song would come to feature a leading melody supported by one or two or three additional parts that provide a harmonic context. And harmony becomes the focus for most activity involving musica ficta. Still, it is important to bear in mind, as we turn to the polyphonic chanson, the analytical model for discursive melody that we have developed in connection with trouvère monophony. For this model may be useful for understanding inflections in polyphonic songs, in spite of the imposing presence of harmonic discourse.

This chapter has two main purposes. It provides a selective review of accidentals in polyphonic chansons by Guillaume de Machaut, and it covers a few basic aspects of the polyphonic chanson, such as will be relevant for the remainder of our survey. To leap directly from the *grand chant courtois* to Machaut's polyphonic *formes fixes* requires that we gloss over what was probably a complicated transition; it is impossible to say exactly how complicated, since the transition is documented so poorly in the scant surviving sources. The polyphonic chanson may well have developed along several independent paths. There is an unusual anticipation of the idiom in *Trouvère MS O*, for example: a trouvère song similar to others in the manuscript is accompanied by a part labeled "tenor" and arranged like a motet tenor, with a regular rhythmic pattern.[1] The example suggests one way of thinking about the polyphonic chanson: the idiom represents a synthesis, of sorts, between a tradition of lyric melody, inherited from the trouvères, and the increasingly complex polyphony of the motet. In his mature style, Machaut does indeed arrive at a successful synthesis of lyric melody with counterpoint. The idea of the polyphonic chanson as a synthetic creation suggests a way to think about accidentals. As a rule, the accidentals that we shall encounter in polyphonic songs have something to do with basic and universally recognized formulas of counterpoint. Yet the formulas are used in ways that call to mind the model of discursive melody sketched out in our study of trouvère song. *Selective use* of the contrapuntal formulas is what the sources indicate, often enough. And for our goal of interpreting lyric expression, particularly important is selective use in the cantus, the leading melody voice, where, potentially, inflections weigh more heavily than they do in the other voices.

"*Vesci l'ordenance que G. de Machaut wet qu'il ait en son livre*" ("Here is the order that Guillaume de Machaut wants his book to have") – so pro-

---

[1] *Trouvère MS O*, f. 21. For a review of the early history of the polyphonic chanson, see Wulf Arlt, "Aspekte der Chronologie und des Stilwandels im französischen Lied des 14. Jahrhunderts," in *Aktuelle Fragen der Musikbezogenen Mittelalterforschung: Texte zu einem Basler Kolloquium des Jahres 1975*, Forum Musicologicum: Basler Beiträge zur Musikgeschichte 3 (Winterthur: Amadeus, 1982), 193–280. See also the important observations in Lawrence Earp, "Lyrics for Reading and Lyrics for Singing in Late Medieval France: the Development of the Dance Lyric from Adam de la Halle to Guillaume de Machaut," in *The Union of Words and Music in Medieval Poetry*, ed. R. Baltzer (Austin: University of Texas, 1991), 101–31.

claims the heading of *Machaut MS A*.[2] For several reasons, Machaut's songs occupy a central place in this book. First is the exceptional source situation, which makes possible a depth and range of understanding for this composer's oeuvre that far exceeds that for all other fourteenth-century composers. For Machaut we enjoy a large body of firmly attributed music, transmitted in a number of very good sources. We have a sense of chronology, and it is possible to witness an expansion of the composer's range of expression and his willingness to experiment. The sources are hardly unanimous in reporting accidentals, but they are consistent enough to support general conclusions about Machaut's practice. We are able to watch a text go through fairly stable transmission in the "principal" Machaut sources ("collected works" manuscripts devoted exclusively to his songs and poetry, and presumably having origins close to the composer) followed by deterioration in the "secondary" Machaut sources (later and diverse anthologies mixing his songs together with those by many other composers).[3] As long ago as Johannes Wolf in 1904 and as recently as Bettie Jean Harden in 1983, scholars have suggested that accidentals in Machaut's oeuvre are reported precisely and completely (with the exception, in Wolf's view, of some cadential situations).[4] Thus, the methodological base for the present study finds its strongest potential field of development with Machaut. Nowhere else can we proceed with quite the same confidence in the assumption that analysis rests upon a secure and (potentially) authoritative musical text. Since, as we are told, Machaut took special interest in how his books were put together, down to the ordering of their contents, one may entertain the idea that he also exerted authorial control over the proper notation of accidentals.

Machaut's presence in modern-day constructions of the history of the chanson is immense, and this is another reason for giving his songs special

[2] Quoted, translated and discussed in Lawrence Earp, "Machaut's Role in the Production of Manuscripts of His Works," *Journal of the American Musicological Society* 42 (1989), 461–503; quotation on p. 461, photograph of the original document on p. 483.

[3] Of the principal sources, six are important musically for our study: *Machaut MSS C, Vg, A, F-G, B*, and *E*. MS *B* is a copy of *MS Vg*, and much of *MS E* is in turn derived from *MS B* (discussed at the end of this chapter). For a recent analysis of the sources and their relationships, see Earp, "Machaut's Role in the Production of Manuscripts of His Works"; and *idem*, "Scribal Practice, Manuscript Production and the

Transmission of Music in Late Medieval France: the Manuscripts of Guillaume de Machaut" (Ph.D. diss., Princeton University, 1983). Presumably, Machaut's music was first recorded not in large manuscripts like these but on small scrolls known as *rotuli*; hence, the principal sources may already be secondary, in one sense. One *rotulus* preserving a lai by Machaut survived into this century; see Earp, "Scribal Practice," 32.

[4] Johannes Wolf, *Geschichte der Mensural-Notation von 1250–1460* (rept. Hildesheim: Breitkopf und Härtel, 1965), 174–5; Bettie Jean Harden, "Sharps, Flats and Scribes: 'Musica Ficta' in the Machaut Manuscripts" (Ph.D. diss., Cornell University, 1983), *passim*.

Example 2.1 *Doulz viaire gracieus* (after *MS C*, f. 203)

attention. His achievement may have extended to innovative use of accidentals; in song after song he takes delight in the unusual gesture, the
inventive design. He may also have been the key figure in working out the
format of a "discant" duet: a leading melody voice ("superius," as it will be
known later, or "cantus," as it is referred to here) is matched by a contrapuntal mate of almost equal importance ("tenor"). This is the core contra-

puntal framework that will continue to dominate the chanson tradition well beyond the period covered in this book. The discant duet may be supplemented by one or two additional parts ("triplum" and "contratenor"). If we imagine Machaut as having forged this way of making chansons, we must also admit that all claims of innovation in the early fourteenth century necessarily depend on a great deal of speculation. The early years of the polyphonic chanson – that is, whatever happened before *MS Machaut C*, the earliest source for Machaut's music, dating *c.* 1350–56 – are almost completely obscure.[5] In an often-cited remark that dates from the early fifteenth century, Philippe de Vitry is mentioned before Machaut as having "*trouva la maniere de motets, et des balades, et des lais, et des simples rondeaux.*"[6] Since no songs in the vernacular survive with an attribution to Philippe, it is impossible to know if he exerted an influence on the chanson comparable to that which he certainly exerted on the motet. The sad fact, then, is that an important reason for Machaut's preeminent status in modern historiography is the abnormally fine documentation of his achievement.

A group of sixteen rondeaux by Adam de la Halle stand as one solid landmark in the history of the polyphonic chanson before Machaut.[7] Like Machaut, Adam worked in both the lyric world of the courtly love song and the learned world of the motet. Also like Machaut, Adam enjoyed the recognition of having his compositions collected in a manuscript devoted to him alone. The unassuming, dance-like rondeau of the thirteenth century was a curious choice, perhaps, upon which to lavish polyphonic detail.[8] Adam's settings are short and modest. Attention is drawn to charming details.

Machaut's *Doulz viaire gracieus* (Ex. 2.1) may have been one of his early rondeaux; in any event, it resembles those by Adam in some respects.[9]

[5] On this recent dating of *MS C*, see François Avril, "Les manuscrits enluminés de Guillaume de Machaut: Essai de chronologie," in *Guillaume de Machaut: Colloque-Table ronde . . . Reims (19–22 Avril 1978)*, Actes et Colloques 23 (Paris: Klincksieck, 1982), 117–33; cited by Earp, "Lyrics for Reading and Singing," 124, n. 48.
[6] On this passage and the likelihood of Machaut's greater significance in the evolution of the polyphonic chanson, see, most recently, Earp, "Lyrics for Reading and Singing."
[7] The sixteen rondeaux (one of which we would call a virelai and another of which we would call a ballade, though all are labelled rondeaux in the source) are edited by Nigel Wilkins, *The Lyric Works of Adam de la Hale*,

Corpus Mensurabilis Musicae 44 (Dallas: American Institute of Musicology, 1967).
[8] By accident, its relatively "low" status made it available for this treatment: unlike the *grand chant courtois*, the rondeau came with measured rhythms, and this may have made it easier for the genre to be taken up into polyphonic settings. Perhaps there was even a touch of irony in the idea of surrounding a humble refrain song with the trappings of learned polyphony.
[9] For a brief summary of research on the chronology of Machaut's music, with references to and comments on the secondary literature, see Lawrence Earp, *Guillaume de Machaut: a Guide to Research* (New York: Garland, 1995), 273–7.

Machaut's interest in accidentals is evident, even in this modest piece. The first chord, marked by *F*-sharp/*a* in tenor and cantus, supplemented by *c*-sharp in the triplum, is preparatory, both rhythmically and harmonically. Adam begins *A jointes mains vous proi* in a similar way, with a preparatory chord built on *G/b/e*.[10] Details like these stand out in this unassuming idiom. Adam's refrain of only six measures ends where one would expect, given the initial sonority: it ends on *F/c/f*. Machaut's twelve-measure refrain has five signed *F*-sharps, and these straightforwardly emphasize *G*; but the refrain and hence the song ends unexpectedly on *b*-flat/*b*-flat/*f*. When *Doulz viaire gracieus* is performed according to its ABaAabAB rondeau form there will be two leaps of a diminished fourth in the tenor, from the last note of the refrain back to the first note. Machaut's restless exploration of both chromaticism and idiosyncratic detail in design is evident.[11]

Doulz viaire gracieus resembles Adam's earlier rondeaux not only in its brevity but also in scoring.[12] The voices are distributed in a way that suggests the labels triplum/cantus/tenor (Adam's source gives no labels; Machaut's sources identify triplum and tenor). All of Adam's polyphonic rondeaux are transmitted "in score," with text given below the bottom voice, a format well established for the polyphonic conductus and a sensible way to present the heavily note-against-note idiom. *Doulz viaire gracieus* is not presented in score, and text is given for the cantus only. But Machaut, like Adam, is thinking less in terms of a leading melody with accompaniment and more in terms of a polyphonic texture in which the voices are of almost equal status. *Doulz viaire gracieus* even has brief imita-

---

[10] Ed. Wilkins, *The Lyric Works of Adam de la Hale*, 56.

[11] Vertical dissonances are prominent: they include two augmented fourths (mm. 4 and 8), two minor sevenths (mm. 6 and 10), a combined major seventh and augmented fifth (m. 7), a major seventh (m. 11) and – most audaciously – the diminished octave, *F*-sharp in the tenor against *f*-natural in the triplum (m. 3). This was one of the first pieces by Machaut known to early nineteenth-century German musicologists like Raphael Kiesewetter, who reacted to the counterpoint with disgust, quoting Cicero: *O tempora! O mores!*; cited by Earp, *Guillaume de Machaut: a Guide to Research*, 277–9. Regarding the diminished octave, this is implied by the assumption that *F*-sharp in the tenor at measure 1 still holds through measure 3. Sarah Fuller questions the diminished octave; see "Tendencies and Resolutions: the Directed Progression in *Ars Nova* Music," *Journal of Music Theory* 36 (1992), 255, n. 27. She suggests that the signed *f*-natural in the triplum (which is signed consistently in the sources) may have been a scribal mistake. She properly asserts the primacy of the cantus–tenor pair and is reluctant to adjust this pair because of an inflection in the triplum; this is a fundamental assumption with which I agree, and which I will try to build upon in Chapter 3. But given the heavy emphasis on vertical dissonance in this song (much of it, though not all, caused by the triplum), one may be inclined to accept the diminished octave. On the other hand, the notated augmented octave in measure 2 (cantus against triplum) seems highly unlikely, especially since both voices resolve, presumably in parallel octaves, to *G*. MS *C* is the only one of the principal sources to lack *b*-flat in the triplum for measure 5.

[12] As suggested by Jeremy Yudkin, *Music in Medieval Europe* (Englewood Cliffs: Prentice Hall, 1989), 498.

tion through all voices. The cantus has a humble role in a piece that features counterpoint (including some crunching counterpoint) and an unexpected design (motion from *G* to *B*-flat). Machaut is not thinking in terms of a dominating lyric melody with supporting polyphony.

But he will be doing that, and with splendid results, by the time he composes a group of rondeaux that appear to date very near the compilation of *MS C*. The celebrated *Rose, lis* shows the mature style, fully formed and brilliantly executed.[13] The core duet of cantus–tenor is given in Ex. 2.2. The sources also transmit a triplum and two contratenors (one of them surely not authorial).[14] These voices have been left out of the example in order to make a point cleanly about how accidentals work in terms of the discant framework of leading melody with harmonic support. Questions about the essential or inessential natures of contratenors and triplums are complicated, and by excluding these voices from the example I do not mean to imply a simple answer. The problem obviously bears upon our understanding of accidentals, and it will be considered from several angles in the next chapter. As I have argued in the Introduction, it seems likely that composers often worked mainly with the discant duet and then secondarily

[13] Modern edition of *Rose, lis* in Leo Schrade, ed., *The Works of Guillaume de Machaut: Second Part*, Polyphonic Music of the Fourteenth Century 3 (Monaco: L'Oiseau-Lyre, 1956), 152; this edition is cited hereinafter as PMFC 3. On problems in the rhythmic notation of this song, see Richard Hoppin, "Notational Licenses of Guillaume de Machaut," *Musica Disciplina* 14 (1960), 13–28. On the unordered sections of *MS C*, to which *Rose, lis* belongs, and the likelihood that these sections represent additions to the manuscript that are nearly contemporary with its time of copying, see Earp, "Scribal Practices," 76 ff, 138 ff, and further literature cited there. *Rose, lis* is copied over two gatherings, implying a late time of entry; musically, it and some of its companion rondeaux are distinguished by innovative rhythmic notation and a four-voiced texture. For an analysis of this song differing from that offered here and featuring hexachordal parsing, harmonic reduction, and "structural prolongation," see Daniel Leech-Wilkinson, "Machaut's *Rose, lis* and the Problem of Early Music Analysis," *Music Analysis* 3 (1984), 9–28. I welcome Leech-Wilkinson's argument that modern analysis of late medieval polyphony need not be limited to concepts firmly articulated during the time the work was written, and I would suggest that the emphasis on hexachords in his analysis could be modified in this light. At the same time that he uses hexachordal analysis, Leech-Wilkinson downplays the technique: "Such a description, eminently respectable in its period antecedents, is closely comparable in analytical function to chord-labelling a tonal work, and as will be seen, about as revealing" (27, n. 23). In my view, hexachordal analysis is *much less* revealing than chord-labeling a tonal work, since the latter engages the analyst with musical syntax, even if only in a rudimentary way, and since (as I have argued in the Introduction) it is doubtful that hexachords have any syntactical significance in late medieval polyphony. Leech-Wilkinson's hexachordal parsing leads him to the problematic assumption that "the listener is left in no doubt that the descending hexachord, at least on the level of musical surface, is the subject of *Rose, lis*" (p. 18). See also my comments in the Introduction, note 70.

[14] *Machaut MS C*, the earliest of the principal sources, lacks the triplum but includes, uniquely, the voice labeled "Contratenor II" in Schrade's edition. Bettie Jean Harden argues that this voice can "surely be excluded entirely from serious consideration"; "Sharps, Flats and Scribes," 133. Leech-Wilkinson, "Machaut's *Rose, lis*" (p. 21), says that the "Triplum, although surely conceived together with the other voices, is nevertheless disposable. *Rose, lis* may be performed with or without it."

Example 2.2 *Rose, lis,* cantus and tenor (mainly after *MS F-G,* f. 151v)

with a triplum or contratenor. That working method would have made it possible to gain control over the special demands of crafting a dominant melody within a polyphonic texture. Triplums and contratenors are supplemental in the sense that it is usually possible to remove them completely and be left with an attractive, self-sufficient duet.[15]

Rose, lis offers a splendid musical expression of the sweetness that manifests in rose, lily, and springtime, sweetness surpassed only by the poet's *belle*, to whom the song is addressed. One component of this musical sweetness, perhaps a necessary component, is stability. From the initial unfolding out of unison *c* through the octave leap in the tenor at the end of phrase 1 (mm. 10–11), the duet is crafted as a display of melodic, harmonic, and contrapuntal balance. There is no lack of variety, but the variety is firmly anchored by strategic returns to the main pitch. When the composer introduces E-flat in cantus and tenor (m. 14), the inflection stands as a rich digression that benefits from the stable design. There are several textual problems involving accidentals in *Rose, lis*, but these E-flats at measure 14 are not among them.[16] This digression is perhaps the main event in the song.

It is essentially a *melodic* inflection; this is a point to emphasize. Obviously, it is a polyphonic event, since cantus and tenor have the same inflection at precisely the same moment. But there is no contrapuntal or (as I shall shortly explain) harmonic basis for this digression from the pitch field of phrase 1. Thus, we may read the inflection as a polyphonic manifestation of the model of discursive melody already developed, in Chapter 1. The event is unlike *Doulz viaire gracieus*'s F-sharps, which are harmonically generated. There is no shortage of harmonically based inflections in Machaut's mature style; so we should not make too much out of this comparison between the vertically oriented *Doulz viaire gracieus* and the cantus-dominated *Rose, lis*. It should be emphasized, however, that prominent, melodically based inflections will come more readily in a cantus-dominated idiom. In contrast, digressions like this are foreign to earlier motets, and *Doulz viaire gracieus* stands a step closer to that tradition.

---

[15] I have sketched out my approach to the problem of hierarchies of voices in chansons in the Introduction. I am not suggesting that Machaut was incapable of working with more than two voices in a polyphonic texture at once. And I am not suggesting that triplums and contratenors in Machaut's polyphonic songs are wholly inessential, and that they may be disregarded at will. In the next chapter I shall comment more fully on accidentals and this model of a hierarchy of voices.

[16] It seems to me that, with respect to accidentals, the only emendation required of the reading provided by *MS F-G* (as given in Ex. 2.2) is *e*-flat in the cantus at measure 22. This inflection is carried by *MS C*. I assume that by durational rules, *e*-flats hold for the cantus in measures 34 and 35.

It is fair to say, I think, that the digression from *e*-natural to *e*-flat within an overall context of stable *C* stands as the most salient musical idea of *Rose, lis.* But it would be unfair to characterize the song as nothing more than melody with accompaniment. The success of the piece flows not only from Machaut's control of melody but also from his control of harmony. Machaut's clever command of the new idiom of the polyphonic chanson is evident when he turns the melodic inflection of *E*-flat into a harmonic event. This happens as early as measure 16, where *E*-flat/*c* moves to *D*/*d* – assuming, as I think one must, that *E*-flat from measure 15 in the tenor holds through this cadence. The same gesture is repeated at the midpoint of the rondeau (mm. 24–5; again assuming that the earlier *E*-flat, from measure 22, holds through the cadence). *E*-flat returns in its more linear identity at measures 22 and 34. There could be no better demonstration of how accidentals in the polyphonic chanson must be understood in terms that are neither strictly melodic nor strictly harmonic but, rather, some fluid mix of the two. This is a basic fact that underlies several lines of interpretation that we shall pursue: inflections in the leading melody voice are, by definition, melodic, but they often have a harmonic basis. In this sense, harmony and melody cannot be separated. In the end, the most interesting point to consider will be: how are the harmonic formulas used selectively, as a tool for design that contributes to the discursive model, as articulated by the cantus, especially?

To develop this line of analysis further, it will be useful to review the topic of harmony in the ars nova at a general level. This will provide us with a good analytical base from which to consider the majority of inflections in the chanson, through the mid-fifteenth century.

Harmony

Our modern-day notion of musical "harmony" easily finds a place in discussion of late medieval polyphony, so we should not be shy about using the word, even though it obviously holds anachronistic dangers. Similarities between late medieval harmonic practice and that of common-practice tonality can be misleading, but the connection is unavoidable. Late medieval harmony provides the historical antecedent for dominant–tonic function in the common-practice, and it also provides a point of entry into the style for the modern ear. Musica ficta plays a large role, so the phenomenon is central to our study of accidentals.

We may think of harmony in two different ways: as a static phenomenon and as a dynamic one. Hucbald defines the former when he says that "Harmony is the proper union of two notes." Not too much should be made, perhaps, out of the word *harmonia* here, but the usage does point up the basic fact that the modern-day notion of harmony is based on the medieval regard for vertical consonance.[17] Yet we use "harmony" to mean something more than the proper union of two notes; the technical sense of the word involves attendance to a proper arrangement of vertical sonorities. The medievals, too, developed a technique for arranging vertical sonorities, and it would surely surprise them to discover how much later centuries made of the practice they invented, though it should not surprise us that the modern practice traces its origins to this period, the source of so much that happened later.

Late medieval harmonic syntax was fully formed by the early fourteenth century. Marchetto of Padua (1318) may be read as transforming the discourse pertaining to a traditional, static conception into a way of speaking about the new, dynamic conception. Marchetto cites Boethius:

> Boethius writes, "A dissonance occurs when two pitches struck together do not wish to be mixed. Each, rather, strives to flee," that is, each pitch seeks to go to the location where it will produce a pleasant, amicable, sweet mixture, that is, a consonance.[18]

But this is not quite what Boethius says:

> Consonance is a mixture of high and low sound falling pleasantly and uniformly on the ears. Dissonance, on the other hand, is a harsh and unpleasant percussion of two sounds coming to the ear intermingled with each other. For as long as they are unwilling to blend together and each somehow strives to be heard unimpaired, and since one interferes with the other, each is transmitted to the sense unpleasantly.[19]

Boethius views consonance and dissonance as static qualities; Marchetto is interested in the dynamic relationship between the two. For Marchetto and his age, the imperfect consonance – a special kind of dissonance, in the terminology used by this theorist – has become very useful.

---

[17] Quotation from Hucbald, as cited by Marchetto of Padua; see the *Lucidarium in arte musice plane*, ed. and trans. Jan W. Herlinger (Chicago: University of Chicago Press, 1985), 204–5. As Marchetto observes, *armonia*, *euphonia*, *simphonia*, and *consonantia* are simply different words for describing the same thing; Herlinger, ed., *ibid.*, 206–7. In this reference to Hucbald and in the following reference to Boethius, it is Marchetto's likely reading of the theorists that interests me most; quite possibly, the vertical orientation we (and presumably

Marchetto) bring to these passages would have been foreign to Boethius and even Hucbald.

[18] "Boetius: Dissonantia fit cum duo soni simul pulsi sibimet permisceri nolunt, sed sibi quisque gliscit ire, hoc est quod uterque sonus ad locum ire cupit ubi est permixtio iocunda, amicabilis, et suavis, hoc est consonantia." See Herlinger, ed., *Lucidarium*, 200–1.

[19] *Fundamentals of Music*, ed. and trans. Calvin M. Bower (New Haven: Yale University Press, 1989), 16.

In its two-sided way, harmony guides placement of the vast majority of accidentals in late medieval polyphony. The static conception, "the proper union of two notes," gives rise to the application *causa necessitatis*. There is no tidy label from the period for inflections used to dynamically relate two vertical sonorities, one to the other. Following the lead of several Italian theorists, it will be referred to here as the "propinquity application."

In theory, the necessity application is a straightforward matter; one may recognize a more complicated situation in practice. Musica ficta is necessary, theorists say again and again, because it makes possible the transformation of diminished and augmented unisons, fifths and octaves into perfect consonances. Thirteenth-century motets follow thirteenth-century theory in using *E*-flat to form a perfect fifth below *b*-flat and *f*-sharp to form a perfect fifth above *b*-natural.[20] During the fourteenth century, necessity applications then expand on both the sharp side and the flat side. The main fact to emphasize about necessity applications in Machaut's songs is how thoroughly they are notated in the principal sources. This notational pattern is one bit of evidence supporting the assumption that accidentals are completely signed in Machaut's oeuvre. Yet, in spite of the consistent notation of necessity-based accidentals, two general problems arise. First, it seems likely that Machaut was willing to violate the necessity rule on occasion. It seems clear that augmented and diminished intervals could be useful to him. Second is the issue of how to deal with troubling inflections when they occur in contratenors and triplums. There are more than a few instances of an inflection in these voices that conflicts with a reading in the cantus and tenor that, by itself, makes good contrapuntal sense. At issue is the significance of textural hierarchy: is it likely that supplemental voices influenced the pitch content of the discant pair, even when that pair makes good sense as notated? Both of these topics are dealt with in the next chapter, where various examples are brought together to make an argument based on practice; but it is important to beflag them here, since they come up in Machaut's music from time to time.

*

It is not possible to postpone discussion of the propinquity application, however, for this technique is of great importance for understanding Machaut's songs. Here we may usefully build on recent advances in analysis of ars nova harmony in general practice, independently of accidentals.

Central to ars nova polyphony is a harmonic syntax in which imperfect

---

[20] For a review of music theory on this topic, see Berger, *Musica ficta*, 93–121.

Example 2.3

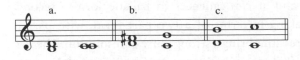

consonances (thirds and sixths and their octave compounds) resolve to perfect consonances (unisons, fifths, and octaves). Three progressions stand as paradigmatic references: minor third contracts to unison, major third expands to perfect fifth, and major sixth expands to perfect octave (see Ex. 2.3). The special status of these three progressions is determined by the basic precepts of counterpoint, as described by contemporary theorists and as confirmed by the way in which composers use the progressions. The influential *Ars contrapuncti secundum Johannem de Muris* explains that these progressions represent the "natural" movement of minor thirds, major thirds, and major sixths.[21] Petrus Frater dictus Palma Ociosa (1336) illustrates these progressions and others through examples, and he makes it clear that musica ficta should be used to alter the intervals when this use brings the progressions in accord with basic precepts. Musica ficta should be applied, for example, when one needs to transform a minor third into a major third as the interval expands outward, to a perfect fifth (as in Ex. 2.3b).[22] In an important aside, Jean de Murs says that the intervals may move contrary to their natural inclinations, for the sake of variety.[23] But these paradigms represent the strongest paths for imperfect consonances to follow, and that is because each path involves contrary motion and resolution by step, in addition to the basic component of the harmonic syntax, movement from imperfect consonance to perfect consonance.

This harmonic syntax emerged out of traditional contrapuntal practice, and that is the context in which theorists discuss it. But composers come to use these progressions as special events, distinguished in the routine

[21] Edmond de Coussemaker, ed., *Ars contrapuncti secundum Johannem de Muris*, Scriptorum de Musica Medii Aevi Nova Series a Gerbertina Altera III (Paris: A. Durand, 1869), 59–60. On the text and Jean de Murs' possible authorship, see Ulrich Michels, *Die Musiktraktate des Johannes de Muris*, Beihefte zum Archiv für Musikwissenschaft (Wiesbaden: Franz Steiner, 1970), 40–2.

[22] Petrus Frater dictus Palma Ociosa, *Compendium de discantu mensurabili*, ed. Johannes Wolf, "Ein Beitrag zur Diskantlehre des 14. Jahrhunderts," *Sammelbände der Internationalen Musikgesellschaft* 15 (1913–14), especially 507–16. Petrus says that minor sixths should be "perfected" by musica ficta to form major sixths; from there the interval may resolve properly, preferably to an octave.

[23] *Ars contrapuncti secundum Johannem de Muris*, 59. On *causa variationis*, see Klaus-Jürgen Sachs, *Der Contrapunctus im 14. und 15. Jahrhundert: Untersuchungen zum Terminus, zur Lehre und zu den Quellen*, Beihefte zum Archiv für Musikwissenschaft 8 (Wiesbaden: Franz Steiner, 1974), 66–9.

contrapuntal flow. They use them, for example, with overwhelming consistency at final cadences and at *clos* cadences in ballade form ("second endings" to part 1, speaking in terms of a two-part form, with part 1 repeated). The core progressions bring a strong sense of resolution. The *Ars contrapunctus secundum Philippum de Vitriaco* puts it this way: "the sixth seeks out the octave, and this rule always holds."[24] As in the harmonic syntax of common-practice tonality, the rules of this syntax are easily perceived by the initiated listener and central to the style. Even though the syntax is locally oriented (unlike harmonic syntax in common-practice tonality), it may have long-range effects. Composers may manipulate it with a keen sense of how it contributes to the design of a song.

Musica ficta plays a role in the new, dynamic conception of harmony, just as it continues to play a role in the traditional, static conception. Inflections enhance the directional tendency that imperfect consonances have acquired. Again, Marchetto, the earliest source:

> The diesis is a 5th of a whole tone, occurring when, for instance, any whole tone is divided in two in order to color some dissonance such as a third, a sixth, or a tenth striving toward some consonance.[25]

Marchetto's idiosyncrasies (a new division of the whole tone, and a new sign, mentioned elsewhere, to notate it) do not obscure the period's standard view. Fourteenth-century theorists recommend the use of musica ficta to adjust an imperfect sonority when it moves to a perfect sonority, so that while one voice moves by semitone the other moves by whole tone. The basis for the application is harmonic; the melodic result is a "leading tone" in one voice (a very high leading tone, in the tuning advocated by Marchetto; it is as if the tuning adds more tension to the imperfect conso-

---

[24] Reference to *Ars contrapunctus secundum Philippum de Vitriaco* given in Richard Crocker, "Discant, Counterpoint and Harmony," *Journal of the American Musicological Society* 15 (1962), 12. For further references to theorists on this topic, see Sarah Fuller, "On Sonority in Fourteenth-Century Polyphony: Some Preliminary Reflections," *Journal of Music Theory* 30 (1986), 44. The historical connection between this harmonic practice and tonal harmony is stressed by Crocker (p. 17): "The formulas of the fifteenth century, then, are indeed functional: they depend upon the two-note progressions of discant. They also sound like the familiar progressions of 'functional harmony,' which simply means that triadic functions and progressions develop in unbroken continuity out of discant." Carl Dahlhaus also recognizes the connection: "And one of the basic ideas of

contrapuntal theory from the 14th through the 17th century is that the variation of intervallic quality – the tendency of dissonance toward consonance, or of imperfect consonance toward perfect consonance – forms the driving force behind music's forward motion. A chain of sixths striving toward the perfection of an octave differs of course in degree, but not in principle, from Rameau's progression of seventh chords whose goal is a triad – an *accord parfait.*" *Studies on the Origin of Harmonic Tonality*, trans. Robert O. Gjerdingen (Princeton: Princeton University Press, 1990), 22–3 and 29.

[25] "Dyesis quinta pars est toni, puta cum aliquis tonus bipartitur propter aliquam dissonantiam colorandam supple terciam, sextam, sive decimam tendendo ad aliquam consonantiam." *Lucidarium*, 140–1.

nance and, hence, more strength to the progressions). French theorists describe the practice, but they say little more. Prosdocimo de' Beldomandi, borrowing, in part, from Marchetto, explains how it works:

> Last, for understanding the placement of these two signs, round b and square b . . . these signs are to be applied to imperfectly consonant intervals – the third, the sixth, the tenth, and the like – as is necessary to enlarge or diminish them to give them major or minor inflections as appropriate, because such intervals ought sometimes to be major and sometimes minor in counterpoint; and if you wish to know the difference – when they should be major and when minor – you should consider the location to which you must move immediately after leaving the imperfect consonance; then you must see whether the location you leave is more distant from that location you intend immediately to reach, making the imperfect consonance major or making it minor: for you should always choose that form, whether major or minor, that is less distant from that location which you intend to reach, and you should, by means of the signs posited above, make a major interval minor or, contrariwise, a minor one major as appropriate. There is no reason for this than a sweeter-sounding harmony. Why the sweeter-sounding harmony results from this can be ascribed to the sufficiently persuasive reason that the property of the imperfect thing is to seek the perfect, which it cannot do except through approximating itself to the perfect. This is because the closer the imperfect consonance approaches the perfect one it intends to reach, the more perfect it becomes, and the sweeter the resulting harmony.[26]

The propinquity application, or the rule of "closest possible approximation," derives directly from the general rule of step-wise motion. It can be understood as a nuance of practice that came to be established as a basic feature of practice. What theorists do not say, but what we may recognize in music by Machaut and others, is that there is room to manipulate the application, just as there is room to manipulate harmonic syntax, generally.

---

[26] "Item ultimo pro noticia collocationis istorum duorum signorum, scilicet b rotundi et b quadri . . . in vocum combinationibus imperfecte consonantibus, sicut sunt tercia, sexta, decima, et huiusmodi, ponenda sunt etiam hec signa secundum quod oportet addere vel diminuere in ipsas reducendo ad maioritatem vel minoritatem opportunas, eo quod tales combinationes in contrapuncto esse debent aliquando maiores et aliquando minores; et si hanc diversitatem scire cupis, quando, scilicet, ipse debent esse maiores et quando minores, considerare debes locum ad quem immediate accedere debes post tuum recessum a tali consonantia imperfecta, et tunc videre debes an locus a quo recedis magis distet a loco ad quem immediate accedere intendis, faciendo talem consonantiam imperfectam maiorem an in faciendo ipsam minorem, quoniam illam semper sumere debes que minus distat a loco ad quem immediate accedere intendis, sive illa sit maior sive minor, et debes tunc facere ipsam per signa superius posita, de maiori minorem vel e contra, scilicet de minori maiorem, secundum quod oportet, cuius ratio non est alia quam dulcior armonia. Sed quare hec dulcior armonia ex hoc proveniat potest talis assignari ratio satis persuasiva, quoniam si de ratione imperfecti sit sui appetere perfectionem, quod aliter esse non potest quam per approximationem sui ad rem perfectam. Hinc est quod quanto consonantia imperfecta magis appropinquat perfecte ad quam accedere intendit, tanto perfectior efficitur, et inde dulcior armonia causatur." Prosdocimo de' Beldomandi, *Contrapunctus*, ed. and trans. Jan Herlinger (Lincoln, Nebr.: University of Nebraska Press, 1984), 79–85.

There is more behind this manipulation than an interest in variety (which, as we have seen, is how Jean de Murs justifies irregular progressions). In Machaut's hands, harmonic manipulation becomes a tool to be used in designing a piece. The composer regularly manipulates all three components of the harmonic syntax – alternating sonority type, contrary motion, and stepwise motion. When they discuss the basic rules of counterpoint, theorists say nothing about these possibilities, so we are left on our own to interpret them. Recent years have seen promising gains in interpretation of ars nova harmony, and we may usefully apply these gains to analysis of accidentals.

Sarah Fuller's work on ars nova harmony, especially, provides a good base for working with propinquity inflections. Fuller's analytical methodology builds on the precept that perfect consonances are stable and imperfect consonances unstable. The methodology provides a way to classify a range of sonority types according to relative degree of stability and instability. From this it becomes possible to rank progressions along a scale ranging from "neutral or non-committed to definitely directed."[27] At one side of the spectrum stands the "doubly imperfect" sonority, for example, *D/F-sharp/b* ("doubly imperfect" because the third and sixth are combined); at the other, the "doubly perfect," for example, *D/A/d* (doubly perfect because of the combined fifth and octave). In between fall mixed sonorities, such as *D/F/a*. Inflections are important: *D/F-sharp/b* is more firmly directed than *D/F/b*. Fuller does not intend to identify a rigid syntactic system. Rather, she seeks to show how the composer distinguishes some harmonic events from others in shaping a piece. The events take their meaning from context as much as they do from the syntactic precepts just sketched.[28] That context involves voice-leading, duration, mensural position, and, above all, organization of pitch in the piece as a whole. Through this line of inquiry, Fuller arrives at a method that is flexible enough to respond to the concerns of the present while being rooted in the normative practice of the past.

Machaut's *Nes que on porroit* is a ballade in which inflections do not play a terribly important role, but it is useful for demonstrating this approach. A good place to begin analysis of the musical side of any ballade is with the

[27] "On Sonority in Fourteenth-Century Polyphony: Some Preliminary Reflections," *Journal of Music Theory* 30 (1986), 35–70, quotation from p. 51.

[28] Fuller: "But in actual practice, the association of objective types with specific qualities can only be considered loosely normative, for multiple factors can act in a compositional context to qualify the effect and function of a sonority" (p. 44); and: "The characterizations advanced here are to be considered as useful guides to norms, not fixed stereotypes to be forced upon musical events" (p. 45).

Example 2.4 *Nes que on porroit:* ouvert and *clos* cadences (the latter a duplication of the final cadence; after PMFC 3: 122)

main "nodal points," the *ouvert, clos,* and final cadences (see Ex. 2.4). These voice leadings are unusual for main cadences: cantus and tenor arrive on their octave *D/d* and *C/c* by moving in similar rather than contrary motion and by leap rather than step. In these two respects, the cadences deviate from the paradigm; hence, we may interpret them as decidedly weak. (In this view, ironically, the leap in the tenor down by a fifth at the *clos* and final cadences, though causing a superficial resemblance to the dominant–tonic cadence, is a mark of weakness rather than strength.) On the other hand, the cadences form, through their respective points of arrival, a traditional pattern. Typically for ballades, *clos* and final cadences match, while the *ouvert* cadence is located one step above (*D-C-C*). This pattern is forth-rightly coordinated with events in the rest of the piece, where *C* is empha-sized, both melodically, through the shape of the elegant cantus, and harmonically, through emphasis on *C/c/c* and *C/G/c.*

Notably, a few clearly directed progressions within the body of the song occur in weak mensural positions – for example, the arrivals on *D/a/d* in measure 4 and *C/G/c* in measure 8. I would acknowledge Fuller's insistence that context must direct analysis of harmonic events by suggesting that, in these cases, mensural position undermines progressions that are otherwise clear and strong. And, indeed, a certain softening quality surfaces through-out the piece. In some progressions, the voices are slightly out of synchrony with one another, as if to decorate the harmony (see Ex. 2.5). The musical atmosphere is conditioned first and foremost by the leisurely 9/8 flow of the cantus. The unusual voice leadings at *ouvert, clos* and final cadences should be understood in the light of these events: the weakness of the cadences is an expressive feature. In light of the poem, one might charac-

Example 2.5 Two cadences from *Nes que on porroit* (mm. 2 and 6)

ize the musical mood as wistful. What is most striking, however, is not musical expression of the poem, which is, after all, of a standard type; rather, it is the persuasive coordination of various musical devices.

*

Today there is considerable momentum behind the position that propinquity inflections were conventionally applied as a performance practice – applied, that is, even in the absence of a sign, and with such universality that the signs were not even needed. This position has deep, nineteenth-century roots (to use an appropriate metaphor) in early musicology. As mentioned already, in the Introduction, Hugo Riemann viewed the situation as one of recovering a practice that was obvious to educated performers of the period.[29] Furthermore, it is clear that, for Riemann, the project was much larger than recovering details of a lost performance practice, for his approach to the phenomenon was inseparable from his ideas about the evolution of tonality. A good case could be made, I think, that the mix of "lost self-evidence" with ideas about rudimentary tonality has remained a potent force through much of the twentieth century.

No theorist from the fourteenth century ever proclaims the existence of an unnotated convention for the propinquity application. So, if the theorists are providing details of a lost performance practice, they do not tell us that this is what they are doing. As we have seen, theorists occasionally state quite plainly that the signs for soft and hard *b* should be used; Prosdocimo does this in the passage quoted above.[30] This combination – the absence of

[29] *Verloren gegangene Selbstverständlichkeiten in der Musik des 15.-16. Jahrhunderts: Die Musica Ficta; eine Ehrenrettung*, Musikalisches Magazin 17 (Langensalza: H. Bayer, 1907).

[30] Petrus Frater dictus Palma Ociosa mentions the signs explicitly and several times. Wolf, ed., *Compendium de discantu mensurabili*, 514–15. For example: "In addition, it should be noted that, generally, when the soft *b* or the hard *b* is placed where it is not customary, it is called musica ficta. And where the soft *b* is put, in the same place and under the same *vox* the semitone is lowered beyond the customary course of melody. And where hard

Example 2.6

direct commentary about unwritten applications and the presence of commentary on written ones – does not prove, of course, that there were no self-evident performance practices. But it does suggest, at the very least, that we should take seriously the readings as they have been transmitted. We shall see how favored notions of conventional performance practices have obscured subtleties of compositional practice, subtleties that draw us into an approach to harmony that is quite a bit different from the approach to which we are accustomed in study of common-practice tonality.

The treatises deal in basic matters of theory and pedagogy, so it would not be surprising to discover that they are of little use for interpreting nuances in complicated works of art. The treatises make it clear, for example, that propinquity adjustments may be made with either sharps or flats; but they do not tell how to choose between the two. There are two ways to turn a minor sixth into a major sixth (see Ex. 2.6). In studies that have been highly influential, Margaret Bent and Andrew Hughes respond to this dilemma by suggesting that codes of performance practice favored *musica recta* over *musica ficta*. When applied to our example, their line of reasoning yields the choice of *b*-flat. This line of reasoning has been effectively critiqued by Karol Berger, who then moves through the theoretical discourse differently in order to produce a different analysis: that theorists seem to favor *mi* inflections over *fa* inflections – that is, sharps over flats. Applied to our example, Berger's analysis gives favor to *g*-sharp.[31]

Berger's insight is confirmed – and also qualified – by manuscript evidence, particularly that for Machaut's songs. In our example, *b*-flat produces, in the language of solmization, a *mi clausula*, a distinctive arrival marked by half step above the lowest sounding pitch (solmizing *a* as *mi*). In modern-day terms, the event could be classified as a "lowered leading tone"

b is put, in the same place and under the same *vox* the semitone is raised beyond the customary course of melody in uncustomary places." (Praeterea notandum est in generali, quod falsa musica dicitur proprie, quando locabitur *b* molle vel ♮ quadratum in locis non usitatis. Et ubi ponitur *b*, in eodem loco et sub eadem voce deprimitur semitonium ultra cantum consuetum. Et ubi ponitur ♮, in eodem loco et sub eadem voce sustinetur

semitonium ultra cantum consuetum in locis non usitatis.)

31 Berger discusses the matter, critiquing the position of Bent and Hughes, in *Musica ficta*, 83–4, citing Bent and Hughes on p. 216, n. 64; see pp. 139–50 for Berger's review of evidence that implies to him *mi* preference over *fa* preference.

or "lowered second" cadence; in modal terms, it could be described as a reference to *deuterus* mode. Patterns of use make clear not only that lowered leading tones hold a minority status, but also that the formula is used for special effect. From a survey of nodal points in ballades and ron-deaux (*ouvert*, *clos*, and final cadences in ballades, midpoint and final cadences in rondeaux) one can see that, when he uses them, Machaut places lowered leading tones exclusively in *ouvert* position.[32] This pattern of use suggests that the lowered leading tone defines a point of arrival that is more tentative, relative to that defined by a raised leading tone. Sometimes, Machaut places an imperfect consonance, loaded with tension, in *ouvert* position; the event is analogous to tonality's "half cadence."[33] It is easy to suggest how these cadential types line up hierarchically: raised-leading tone to perfect consonance makes the firmest arrival, the half-cadence makes the weakest, and the lowered leading tone falls in between. The unnamed composer of *Pour tant se j'ay le barbe grise* (*MS Oxford 213*, f. 47)[34] takes advantage of this hierarchy in an unusual way. Typically, mid-point arrivals for rondeaux are located a step or two steps above final cadences (as in *Nes que on porroit*). In *Pour tant se j'ay le barbe grise*, both midpoint and final arrivals are *D/a/d*. The two arrivals are distinguished from one another by the propinquity applications that precede them: *e*-flat is signed for the *ouvert* midpoint cadence, *c*-sharp for the *clos* final.

In eight songs, Machaut uses another, related formula in *ouvert* posi-tion.[35] Cantus and tenor form a perfect fifth at the arrival, and to get there the cantus moves through what we may refer to, for convenience, as the "lowered sixth" (see Ex. 2.7). The inflection should be regarded as a pro-pinquity application; Petrus Frater dictus Palma Ociosa includes it in his list of formulas.[36] The lowered-sixth application should be regarded as rel-atively weak; it is analogous, in this sense, to the lowered-second applica-tion. There is one more general observation to make about nodal points in Machaut's ballades and rondeaux: it may be significant that even when there is an opportunity for a raised leading tone in an *ouvert* cadence the

---

[32] Lowered-second cadences never occur in final position in Machaut's polyphonic ballades, rondeaux and virelais, and they occupy *ouvert* position in twenty songs (achieved either by signed accidentals or by locating the arrival on *E*). From the ballades, see nos. 1, 5, 8, 10, 13, 14, 18, 23, 34, 36, 39, 41, and 42; from the rondeaux, nos. 3, 5, 6, 10, 17; and from the virelais, nos. 23 and 29 (numberings follow Schrade, ed., PMFC, 3). It probably goes without saying that such an observation depends upon textual decisions arising from unstable transmission from source to source and the difficulty of

being sure about the duration of a sign's effect.

[33] *Ouvert* cadences feature cantus and tenor sounding a held imperfect sonority in the following songs by Machaut (numbers refer to Schrade's edition): ballades 3, 7, 15, 16, 20, 21, 22, 25, 26, 28, 32; rondeau 18; and virelais 26, 28, 30, 31.

[34] Modern edition in Gilbert Reaney, ed., *Early Fifteenth Century Music*, Corpus Mensurabilis Musicae 11/IV (Rome: American Institute of Musicology, 1977), 31–2.

[35] Ballades nos. 4, 6, 40, and rondeaux 2, 7, 9, 11, and 12.

[36] Wolf, ed., *Compendium de discantu mensurabili*, 509.

Example 2.7 *Helas! pour quoy*, midpoint cadence

principal sources never have them signed.[37] Some *ouvert* cadences have no propinquity inflection signed at all. Modern editors have frequently responded to this situation by suggesting the raised leading tone as an editorial "correction," assuming that unnotated propinquity applications were supplied as conventions of performance practice. Alternatively, one could assume that the absence of half-step motion represents yet another technique for making a cadence relatively weak.

The general point to draw from these observations is that accidentals offer a way to rank cadences hierarchically.[38] Berger's statement that "the fourteenth-century evidence, and in particular that of Marchetto and Petrus, argues . . . that where a choice of the leading tone had to be made, the sharp, and not the flat, was the preferred solution" must be qualified.[39] The sharp is the preferred "solution" (backing off from this word because it points, in Berger's statement, to a choice made in performance practice) only in the sense that it is stronger and more commonly used. The flat is secondary because it is held in reserve, for special effect. Patterns of use in

[37] There are three exceptions, two of which can be explained and dismissed. The canonic ballade *Sanz cuer m'en vois/Amis, dolens/Dame, par vous* (Schrade, ed., PMFC 3: 88) is obviously a special case. In *Amours me fait desirer* (PMFC 3: 92), *c*-sharp is signed four measures before the arrival in the cantus on *d*. But there are two arrivals on *d* that come in between the propinquity application and the *ouvert* cadence; more importantly, *b*-flat is signed as the cantus moves up to the *d* in question, as if to cancel the previous *c*-sharp. As noted already, Machaut occasionally features an imperfect consonance at *ouvert* cadences. These half cadences are sometimes inflected with sharps, but that is obviously a different kind of event; the cadence is weak by virtue of having an imperfect consonance featured as the point of arrival. The remaining exception is *Rose, lis*, for which *MS C* uniquely signs *c*-sharp at the midpoint cadence on *d*. The sharp appears to have been entered by a different hand than that which entered the *b*-natural that follows; certainly the spacing of the notes here would have allowed room for a late addition, and it is clear from the

spurious contratenor copied at the bottom of the page that the piece received later attention.

[38] In her dissertation on the principal Machaut manuscripts, Bettie Jean Harden has independently come to a similar position about Machaut's interest in manipulating the propinquity application to achieve a hierarchy of harmonic gestures; see her discussion of the ballade *Gais et jolis*, "Sharps, Flats and Scribes," 230–4. The song has no sharps or flats signed (excepting *b*-natural, signed once in *MS E*), and this leads to a distinction between cadences on *D* and those on *C*, the latter having a raised leading tone and the former lacking one. As Harden observes, the composer achieves a cadential hierarchy by coordinating the design with a pitch field that is limited to the diatonic gamut. Harden was led to this position not through the analytical methodology developed by Sarah Fuller (which was not available in 1983) but by taking the transmitted readings literally, following the assumption that accidentals are completely notated.

[39] *Musica ficta*, 143.

the nodal points of Machaut's ballades and rondeaux are consistent enough to support the idea that the hierarchical distinction is always valid, even for interior cadences, where formal conventions – that is, the difference in status between *ouvert*, *clos*, and final cadences – do not direct the analysis.

In an important article on songs by Trebor, Howard Mayer Brown observes the need to take analysis "beyond the simple formulation of the theorists that a cadence normally involves a sixth expanding to an octave, or a third contracting to a unison, by collecting and classifying what are patently cadences in fully fashioned works of art, information that we can then apply to passages that are less than obvious."[40] From the six surviving ballades attributed to Trebor, Brown identifies thirteen different cadential formulas. His list includes all of the formulas we have just considered – raised leading tone, lowered leading tone, lowered sixth in the cantus, and arrival on an imperfect sonority. Trebor uses precisely the same techniques to mark tentative arrivals in *ouvert* position that Machaut uses. These techniques provide, in each case, a way to identify the *clos* cadence as relatively stronger than the *ouvert*.[41]

The next obvious step is to follow Brown's advice and try to apply these analytical gains to passages that are less than obvious. Two of Machaut's better-known ballades, *Biauté qui toutes autres pere* and *De toutes flours*, will serve to illustrate the composer's interest in manipulating the propinquity application in the service of overall musical design.

Biauté qui toutes autres pere

Biauté qui toutes autres pere (Ex. 2.8)[42] is built around an extraordinary cadential pattern in which the three nodal points each emphasize the same

[40] "A Ballade for Mathieu de Foix: Style and Structure in a Composition by Trebor," *Musica Disciplina* 41 (1987), 75–108. Brown provides an inventory of cadences in Trebor's ballades in Example 2, p. 102.

[41] Trebor's six ballades are all available in modern edition in Gordon Greene, ed., *French Secular Music: Manuscript Chantilly, Musée Condé 564*, 2 vols., Polyphonic Music of the Fourteenth Century 18–19 (Monaco: L'Oiseau-Lyre, 1981–2), nos. 19, 20, 38, 40, 64, and 66. The only exception to my claim about cadential hierarchies in these songs is *En seumeillant* (no. 20 in the edition): *B*-natural and *G*-sharp are signed for the *ouvert* cadence to *A/a*, and there is no raised leading tone for the *clos* and final cadences to *Gamma/G*. The piece is unusual on several counts, especially in being both highly inflected and very unstable; together with the low

scoring, these features suggest a comparison with Solage's celebrated *Fumeux fume*. At the *ouvert* cadence, the contratenor dips down, surprisingly, to *F* below *Gamma*, as if to destabilize what is otherwise a strong arrival.

[42] Schrade, ed., PMFC 3: 74. The song is transmitted as a duet in four of the principal Machaut sources (*Machaut MSS C, A, F-G*, and *Vg*), then with an added contratenor in *Machaut E* (an inferior and later principal source) and *Utrecht 37* (*Utrecht, Universiteitsbibliotheek, 6 E 37*; a late secondary source). On the inferior quality of added contratenors in *Machaut E*, see Wolfgang Dömling, *Die mehrstimmigen Balladen, Rondeaux und Virelais von Guillaume de Machaut: Untersuchungen zum musikalischen Satz*, Münchner Veröffentlichungen zur Musikgeschichte (Tutzing: Hans Schneider, 1970), 74–5.

Example 2.8 *Biauté qui toutes autres pere*, cantus and tenor (after *MS Vg*, f. 298)

Example 2.8 (*cont.*)

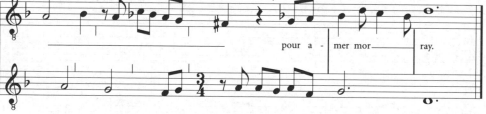

pitch, *D*. The composer distinguishes *ouvert* and *clos* from one another only by the subtle means of contrast between perfect fifth (*D/a*) for *ouvert* and perfect octave (*D/d*) for *clos* and final. (In 1336, Petrus Frater dictus Palma Ociosa codifies a hierarchy of intervals in which octaves are more stable than fifths.[43]) Furthermore, all three cadences are weak, since, in each case, the tenor moves by leap and there is no leading tone in the cantus (recall *Nes que on porroit*). It is a provocative combination: the composer locates the three main cadences on the same pitch, as if to negate large-scale forward direction, and he also makes them weak, as if to say that the arrivals do not really conclude what has come before.

Or at least that is one way to analyze, and I shall try to suggest how these cadences, together with signed accidentals, play a role in the design of the whole piece. *Biauté qui toutes autres pere* makes little sense if we follow the

43 Wolf, ed., *Compendium de discantu mensurabili*, 512.

basic precept of modal theory, "begin analysis with the final."[44] Except for the three main cadences, which emphasize *D*, *G* is emphasized as the most important pitch in this song. The piece is built in a contradictory way, with nodal points and the design of the interior flow at odds with one another. Perhaps this explains the relative weakness of the main cadences: in this context of contradiction, they seem not to conclude what has gone before. And the triple repetition supports the idea that the cadences stand outside of the main discourse of the internal flow, for the repetition negates the sense of large-scale forward direction that one expects from an *ouvert–clos–final* pattern. *D* is associated with closure by virtue of being repeated at the ends of sections rather than by actually satisfying a goal implied through the polyphonic flow.

G is emphasized as the main pitch through a series of melodic and harmonic events in part 1. The opening sonority is *G/d*. And the first important point of arrival is *G* at measure 7 (even though the arrival splits line 2 of the poem). This moment is defined partly by the shape of the cantus, which arrives first on *a*, marking the *ouvert* midpoint of the phrase at measure 4, and which then circles around, making its way to *G* for the *clos* ending of the phrase at measure 7. Accidentals help define this structure: the tenor's *E*-flat (m. 3) provides the lowered leading tone that brings an *ouvert* quality to the midpoint arrival (on *D*), while *F*-sharp in the cantus points to a stronger arrival on *G*.[45]

The sense that measure 7 marks a strong arrival is confirmed by what happens next, for the cantus ascends back to *d* by measure 9; now the two voices are poised precisely as they began, on *G/d*, and this is a fitting way to launch the splendid melisma of measures 9–16. In this melisma, the tenor's syncopations provide steady tension, both rhythmic and harmonic.[46] *G* is

---

[44] This is noted by Jehoash Hirshberg, "Hexachordal and Modal Structure in Machaut's Polyphonic Chansons," in *Studies in Musicology in Honor of Otto E. Albrecht*, ed. John Walter Hill: Bärenreiter (Kassel 1980), 26. Hirshberg discusses the limitations of modal analysis for Machaut's chansons, and his analysis of *Biauté qui toutes autres pere* (26–7, referred to as "Ballade 4") agrees in many details with that presented here. I would not feel the need, as he does, however, to think of the song as "essentially a composition in G Dorian, although its two sections end on D." Also absent from Hirshberg's analysis is the notion that "lowered-second" cadences are weaker relative to "raised-seventh" ones. And finally, to mark the difference in our analyses, I would cite Hirshberg's recognition of sharps "needed to improve interval

progressions." This is a revealing way to sum up biases about harmonic conventions that are mixed together with assumed conventions of performance practice; unconventional progressions are seen as needing improvement.

[45] As usual, the problem of how long accidentals remain in force is troubling. Here I assume that *F*-sharp in the cantus holds through measure 6; *F*-sharp in the tenor would seem to confirm this assumption.

[46] Carl Dahlhaus observes how the consonance-structure of this passage becomes apparent if the tenor is shifted one semibreve backward – that is, if the rest in measure 9 is dropped, and the tenor's *G* is placed under the *D* of the superius, etc. This produces a series of consonances between cantus and tenor in proper discant

again emphasized by the fact that this dissonant, polymensural passage clears out on *F*-sharp (m. 15), which establishes the sense of direction; and *g* is also emphasized by virtue of its position as the high boundary, obtained in measure 10. And when it perches on *a* for the *ouvert* cadence, the cantus seems to predict the conventional stepwise relationship between *ouvert* and *clos* endings, *a-G* – so much is traditional; it is the second ending that is unexpected. Part 2 opens with a digression through several highlighted pitches (*C, B*-flat, *C*), a procedure not uncommon for ballades. Eventually, the importance of *G* is reaffirmed at another structural moment: the sonority that serves to announce the refrain is *F*-sharp/*a* (m. 28). "Rounding" (repetition of music from the end of part 1 at the end of part 2) brings about a slight revision of the polymensural melisma and restatement of the *clos* ending.

Biauté qui toutes autres pere cannot be reduced to a single, dominating pitch. In an ambiguous design, the directional and hierarchical signals provided by accidentals become all the more important – hence, the roles of *F*-sharp and *E*-flat, which together give emphasis to *G* over *D*.[47] The song appears to fall relatively early in Machaut's spectacular period of interest in the ballade; perhaps the restless, experimental flair signals a breakthrough. The young composer flexes his muscles: he demonstrates command of the rhythmic components of the ars nova through polymensural and syncopated rhythms; and he demonstrates command of the harmonic language of ars nova through manipulated propinquity applications. It is all coordinated with an unusual design. In study of *Trouvère MS O*, we have observed how the intervention of accidentals offers various possibilities for manipulating pitch and shaping design. This technique is now channeled

---

fashion. See "'Zentrale' und 'Periphere' Züge in der Dissonanztechnik Machauts," *Aktuelle Fragen der Musikbezogenen Mittelalterforschung: Forum Musicologicum* 3 (Winterthur: Amadeus, 1982), 281.
[47] Compare *Biauté qui toutes autres pere* with *Je ne cuit pas* (Schrade, ed., PMFC 3: 85). This latter ballade is remarkable for its quantitative emphasis on *a*, which, in spite of the emphasis, is clearly established as a secondary pitch through propinquity *b*-flats. Aside from the *clos* and final cadences, *D* is used sparingly, though it is prepared by the tentative arrivals on *A* and by a few important *c*-sharps. *Comment puet* (Schrade, ed., PMFC 3:154) resembles *Biauté qui toutes autres pere* in significant ways. The midpoint cadence of the rondeau (*D*/*F*-sharp/*a*) emphasizes the same pitch as the final cadence (*D*/*a*/*d*). A few inflections lead the piece quickly

through various areas: *D* is established immediately, through *c*-sharp, but *b*-flat, emphasizing *a*, and then *b*-natural, emphasizing *c*, quickly follow. (Schrade's *c*-natural in measure 3 is surely incorrect; several sources make it clear that the sign is *b*-flat, which makes good sense and stands as a more characteristic inflection, since cancellations of *c*-sharp are rare.) Just as quickly, *D* returns for the conclusion of the first phrase. In phrase 2, inflections in the descending sequence – a sequence not unlike that of the melismatic one from *Biauté qui toutes autres pere* – carry on the steady instability. The nod towards *G* in this phrase provides a way to hear *D*/*F*-sharp/*a* at the midpoint. The last few phrases bring the song through *C* and *G* before it finds its way back to *D*. This song shows an "essential" contratenor that fully participates in the harmonic organization of the piece.

through the harmonic syntax of the ars nova. Some 75 years later, Du Fay works with a conception close to that of *Biauté qui toutes autres pere*. In his ballade *Je me complains*, *d* is emphasized, and *c*-sharps strengthen the sense that it is the main pitch.[48] Yet the three main cadences end on *a/aa*. *c*-sharps sound above *a* three times to form "half cadences" (mm. 7, 10, and 28), confirming the association of *a* with instability. The traditional cantus–tenor framework is abandoned in favor of equal-range voices marked *primus*, *secundus*, and *tertius*. Traditional discant cadences are irregular and scattered. As if in response to an unusual format, Du Fay works out this plan of clearly directed half-cadences, regularly placed strong sonorities built on *D*, and weak arrivals at the main nodal points on *a/aa*. As in *Biauté qui toutes autres pere*, a few carefully placed accidentals play an important role in an ambiguous design.

De toutes flours

Machaut's *De toutes flours* (Ex. 2.9) draws out the central problem of unnotated conventions for the propinquity application, mainly because the musical text, which is stable through the principal sources, contradicts familiar assumptions. Dropping those assumptions, we may read the text as a further display of Machaut's interest in manipulating basic components of harmony. The song has been analyzed by Fuller. As already acknowledged, Fuller's work on harmony provides a strong base for interpreting accidentals; yet the present interpretation of this song will differ fundamentally from her published account.[49]

The song is transmitted by five principal and four secondary sources. Fuller draws attention to one vexing situation (m. 15 of the edition):

[48] Modern edition in Heinrich Besseler, ed., *Guillaume Dufay: Opera Omnia*, Corpus Mensurabilis Musicae 1/VI (Rome: American Institute of Musicology, 1951–66), 29.

[49] Sarah Fuller, "Guillaume de Machaut: *De toutes flours*," in *Models of Musical Analysis: Music Before 1600*, ed. Mark Everist (Cambridge, Mass.: Basil Blackwell Ltd, 1992), 41–65; edition of the three-voiced version of the piece on pp. 59–61. A triplum is given in two sources; see Fuller, 62–4 for the four-voiced transcription. Fuller is undoubtedly correct in her assertion that "This triplum is doubtless a later accretion to the three-voice setting and was probably composed by someone other than Machaut" (p. 41). See Friedrich Ludwig, *Guillaume de Machaut: Musikalische Werke* (Leipzig: Breitkopf und Härtel, 1926–9), II: 48, for a concordance table, including references to two lost sources, *Paris, Bibliothèque Nationale n.a.f. 23190*, no. 27 (the "*Trémoïlle manuscript*"), and *Strasbourg, Bibliothèque Municipale, MS 222 C.22*, no. 168. There is also a keyboard arrangement of *De toutes flours* in *MS Faenza, Biblioteca Comunale, Cod. 117*, ff. 37v/38v. The arrangement is very free, making the source of little apparent value to our discussion of the transmission of Machaut's accidentals. Although it is difficult to tell for sure, it appears from my microfilm copy of *MS A* that *D*-flat is signed in the tenor for the *clos* ending. If so, the accidental is probably a mistake, and it has been dropped from Example 2.9. Yet it should be noted that later fourteenth-century songs do show, occasionally, the vertical mix of sharps and flats; see Chapter 3.

Example 2.9 *De toutes flours*, part 1, three-voiced version (after *MS A*, f. 470)

Example 2.9 (*cont.*)

gier fors u – ne seu – le ro———
ne qui du – re-ment s'o po———

se

sc

Some problems are especially thorny. For instance, at the end of phrase two, on *vergier* (breve 15) a notated B flat in the cantus in two principal sources contradicts the normal inflection (major sixth D–B natural to octave C) expected at a cadence and specified at other C endings in this song. In other copies where B flat stands as a "signature" in the cantus, the flat is not specified. Trained performers working from these sources would surely sing B natural to provide the conventional cadence progression, to fulfill the resolution of the B natural at breve 14, and to be consistent with the other C cadences in the piece. Does the notated B flat on *vergier* signify an express desire on someone's part to override the conventional performance mode, or is it a scribal lapse, a premature indication of a restored "signature" B flat? Although a good case can be made for the second position, based on specific disposition in the two principal sources, patterns of voice-leading and Machaut's normal practice elsewhere, the other view cannot be completely ruled out.[50]

Admitting that our understanding of fourteenth-century performance practice is not as solid as we would like it to be opens up the possibility of accommodating contradictions and exceptions. In an idiosyncratic piece, especially, it is good to take seriously a literal reading.

Measure 15's *b*-flat is interesting for two reasons: it "cancels" *b*-natural in the cantus of two measures earlier, before this pitch has a chance to resolve to the implied *c*; and it undermines the arrival on *c* in measure 16 by creating a whole step instead of a half-step leading tone. It is easy to understand how the flat could have been dropped by a skeptical scribe (and Fuller shows herself to be one when she drops it from her edition of a source that includes it). But the transmission of the sign is not weak. It is firmly communicated by the principal sources, and it is dropped only by the secondary sources (Table 2.1).[51] That all of the principal Machaut manuscripts are corrupt at measure 15 while the later and secondary manuscripts give an authoritative reading seems highly unlikely.

---

[50] Fuller, "Guillaume de Machaut: *De toutes flours*," 57, n. 6.

[51] Four of the principal Machaut manuscripts carry the sign explicitly notated at this place. The fifth (*Machaut MS F-G*) has *b*-flat notated at the beginning of the staff as a signature, indicating the inflection of all pitches on that line or space. There is no direct evidence that signature-accidentals are weaker than internally signed accidentals. There is no direct evidence that signatures are anything other than inflections governing an entire line or space (there is no evidence, for example, that they serve more casually, as loose guides to solmization). The Parisian Anonymous of 1375: "whenever any of these signs for the *coniuncta* is placed at the beginning on whatever line or space, all syllables on that line or space ought to be sung according to the sign placed at the

beginning – unless it is removed by something more particular in the middle or elsewhere. . ." ("quandocumque aliquod istorum signorum pro coniuncta ponitur in principio regule vel spacii cuiuscumque, omnes voces illius regule vel spacii cantari debent virtute illius signi in principio positi, nisi per aliud specialius in medio vel alibi hoc tollatur. . ."; Oliver B. Ellsworth, ed. and trans. *The Berkeley Manuscript*, 52–3.) And Bartolomeo Ramos de Pareia (1482): ". . . if the sign is put at the beginning such a nomenclature must be followed throughout the entire song. If, however, it is not put at the beginning but in the course of the song, they say that the nomenclature of the sign to be sung is only applied on the note to which it is added." *Musica practica*, ed. and trans. Clement Miller (n.p.: American Institute of Musicology, 1993), 88.

Example 2.10 Johannes Cesaris's *Bonté biaulté*, mm. 25–6 (after Reaney, ed., *EFCM*, I: 30)

Similar events occur in two songs by later composers. Solage's use of the same *b*-flat to weaken a cadence to *c* in *Le Basile* has been noted in the Introduction. The resemblance to *De toutes flours* is striking. It is more than ironic to discover that this flat, too, has been dropped from a modern edition. The event makes sense in terms of large-scale musical design, for it forms part of a gradual destabilization in which the polyphony flows away from the firmly established *C* of the beginning. Then, logically enough, *C* returns with the *clos* ending of part 1. There is movement from stability (associated with *C*) to instability (associated with several inflections and harmonic turns) back to stability (again associated with *C*). Some years later, Johannes Cesaris uses a similar gesture in his ballade *Bonté biaulté* (see Ex. 2.10). Again the formal logic is clear. Moving to *cc* through *bb*-flat weakens the arrival (as does the contratenor's *e*, bringing harmonic "imperfection"), as if to work against the strength of the voice leading. The tentative arrival is well suited to a cadence in this position, for this chord serves to announce the ballade's refrain (recall m. 28 of *Biauté qui toutes autres pere*, where an imperfect consonance was used for the same purpose). The refrain that follows brings the piece to a strong concluding cadence on the main pitch, *F*.

It is unlikely that all three of these texts are corrupt and likely that they show the same interest in using accidentals as a tool in overall design. Rather than imagining, as Fuller does, that trained singers knew how to "correct" unconventional cadences, I imagine them being skillful in negotiating those cadences as written. A raised leading tone makes an arrival stronger – the theorists all agree on that; it follows that its absence makes an arrival weaker. This technique offers the composer another way to distinguish various arrivals on the same pitch from one another hierarchically. Music always offers the potential to work on two levels and even in two contradictory ways at once. With this technique, the composer marks a point of arrival without stopping forward motion. Machaut's dangling *b*-natural in *De toutes flours* makes the event even more forceful. Jean de Murs gives us one opportunity to ground this event in contemporary theory when he says that variety is gained when intervals do not resolve to their "natural" places. But Machaut has gone well beyond the rudimentary concerns of the discant treatises, and he uses irregular events with a sense of how they may serve larger purposes.

I would invoke *difficilior lectio potior*, a basic principle of textual criticism, to explain the instability of *De toutes flours*'s musical text. This principle, which has been scarcely applied in study of accidentals, follows the assumption that idiosyncratic readings tend to become conventionalized over time.[52] Table 2.1 charts a process in which the musical text becomes increasingly trivialized. The table implies a conceptual (not necessarily a chronological) sequence, in which the unsettled quality of the piece is gradually washed away. The principal sources notate a highly discursive piece, with unexpected turns. Of the secondary sources, *Florence P 26*, *PN 568*, and *Modena A* preserve most of the inflections notated in the principal sources; they lack mainly the *b*-flats of measures 15–22. For the scribe of *PN 6771*, the piece is humdrum: *e*-flat disappears from the superius entirely (not only in part 1, as indicated in the chart, but throughout the piece), and after the first phrase the manuscript preserves few *b*-flats. If we knew only this version we would have no clue about essential ingredients of the composer's conception – and one can only wonder how many times that has actually happened throughout the surviving polyphonic corpus.

The troubling *b*-flat finds a place in analysis of the song. The cantus opens and ends the first musical phrase (mm. 1–8) on *c*, and the phrase closes with what looks like a traditional cadential gesture to *c*, with the voices moving in contrary motion from a doubly-imperfect sonority to a doubly-perfect sonority. Yet a *b*-flat signature governs this pitch (all of the sources agree), so the arrival is relatively weak. The sources do not contradict this signature until measure 14, where *b*-natural is signed (all but two of the sources agree). And, as we have just seen, several sources immediately contradict the *b*-natural, so that the cadence in measure 16 lacks a leading tone, just as the cadence in measure 8 does.

The composer may have good reasons for not wanting all arrivals on *c* to be the same. During the first phrase, several events weaken the sense of any

---

[52] Lee Patterson's summary of this principle – "scribes habitually trivialize their texts" – seems especially apt for the present situation: *Negotiating the Past: the Historical Understanding of Medieval Literature* (Madison: University of Wisconsin Press, 1987), 95.

Table 2.1

Distribution of accidental signs in the cantus line of *De toutes flours* (part 1 only).

Signature-accidentals are marked by parentheses, as they apply to each pitch on the given staff until there is a cancellation on that staff.

measure	5	7	10	14	15	20	22	23	27	29 (1st end)	29 (2nd end)
Machaut A	(b-flat)	(b-flat)	e-flat	b-nat.	b-flat	b-flat	—ᵃ	e-flat	—	b-nat.	b-nat.
Machaut F–G	(b-flat)	(b-flat)	(e-flat)	b-nat.	(b-flat)ᵇ	b-flat	(b-flat)	e-flat	—	b-nat.	—
Machaut Vg	(b-flat)	(b-flat)	e-flat	?ᶜ	b-flat	(b-flat)	(b-flat)	e-flat	(b-flat)	b-nat.	—
Machaut B	(b-flat)	(b-flat)	e-flat	b-nat.	b-flat	(b-flat)	(b-flat)	(e-flat)ᵈ	(b-flat)	b-nat.	—
Machaut E	(b-flat)	(b-flat)	e-flat	b-nat.	b-flat	(b-flat)	(b-flat)	e-flat	(b-flat)	b-nat.	b-nat.
Fp 26	(b-flat)	(b-flat)	e-flat	b-nat.	—	—	—	(e-flat)	(b-flat)	(b-flat)	(b-flat)
PN 568	(b-flat)	(b-flat)	e-flat	b-nat.	—	—	—	(e-flat)	(b-flat)	(b-flat)	—
Modena	(b-flat)	(b-flat)	e-flat	b-nat.	—	—	—	(e-flat)ᵉ	(b-flat)ᶠ	(b-flat)	(b-flat)
PN 6771	(b-flat)	(b-flat)	—	(b-flat)	(b-flat)	(b-flat)	(b-flat)	—	b-flat	(b-flat)	(b-flat)

Notes:

ᵃ Here the question of how long a sign remains in force comes into play: the flat before the b of m. 20 may be taken as holding still for the b of m. 22, since the pitches follow one another so closely. In any event, m. 22 is governed by b-flat signature in the other Machaut sources, as the table shows.

ᵇ The situation for this important place needs to be spelled out: the staff is governed by a b-flat signature, and the b of m. 15 is the first pitch of the line. Hence, the flat sign could be read as either a signature or a sign referring to a specific pitch – or both.

ᶜ The microfilm copy of this source available to me is difficult to read. It appears to me that there is space provided for b-natural at m. 14, and it seems as though there is some mark on the page; but it is difficult to say anything more. Since MSS Machaut B and Machaut E are thought to have been dependent upon Machaut Vg, there would seem to be a good chance that the sign is actually there, as it is in the two later manuscripts. Furthermore, the sign is included in the edition of the piece by Ludwig, who used MS Vg as his primary source and who was able to see the manuscript in person.

ᵈ In what must be a copying error, the source has mm. 23–8 transposed down a third; hence, the chart assumes that what the source signs as a b-flat is a copyist's attempt to make sense of his error and that the correct reading is e-flat, like the other sources.

ᵉ Modena, Fp 26, and PN 568 each carry an e-flat signature here, providing e-flats for mm. 24 and 25. Hence, according to the stated guidelines, entries for e-flats in mm. 24 and 25 should be made; the entries are dropped for clarity. One assumes that the other sources imply e-flats for these pitches, even in the absence of a signature; i.e., that the e-flats signed in mm. 9 and 23 carry for the two pitches that follow immediately, in each case.

ᶠ e-flat is given as a normally placed signature, but b-flat is given before the clef, in the margin, on this staff and the next. Such placement occurs fairly often in this manuscript.

clear hierarchy among the pitches. The cantus begins on *c*, but it is harmonized by *F* in the tenor. And in measure 6, *F* is again emphasized, now as the
lower and prominent boundary of the cantus; the cantus reaches this *F*,
significantly enough, by turning away from *c* through *b*-flat.[53] As often
happens in late medieval songs, pitch is organized dynamically and unpre-
dictably, and that is one reason why it is misleading to label this or that
phrase or piece as "in" a certain modality or tonality.

Phrase 2 juxtaposes *b*-natural (mm. 9 and 14) with *e*-flat (mm. 10 and
13), implying a diminished fourth and increased harmonic tension. (That
the *e*-flat signed in the cantus carries through the phrase seems evident;
durational problems are addressed generally below.) The pitch field has
shifted: *b*-flat and *E*-natural both sound in phrase 1 (though not in the
same voice), and this is followed by the juxtaposition of *b*-natural with *e*-
flat in phrase 2. The alterations serve not only to generate harmonic tension
but also to turn the piece decisively away from *F*. *b*-naturals imply a strong
arrival on *c*, but, as we have seen, the cantus turns through *b*-flat in measure
15, and full closure is denied.

As in *Biauté qui toutes autres pere*, an elaborate melisma brings a flourish
to the conclusion of part 1. In the melisma, the cantus turns twice more
through *b*-flat (mm. 20 and 22), the second time as part of another undermined progression to *C/c*. Harmonic tension is not fully resolved until the
clos ending, where *b*-natural is signed.[54] Part 2 begins with a fresh chord
built on *B*-flat, establishing a sense of digression that is characteristic of
this moment in ballade form. Yet, when *b*-natural follows (m. 35), the event
seems designed to restate tension between the two locations of *B*. Other
references to the material of part 1 follow: *e*-flat and *b*-natural sound in the
cantus, and the cadence that serves to announce the refrain (mm. 46–7)
duplicates the harmonic sense of part 1's *ouvert* ending.[55] The refrain con-
centrates harmonic tension into a single dramatic sweep. The cantus leaps
to high *aa*, expanding from the previous high boundaries of *f* followed by *g*.
And since, in this phrase, the cantus also highlights *e*-flat (m. 49) and *b*-
natural (m. 57), it indirectly defines an augmented fourth, a minor seventh,

[53] The companion pieces that should be cited in support
of this analysis of the opening phrase of *De toutes flours*
are *Il m'est avis* (Schrade, ed., PMFC 3: 98) and *En amer
a douce vie* (PMFC 3: 138). In each ballade, the cantus
starts on *c* and ends on *c*, and it uses *b*-flat in the first
phrase, on the way to a cadence on *F*. PN 6771's reading
of *Il m'est avis* lacks all internally signed accidentals
(again representing a parallel with *De toutes flours*).

[54] Three of the Machaut manuscripts sign *b*-natural
only at the first ending and not the second ending; the

layout on the page makes it easy to imagine the sign
carrying through to the second ending.

[55] This is, I think, how this moment should be parsed: it
is an *ouvert* cadence that serves to announce the refrain
and to predict a final resolution on *C*. Contrast this with
Fuller's interpretation of a "shift in tonal orientation" to
D and her suggestion that "the task of the refrain is to
re-establish the *C-G-c* sonority that has just been
supplanted" ("Guillaume de Machaut: *De toutes flours*,"
56).

and a diminished fourth. *D/F*-sharp/*b*-natural (m. 57) is stretched out as if to summarize the cumulative tension that is resolved ultimately in the final measure.

Machaut shows his ability to integrate nuances in use of accidentals with a broader sense of design.[56] Sarah Fuller's perspective on this period leads her to an important hypothesis, one that properly, in my opinion, places harmony at the expressive center of ars nova polyphony: "An issue-oriented history of compositional technique might indeed claim that a primary task of 14th-c composers was to develop control over new harmonic resources forced to the fore by novel rhythmic practices."[57] This puts things nicely. A complementary view would be that composers discovered ways to take advantage of the inherent flexibility of the harmonic syntax that had become a central part of polyphonic music. Their efforts may well have been trampled through the rough paths of transmission that often shaped the anthologies. The trampling is evident in the transmission of *De toutes flours*; for most other composers, one imagines, it is likely to remain hidden. There is a conceptual problem, too: when analysis is conditioned too heavily by the analogy with common-practice tonality, the nuances and flexibility of fourteenth-century harmonic syntax may disappear altogether.

For what is most striking about these and other songs by Machaut is the composer's selective use of the basic precepts. No matter to what degree they are inconsistent with each other, this is the message of the principal sources: for this composer, the propinquity application is an option.[58]

[56] For *De toutes flours*, it is possible to argue that Machaut's manipulation of the propinquity application that I am trying to legitimize and interpret on musical grounds serves also to highlight the syntax of the poem. Cadential hierarchies may be read as providing a technique for musical punctuation that echoes verbal punctuation. For an introduction to this general topic, see Harold Powers, "Language Models and Musical Analysis," *Ethnomusicology* 24 (1980), 1–60. Powers cites (pp. 49 and 50–1) the *Musica enchiriadis* and other treatises in which concepts of *cola* and *comma*, varying degrees of stops and articulations, are used in musical analysis. Accordingly, one would see the lack of a full stop in the polyphony for each run-through of part 1 in *De toutes flours* as musical articulation of the lack of a full stop in the poetry. Fuller makes the following observation concerning this poem ("Guillaume de Machaut: *De toutes flours*," 43): "Despite the rhyme-stopped endings, thought units frequently continue across line boundaries in the poem. The continuity (technically known as

enjambment) is sometimes disregarded in the music, as in stanzas 1 and 2 where a decisive cadence at the end of line 4 (breve 30b) denies the patent syntactic thrust from this line into the next. But Machaut does frame his music to take some continuities of the first stanza into account." I thank Alejandro Enrique Planchart for suggesting this textual-musical analysis to me.

[57] "On Sonority in Fourteenth-Century Polyphony: Some Preliminary Reflections," 38.

[58] In his survey of fourteenth- and fifteenth-century theorists, Klaus-Jürgen Sachs concludes that the propinquity application was neither universally followed in practice nor universally prescribed in theory. Sachs sees evidence suggesting that the propinquity application was optional, in contrast to the necessity application. See "Die Contrapunctus-Lehre im 14. und 15. Jahrhundert," in *Die mittelalterliche Lehre von der Mehrstimmigkeit*, ed. Frieder Zaminer, Geschichte der Musiktheorie bd. 5 (Darmstadt: Wissenschaftliche Buchgesellschaft, 1984), 199–208.

Example 2.11 *Rose, lis,* mm. 26–30, cantus, tenor, and contratenor

Analyzing in this way, we may fold the propinquity application into *causa pulchritudinis*. The application is used here but not there, now with this formula now with that one. The guide is the composer's sense of design – that is, his sense of beauty. In this way, the linear model of using inflections in the service of discursive melody may be transferred to polyphony.

Further notes on style and transmission

Machaut is given to experimentation, so it is not surprising to learn that he preferred to release his songs only after he was able to hear them performed.[59] Accidentals are used to generate tension that sustains forward drive. The event may have only local significance, or it may function on the larger scale. The composer violates basic precepts in his bold use of dissonances and "difficult" intervals. The vertical tritone, for example, marks one of the loveliest stretches from *Rose, lis* (Ex. 2.11). Harmonic tension initiated by *D/b*-natural is prolonged and increased, first by the vertical tritone, *F/b*, then by the doubly-imperfect *D/F*-sharp/*b*, held for two full measures. Meanwhile, the cantus flirts with the note of resolution, *c*, as part of a delayed resolution to a propinquity inflection.[60]

[59] Letter to the elusive Peronne, Letter 33 of the *Voir Dit*; quoted in Friedrich Ludwig, *Guillaume de Machaut: Musikalische Werke,* II: 56*.

[60] I would suggest that the cantus should sing *b*-natural in measures 15–16 (contrary to Schrade's editorial recommendation of *b*-flat), even though it forms an augmented fifth against the tenor's *E*-flat. By the same logic, the cantus should sing *b*-natural against the tenor's *F* in measure 24. Harmonic organization implies *b*-natural; hexachordal solmization (taking *e*-flat as *fa*) would demand *b*-flat and destroy the harmonic implications toward *c*. For use of delayed resolutions similar to these that might predate Machaut, see Philippe de Vitry's motet *In Arboris/Tuba sacre*, modern edition by Leo Schrade, PMFC 1: 88–90. Hocket disrupts the normal resolution of *b/d/f*-sharp in measure 25, and the duplum's *f*-sharp of measure 31 does not resolve until measure 37.

Machaut also uses difficult leaps. Some are formally highlighted. A leap from *G* to *c*-sharp opens *Amours me fait desirer*. In *Je sui aussi*, the same tritone is featured at the break between parts 1 and 2 of the ballade stanza. During the refrain of *Ne penses pas* the cantus moves in perfect longs from *f*-sharp to *c*. [61] We should surely be cautious about applying, as an assumed convention of performance practice, the prescription against indirect tritones to music by a composer so fond of direct tritones.[62] A general argument presented in Chapter 1 applies here with even greater force: the composer enjoys the possibility of working against, rather than in step with, the standards of intervallic decorum suited to plainchant. The performance practice of applying unnotated inflections in order to smooth out the rough contours of Machaut's lines may not have been part of this tradition at all; to the contrary: one can easily imagine a performance practice that highlights difficult leaps with a dramatic flair. The first phrase of *Honte, paour, doubtance* features a displaced-octave resolution to a propinquity inflection, which may have been designed to highlight the poetic caesura at the fourth syllable (see Ex. 2.12). Judged by standards of melodic decorum associated with plainchant, Machaut can be an inelegant com-

[61] Modern edition of *Amours me fait desirer* in Schrade, ed., PMFC 3: 92. The vertical tritone *b*-flat/*e*-natural sounds between cantus and tenor in measures 3, 6, and 10. Edition of *Je sui aussi* in PMFC 3: 94. Placement of *c*-sharp at the beginning of part 2 on the word "Fors" (m. 17) is neatly coordinated with placement of *f*-sharp on the same word at the beginning of the refrain (m. 36). Both sharps are leapt to, emphasizing the symmetry. And both events are followed with vertically sounding augmented intervals, *b*-flat against *c*-sharp (m. 19) and *b*-flat against *f*-sharp (m. 38), in an eighth-note neighbor-motif. The respective implications towards *d* and *g* articulated by these sharps mirror the respective roles of these two pitches in the hierarchy of the piece, *g* as most important and *d* as secondary. Edition of *Ne penses pas* in PMFC 3: 81; the leap is between measures 48 and 49. The sharp is not signed at this particular *f*, but it is signed just before. The full resolution of *a*/*f*-sharp would seem to come only at measure 50, implying that the inflection holds through measure 48. Beneath the *f* of measure 48 is signed *b*-natural in the tenor, strengthening the case.

[62] For an example of an indirect diminished fifth see *Vos doulz resgars* (PMFC 3: 148), which has *b*-flat to E-natural in the cantus, measures 26–7. To mention a few more of Machaut's augmented and diminished intervals: *Dame, se vous n'avez* (PMFC 3: 156), mm. 7–8 features a

tritone leap, *F* to *b*-natural, in the cantus. *Vos doulz resgars* (PMFC 3: 148) features a diminished fifth leap, *b*-natural to *F*, in the tenor (mm. 32–3). *Ce qui soustient moy* (PMFC 3: 155) opens with a harmonic tritone, *b*-flat/*e*-natural, between tenor and cantus. *On ne porroit penser* (PMFC 3: 72) has a harmonic diminished fourth, *F*-sharp/*b*-flat (m. 7), and a melodic tritone, *G* to *c*-sharp, in the cantus (m. 16). For *Cinc, un, treze* (PMFC 3: 146) Schrade, as editor, is willing to accept, as he should, the leap of a diminished fifth from *c*-sharp to *g* (mm. 8–9) and the occurrence of these same pitches simultaneously later in the piece (m. 25); he unnecessarily balks at the harmonic augmented fifth *F*/*c*-sharp in measure 2. The leap of an augmented second from *b*-flat to *c*-sharp is used in *N'en fait n'en dit* (PMFC 3: 82, mm. 10–11), *Amours me fait desirer* (PMFC 3: 92, mm. 8–9), and *Je sui aussi* (PMFC 3: 94, mm. 5–6). An augmented second from *f* to *g*-sharp is featured in *Ploures, dame* (PMFC 3: 120), measures 31–2. Schrade's suggestion of editorial *f*-sharps and *g*-sharps in measure 31 weakens the effect of measure 32's *g*-sharp; the cross relation and the augmented second give added punch to this important harmonic moment. In his study of Machaut's polyphonic Mass, Daniel Leech-Wilkinson also concludes that augmented and diminished intervals are idiomatic; see *Machaut's Mass: an Introduction* (Oxford: Clarendon Press, 1990), especially 98–103.

Example 2.12 *Honte, paour, doubtance*, mm. 1–5 (after PMFC 3: 106)

poser. The author of *Summa musice* (*c.* 1200), who described the leap of a ninth as the "braying of an elephant," would not have condoned the "hateful dissonances" that stand out in exotic creations like Machaut's cantus lines.[63] Though it may be an oversimplification that is caused by a lack of evidence for historical context, it is attractive to imagine Machaut as a composer who thrived on the opportunity to forge an independent expressive identity for the polyphonic chanson.

Honte, paour, doubtance also shows prominent juxtaposition of flats and sharps, a technique Machaut uses occasionally.[64] In part 1, the cantus sings both *e*-flat and *c*-sharp, one after the other, as alternative propinquity inflections to *d*. In part 2, a prominent *e*-flat follows an equally prominent *e*-natural. Chromatic juxtaposition of *fa* and *mi* degrees also occurs in several *C*-pieces that feature *e*-flat in the cantus. *Rose, lis, De toutes flours, En amer a douce vie*, and *De petit po* each use *e*-flat near *b*-natural in the cantus at least once and with some prominence. On the other hand, it is interesting to note that none of these songs has *f*-sharp (or *F*-sharp) in the cantus. I doubt that the avoidance of this inflection has anything to do with any reluctance to mix certain accidentals with one another. Rather, it probably has to do with the composer's interest in working with similar techniques and similar designs through a group of pieces.

[63] The treatise is translated and edited by Christopher Page, *The Summa Music: a Thirteenth-Century Manual for Singers* (Cambridge: Cambridge University Press, 1991), references on pp. 84, 86, 167, and 168. A disadvantage of all-vocal performance is that a dramatic leap like this one in *Honte, paour, doubtance* will be lost or obscured, since the tenor rises above the cantus in measure 3.

[64] Other examples among Machaut's songs include *Pour ce que tous mes chans* (PMFC 3: 83, mm. 13–16), and *De petit po* (PMFC 3: 90, mm. 16–17); both show close juxtaposition of *e*-flat with *b*-natural. *Doulz amis* (PMFC 3: 77) juxtaposes *b*-flats (dropped from Schrade's edition but preserved in *Machaut MSS Vg, B* and *E*) with *G*-sharp (mm. 16–17); *Esperance qui m'asseure* (PMFC 3: 84), juxtaposes *b*-flat with *F*-sharp and *c*-sharp.

For in another group of *C*-pieces, *f*-sharp is used and *e*-flat is avoided in the cantus.[65] It is possible to suggest a few generalizations that hold, more or less, for the songs in these two groups. In the cantus lines that use *f*-sharp but not *e*-flat, there is a stronger sense of downward melodic flow. The high sharp emphasizes *g* as a secondary pitch, and the effect of this is to reinforce the sense of high tension moving to low resolution. In the earlier songs especially (*Helas, tant ay dolour, Riches d'amour*), this way of organizing the melody is strong. In the later songs, the same technique is more localized, but the effect of the inflection is there. In the four *C*-pieces using *e*-flat (*Rose, lis, De toutes flours, En amer a douce vie*, and *De petit po*), melodic direction is more balanced and less bound to the prototype of downward resolution. These are two separate tendencies: high *f*-sharp reinforces the peak of a phrase, highlighting its distance from the final; *e*-flat interrupts progress to the final, which has almost arrived.

I would resist the temptation to project the idea of "tonal type" upon tendencies such as these. Better to think of Machaut working according to a simple, time-honored practice of composers everywhere: when he finds an expressive device that pleases him, he repeats it and develops it in other pieces. Over the course of time, his attention shifts through different techniques. The search for tonal types – though only in its first stages, still, and perhaps holding promise of future gains – can be misleading when cast too strongly in systematic terms.[66]

---

[65] *Helas, tant ay dolour* (PMFC 3: 70), *Riches d'amour* (PMFC 3: 76), *Ne penses pas* (PMFC 3: 81), *Tres douce dame* (PMFC 3: 104), *Donnez, signeurs* (PMFC 3: 108), *Nes que on porroit* (PMFC 3: 122), *Certes, mon oueil* (PMFC 3: 158).

[66] See the important article by Peter Lefferts, "Signature-systems and Tonal Types in the Fourteenth-Century French Chanson," *Plainsong and Medieval Music* 4 (1995), 117–48. Though he admits that these pieces are hard to classify (and he also admits his dependence on modern editions, which in this case, especially, becomes a problem), Lefferts groups *De petit po, De toutes flours, En amer a douce vie*, and *Rose, lis* in his "two-flat *C*" tonal type (meaning that the final of the cantus is *c* and that the signature has *b*-flat and *e*-flat; see Appendix, p. 145). Elsewhere he contradicts these classifications: *De petit po* (designated "B18") is classified as both the "natural *C*" tonal type (meaning that the final of the cantus is *c* and that there are no sharps or flats in the signatures) and the "two-flat *C*" tonal type in Example 8. Neither the "Machaut sources" nor the edition by Schrade carries

any signature flats for this piece (*b*-flat is signed only once, in *MS E*). Furthermore, it is not true that all four of these pieces shift from "an opening phrase in natural-system *C* to subsequent language in two-flat *C*" (p. 133): *De toutes flours* and *En amer a douce vie* both begin with *b*-flat in the cantus; for *De toutes flours*, this information is missed in Table 3. Also, it is an exaggeration to describe part 2 of *En amer a douce vie* as "two flats," since *b*-natural is more prominent. Again contrary to Table 3, *Rose, lis* does not move from natural to two-flat, but, rather, from natural to natural, with *e*-flats making an appearance in the cantus in both parts of the rondeau, and *b*-flat appearing in only one of the six sources (*MS Machaut B*), at the very end. All of this, I suggest, implies that Machaut is not thinking in the systematic terms Lefferts has developed. As I have argued, *b*-natural is importantly juxtaposed with *e*-flat in all four songs. *E*-flat is used regularly, in both cantus and tenor, to define *mi*-cadences on *D*, and to establish the open quality of this pitch, not only at the medial cadence but elsewhere. It is true that this harmonic logic confirms the systematic

*

The reader will recall, from discussion of *De toutes flours*, the textual problem of deciding how long *e*-flat remains in effect. In phrase 2, for example, the flat is given only once, but it is hard to imagine anyone arguing that it holds for any duration less than the entire phrase, during which it will be sung four times in the cantus. In Machaut's songs it is rare to find accidentals repeated in situations like this and common to come to the conclusion that the "once only" rule for accidentals does not apply. Yet, unlike *Trouvère MS O*, the principal Machaut sources do not consistently imply, through patterns of restatement, that accidentals hold for the duration of the staff upon which they are placed. Occasionally, the same stretch of music is notated in one source without a repeated sign, suggesting that a single sign governs an entire phrase, while, in another source, the sign is repeated following an earlier staff break. But one often suspects that the scribes of the principal manuscripts were less than careful about this. Discrepancies in staff lengths between exemplar and copy-in-progress may have been a main cause of corruption.[67]

expectations Lefferts has established. My view is that the evidence does not imply the influence of a tonal type; rather, it reflects the composer's recurring interest in three techniques: manipulation of *mi* cadences, tension from the indirect diminished fourth, and alternation between *e*-flat/*e*-natural. Rather than bend the pieces to make them fit into tonal types, I am inclined to emphasize how flexible Machaut's vocabulary is, as he uses similar expressive devices in the service of various designs. The same problem surfaces in Lefferts's analyses of other songs by Machaut, to greater or lesser degree. For example among the "*G* with one flat" type (Appendix, p. 145), consider the ballade *Se je me pleing* (PMFC 3: 86): this song moves through *b*-natural to *c* for the first phrase; *e*-flat follows, and *b*-flat follows later (though the sources disagree on *b*-flats), well after *B*-flat in the tenor at measure 13. Likewise, *b*-natural governs phrase 1 of *Je sui aussi* (contrary to the edition in PMFC 3: 94), and *b*-flat is used sparingly in part 1 (mm. 2 and 12), more regularly in part 2. Also irregular is the lovely rondeau *Ce qui soustient moy* (PMFC 3: 155): *e*-natural sounds against *B*-flat at the opening (the sonority is echoed in m. 13, with *F*-sharp against *C*), and *b*-flat is used mainly as a propinquity inflection (*G/b*-flat moving to *D/a*).

[67] For example, consider the cantus of *Doulz viaire gracieus* (Ex, 2.1 above), which is copied on one staff only in *MSS Vg* and *A*, with a *b*-flat signature. It is copied on

two staves in *MS C*, and the *b*-flat signature is restated for the second staff, implying a reading that matches *MSS Vg* and *A*. It is copied on three staves in *MS G* and with a twist: the first staff has a *b*-flat signature; the second does not, but the flat is placed well before the first *b* of this staff (measure 9 of the edition), certainly with the intention of inflecting both *b*'s on this staff; and the third staff consists of one pitch, the final *b*, which is obviously to be sung as *b*-flat – yet no flat is given. Signs are very commonly pre-placed in the principal Machaut sources. Occasionally, the practice extends to pre-placement on the previous staff. For example, *MS F-G* has *e*-flat in the triplum of *Rose, lis* at the end of the second staff, before *e* sounds for the second note on the third staff (the flat is repeated for the third staff); *MS F-G* has a similar placement of *b*-flat in the cantus, at the end of the third staff for *Vos doulz resgars* (PMFC 3: 148); and *MS A* has *e*-flat signed for the cantus of *Rose, lis*, again at the end of the second staff, to inflect *e* as the fourth note on the third staff. It should also be noted that clef changes and sectional markers (placed, for example, after a *clos* ending) are sometimes accompanied by signature accidentals; this adds another feature to be factored in when considering durational issues. Durational issues are discussed by Bettie Jean Harden, "Sharps, Flats and Scribes," 301–19 and elsewhere. Daniel Leech-Wilkinson makes this observation regarding the transmission of Machaut's polyphonic Mass: "the scribe of *MS G*,

It would be nice to have a quantifiable rule for establishing the duration of accidentals, but at the moment it is difficult to make progress. It is hard to avoid falling back on subjective parsing of musical design: the inflection seems to govern until the logic of which it forms part has been brought to a conclusion. It is easy to apply this guideline with confidence when the resolution of a propinquity application is delayed.[68] That is not the case, however, in the second phrase of *De toutes flours*, where the harmonic logic is not so clear, since *e*-flat does not function as a propinquity inflection. I would argue, however, that this inflection still has a harmonic rather than a purely melodic function, since what is most important is the juxtaposition *e*-flat/*b*-natural and the implication of a diminished fourth.[69] Tinctoris's well-known recommendation that accidentals hold as long as a line remains in the same hexachord can be invoked as evidence that the "once only" rule was not universally acknowledged.[70] Tinctoris places the textual matter in the realm of solmization. But solmization will not get us very far

working perhaps twenty years after *A* and *Vg* . . . seems to have copied sharps and flats assuming that they lasted until the end of the line. *A* and *Vg* suggest that this was not Machaut's view." *Machaut's Mass: an Introduction*, 101, n. 6. It is not clear to me how extensively this observation correlates with the chanson repertory, since it often seems to be the case that accidentals govern for the duration of the staff in all the manuscripts, and since there are some examples of the same accidental being repeated on the same staff in *MS F-G* (see, for example, *F*-sharps in the cantus of *Puis qu'en oubli*, and *b*-naturals in the contratenor of *Dix et sept, cinq*).

[68] Consider placements of signs in *Se quanque amours* (PMFC 3: 96). The cantus has signed *c*-sharps for measures 1, 6, 14, 29, and 37 of Schrade's edition. *D* is clearly the main pitch of the song, so *c*-sharp is the main propinquity inflection. *c*-sharp resolves irregularly a few times (for example, mm. 1–2, 6–7, 24–5). According to the principle that I have just proposed, that an inflection lasts until the musical logic in which it takes part has been brought to a conclusion, these signs carry through additional *c*'s in measure 4 (the resolution in measure 2 being weakened by the tenor's move to *G* under the cantus's *d*), measure 15 (a delayed resolution), measure 30 (likewise), and measure 39 (likewise, again). To assume that this is how duration was negotiated, one has to assume a keen sense of harmony guiding the singer. This reading leaves *c*'s in measures 17 and 32 uninflected and logically enough, since they do not take part in harmonic motion towards *d*. It also leaves the *clos* ending uninflected; the progression is relatively weak, with

similar motion between cantus and tenor and disjunct motion in the tenor. (Note that Schrade's *g* for the cantus in measure 34 is inferior to the *e* that is carried by *MSS Vg* and *C*.) In this reading, directional *c*-sharps in the cantus are inflected and no other pitch is inflected. This implies that the omissions of *f*-sharp in measures 27 and 38, for example, are purposeful: that the progressions to *G* are of secondary importance to the resolutions on *D* (the first arrival is already weakened by the appoggiatura leap to *aa*). *G*-sharps, *C*-sharps and an *F*-sharp in the contratenor lend support to harmonic events established by cantus and tenor.

[69] The opposite position is taken by Jehoash Hirshberg, "The Music of the Late Fourteenth Century: a Study in Musical Style," 399–404. Hirshberg parses the song hexachordally, and he associates the *b*-flat signature in the cantus and the *e*-flat inflections with a transposed gamut.

[70] The problem and Tinctoris's remarks are discussed by Berger, *Musica ficta*, 19–20; for Tinctoris's remarks see *Liber de natura et proprietate tonorum*, Cap. viii, p. 54. The Parisian Anonymous of 1375 comes close to saying the same thing Tinctoris says; see Ellsworth, ed. and trans., *The Berkeley Manuscript*, 52–3. I would read Tinctoris less as trying to reform contemporary practice (as Berger reads him) and more as responding to the reality of contemporary practice with a rule that is tidier and more precise than practice allows; that is, Tinctoris is once again attempting to systematize a practice that was probably haphazard and inconsistent.

in textual criticism of accidentals in Machaut's polyphony, since the
inflections are harmonically based, as a rule.

*

Machaut bestows upon the cantus of *Pas de tor en thies pais* a series of
inflections, leading the piece through an unstable polyphonic flow: *c*-sharp
is followed by *f*-sharp and *b*-flat. In part 2 of the ballade, the cantus moves
through the same inflections once more. Many of the signs clearly govern
more than one pitch.[71] Yet a few textual problems stand out. Perhaps it
didn't matter so much whether, for example, *f*-sharp in the cantus holds
through measure 14 (and, analogously, through measure 33). Here we must
puzzle over the possibility that the inflection holds until the harmonic logic
upon which it is based is brought to conclusion, and whether it is then
automatically dropped as the line descends away from the pitch of resolution, *g*. Perhaps these two inflections are so fleeting that it doesn't matter.

On the other hand, the final cadence (Ex. 2.13) would seem to matter a
great deal, and the fact that it is uninflected in all four principal sources
demands our careful attention. One cannot easily make the argument that
an earlier *c*-sharp (measure 44) holds through the final cadence. If signs
govern through a passage as long and complicated as this one, then why are
they uniformly repeated elsewhere in the song? The four sources all agree
on *c*-sharps for measures 4, 15, 37, and 44, and they all agree on *f*-sharps
(and *F*-sharp) for measures 11, 30, and 39. Did the scribes know that it was
unnecessary to notate the final inflection, since it was obvious to everyone
to apply it there automatically, without a sign?[72]

There are good reasons to doubt that this assumption holds for this
passage (and for the precisely matched passage, the *clos* ending of part 1).[73]

---

[71] Modern edition in PMFC 3: 116; a better edition,
with corrections of the *ouvert* ending, is given by
Elizabeth Keitel, supplement to *Early Music* 5 (1977).
Several times, a single sign marks a propinquity
inflection that finds its way gradually to resolution. For
example, even though no source repeats the sign, we may
assume that *c*-sharp from measure 4 in the cantus holds
through measure 7, after which the inflection will finally
resolve directly to *d*. A fresh digression is signaled by *f*-
sharp in the cantus at measure 11, and, again, this
inflection surely holds for the next few measures, though
the sign is not repeated in any source. It holds, one must
assume, through measure 12, where cantus and tenor
fleetingly form the octave *G/g*. The main chromatic event
of the next phrase is the introduction in the cantus of *b*-
flat, which moves to *a* at measure 17 (a propinquity
application producing a weak progression that Machaut

sometimes uses in *ouvert* position, as we have seen).
[72] It is also possible that the final cadence of *Pas de tor*
is weak because the composer wants the piece to sound
unresolved, and that he plays with ambiguity; the
conception would be similar to that of *Biauté qui toutes
autres pere*.
[73] Schrade signs *c*-sharp for the cantus and *F*-sharp for
the tenor in the *clos* ending, but I do not see either
inflection on the microfilms. Ludwig reports that this *c*-
sharp is signed in *MS Vg*, but the sharp appears to me –
again, through a poor microfilm – to be *b*-natural; this
reading is supported by *MS B*. The same *b*-natural is
used in precisely the same arrangement in *MS F-G*'s copy
of *Mes esperis se combat* (PMFC 3: 134), at the *clos*
ending on *d* – and in this case, too, the sign is not given
for the analogous cadence at the end.

Example 2.13 *Pas de tor en thies pais*, mm. 49–end (after PMFC 3: 116)

The situation represents what has become, for the twentieth century, a classic sort of "musica ficta problem." By the necessity rule, *b*-flat in the tenor at measure 55 generates *b*-flat in the cantus (and there is, indeed, a *b*-flat signed, only a few measures earlier, in all sources). If both *b*-flat and *c*-sharp are applied in the penultimate measure, then the cantus must sing an augmented second (this is Schrade's suggestion). Augmented seconds may have been acceptable in this idiom, but they are hardly commonplace. It is hard to imagine that performers were expected to resolve contradictory situations like this by themselves. Why would contradictory situations have been left to the performer to work out, while straightforward inflections elsewhere in the same piece were notated explicitly? To solve the problem, the performer would have had to balance notated evidence from several parts along with two precepts of contrapuntal theory; he would then have had to ponder the problem of the augmented second. There is no evidence that performers were expected to do this; certainly the surviving treatises would not have helped them.

It may be significant that a good number of songs ending on *D* and *G* lack propinquity accidentals for final cadences.[74] In a few cases, there is an earlier inflection that one might take as still governing to the end.[75] In a few others, the leading tone is a very short note (though it is not clear to what extent this might have been a factor, since there are more than a few instances in Machaut's oeuvre of inflected short notes; see, for example, *E*-flats in *De petit po*). Perhaps final cadences were special. It would have been easy for conventions of performance practice to grow around them. On the other hand, it is possible that the composer did not notate accidentals at final cadences because he did not want them there. He may have wanted a non-inflected sound, one that would give the piece a special identity. I refer, of course, to modal identity.

Writing just before Machaut's death, the Parisian Anonymous of 1375 briefly sketches a way to analyze mode in polyphonic songs:

> And now, it remains to clarify some things about other songs (for example, motets, ballades, and the like) with respect to the judging of their tones or modes. Let the judgment therefore be with respect to every final of the tones or modes of any song – motets, ballades, rondeaux, virelais, and the like. First, every song of this type that ends on any re, on sol B quadratum, on la naturalis, or on sol or la B mollis, is in the first or second tone. Every song of this type that ends on any mi or on la B quadratum is in the third or fourth tone. Every song of this type that ends on fa naturalis or on fa or ut B mollis is in the fifth or sixth tone. Every song that ends on sol or ut naturalis or on fa or ut B quadratum is in the seventh or eighth tone.[76]

---

[74] Of the *D* pieces, in addition to *Pas de tor*, see *Se vous n'estes* (PMFC 3: 146), *Comment puet* (PMFC 3: 154), *Plus dure que un dyamant* (PMFC 3: 187), *Se quanque amours* (PMFC 3: 96), *De fortune* (PMFC 3: 101), and *Mes esperis se combat* (PMFC 3: 134). Of the *G* pieces, see *Puis qu'en oubli* (PMFC 3: 161), *Moult sui de bonne heure nee* (PMFC 3: 190), *S'Amours ne fait par* (PMFC 3: 68), and *Je sui aussi* (PMFC 3: 94).

[75] Though I have just argued against this explanation for the lack of a final propinquity inflection in *Pas de tour*, the duration problem must always be considered. To put the matter in a slightly different light, consider *Dame de qui toute ma joie* (PMFC 3: 140). *B*-flats in the tenor at the ends of parts 1 and 2 are not signed, though they obviously need to be sung. In both cases, most of the principal sources sign the flat for a previous *B* (mm. 22 and 38) and this flat would seem to carry through. On the other hand, it is possible to argue for the final cadence that *E*-flat signed in measure 44 generates *B*-flat through solmization, *E*-flat sung as *fa* and *B*-flat, as a

result, sung as *ut*. This would represent a very particular application of the theory that inflections signal hexachordal organization, which must be used to construct the musical text.

[76] "Restat et nunc quidem de cantibus aliis, puta motetis, baladis, et huiusmodi, de quibus tonis sive modis iudicandi fuerint aliqua declarare. Sit igitur finale iudicium omnium tonorum seu modorum cuiuslibet cantus, videlicet motetorum, baladarum, rondellorum, vireletorum, et huiusmodi istud. Primo quod omnis cantus huiusmodi finiens in re quocumque, aut finiens in sol B quadrati, aut in la naturale, aut in sol vel in la B mollis, est primi vel secundi toni. Item omnis cantus huiusmodi finiens in mi quocumque, aut finiens in la B quadrati, es tercii vel quarti toni. Item omnis cantus huiusmodi finiens in fa naturale, aut finiens in fa vel in ut B mollis, est quinti vel sexti toni. Item omnis cantus finiens in sol vel in ut naturale, aut finiens in fa vel in ut B quadrati, est septimi vel octavi toni." Ellsworth, ed. and trans., *The Berkeley Manuscript*, 84–5.

This statement stands against Grocheio's caution, 75 years earlier, about the insignificance of modes to polyphony and vernacular monophony. Then, a century later, with Tinctoris in 1475, we are confronted with an argument favoring modal analysis of polyphony that is made with more conviction than ever before. Tinctoris's approach (see Chapter 4) is explicitly tied to the "species" definition of modality: each mode is defined as a unique combination of scalar modules that form patterns of fourths, fifths, and octaves; the modules differ from one another in their sequences of half and whole steps. It would be pointless to apply species analysis to Machaut's songs, since the inflections of which the composer is so fond constantly disrupt the abstract modules upon which the theory is based. The Parisian Anonymous says nothing about species of fourths, fifths, and octaves, and there is no reason to believe that he is thinking about modality in this way. His brief statement emphasizes the final and surrounding intervals. This is a more traditional approach to modality, one that is usually (though not here, significantly enough) completed by discussion of range. Elsewhere in his treatise the theorist shows himself to be keenly interested in theoretical accommodation of musica ficta. By comparison, these brief and problematic observations about modality in songs come off as half-hearted. Others have noted how the classifications do not correlate very well with compositional practice.[77]

Yet to read the theorist more sympathetically, we may imagine the possibility that he was hearing final cadences that sounded modal, in the sense that they conformed to a particular intervallic pattern around the main final pitch – that is, that they moved without propinquity inflections, and in this way suggested *protus* and *tetrardus* (with *tritus* having a raised seventh by virtue of diatonic melody and *deuterus* being

---

[77] See, most recently, Peter Lefferts, "Signature-systems and Tonal Types in the Fourteenth-Century French Chanson," 142, n. 36; Ellsworth, ed. and trans., *The Berkeley Manuscript*, 2–4 and 84–7; Howard Brown, "A Ballade for Mathieu de Foix," 90–3; Jehoash Hirshberg, "Hexachordal and Modal Structure," 19–21; and Richard Crocker, "A New Source for Medieval Music Theory," *Acta Musicologica* 39 (1967), 161–71. Lefferts includes thoughtful observations about using modal classifications, and his remarks on typical uses of range in cantus lines (and in trouvère songs) are especially valuable. Still problematic, however, are some of the classifications and the tendency to over-systematize (as I have mentioned above). For example, in Table 1 (p. 121), which seeks to associate authentic cantus lines with tenors that end at the unison or underfifth, the list of "anomalies" should be expanded. Considering only Machaut's songs: the cantus of "B2" (*Helas, tant ay dolour*), dips down to G and up to only a quick b, with c as final; the same is true for "B5" (*Riches d'amour et mendians*); the cantus of "V24" (*En mon cuer a un descort*) goes down to E and up to f, with c final; the cantus of "V30" (*Se je souspir*), goes down to C and up to f, with F final; and the cantus of "B12" (*Pour ce que tous mes chans*) dips down to C below the final F. With these additions to the "anomaly" column of Table 1, Machaut appears to be less systematic than we might like him to be; again, his music resists analysis according to "tonal types."

avoided). In the end, there are only a few good candidates among Machaut's songs for this kind of analysis, so we may be inclined towards alternative explanations: there may indeed have been a performance practice that relieved the scribe from the (very modest) burden of notating sharps. Or, some pieces may end weakly. In any event, these various possibilities easily get lost when focus is shifted to universal conventions for applying the propinquity inflection as a performance practice. For future research, these will be the possibilities to consider when studying propinquity applications, particularly at final cadences: Are there tendencies in a given repertory (and within a coherent layer of redaction) towards modal definition at final cadences? Can the lack of propinquity inflections at the final cadence be explained in terms of weak endings (an attractive possibility when there are other, equally perplexing practices close at hand, such as irregular endings)? Is there evidence to suggest that propinquity inflections at the final cadence and perhaps other nodal points were not notated because they (but not other cadences, perhaps) were implied to performers? As I have said before, the best way to advance on these issues is by placing manuscript evidence at the center of the inquiry, even though that approach is likely to yield conclusive results only in a small number of cases. Perhaps a few strong cases will be enough, eventually, to supply working generalizations for the repertory as a whole.

*

Among the principal sources of Machaut's music, various lines of dependence and independence emerge, some clearly and some as dimly imagined possibilities. *MSS Vg, B,* and *E* stand, at least partly, in a stemmatic line. *Vg* served as the exemplar for *B,* a hastily and often poorly executed paper manuscript. *B* in turn served as the exemplar for at least some of *E,* which was owned by and perhaps commissioned for Jean, Duke of Berry, well after Machaut's death. *E* omits many signs and it shows confusion in placement of a good many more.[78] In a study of these three manuscripts, Margaret Bent rescues *E* as an important source that should not be ignored. She argues that the scribe had access to secondary sources, and that he was

---

[78] Margaret Bent observes that the scribe of *MS E* has a "habit of inserting an accidental when he encounters one in *B*, but placing it at the vertical register of the immediately-following note rather than at that of the note to which it properly applies. He almost never supplies ficta signs not present in his exemplar, but such observation of his habits should guide our interpretation of his placing in cases where we do not have his exemplar." See "The Machaut Manuscripts *Vg, B* and *E*," *Musica Disciplina* 37 (1983), 71.

not exclusively dependent on *B*.[79] Here and there, accidentals confirm that *E* makes occasional use of a secondary line of transmission.[80]

MS E's mixed layers remind us to be cautious about crudely characterizing the division between principal and secondary sources for Machaut. Less than a third of Machaut's 70 known polyphonic ballades, rondeaux, and virelais found their way into surviving secondary sources, so in most cases there is nowhere to turn but to the principal sources. Given likely rates of loss and given the large number of surviving principal sources, a great many more of them must have been made. Principal sources may have experienced the same gradual deterioration that secondary sources presumably experienced. Lawrence Earp demonstrates how *MS Cambrai 1328*, a collection of fragments representing what was once a large and diverse anthology from the later part of the fourteenth century and from the North, preserves a reading for a motet by Machaut superior to that of the principal sources.[81] But most secondary sources do not enjoy this chronological and geographical proximity to the composer, and the clear trend for them is to lack accidentals that the principal sources record with some consistency. In Chapter 1, we observed a model of transmission in which added accidentals were used to enhance the discursive flow of melody. For Machaut's music, the opposite trend seems to characterize transmission through the secondary sources. The *difficilior lectio potior* argument, which fits *De toutes flours* so neatly, may well be applicable to other variants in the secondary sources.[82] When the secondary sources lack

[79] See Bent, "The Machaut Manuscripts *Vg*, *B* and *E*," especially Table 2 on p. 78.

[80] In its description of *Honte, paour, doubtance,* for example, *MS E* agrees with *Florence P 26* in lacking *c*-sharp at measure 11. These two manuscripts are also the only ones to carry a sharp for *e* in measure 20 and *F*-sharp in the tenor for the *ouvert* ending.

[81] See Earp, "Machaut's Role in the Production of Manuscripts of His Works," 494–7. *MS Cambrai 1328* has two polyphonic songs by Machaut, *De petit po* and *Se vous n'estes.* Judging from Friedrich Ludwig's critical report on the variants for *Se vous n'estes* (the photographs of *MS Cambrai 1328* to which I have access are illegible), the manuscript agrees with the principal sources in important details; see Ludwig, *Guillaume de Machaut,* I: 57. Several important variants involve accidentals; for example, the placement of *F*-sharp in measure 7, the placement of *b*-flat in measure 16 (in *MSS C* and *A*) as an early prediction of the *ouvert* arrival on *a*

in the cantus, and the use of *B*-flat in the second part of the song. For a list of songs by Machaut that circulated in secondary sources, see Earp, "Scribal Practice, Manuscript Production and the Transmission of Music," 14–15.

[82] For example, consider *c*-sharp for measure 11 of *Honte, paour, doubtance*: the *c*-sharp is juxtaposed with *e*-flat in four of the principal sources, but the inflection is absent in *Florence P 26* and *MS E*. As an example of a secondary source reporting accidentals that have, most likely, been added to an authorial reading, consider the tendency of *Florence P 26* to add sharps, particularly for imperfect consonances in *ouvert* position. The manuscript uniquely has *F*-sharp in the contratenor of *Se vous n'estes* (PMFC 3: 146) at the *ouvert* midpoint cadence (m. 20); it has the same sharp uniquely at the *ouvert* cadence of *Honte, paour, doubtance,* in the tenor; and it has the same sharp uniquely in the tenor of *De petit po* (PMFC 3: 90), measure 40.

a sign that the principal sources agree on it will be hard to trust the reading of the former, even if the latter is problematic.

What is most notable about the principal sources is the extent to which they agree with one another. Variants tend to be minor, infrequent, and relatively easy to deal with; they may often stem from durational issues (where the sign is placed, how often it is repeated). Variants can be dealt with easily when a stemmatic relationship is involved, as in the line from *MSS Vg* to *B* to *E*. There are other, less certain connections. *MS C* is the oldest principal source, dating before 1356. Earp surveys the evidence that Machaut revised his exemplars after this manuscript was compiled. If there was such a revision, then *MSS A, F-G,* and *Vg* may have followed revised exemplars, which could have been superior, inferior, or simply different, depending on whether they were corrected, mistaken, or rewritten.[83] In some places where a reading from *C* is isolated, it does seem possible that a revised exemplar corrected a reading that was sketchy or incorrect.[84] Elsewhere, *C* appears to have a superior reading in isolation.[85] But cases like this are few. For the most part, *C*'s readings are supported by at least one other source.

Friedrich Ludwig long ago cited *Vg* as having the best musical readings

[83] These issues are dealt with by Earp, "Machaut's Role in the Production of Manuscripts of His Works."

[84] For *S'Amours ne fait par* (PMFC 3: 68), *MS C* has *b*-natural for the tenor at measure 70, while *MSS A, F-G,* and *B* (and, by implication, *MS Vg,* though the sign cannot be seen on microfilm) have *c*-sharp. Either reading is plausible, *b*-natural for necessity in measure 72 and *c*-sharp for propinquity in measure 73. The passage is dissonant either way: with *c*-sharp, there is a diminished fifth, *c*-sharp/*g*, at measure 71; with *b*-natural, there is an augmented fourth, *c*/*f*-sharp, at measure 73. *c*-sharp would seem preferable because of the arrival on *d* at measure 75. The intervention of *c*-sharp at measure 19 in the cantus of *Dame, ne regardes pas* (PMFC 3: 80) makes a striking effect, given the prominence of *c*-natural in this voice; the sharp is absent from *MS C* but present in *MSS A, Vg,* and *F-G.* On *MS C*'s shorter staff lengths and its tendency to have more signature accidentals than other sources, see Harden, "Sharps, Flats and Scribes," 122–37.

[85] My favorite variant from *MS C* occurs in *Rose, lis* (Ex. 2.2), where *e*-flat is introduced in the cantus at measure 22 and, analogously, at measure 34. Other manuscripts have it earlier; but, in doing so, they reduce the strength of the resolution to *F*/*f* at measures 21 and 33, and they reduce the impact of the *e*-flat by taking away the close

cross relation. On the other hand, *MS C* carries *c*-sharp for measure 24, which is most likely corrupt (presuming *E*-flat in the tenor; see, however, comments in Chapter 3 on vertically combined sharps and flats). Hoppin, "Notational License," 15, notes that only *MS C* has the correct mensural notation for a passage from *Rose, lis*; cited by Earp, "Scribal Practice, Manuscript Production and the Transmission of Music in Late Medieval France," 308. Earp reports that *MSS F-G* and *A* are sometimes closely connected and may have derived from the same exemplar; they share some *unica* and some important variants, particularly in the longer poems. I see no situations where this connection helps to sort through significant omissions or inclusions of accidentals. As a rule, points of agreement between *MSS F-G* and *A* are supported by at least one of the other principal sources. The few stray exceptions to this rule may be coincidental: for example, consider the necessity application of *E*-flat in the tenor at measure 32 of *Amours me fait desirer* (PMFC 3: 92), and stray *b*-flats in the tenor at measure 15 and the cantus at measure 31 of *Je sui aussi* (PMFC 3: 94). For later songs which are not included in *MS C*, however, the comparison loses strength, since *MSS B* and *E* are dependent upon *MS Vg*, the only other principal source.

among the principal manuscripts. Occasionally, *Vg*, *B*, and *E* lack an accidental that is included in *C*, *A*, and *F-G*. Since *C* may be independent of *A* and *F-G* (which show various connections), one might lean towards the hypothesis that, in the situation just described, *Vg* is mistaken, and that the mistake was carried into *B* and *E*.[86] Still, given its favored status, *Vg* may have authorial readings even when it is isolated. Research on this problem will undoubtedly advance when reasonable scholarly access to the manuscript is permitted.

And that is a fitting note upon which to take leave of this rich body of music. There is far more to say about accidentals in Machaut's songs than I have been able to cover, and at nearly every turn one sees promising paths for future research.[87] If the composer was as important to the development of the polyphonic chanson as modern historiography has imagined, then his creative use of accidentals may be counted among his contributions. We shall not enjoy the same security of readings with any other composer, and that means that it will be difficult to project this same innovative importance onto anyone else. But there is a great deal of chromatic beauty in the chanson tradition from composers of the next few generations, and compositional practice does not stand still. Whether later composers knew it or not, they were probably indebted to Machaut's innovation, both to its detail and to the attitude of stepping beyond convention that he seems to have cherished.

---

[86] The *lectio difficilior* argument may be applicable to *Mors sui, se je ne vous voy* (PMFC 3: 185), measure 2 of the cantus, where MSS *C*, *A*, and *F-G* have *b*-flat, forming a forceful juxtaposition with *c*-sharp from a measure earlier; the *b*-flat is absent from MSS *Vg*, *B*, and *E*. Similarly, *d*-sharp (not *c*-sharp, as Schrade transcribes it) is signed in MSS *F-G*, *A*, and *C* but not in MSS *Vg*, *B*, and *E* at measure 15 of *Riches d'amour* (PMFC 3: 76); Harden, "Sharps, Flats and Scribes," 217, observes that this is the only *d*-sharp in Machaut's songs.

[87] Among topics I have not covered, the occurrence of stray *b*-naturals needs to be mentioned. If we assume, as I have done, that unsigned *b*'s represent *b*-natural, then pieces like *Ploures, dames* (PMFC 3: 120), which has six signed *b*-naturals and no *b*-flats in the contratenor, demand an explanation. Five of the *b*-naturals are part of a turning figure around *a*, and since this figure often brings *b*-flat (see *Nes que on porroit*, for example), the signs may serve to prevent what may have appeared as a conventional inflection. Exactly why the composer wants *b*-natural and not *b*-flat in these figures is hard to say;

perhaps it has something to do with the importance of *C* in this song, and the relatively weak standing of *D*, in spite of *clos* and final endings. When *b*-natural is important for propinquity or necessity it tends to be signed, especially in a contratenor; see, for example, *En amer a douce vie* (PMFC 3: 138), *Phyton le mervilleus serpent* (PMFC 3: 132), *Mes esperis se combat* (PMFC 3: 134), *Quant Theseus* (PMFC 3: 124), *Dix et sept, cinq* (PMFC 3: 160). *Tres bonne et belle* (PMFC 3: 182) presents an interesting case. All of the principal sources indicate *b*-natural for the cantus in measure 8 and for the tenor in measure 27. The first inflection may be designed to prevent *c*-sharp and to make the cadence to *D/a/d* in measure 9 relatively weak; see Sarah Fuller, "Guillaume de Machaut: *De toutes flours*," 58, n. 33, for a similar analysis. The tenor's *b*-natural at measure 27 of *Tres bonne et belle* would seem to be designed to prevent the lowered-second for the cadence on *a/aa* (with *D* in the contratenor underneath). For further discussion of the phenomenon see Harden, "Sharps, Flats and Scribes," 243 ff.

Our focus now shifts from the work of a single composer back to a broad and diverse repertory that includes the work of many composers, some anonymous and most barely identifiable. Consequently, we also turn back to an emphasis on anthologies. Most of the songs discussed in this chapter were copied into one of two large and important sources for polyphonic music from the decades surrounding 1400 – *MS Chantilly, Musée Condé 564 (c. 1410–15)* and *MS Oxford, Bodleian Library, Canonici Misc. 213 (c. 1426–36)*.[1] These sources are justly famous, *Chantilly 564* as a spectacular repository of complicated late fourteenth-century songs and *Oxford 213* as a wide-ranging anthology that is crowned, on its most recent end, by 40 of Du Fay's early songs. *Chantilly 564* includes earlier music going back to Machaut, and *Oxford 213* has music dating as early, perhaps, as the 1370s. Thus, the two anthologies yield a wide chronological range, suiting well our purpose of sampling the use of accidentals between Machaut and Du Fay.

There survives from this period a considerable quantity of music, yet we know relatively little beyond the bare notes on the page, and much of the context for the music remains obscure. Rarely do songs survive in more than one or two manuscripts. More than occasionally, one discovers good reasons to question the reliability of sources, which, as a rule, preserve a repertory that is eclectic both geographically and chronologically. *Chantilly 564* and *Oxford 213* were both copied in northern Italy, and most of their songs that will be of interest to us here were probably composed elsewhere; these Italian manuscripts are, in fact, our two main sources for French music during this period. The contrast with the transmission of Machaut's oeuvre could not be stronger. While Machaut is well represented

---

[1] On *Chantilly 564*, see Charles Hamm, gen. ed., *Census-Catalogue of Manuscript Sources of Polyphonic Music, 1500–1550*, 5 vols. (Neuhausen-Stuttgart: American Institute of Musicology, 1979), I: 147. John Nádas (personal communication) has considered the possibility of a late date *c.* 1410–15, based on archival discoveries concerning some composers represented in the manuscript. On *Oxford 213*, see *Census-Catalogue of Manuscript Sources of Polyphonic Music, 1500–1550*, II: 275. This manuscript, particularly, has inspired a series of close codicological studies, including David Fallows, *The Canonici Codex: a Facsimile of Oxford, Bodleian Library, MS. Canon. Misc. 213* (Chicago: University of Chicago Press, 1995); Graeme Boone, "Dufay's Early Chansons: Chronology and Style in the Manuscript Oxford, Bodleian Library, Canonici misc. 213" (Ph.D. diss., Harvard University, 1987); and Hans Schoop, *Entstehung und Verwendung der Handschrift Oxford Bodleian Library, Canonici misc. 213*, Publikationen der Schweizerischen Musikforschenden Gesellschaft 2/24 (Berne and Stuttgart: Paul Haupt, 1971).

by a variety of sources that we are encouraged to have confidence in, the period that follows him is poorly represented by sources that we should automatically be suspicious of. There are some slight exceptions, but they mainly come with the younger generation: *MS Escorial A* is an unusually good source for Binchois, for example, and scholars have speculated about Du Fay's possible connections to *Oxford 213*. Yet even in these cases there are relatively few close concordances, and the situation remains far less favorable than it is for Machaut.

The period between Machaut and Du Fay – or Binchois, if one thinks of this master as slightly older than Du Fay and perhaps taking a leading role in forging a new style – seems to lack the presence of a single, dominating figure. Gustave Reese described it as "a transition between two peaks."[2] That image would not come to mind so quickly, perhaps, in today's historiographic climate, but it does have the benefit of signaling the dimness of view with which we must still reckon. Among northern composers of chansons, the shadowy Solage and the much-debated Baude Cordier lead the way in number of surviving attributions, with ten each. All but one of Solage's ten songs survive only in *Chantilly 564*; Baude Cordier's oeuvre is supported only slightly better. There is stylistic plurality in the work of these two composers and many others, and this encourages one to project upon the composer an attitude of experimentation, a search for some elusive stylistic solution. It is hard to know the extent to which this impression is produced by lack of context – lack of chronology, attributions, and identifiable lines of influence.

The spectacular rhythmic complexities that condition the surface of so many chansons from this period provide an additional point around which historiographic confusion spins. Ursula Günther's felicitous label "ars subtilior" has gained currency because it brings a positive focus to this practice.[3] Reinhard Strohm forges a historiographic model that highlights a central French tradition and various peripheral traditions, the latter working through different kinds of relationships with the former.[4] One thing that is central about the French tradition is that it presumably develops, in part, by moving through more and more rhythmic complexity, while the peripheral traditions participate in this development less consistently or not at all. Music by Philippe de Vitry and Machaut, the two leading figures of the ars nova, had, presumably, a late-century presence that gave shape to developments in the central tradition. This model suggests a pos-

---

[2] *Music in the Renaissance* (New York: Norton, 1959), 10.

[3] Günther, "Das Ende der Ars Nova," *Die Musikforschung* 16 (1963), 105–20.

[4] *The Rise of European Music, 1380–1500* (Cambridge: Cambridge University Press, 1993), especially 1–106.

sible way to think about accidentals in the chanson: to what extent does the period follow Machaut's practice, in particular details and in general conception? "Ars subtilior" suggests intensification of the rhythmic paradigm of the ars nova; a similar process may have taken place in melodic and harmonic design, including techniques for using accidentals.

On the other hand, Strohm's observation that ars subtilior was not a universal phenomenon leads him to the useful category of "ars subtilior essay." This categorizing approach may shed light on pieces that feature exceptionally intense use of accidentals; by analogy, we may speak of the "musica ficta essay." And with these models in hand we are prepared to deal with a diverse situation. It is unlikely that the period witnessed a uniform and steady development through music of greater and greater complexity until, suddenly and radically, a reaction set in, launching a fresh style period. There may have been some tendencies along these lines, but it is also possible that the pluralistic profile associated with the surviving oeuvres for Solage and Baude Cordier accurately reflects the period, to some degree. There must have been more than one way of moving stylistically between Machaut and Du Fay. Any connections that we are able to draw within groups of pieces that use accidentals in similar ways will play into this pluralistic profile; if the connections do not yet yield a coherent analysis of the flow of music history, they may eventually provide one basis among several for that elusive project.

Solage and the "musica ficta essay"

"Ars subtilior" may be used to describe not a style period but a type of piece, one marked by rhythmic complications beyond the paradigm of ars nova. In southern France (and, in emulation, in northern Italy) ars subtilior may have been more pervasive than it was in northern France, where, through Du Fay, composers may have each written a few songs or just a single song marked by dazzling rhythmic display; this is one way to read a poorly documented (and certainly fragmentary) situation. Simpler styles may have survived continuously, alongside the complicated style, during the period between Machaut and Du Fay. If true, then the simple rondeau style that came into fashion during the early decades of the fifteenth century did not have to be reinvented out of whole cloth, as an antidote to hyper-refinement.

The surviving songs attributed to Solage and Baude Cordier encourage this point of view. It appears that each composer developed a diverse port-folio, though there is surely room for difference of opinion about how to interpret these diversities. A debate about Baude Cordier centers on Craig Wright's suggestion that this composer also went by the name Baude Fresnel, who was dead by 1398.[5] That *terminus ante quem* for Baude's lightly textured rondeaux makes them surprisingly early antecedents to the Binchois–Du Fay idiom. Of Baude's ten surviving songs, *Amans amés, Pour le default,* and *Dame excellent* count as ars subtilior essays, with frequent changes in mensuration and some complexity in rhythm. Solage shows less interest in such practices.[6] From his ten surviving songs, only *S'aincy estoit* counts as a fully formed ars subtilior essay; there are complicated rhythms also in *Calextone, qui fut dame,* but they are much less dominant. Sadly, Solage is little more than a name attached to a small collection of songs. Slender hints about his biography come from the poems he set, which include allusions to Jean, Duke of Berry, and to the Parisian literary circle of the *fumeux*. At issue is what to make of the apparently slight interest in ars subtilior. It has been suggested that his slight interest indicates that he was older, and that he made only a few attempts to keep up with modern trends. If not older, he may have been conservative. Alternatively, he may represent a northern French tradition in which ars subtilior is only one strand of a diverse portfolio. The older layers of *Oxford 213*, which include a number of Baude's songs, may preserve a high concentration of music from northern France and the Burgundian realm. The juxtapositions of style in these older layers, with complicated songs and simpler songs sitting side by side, support this line of analysis. Cesaris (*Se par plour/Se par plour*) and Velut (*Laissiés ester vostres chans*) are each represented by only isolated ars subtilior essays, for example. This trend may be detected even into the more recent layers of the manuscript, which include an ars

[5] See Craig Wright, "Tapissier and Cordier: New Documents and Conjectures," *The Musical Quarterly* 59 (1973), 177–89. Doubting Wright's hypothesis is Ursula Günther, "Unusual Phenomena in the Transmission of Late 14th Century Polyphonic Music," *Musica Disciplina* 38 (1984), 87–109 (especially pp. 89–92; additional references cited). Supporting Wright's hypothesis is Reinhard Strohm, *The Rise of European Music,* 55, 58, and 141–4. See also *The Lucca Codex: Codice Mancini Lucca, Archivio di Stato, MS 184, Perugia, Biblioteca comunale Augusta, MS3065,* introductory study and facsimile edition by John Nádas and Agostino Ziino (Lucca: Libreria musicale italiana, 1990), 44, n. 77.

Modern editions of all ten songs by Baude Cordier in volume I of Gilbert Reaney, ed., *Early Fifteenth-Century Music,* Corpus Mensurabilis Musicae 11 (Rome and Stuttgart: American Institute of Musicology, 1955–83); this series will be cited hereinafter as *EFCM* . The lighter rondeau style has also been associated with the Parisian *cour d'amour,* founded in 1401; see Strohm, *The Rise of European Music,* 64 and 131.

[6] Modern editions of all ten songs by Solage in Gordon Greene, ed., *French Secular Music: Manuscript Chantilly, Musée Condé 564,* Polyphonic Music of the Fourteenth Century, 18–19 (Monaco: Oiseau-Lyre, 1982); this series will be cited hereinafter as PMFC.

subtilior essay by Du Fay (*Resvelliés vous*) and one by Hugo de Lantins (*Je suy extent*).[7]

Solage is best known today not for his ars subtilior essay but for his rondeau *Fumeux fume*.[8] Heavy chromaticism renders a musical depiction of the mental fog described in the vague poem, which yields three different translations.[9] In this case, unquestionably, musical analysis must follow literary analysis, and in his ambition to musically articulate the mental fog of the poem Solage is surely successful. It is not that the music lacks design, but the design is less important than the shock of continuous and unpredictable chromaticism. Both the range and density of inflections are extraordinary. The composer determinedly moves through (in order of first appearance) *B*-flat, *C*-sharp, *F*-sharp, *B*-natural, *E*-flat, *A*-flat, *D*-flat, *E*-

[7] Modern editions of *Se par plours/Se par plours* in Reaney, ed., *EFCM*, I: 22; *Laissiés ester vostres chans* in *EFCM*, II: 122; *Resvelliés vous* in Heinrich Besseler, ed., *Guillaume Dufay Opera Omnia*, Corpus Mensurabilis Musicae 1 (n.p.: American Institute of Musicology, 1951–66), VI: 25–6; *Je suy extent* in Charles Van den Borren, ed., *Pièces Polyphoniques Profanes de Provenance Liégeoise (XVe Siècle)*, Flores Musicales Belgicae (Brussels, Editions de la Librairie Encyclopédique, 1950), 53. David Fallows suggests that the two pieces might have been written as a result of a friendly rivalry between Du Fay and Hugo de Lantins; see *Dufay* (London: Dent), 278, n. 21. Du Fay uses three different mensuration signs in *Resvelliés vous*; "2" designates *dupla* proportion and "3" designates *sesquialtera* at the minim level. The notation resembles that used in *Medée fu* (discussed below) where minims are also reduced via numbers: "3" used in exactly the same way, "4" is used for *dupla*, and "2" is used for *sesquitertia*. The two songs stand ten folios apart from one another in *Oxford 213*. For analysis of the rhythmic order and notation of *Medée fu*, see Reinhard Strohm, *The Rise of European Music*, 46–53. In this comparison, one might also stress the use of "dangling" *g*-sharps and *c*-sharps in both *Medée fu* and *Resvelliés vous* (discussed below). For references to further work on the older layers of *Oxford 213* and these historiographic problems, see my "Sharps in *Medée fu*: Questions of Style and Analysis," *Studi Musicali*, forthcoming. Fallows observes musical connections between the first phrase of *Resvelliés vous* and a polyphonic setting of a Mass cycle by Du Fay; see *Dufay*, 165 ff.

[8] For a thoughtful discussion of textual and analytical problems surrounding *Fumeux fume*, see Peter M. Lefferts, "*Subtilitas* in the Tonal Language of *Fumeux*

fume," *Early Music* 16 (1988), 176–84. I find Lefferts's comments on the design of the piece helpful, though I am bewildered by his notion that the singer of *Fumeux fume* would have been expected to "follow through the full hexachordal implications of these accidentals" (p. 178). As I have said already (in the Introduction), I find this point of view to be generally irrelevant in the song tradition under study here; it would seem to be especially irrelevant in this song, which is so relentlessly unstable and so harmonically oriented in its chromaticism. It is hard to imagine a song less suited to hexachordal solmization. I see no evidence that it has influenced Lefferts's editorial suggestions for accidentals in his published edition; mainly, these suggestions are based on the necessity rule, on durational problems, and on avoidance of melodic diminished fifths and augmented fourths. (There is no support from any of these guidelines for Lefferts's suggestion of *b*-flat for the cantus in measure 28, however; there is no hexachordal basis for the emendation, either.) Lefferts also makes some unlikely transcriptions: *a*-flat in the cantus at measure 30 should be read as *G*-flat for the following *G*, thus "cancelling" the previous *G*-sharp – otherwise there is no resolution for the *G*-sharp; likewise, *D*-flat in measure 34 should be read as *C*-flat, cancelling the previous *C*-sharp. As anyone who has worked with the manuscript knows, placement of accidentals is a routine problem in *Chantilly 564*. Since Solage writes bold chromaticism so often, it is particularly unfortunate that we are completely dependent on this manuscript for readings of his music (with the exception of one piece).

[9] Lefferts, "*Subtilitas* in the Tonal Language of *Fumeux fume*," presents three translations, credited to Sylvia Huot; see p. 182, n. 10.

natural, *G*-flat, and *G*-sharp. Unexpected harmonic turns follow one after the other. There is a long descending sequence through various flat degrees; in other sequences, flats and sharps are jarringly juxtaposed. *Le mont Aon* – also in *Chantilly 564* and, perhaps not coincidentally, showing various connections to Solage's songs, as we shall see – features a chromatic sequence that recalls *Fumeux fume*. The sequence generates (in order of first appearance) *b*-flat, *f*-sharp, *a*-flat, *f*-natural, *e*-flat, *G*-flat, and *D*-flat.[10] If one is looking for examples of late fourteenth-century intensification of Machaut's practice, here is a possibility. These chromatically inflected sequences recall passages from Machaut's *Comment puet* and *Biauté qui toutes autres pere.*[11]

The foggy *Fumeux fume* and the ars subtilior essay *S'aincy estoit* are each, in their respective ways, isolated in Solage's surviving oeuvre. It seems appropriate, therefore, to think of them as two different kinds of display pieces. The ars subtilior rubric hardly seems to fit *Fumeux fume*, for there is nothing subtle about it.[12] A handful of additional songs, scattered here and there (and usually in only one source, implying limited circulation for this kind of piece and the likelihood that there must have been more of them that do not survive), fit the category of "musica ficta essay." The manuscript *Florence P 26* preserves the anonymous *Le Firmament* and Johannes Cesaris's *Bonté bialté.*[13] In *Oxford 213* there is the anonymous *Arriere tost* and the more modest *Ma chiere mestresse* (and the related *Or avant, gentilz fillettes*) by Guillaume le Grant.[14] *Oxford 213* also transmits the lovely *Confort d'amours*, which, with its rich texture and careful treatment of cross relations, is one of the best songs in the older layers of the manuscript.[15] Solage's *Fumeux fume* is conceived as a musical illustration of a poetic idea, but this is not true for the others. Perhaps this suggests that the first musica ficta essay was sparked by the idea of musical illustration of a poem, and that the small tradition began with Solage.

Other songs (like *Le mont Aon*) use heavy chromaticism only for a phrase or so, and to extend the point of analogy one may note that precisely

---

[10] The similar use of chromatic sequences in *Le mont Aon* and *Fumeux fume* is noted by Lefferts, "*Subtilitas* in the Tonal Language of *Fumeux fume*," 179. An edition of *Le mont Aon* is given by Lefferts and Sylvia Huot, *Five Ballades for the House of Foix* (Newton Abbot: Antico, 1989).

[11] *Comment puet*, mm. 8–17 of the edition in Schrade, ed., PMFC 3: 154; *Biauté qui toutes autres pere*, mm. 10–15 of the edition in PMFC 3: 74.

[12] For recent analysis of fourteenth-century usage of the term "subtilitas" and its relevance for musical notation, see especially Anne Stone, "What is Subtler about the Ars Subtilior?" (forthcoming in *Rivista italiano di musicologia*) and further references cited there.

[13] Modern edition of *Le Firmament* in PMFC 22: 150; *Bonté bialté* in EFCM, I: 30.

[14] Modern edition of *Arriere tost* in EFCM, IV: 56; *Ma chiere mestresse* in EFCM, II: 49; *Or avant, gentilz fillettes* in EFCM, II: 50.

[15] Modern edition in EFCM, IV: 18.

the same thing happens with ars subtilior rhythms. To be sure, the number of songs that one is willing to classify as musica ficta essays is far fewer than those that fit the category of ars subtilior essay. It is possible, of course, that heavily inflected songs arose coincidentally and independently of one another, with no coherent tradition. Yet one is reluctant to dismiss a potential thread of tradition for a period in which so few threads emerge, especially since this thread, slender though it is, moves into Du Fay's generation. *Helas ma dame* (which will be considered closely in the next chapter) is exceptional within Du Fay's oeuvre, just as *Fumeux fume* is exceptional within Solage's oeuvre. And if we think of Du Fay's *Resvelliés vous* as an ars subtilior essay, in the tradition of Solage's *S'aincy estoit*, then these two composers suddenly have more in common than familiar historiographic models would suggest. *Resvelliés vous* and *Helas ma dame* date from early in Du Fay's career, probably from the early and mid-1420s.[16] Cesaris, with his ars subtilior essay *Se par plour/Se par plour* and his musica ficta essay *Bonté bialté*, provides one possible link in these parallel chains, from Solage to Du Fay. Encouraged by Martin le Franc's famous, though very loose, linking of Cesaris with Du Fay, Heinrich Besseler suggested influence from *Bonté bialté* to Du Fay. I see no reason to believe that Cesaris provided Du Fay with particular strategies for organizing a piece, but it is always possible that he did provide the young, open-eyed composer with an example of what a musica ficta essay could be.[17]

*

One associates with Solage's music a quality of leisurely expansion; in this, he is a leading representative of late-century trends. The musical phrases expand without too much regard for the poetic phrases, and there are frequent melismas; these techniques contribute to the elevated tone. Again, one is encouraged to think of Solage as elaborating upon Machaut's model for the ballade. I have commented already on accidentals in *Le Basile* (excerpted in the Introduction as Ex. 1.4), where *b*-flat is signed in the cantus before an arrival on *c*; the event recalls a controversial moment from Machaut's *De toutes flours*. Part 1 of *Le Basile* begins stably, with *c* clearly

---

[16] *Resvelliés vous* was composed for the wedding of Vittoria di Lorenzo Colonna and Carlo Malatesta da Pesaro, July 18, 1423; see Fallows, *Dufay* 22–3 and 165–8. Graeme Boone suggests that *Helas ma dame* may date from 1426–7; see "Dufay's Early Chansons: Chronology and Style in the Manuscript Oxford, Bodleian Library, Canonici misc. 213" (Ph.D. diss., Harvard University,

1987), 192 ff.

[17] Modern editions of all surviving pieces attributed to Cesaris in *EFCM*, I. Besseler's remarks are in *Bourdon und Fauxbourdon* (Leipzig: Breitkopf, 1974), 53–4; see also his article "Cesaris" in *Die Musik in Geschichte und Gegenwart* (Basel, 1952), II: cols. 987–8.

Example 3.1 *Corps feminin*, mm. 1–4 (after Greene, ed., PMFC 18: 66)

established, and this makes it unsurprising that part 1 ends with a firm arrival on *c* at the *clos* cadence. The inflections *b*-flat, *f*-sharp, *a*-flat, and *c*-sharp lead the cantus in its interior phrases through various digressions. *b*-flat in the cantus before the cadence on *c* at measure 25 should be understood as an element of instability within a context that is stable, overall. In this regard, the conception is close to Machaut. Though late fourteenth-century composers may be read as expanding upon Machaut's achievement by taking the ballade in the direction of greater expansivity, it is significant that such intensification of the received model rarely extends to chromatic practice. There is some evidence of direct modeling, as in *Le Basile*.[18] With the glaring exception of *Fumeux fume*, Solage may even be more conservative than Machaut in use of chromaticism, and since Solage is one of the late-century composers most keenly interested in accidentals, this is a telling comment on trends of the time.

In *Corps feminin* (Ex. 3.1), Solage features a technique that turns up in a number of songs from *Chantilly 564* and *Oxford 213*: this is the use, in the first phrase, of a sudden, dislocating sharp. Again there is a possible model from Machaut – phrase 1 of the ballade *Ploures, dames*.[19] *Corps feminin* begins on *b*-flat/*f*, and the first phrase arrives on *F/c/f* with a sense of closure. But the sudden turn in the cantus through *f*-sharp at the midpoint of the phrase disrupts the stability of the whole. The overall stability of the phrase makes it useful as a component in an expansive design for the entire

[18] Modern edition of *Le Basile* in PMFC 19: 79. It is tempting to imagine other echoes of Machaut in this song. The syncopated line at measures 63–7, which moves through *e*-flat, *b*-flat, and *b*-natural, recalls melismas in *De toutes flours*. And the descending sequence marking the ends of parts 1 and 2 (mm. 29 ff

and mm. 68–73) recalls the descending sequence of *Biauté qui toutes autres pere*; though the figure is not unusual in late-century songs, Solage places it here at exactly the same moment in the form as Machaut does.

[19] Schrade, ed., PMFC 3: 120.

Example 3.2 Suzoy's *Prophilias*, mm. 1–7 (after Greene, ed., PMFC 18: 136)

piece; the interior sharp causes a degree of inner tension. During the rest of the piece, the cantus has three more *f*-sharps, each used in a similar way.

This technique of using a sudden, dislocating sharp in the first or first few phrases surfaces also in *Le mont Aon* (one folio away from *Corps feminin* in *Chantilly 564*) and in precisely the same way: the sharp unexpectedly inflects the main pitch of the phrase. Another example is Suzoy's *Prophilias* (now the sharp is in the tenor). The inflection is not properly resolved, and this increases its impact (see Ex. 3.2). Suzoy brings the event back toward the end of part 2 of the ballade, as a tension chord poised to announce the refrain.[20] Du Fay comes upon a similar idea in a ballade we have already had cause to mention, his ars subtilior essay, *Resvelliés vous* (see Ex. 3.3). Like Suzoy, Du Fay brings his dislocating sharps back at the end of the ballade's second part. He places them prominently at the beginning of the refrain (rather than just before it, as happens in

[20] According to Greene's critical report, PMFC 18: the sharp is not present in the only concordant source, *MS NL-Uu 37*, f. 21

Example 3.3 Du Fay's *Resvelliés vous*, mm. 1–7 (after Besseler, ed., *Guillaume Dufay Opera Omnia*, VI: 25)

Prophilias), where they give an added charge to the proclamation of the dedicatee's name. Given the fact that this technique occurs in this piece – the piece that stands most clearly as Du Fay's representative ars subtilior essay – the possibility of complete coincidence seems unlikely. This must have been Du Fay's first dedicatory ballade, and he must have been aware of precedents. Sitting down to write it, Du Fay looks to older composers and their gestures of display.

Sharps in Medée fu

In recent decades, the ballade *Medée fu* has become an exceptionally well-known ars subtilior essay. Whoever the composer was, he deserves every bit of his modern-day success. Historians have emphasized rhythm, but the song is no less interesting in its melodic and harmonic design, with accidentals playing an important role. Various textual problems involving acci-

Table 3.1

Accidentals in the cantus of *Medée fu*

measure	8	11	39	42	45	51
FP 26	g-sharp	c-sharp	—	g-sharp	g-sharp	c-sharp
Chantilly 564	g-sharp	c-sharp	—	g-sharp	g-sharp	—
Ox 213	—	—	c-sharp	g-sharp	g-sharp[a]	—

Note:

[a] Pre-placed, implying (presumably) inflection of *g* in both m. 44 and m. 45.

dentals arise. At the micro level, textual problems mix with issues of scribal practice. Then, at a broader level, analysis of the piece mixes with style analysis in a way that is particularly rewarding; a handful of songs that experienced similar patterns of transmission show a group of composers working with similar ideas. Interpretation of how sharps work integrates the various levels of study, and this makes *Medée fu* a splendid case study. The song is also very beautiful, so our careful attention will be more than compensated.

There are five recent editions of the song.[21] These editions differ in their presentation of accidentals, and the differences stem only partly from the fact that the three surviving sources (*Chantilly 564*, f. 24v; *Oxford 213*, f. 116v–117; and *Florence P 26*, f. 107v) have slightly different readings. Table 3.1 is an inventory of accidentals signed in the cantus.

For tenor and contratenor, the sources report only one additional accidental, *c*-sharp in the contratenor at measure 53 (present in both *Florence P 26* and *Oxford 213* but absent from *Chantilly 564*). Based on the following analysis of the piece, I am inclined to believe that all of these accidentals are authorial, and that collectively the sources give a complete reading. The transcription given in Example 3.4 is a conflation: for the cantus, *Oxford 213*'s *c*-sharp, for measure 39, has been added to the five sharps given by *Florence P 26*. With few sources and no reason to have firm confidence in any of them, it does not seem reasonable to impose the dictum of exclusive reliance upon a "best source." In many cases it must be true that no surviving source is complete. Instead of relying exclusively upon one of three

[21] Reaney, ed., *EFCM*, IV: 51; Willi Apel, ed., *French Secular Compositions of the Fourteenth Century*, Corpus Mensurabilis Musicae 53 (Stuttgart: American Institute of Musicology, 1970–2), II: no. 165; Richard Hoppin, ed., *Anthology of Medieval Music* (New York: Norton, 1978), 165 (commentary on the piece by Hoppin in *Medieval Music* [New York, 1978], 483–4); Gordon K. Greene, ed., PMFC 18: 74; Strohm, *The Rise of European Music*, 47. *Medée fu* is one of the two songs shared by *Chantilly 564* and *Oxford 213*; *Ma douce amour*, by Hasprois, is the other.

Example 3.4 *Medée fu*

Example 3.4 (*cont.*)

Example 3.4 (*cont.*)

- iè _____ re, ne _____ bien _____

_____ mon ____ dain _____ a _____ voir tors _____

son a _____ my: Ma _____ da ____

Example 3.4 (*cont.*)

large anthologies – each compiled in northern Italy and, most likely, geo-graphically removed from the composer – as an accurate witness we may attempt to blend textual criticism with higher criticism, each informing the other. This method is neatly defended by Karol Berger:

> Armed with the results achieved by higher criticism, we will be able to descend back to the level of textual criticism and make the choice between available variants. The process is going to be circular, of course, but this should not deter us, since the circle is of the benign, hermeneutic kind, not a vicious one. The process simply reflects the well-known hermeneutic fact that we often must already partially understand a text before we can fully have it, since, in the process of interpretation, detail and totality are related in a circular fashion; to understand the whole, one has to understand the parts, but to understand the parts, one must have some idea of the meaning of the whole.[22]

In *Medée fu*, sharps play an important role in a fairly systematic approach to design. If *Oxford 213*'s c-sharp at measure 39 is not authorial, then it was contributed by someone who understood the piece very well.

Textual analysis of both the old sources and the modern editions of those sources calls forth several problems, each more or less traditional: (1) uncertainty about which pitch the sign is supposed to inflect; (2) uncertainty about what importance to place on conflicts between voices; (3) whether or not augmented and diminished intervals are idiomatic; (4) whether or not true chromaticism is idiomatic. The problems gather par-ticularly around two locations. First, there is g-sharp in measure 8, which two modern editors have interpreted as f-sharp for measure 7. The decision may have been based on two perceived problems: the contratenor seems to contradict g-sharp and favor g-natural; plus, the leap in the cantus of an augmented second, from f-natural to g-sharp, may seem awkward. In reading f-sharp, the editors assume post-placement of the sign, for it is located between f and g in the two sources that have it. The second problem area is measures 44–5, where our edition shows g-natural followed by g-sharp; two of the five recent editions inflect both g's, one has the sharp in parentheses (communicating the editor's doubt about it), and another drops the sharp altogether. At issue is whether or not true chromaticism is intended. Again the matter of placement arises, for the sign is placed between the two g's in *Florence P 26* and *Chantilly 564*, while *Oxford 213* has the sharp placed before both g's (in front of bb, measure 44).

Thus the scribal issue of placement goes hand in hand with issues of style. Pre-placement, post-placement, under-placement, over-placement,

---

[22] Berger, *Musica ficta*, 187.

and uncertain vertical placement – there are examples of every one of these in *Chantilly 564* and *Oxford 213*. Placement of accidentals can be so obscure that it is sometimes hard to imagine how the intention was understood by scribes and performers. It is safe to assume that this problem generated many variants, as the scribes of the large anthologies tried to make sense of obscure readings that came across their desks. Scribes may have worked rapidly, and they may have worked by eye rather than by ear; there are some clear examples of this.[23] In the case of *Medée fu*, g-sharp performs such an important function that we are encouraged to believe that the sharp in measure 8 manifests pre-placement, which is by far the most commonly used method. Certainly post-placement is a possibility, but it is much less likely.

The placement in *Chantilly 564* and *Florence P 26* of the sharp between two *g*'s at measures 44–5 calls forth an even more obscure possibility of scribal practice. In his study of the *Old Hall* manuscript, Andrew Hughes wonders whether this kind of placement is a means for "circumventing the 'once-only' principle for accidentals."[24] Hughes would interpret the single sign as placed to inflect both the pitch that comes before and the pitch that comes after. The alternative is direct chromaticism. In *Medée fu*, it seems important that the first *g* sounds above *c*. The chromatic design follows the harmonic logic that g-natural is used to make a perfect fifth with the tenor, while g-sharp makes a major sixth with the tenor to establish the clear implication of resolution to *a/aa*. Melodic chromaticism is coordinated with the progression of intervals, perfect fifth to major sixth. There is every reason to believe that augmented intervals (including fifths) were in the air during this period, so it is not a question of insisting that *c/g*-sharp is unstylistic. Important is the fact that precisely this progression is encountered several times in contemporary songs. In *Cine vermeil* – linked to *Medée fu*, since both belong to a group of eight chansons shared by *Florence*

[23] For example, Binchois' *Adieu, Adieu, mon joieulx souvenir*, modern edition by Wolfgang Rehm, *Die Chansons von Gilles Binchois*, Musikalische Denkmaler 2 (Mainz: Schott, 1957), 1. The contratenor shows two lines of transmission, one through *Oxford 213* and *Rome 1411*, the other through *Escorial A* (echoed in later sources). *Escorial A* is surely correct in reporting c-sharp for measure 28, where the other two manuscripts have *d* – and with the sharp still intact, even though it makes no sense. The scribes have copied by eye rather than by ear, and their mistake produces a nonsensical sharp. The situation is described by Dennis Slavin, "Questions of

Authority in Some Songs by Binchois," *Journal of the Royal Musical Association* 117 (1992), 27, n. 20.

[24] Andrew Hughes, *Manuscript Accidentals: Ficta in Focus 1350–1450*, Musicological Studies and Documents 27 (Rome: American Institute of Musicology, 1972), 69. Lewis Lockwood, working with a much later repertory, observes a sharp that may be placed below the inflected pitch as a way to inflect two notes instead of one; see "A Sample Problem of *Musica Ficta*: Willaert's *Pater Noster*," in *Studies in Music History: Essays for Oliver Strunk*, ed. H. S. Powers (Princeton: Princeton University Press, 1968), 179, n. 23.

P 26 and *Chantilly 564* – the cantus moves from *f* to *f*-sharp while the tenor moves underneath from *B*-flat to *A*.[25] Hymbertus de Salinis's *En la saison* has exactly the same situation (twice).[26] Johannes Cuvelier's *Se galaas* has *cc* to *cc*-sharp in the cantus over *f* to *e* in the tenor.[27] Senleches's *En ce gracïeux temps* features movement from *f* to *f*-sharp in the cantus against *F* to *D* in the tenor.[28] *Revien a moy* has a contratenor moving in exactly the same way.[29] *Arriere tost* shows the pattern at the final cadence, where the cantus moves from *c* to *c*-sharp while the tenor moves from *F* to *E*.[30] The repeated use of this formula in a group of songs that experienced similar patterns of transmission assures us of its legitimacy. Most likely, it is *Oxford 213*'s pre-placement of the sharp that is intended to inflect both *g*'s, not the middle placement of *Chantilly 564* and *Florence P 26*.[31]

Earlier (in the Introduction and in Chapter 2), I have endorsed the more-or-less traditional view that the polyphonic chanson is marked by a hierarchy of voices. The cantus is the leading melody voice, and it is supported primarily by the tenor, with which it forms good strong counterpoint and with which it supplies structural cadences. Contratenors and triplums supplement this primary duet. The result is a three-tiered hierarchy. The composer may take an interest in integrating all of the voices, and in doing so he may conceal the traditional hierarchy. Nevertheless, analysis will still be able to uncover it, and for the period of the polyphonic chanson emphasized in this book, the hierarchy is usually obvious. In my view, this hierarchy is such a fundamental aspect of the tradition that it should weigh heavily in analysis of conflicts between voices that involve accidentals. Such conflicts often involve augmented and diminished intervals. These would seem to invoke the necessity rule, which more than a few musicologists have taken as a rule that overrides everything else. My inclination is to lower the necessity rule from its esteemed position and to sort through nuances in compositional practice, however fitfully they may be recorded

---

[25] *Florence P 26* (f. 101v) describes this situation; *Chantilly 564* (f. 56) has the sharp placed before the first *f*. Modern edition by Greene, PMFC 18: 143.

[26] *Chantilly 564* (f. 46); modern edition by Greene, PMFC 19: 74. A third occurrence (in the *clos* ending) features placement of the sharp in front of the first *f* rather than between the two *f*s.

[27] *Chantilly 564* (f. 38); modern edition by Greene, PMFC 19: 13.

[28] As preserved in *Modena, Biblioteca Estense, MS α M. 5. 24 (lat. 568)*, f. 25v; *Paris, Bibliothèque nationale, nouv. acq. fr., MS 6771* (f. 58v) lacks the sharp. Modern edition by Greene, PMFC 21: 9.

[29] *Oxford 213* (f. 94v); modern edition by Reaney, *EFCM*, IV: 5.

[30] *Oxford 213* (f. 43v); modern edition by Reaney, *EFCM*, IV: 56.

[31] It should be noted that precisely the chromatic pattern that I am claiming is given in musical examples (and hence legitimized) by Marchetto and by later theorists; on the theory, see Karol Berger, *Musica ficta*, 85–6. Margaret Bent gives a similar example from the *Old Hall* Manuscript in "Musica Recta and Musica Ficta," 82.

in the notated record.[32] Instead of automatically falling back on the imagined application of necessity inflections, one might factor into the analysis
of textual problems the importance of the standard hierarchical arrangement of voices.

The contratenor of *Medée fu* raises two questions: do its *G*-naturals in
measures 8 and 45 make *g*-sharps in the cantus less likely? And do its *F*-nat-
urals in measures 11, 39, and 51 cast doubt on *c*-sharps in the cantus above?
I resist the idea that a contratenor should guide editorial decisions about
inflections in the cantus and tenor, especially when those two voices, taken
as a self-sufficient contrapuntal pair, make good musical sense. For it is the
business of contratenors to routinely move *against* the primary logic of this
pair. The contratenor is routinely displaced against the duet in vertical consonance (causing dissonance), rhythmic synchronization (causing syncopation), and location of phrase endings (causing enjambment of
phrases). Of course, the contratenor will just as routinely fall in step with
the duet in each of these areas. We may think of the contratenor as a voice
that is called upon to fulfill two different functions: it will both reinforce
and depart from the activity of the two main voices, confirming their logic
here, disrupting it there. This basic behavior identifies it as a supplemental
voice. Contratenorial displacement happens so often on the levels of rhythmic detail and phrase design that the point is obvious. With harmonic dissonance it may be more difficult to accept the analysis, but this practice,
too, is commonplace. Consider the detail in Example 3.5 from Guillermus
Malbecque's *Adieu vous di* (*Oxford 213*, f. 21). The cantus and tenor make a
fine cadence, while the contratenor is slightly out-of-sync. This happens
rhythmically: the contratenor fills in twice on the minim-subdivisions of
the beat (the fifth pulse of measure 6 and the second of measure 7), and it
rests at the very moment of cantus–tenor cadential arrival. And it happens
harmonically: the contratenor is consonant with the duet with the exception of *G* sounding against *f*-sharp. In the only modern edition of this
piece, the editor has dropped the *f*-sharp, and one would assume that the
dissonance led to this decision. Yet the emendation does not "correct" the
counterpoint, so it is hardly warranted. It is possible, of course, that the
source is in error; if not, then perhaps Malbecque either liked the dissonance or did not care about it. Since it is not unusual to find contratenors
that create dissonance, the latter explanations hold some appeal. The most

---

[32] Peter Urquhart gives a persuasive account of how
undue emphasis on the necessity rule, along with
unwillingness to tolerate cross relations, has generated a
variety of unlikely modern-day trends in scholarship,
especially "cyclic" tendencies of imagined inflections
generating more and more inflections; see "Cross-
Relations by Franco-Flemish Composers after Josquin,"
especially 22–6.

Example 3.5 Malbecque's *Adieu vous di* (after Reaney, ed., *EFCM*, II: 100 [with adjustment according to *MS Oxford 213*, f. 21])

unappealing response is to think that the dissonance causes suspicion about the tenor's *f*-sharp, which follows the standard logic of a propinquity inflection, defined by the cantus–tenor duet.

Likewise, the contratenor of *Medée fu* is sometimes out of-sync with the contrapuntal logic of the cantus–tenor duet. It is not a matter of arguing that the contratenor is "inessential"; the familiar debate around that traditional idea seems to miss the point. Strohm has analyzed its important role. But no matter how important that role is, it should not, in my opinion, elevate the contratenor's status to a level where it would dictate the text of the primary duet. In this view, the contratenor's *G*-naturals in measures 8 and 45 have no bearing upon *g*-sharps in the cantus. Current tastes for *a cappella* scoring should not obscure the real possibility – until recently, it seemed the most likely possibility – that the contratenor carried out its contrary activity on a plucked instrument. The contrapuntal hierarchy in the composer's mind may have been fused with a timbral hierarchy in performance. Dissonant events may well have found their place in the sonic background of a song.[33]

The contratenor may add harmonic tension, and this is the way to read the augmented fifths of measures 11, 39, and 51. The hegemony of the

---

[33] For example, the part may be taken by a plucked lute while the tenor is played on a vielle. This arrangement is elegantly demonstrated in a recorded performance of *Medée fu* by Ensemble Project Ars Nova: *Ars Magis Subtiliter: Secular Music of the Chantilly Codex*, New Albion Records, Inc., NA 021 CD DDD, recorded at Wellesley, MA, July 20–22nd, 1987. A comprehensive study of accidentals in contratenors throughout the fourteenth and fifteenth centuries promises important rewards, since one often finds special patterns of inflection in this part. An interesting testament to the kind of medial role (as a voice that is designed to express agreement as well as disagreement with the primary pair) of contratenors is given by Anonymous 11, who speaks of *contradiscordantia* in contratenors that cause dissonance with the discant but not the tenor; see Richard Wingell, ed., "Anonymous XI (CS III): an Edition, Translation, and Commentary" (Ph.D. diss., University of Southern California, 1973), 146.

necessity rule in late medieval music theory is undermined by the notated record, which receives just enough support from incidental comments implying that augmented and diminished intervals were used and heard. Tinctoris protests too much against vertical diminished fifths when, in a well-known passage, he identifies composers who use them; his protest allows Karol Berger to analyze one context for legitimizing them.[34] Bartolomeo Ramos de Pareia describes how to sing an augmented second (the interval that concerns us at measures 7–8 of *Medée fu*) by thinking of it as enharmonically equivalent to a minor third.[35] This and other "difficult" melodic leaps occur in many songs transmitted by *Chantilly 564* and *Oxford 213*.[36] Prosdocimo de' Beldomandi, who advocates the application of musica ficta only "where necessary, because in art nothing – least of all a feigning – is to be applied without necessity," describes "necessary" applications in some detail and leaves melodic tritones out of the discussion; as has been pointed out many times, his examples include a melodic tritone.[37] John Hothby says that the diminished fifth is avoided especially in plainchant (*maximamento in nel canto legale*); putting things that way implies tolerance of the interval in polyphony and other kinds of music.[38]

---

[34] Tinctoris, *Liber de arte contrapuncti*, lib. II, cap. 33; edition by Albert Seay, *Opera theoretica*, Corpus Scriptorum de Musica 22 (n.p.: American Institute of Musicology, 1975), I: 143 ff; translated edition by Albert Seay, *The Art of Counterpoint*, Musicological Studies and Documents 5 (Rome: American Institute of Musicology, 1961), 130. See the discussion in Berger, *Musica ficta*, 95–100. Berger also recognizes (p. 113) the remarks of Johannes Boen (*c.* 1357) sanctioning vertical diminished sevenths, and those from Bartolomeo Ramos de Pareia, who describes vertical diminished fifths in small note values (pp. 100 ff). On Tinctoris, see also Urquhart, "Cross-Relations by Franco-Flemish Composers after Josquin," 29.

[35] *Musica practica*, translated edition by Clement A. Miller, Musicological Studies and Documents 44 (Neuhausen-Stuttgart: American Institute of Musicology, 1993), 89.

[36] To cite only a few examples: the melodic augmented second is used twice in Gilet Velut's *Laissiés ester vostres chans* (*Oxford 213*, f. 100; ed. Reaney, *EFCM*, II: 122, mm. 24–5 and 30); note also the augmented fifth between cantus and tenor in measure 54 and the augmented octaves between cantus and tenor (and contratenor) in measures 26 and 53; also the brief augmented fifth (m. 25), augmented ninth (m. 30), and diminished fourth (m. 34) between contratenor and cantus. The melodic

augmented second is used twice in *Il n'est dangier que de villain* (*Oxford 213*, f. 108; ed. Reaney, *EFCM*, IV: 49), first in the tenor, *E*-flat to *F*-sharp (mm. 20–1; Reaney drops the sharp from his edition), and then in the cantus (m. 23). Reaney interprets *G*-sharp in the contratenor at measure 3; most likely, this is *F*-sharp for measure 4.

[37] See *Contrapunctus*, ed. and trans. Jan Herlinger, Greek and Latin Music Theory 1 (Lincoln, Nebr., and London: University of Nebraska Press, 1984), 84–5. Andrew Hughes, *Manuscript Accidentals: Ficta in Focus*, 85–6, reads the passage as allowing melodic tritones.

[38] Hothby, *La caliopea legale* in E. de Coussemaker, ed., *Histoire de l'harmonie au moyen âge* (Paris: Librairie Archéologique de Victor Didron, 1852), 347. Karol Berger's presentation of the evidence related to this topic involves references to plainchant, mainly: *Musica ficta*, 70–92. Andrew Hughes's observations on melodic tritones are well worth quoting: "Almost no evidence of the period supports the conventional modern claim that melodic tritones were prohibited in early music: if anything, there are more hints suggesting the opposite conclusion in certain circumstances. . . . Sources of polyphony, and indeed occasionally plainsong, transmit numerous instances of tritones caused by written-in accidentals, and these normally occur when the line continues in the same direction, or at cadence points, where the inflected pitch serves as a leading note. It is my

These innuendoes and begrudging acknowledgments that there is a place for difficult intervals in advanced polyphony are enough, I think, to suggest that the notated descriptions in the practical sources do not all need correcting. What is needed is identification and analysis of patterns of use. Sharps and flats are sometimes juxtaposed melodically as a means to generate pre-cadential tension. In Hasprois' *Ma doulce amour,* not only is there juxtaposition, but flats and sharps are also signed simultaneously to generate pre-cadential augmented sixths; other composers do this, as well.[39] Guillaume le Grant juxtaposes flats and sharps as a general feature of style in three songs that may have formed a cycle.[40] Difficult leaps in cantus lines are sometimes coordinated with stanzaic form and phrase form (as we have observed in Chapters 1 and 2); the leap has the effect of energizing the new section or phrase.[41] Near the beginning of *Puis que je sui fumeux,* Hasprois uses the bold stroke of a major-seventh leap in the tenor to *c*-sharp, sounding against *f* and then *g* in the cantus.[42] This is the main event in a distinctive first phrase, whose energy seems to linger through the

belief that there is more evidence from all areas to suggest that the interval was melodically acceptable in certain contexts, and that within them the evidence of the music and of manuscript accidentals unmistakably confirms its not infrequent use . . ." *Manuscript Accidentals: Ficta in Focus,* 85–6.

[39] In *Ma doulce amour* (*Chantilly 564* f. 34, *Oxford 213,* f. 123, and *Modena A,* f. 28; modern edition by Greene, PMFC 18: 128), *g*-sharp is juxtaposed with *bb*-flat in the cantus (mm. 15–16), but only in *Chantilly 564*; this *g*-sharp sounds against *c* in the contratenor and several different dissonances in the tenor. Then, at measure 39, *g*-sharp is notated in the cantus against *b*-flat in the tenor in both *Chantilly 564* and *Oxford 213.* Melodic and harmonic combinations of flats and sharps occur also in Jacques Vide's *Puisque je n'ay plus de maystresse* (*Oxford 213,* f. 49v; ed. Marix, *Les musiciens de la cour de Bourgogne* [Paris: Droz, 1937], 24): the cantus leaps from *f*-sharp to *b*-flat, while the *f*-sharp sounds against *b*-flat in the tenor. Sharps and flats are vertically signed together in four songs by Trebor: *Se Alixandre, Passerose, Quant joyne cuer,* and *Se July Cesar* (all in *Chantilly 564*; Greene, ed., PMFC 18: 50, 103, and 111, and PMFC 19: 52). For *Passerose,* Greene's *b*-natural for the cantus of measure 39 should be read as *c*-sharp for measure 35 (against *E*-flat in the tenor); and I think it is plausible that *c*-sharp should stand in the cantus at measure 13 (against *F* in the tenor), while *G*-sharp should stand in the contratenor at measure 58 (against *e*-flat in the cantus and *E*-flat in the tenor). For *Se July Cesar, c*-sharp

for the cantus at measure 36 seems plausible (against *F* and *E*-flat in the tenor). Charité's *Jusques tant/Certes/Puisqu'ensy est* (*Oxford 213,* f. 90v; Reaney, ed., *EFCM,* II: 20) features precadential dissonances, including diminished fifths and augmented fourths, regularly on "weak beats."

[40] *Pour l'amour, Ma chiere mestresse,* and *Or avant, gentils fillettes* (*Oxford 213,* ff. 94, 96v, and 111v); editions by Reaney, *EFCM* II. Reinhard Strohm suggests that the three songs were conceived as a group: *The Rise of European Music,* 150.

[41] In Vaillant's *Pour ce que je ne say gairez* (*Chantilly 564,* f. 26; Greene ed., PMFC 18: 85), an augmented-fourth leap in the cantus occurs at the beginning of a melisma on the word "venus." In Galiot's *En attendant d'amer* (*Chantilly 564,* f. 40; Greene, ed., PMFC 19: 28), the abruptness of a prominent leap from *c*-sharp to *g* in the cantus is reinforced by the abruptness of the rhythmic syncopations. The leap emphasizes the long delay in resolution of the *c*-sharp propinquity inflection – a delay that extends to measure 16 (certainly, the sharp holds through measure 15). The delay in harmonic resolution is coordinated with delay in mensural completion, caused by the syncopation. A similarly extended delay – and the same emphasis of it by using the same leap of a diminished fifth, *c*-sharp to *g* – is used by Du Fay in *Je me complains* (*Oxford 213,* f. 18; ed. Besseler, *Guillaume Dufay Opera Omnia,* VI: 29).

[42] *Chantilly 564,* f. 34v; Greene, ed., PMFC 18: 131.

entire stanza. In *Medée fu*, the function of the augmented fifths below *c*-sharp in the cantus is to heighten the harmonic tension of this important propinquity inflection, which has a central role in the overall design, to which we now turn.

*

In part 1, the cantus quickly lays out a basic shape, descent from *aa* to *d*, that will be important throughout the ballade. Except for a brief drop to *a* before the *ouvert* and *clos* endings, a gesture that neatly provides balance and still firmer definition of *d*, this shape controls the cantus for the duration of part 1. Part 2 begins with a departure from the established order, a formal move typical of ballades, when the cantus moves from *f* through *c* (m. 22) to *g* (m. 24). There ends the brief digression, and once again the cantus finds its basic shape, movement between *aa* and *d*, again balanced by the dip down to *a*; there is room for a brief nod toward *g* in measure 48, recalling the digression of measure 24.

The extravagant rhythmic display released by cantus and contratenor (analyzed by Strohm)[43] serves to variously ornament this outline, which is also made more interesting by sharps. Only two degrees, *g* and *c*, are inflected. Their respective functions could not be clearer, for they serve as leading tones to the two boundary-pitches of the "basic shape," *aa* and *d*. First, the prominent *g*-sharp of measure 8 gives extra weight to *aa*, which has already been emphasized since the cantus begins on it and then spends some time circling around it (mm. 6–9); *aa* will continue to be emphasized, for after the obligatory (from an overall, structural point of view) descent to *d* (m. 12), it quickly reappears (m. 13). In one way of looking at the design of the song, the arrival on *g*-sharp in measure 8 produces the moment of high tension for part 1. For if *aa* implies descent to *d*, then *g*-sharp stands one step removed from the main descent; by association, it gains an identity as the pitch that prepares the descent. The fact that *g*-sharp stands an augmented fourth away from the main pitch, *d*, reinforces the point that this is a moment of high tension, one which occurs roughly at the temporal midpoint of part 1. Given such an overtly logical plan, we may use the four main structural pitches to make a reductional graph (see Ex. 3.6).

Harmony is used to clarify and to complement this basic melodic design. Harmony tells us that *aa* at the very beginning of the song is not in fact the main structural pitch, since it is harmonized by *d*; that *g*-sharp should resolve directly to *aa* since it is accompanied by *b* (which must resolve to *a*); that *c*-sharp should resolve directly to *d* since it is accompa-

---

[43] *The Rise of European Music,* 46–53.

Example 3.6 *Medée fu*, mm. 1–13 of the cantus, reduced

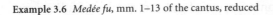

nied by *a* and then *E*; that *d* in measure 12 does not bring satisfactory closure, since it is accompanied by *F*; and that *d* in measure 13 does achieve closure, since it is accompanied by *D*.

I have burdened the reduction in Example 3.6 with arrows in order to establish the main point that I wish to make about *Medée fu*, that *aa*, *g*-sharp, and *c*-sharp become firmly associated with directional tendencies. Cleverly, the composer takes advantage of these associations in part 2 of the ballade. Through the simple logic of the basic melodic shape, *aa*, *c*-sharp, and *g*-sharp each imply motion toward *d*. Only *c*-sharp points there directly; as I have said already, *aa* implies a descent to *d* that includes the intervening diatonic steps, and *g*-sharp is removed one step further, for it implies first the *aa*, then the descent to *d*.

These simple associations allow the composer to work with implied direction in part 2 and to shape the final section of the ballade as a grand conclusion. *c*-sharp in measure 39 recalls measure 11; emphasizing this connection is the fact that both *c*-sharps are accompanied by *F* in the contratenor, forming tense augmented fifths. There follows a quick ascent to *aa* and then *g*-sharp; a pause on this pitch for a full breve (m. 42) becomes a fitting way to announce the refrain. Many fourteenth-century ballades feature harmonic tension at this formal moment. Often, this is achieved by locating a perfect sonority – rather than an imperfect sonority, as happens in *Medée fu* – one step (or two steps) above the final; often this structure duplicates the *ouvert–clos* relationship for the two endings of part 1. Sometimes an imperfect sonority occurs in this position, and when this happens there is almost always a leading tone that points toward the final and main pitch. The composer of *Medée fu* takes this idea one step further: the refrain is announced by a leading tone that points not toward the final and main pitch (*D*) but toward a secondary pitch (*aa*), which, in turn, implies resolution to the final.[44] The composer builds formal strength by using this striking yet simple idea to draw connections between the two parts of the ballade. He also creates the opportunity for an extraordinary

[44] A song that comes close to *Medée fu* in this respect is Suzoy's *Prophilias*, already cited for its use of a dislocating sharp in the first phrase. The lovely refrain is announced by *E/c-sharp/aa*; it is the job of the refrain to gradually bring the piece back to the main pitch, *F*. Even closer – so close, in this and other aspects, that there can be no question but that there is some connection between this piece and *Medée fu* – is Solage's *Pluseurs gens voy* (discussed below).

spinning out from the harmonic tension of *g*-sharp, a delay of full resolution that lasts through virtually the entire eighteen-measure refrain.

This refrain shows the touch of a master. What makes the passage effective is the fact that *g*-sharp so clearly implies the two-stage process of resolution through *aa* to *d*, as outlined in Example 3.6. The power of the passage flows from the composer's manipulation of both harmonic syntax and the associations that have accumulated around the main structural pitches. I would highlight the following details:

> Measures 42–3 feature an "evaded cadence,"[45] as both tenor and contratenor resolve irregularly, undermining the resolution of the cantus to *aa*.
>
> While the cantus rocks around its familiar *aa*, the tenor and contratenor follow in step, returning from their unexpected *F/c* back to *E/b* (compare measures 42 and 45). The harmonic drift reinforces the melodic whimsicality of the cantus.
>
> Measure 47 brings about a proper harmonic resolution to *a/aa*, and this initiates the basic structural descent. The descent includes a brief nod to *g* (m. 48), recalling the role of this pitch in the digression at the beginning of part 2 (m. 24).
>
> Measure 51 brings *c*-sharp, which is again accompanied by *F*. Measures 45–51 may be read as duplicating the logic of measures 8–12, which, in the meantime, was inverted in measures 39–42. Expressed in reduction:

Example 3.7 *Medée fu*,
(a) reduction of mm. 8–12
(b) reduction of mm. 39–42
(c) reduction of mm. 45–51

> Complete resolution is delayed (partly through another evaded cadence in measure 52) until the final cadence. The composer makes room for a drop down to *a* in the cantus and a grand octave descent in the tenor. Traditional rounding associated with ballades has been abandoned in favor of this elegant spinning out from the high tension articulated at measure 42.

---

[45] Zarlino refers to "*fuggir la cadenza*"; see the discussion in Berger, *Musica ficta*, 134–7.

*

Just as higher criticism and textual criticism profitably inform one another, so may stylistic analysis be entered into the mix. If any question remains concerning the legitimacy of the disputed *g*-sharps in *Medée fu*, the matter will be put to rest by the cumulative weight of a handful of songs that likewise use *g*-sharp in the context of hierarchically distinguished *D*. Patterns of transmission suggest the possibility that these pieces emerged from the same milieu.

The strongest resemblance is between *Medée fu* and Solage's *Pluseurs gens voy*.[46] The latter features an initial descent from *aa* to *d* that lasts twelve breves; *g*-sharp enters right away, when the cantus sings *aa*, *g*-sharp, *aa*. *Pluseurs gens voy* and *Medée fu* share the same recurring emphasis on *g*-sharp and *c*-sharp at primary structural moments, as well as secondary details like a digression to *g* in the second part and a quick leap from *f* to *g*-sharp in the cantus. As in *Medée fu*, *E/b/g*-sharp is used to announce the refrain, which then begins on *aa* and descends to *c*-sharp before finding its ultimate resolution on *d* at the final cadence; we have noted already how unusual this design is. There can be little doubt that the composer of one of these songs knew the other song. *Medée fu* benefits from a tighter design throughout.

Baude Cordier's *Tant ay de plaisir* (Ex. 3.8a), preserved uniquely in *Oxford 213*, features *g*-sharp in the same opening descent, *aa* to *d*.[47] As in *Medée fu*, the contratenor provides harmonic tension: it contributes *c*-sharp in measure 3 and *F* in measure 4, making a diminished fourth and an augmented fifth with the cantus. Thus, harmonic tension is established and reasserted over a series of three downbeats (beginning in measure 2), with full resolution coming only at the downbeat of measure 5.

Gilet Velut's *Jusqu'au jour* (Ex. 3.8b; the first song in fascicle 7 of *Oxford 213*, the same fascicle that preserves Cordier's *Tant ay de plaisir*) also features a cantus that opens on *aa* and descends gradually to *d*.[48] *G*-sharp is withheld until the *ouvert* ending of part 1 of the ballade (m. 13 of the modern edition), where it is poised to resolve either back to the beginning, for the repeat of part 1 or, after the repeat, into the extended *clos* ending. This phrase (mm. 14–18) recapitulates the outline of the opening descent;

---

[46] *Chantilly 564* (f. 58), and *Florence P 26* (f. 106v); Greene, ed., PMFC 19: 156.

[47] *Oxford 213*, f. 111; modern edition by Reaney, *EFCM*, I: 6. Reaney's edition mistakenly lacks *c*-sharp in the cantus at the downbeat of measure 4.

[48] *Oxford 213*, f. 101; modern edition by Reaney, *EFCM*, II: 125. It is possible that the sharp signed before the *g* in measure 14 is actually intended to inflect this *g* and not *f* in the next measure, where the editor has placed it. *f*-sharp does make sense, following *causa necessitatis*, but given the importance of *g* in the piece (and in the previous measure, measure 13) *g*-sharp seems possible.

Example 3.8

(a) Baude Cordier, *Tant ay de plaisir*, mm. 1–4 (after Reaney, ed., *EFCM*, I: 6)

(b) Gilet Velut, *Jusqu'au jour*, mm. 12–13 (after Reaney, ed., *EFCM*, II: 125)

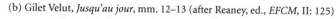

there is the added touch of a drop down to *a* before the arrival on *d*, resembling *Medée fu*. *g*-sharps have been deleted from the edition of the song in *Early Fifteenth Century Music*. Perhaps that decision was based on dissonances between cantus and contratenor (which sounds *G* against the cantus *g*-sharp, resembling *Medée fu*); or, perhaps it was based on felt awkwardness of an augmented-second leap in the cantus, *f* to *g*-sharp (again resembling *Medée fu*).

Three more examples bring our count of songs using *g*-sharp in connection with ascent from *aa* to *d* to seven.[49] It gives one pause to realize that the sharps have been suppressed in modern editions of four of the seven. The cumulative weight of these songs provides the strongest evidence that we will ever get suggesting that, first, the prominent use of *g*-sharp in a piece that features movement from *aa* to *d* is idiomatic; and second, that if the contratenor is dissonant against the *g*-sharp, that is no reason to doubt or cancel the inflection when it makes good harmonic sense, according to the workings of the cantus–tenor pair.

Elsewhere I have reviewed the possibility that these songs, together with a few others shared by *Chantilly 564* and *Florence P 26*, emerged from a coherent group of composers.[50] The older layers of *Oxford 213* may be the strongest witness we have to the northern tradition *c.* 1400 and through the first decades of the fifteenth century. Idiosyncratic techniques for using accidentals suggest common origins that are also hinted at through patterns of transmission. *Medée fu* is the most brightly ornamented jewel among this group of songs, and it has properly taken a recognized place among the leading achievements of the period. Here is the beautiful use of accidentals in the hands of a first-rate composer – sadly, a composer whose name may never be recovered.

Fuions de ci *and conflicting signatures*

Jacob Senleches's *Fuions de ci*, a lament for the deceased Eleanor of Aragon (d. 1382), comes to us in three sources, *Chantilly 564*, the *Reina Codex*, and *Modena A*.[51] Each source gives the same array of "signature" accidentals –

---

[49] Baude Cordier's *Amans, amés* (*Oxford 213*, f. 123; modern edition by Reaney in *EFCM*, I: 7) features *g*-sharp in measure 7 to form an opening section that closely resembles measures 1–10 of *Medée fu*. The second part of this brief rondeau is marked by descent to *c*-sharp and then *a* before the ultimate close on *d*. *De tous les biens* (*Oxford 213*, f. 107v; modern edition in *EFCM*, IV: 47) also uses the familiar opening pattern, complete with prominent *g*-sharp; the stability of *D* which defines the opening phrase yields eventually to *G*, where the song ends. Once more we discover editorial resistance to *g*-sharp, which is placed in parentheses in the modern edition. As before, one is inclined to attribute the resistance either to the contratenor, which supplies *c* underneath to form an augmented fifth, or to the augmented-second leap to the *g*-sharp from *f*

(resembling *Medée fu* on both counts). *Lamech, Judith et Rachel* (anonymous; *Chantilly 564*, f. 45; modern edition in PMFC 21: 66) should probably be added to this list. In the opening gesture, a sharp between *aa* and *g* is placed low, suggesting to a modern editor that it inflects not *g* but the following *f*. But casual placement of lower-neighbors is very common, and in the harmonic logic of the cantus–tenor pair *g*-sharp makes perfect sense, while *f*-sharp no sense. Again, the editor may have been led to question the accidental because of the contratenor, which sounds *G* against the cantus's *g*-sharp.

[50] See my "Sharps in *Medée fu:* Questions of Style and Analysis," forthcoming in *Studi Musicali*; references to work on this group of songs by Ursula Günther, Paula Higgins and others are cited there.

[51] Greene, ed., PMFC 18: 28.

b-flat in the cantus, and *b*-flat and *E*-flat in tenor and contratenor. *Chantilly 564* and the *Reina Codex* show no internally signed accidentals in any voice. *Modena A*, on the other hand, has six unique sharps (see Ex. 3.9). There is no obvious pattern of dependence between *Chantilly 564* and the *Reina Codex*, so the question arises whether there is a way to evaluate the two different readings. My effort here is to relate the problem to internal analysis of the piece and to modern-day interpretations of the widely used format of conflicting signatures. Typically, in fourteenth- and early fifteenth-century chansons, cantus voices have one less flat than tenor voices. Just as typically, songs that end on and emphasize *B*-flat use the signature format that is used in *Fuions de ci*. In this regard, the song represents general trends.

It is possible to approach the typical format for conflicting signatures from two different directions: we may ask why there is one less flat in the cantus, or we may ask why there is one extra flat in the tenor. This piece yields an analysis that allows one to respond to both questions with one answer: the format automatically generates a useful array of cadential formulas, used for the purpose of establishing cadential hierarchies. In Chapter 2, we observed how leading tones are manipulated as a way to distinguish harmonic progressions hierarchically; the hierarchy then serves the composer's sense of overall design. In *Fuions de ci*, the absence of *e*-flat in the cantus means that *e*-natural serves as leading tone to *f*. The presence of *E*-flat in the tenor generates the lowered leading tone to *D*. And since *a*-natural is sung throughout, it serves as leading tone to *b*-flat. The standard signature format automatically produces this simple and effective cadential hierarchy. Senleches uses the lowered leading-tone cadence on *D* in *ouvert* position at the end of part 1 and in a few other places (mm. 15, 31, 34, 43). There are a number of cadences on *b*-flat, the main pitch, and they are usually strong in all respects. Cadences on *f* represent an alternative strong point of arrival in part 2 (mm. 29 and 39).

As Example 3.9 shows, *Modena A* provides additional inflections of *b*-natural and *f*-sharp. The other two manuscripts lack notated leading tones for cadences on *C* and *G*, making these arrivals automatically weaker than those on *B*-flat and *F*. And they are automatically distinguished from cadences on *D*, where the lowered leading tone defines an *ouvert* status. Thus, the composer does not need any additional inflections if he wants a clearly defined cadential hierarchy; the conventional format for conflicting signatures gives him the basic tools of harmonic organization. If we put ourselves in the imaginary mind-set of a meticulous composer who values subtle distinctions in a cadential hierarchy, then we may come to the

Example 3.9 Excerpts from Senleches's *Fuions de ci* (after Greene, ed., PMFC 18: 28–30).
(a). mm. 10–11; (b) m. 16; (c) mm. 26–8; (d) mm. 36–8; (e) m. 40

conclusion that the additional sharps in *Modena A* muddy what is other-wise a clear arrangement.

The conventional format for conflicting signatures, with one additional flat in the tenor, may not have been conceived originally as a way to gener-ate cadential hierarchies, but the original conception of a phenomenon never limits its later use. "Extra" signature-flats in the tenor commonly generate *mi* cadences in *Chantilly 564* and in the older layers of *Oxford 213*.[52] A general point to make here is that we have discovered a *harmonic* explanation for the conventional format.[53] Several scholars, especially Edward Lowinsky and Karol Berger, have previously argued in the same direction. Lowinsky was keenly interested in how changes in signature formats correlate with changes in cadential formulas.[54] Berger argues that, since the tenor moves generally in a range a perfect fifth below the cantus, the extra flat that it carries serves to eliminate the likely occurrence of verti-cal diminished fifths.[55] *Fuions de ci* allows us to take this harmonic orienta-

[52] Many songs in *Chantilly 564* and *Oxford 213* show *mi*-cadences in *ouvert* position that have been generated by the "extra" flat signature in the tenor. For example, in *Chantilly 564*, see *Toute clerté* (f. 13; PMFC 18: 7), Solage's *Corps feminin* (f. 23v; PMFC 18: 66), Suzoy's *Pictagoras* (f. 30v.; PMFC 18: 107), Hasprois' *Ma douce amour* (f. 34; PMFC 18: 128), Suzoy's *Prophilias* (f. 35v; PMFC 18: 136), Johannes Cuvelier's *Se Galaas* (f. 38; PMFC 19: 13) and Trebor's *Helas! pitié envers moy* (f. 42; PMFC 19: 46). And in *Oxford 213*, Grenon's *Je suy defait* (f. 32v; *EFCM*, VII: 3), *Espris d'amours* (f. 125; *EFCM*, IV: 26), *Il n'est dangier que de vilain* (f. 108; *EFCM*, IV: 49), *Par un regart* (f. 95v; *EFCM*, IV: 8) and Fontaine's *Pour vous tenir en la grace amoureuse* (f. 95; ed. Marix, *Les musiciens de la cour de Bourgogne*, 13).

[53] My harmonic orientation towards conflicting signatures (and towards accidentals, generally) stands, on several counts, in contradiction to Edward Kottick's view: "The problem of flats, modality, and musica ficta in the early Renaissance chanson can be explained if we agree that melodic requirements did indeed take precedence over harmonic considerations. The composer used flats so that his melodies, which he wrote in a desirable range, might be sung smoothly and correctly avoiding awkward intervals and melodic patterns, and fitting well with the other voices of the piece. . . . Furthermore, some melodies sounded just as smooth with fewer flats as they did with more, which is another way of saying that they may sound as well in one modal framework as another. Hence partial signatures, varying

signatures, varying internal flats, and floating signatures, along with the art of musica ficta, often reflect the freedom of choice the composer yielded to the scribe and the performer." Edward Kottick, "Flats, Modality, and Musica Ficta in Some Early Renaissance Chansons," *Journal of Music Theory* 12 (1968), 271.

[54] Well known is a series of exchanges between Edward Lowinsky and Richard Hoppin, which ranges over association of the different formats for conflicting signatures with cadential types, as well as the possibility of understanding them in terms of modality. Berger (*Musica ficta*) gives references on p. 210, n. 38. Lowinsky's essays are conveniently gathered in *Music in the Culture of the Renaissance and Other Essays*, ed. Bonnie J. Blackburn (Chicago: University of Chicago Press, 1989), 647; see also the thoughtful additional essay, written for this volume, by Hoppin, "Conflicting Views in Retrospect," 678 ff.

[55] *Musica ficta*, 58–69. For further commentary on Berger's analysis and on modal theories of conflicting signatures, see my "Genre, Style and Compositional Technique in French Music of the Fifteenth Century" (Ph.D. diss., University of California, Berkeley, 1991), 108–34. Mention should be made here of two songs discussed in the Introduction to this book: Lebertoul's *O mortalis homo/O pastores/O vos multi* and the anonymous rondeau *Aylas! Quant je pans*, from *MS Lucca, Archivio di Stato, 184*. Both manifest in a fresh way the presumed logic of the conventional format for conflicting signatures by using "extra" sharps (signed

tion a step further, to the level of cadential hierarchies. Like Lowinsky and Berger, I am skeptical about the potential for melodic explanations for conflicting signatures. The two ways of thinking are not necessarily exclusive of each other. But melodic explanations have usually led in one of two directions, both offering fundamental challenges to how we conceive of pitch relations in this repertory and both raising further problems: there is an interest in bi-modality and there is interest in the role of signatures as markers of hexachords. Interest in hexachordal interpretation is more current and probably more widely accepted. We need to consider its implications, at least on a general level.

A hexachordal orientation to conflicting signatures is advocated especially by Margaret Bent and Andrew Hughes, in influential studies that appeared in 1972.[56] Theorists simply say that a signature-accidental serves to inflect the designated pitch for the duration of the staff upon which the signature is placed; they explain signatures in terms of inflection, and they explain the difference between signature-accidentals and local accidentals as a matter of duration. Bent and Hughes seek to make something different out of signature accidentals (and indeed all accidentals) by reading them as hexachordal markers that guide solmization. Bent emphasizes: "*flat signatures bring about a transposition of the basic* recta *system of three hexachords one degree flatwards for each note flattened in the signature.*"[57] In this view, a signature *b*-flat makes *e*-flat more likely – it makes it a "*recta note*," in Bent's way of thinking about hexachordal transposition – and a signature of *E*-flat makes *a*-flat more likely. Conflicting signatures, then, indicate movement through different though overlapping sets of hexachords in the differently signed voices.[58] This hexachordal orientation to the signs becomes the basis for uncovering an unnotated system for inflecting. Bent and Hughes each give the example of expansion of sixth *E/c* to octave *D/d*: with a *b*-flat signature in the lower part, they say, the singer who chooses to inflect according to the propinquity rule is encouraged to alter *E* to *E*-flat rather

cryptically by Lebertoul with "*G*-flat" and signed redundantly in *Aylas! Quant je pans* with both *G*-flat and *F*-sharp and both *D*-flat and *C*-sharp) in the upper voice for harmonic necessity and propinquity.

[56] Bent, "Musica Recta and Musica Ficta"; Hughes, *Manuscript Accidentals: Ficta in Focus 1350–1450.*

[57] "Musica Recta and Musica Ficta," 98.

[58] Though I am arguing against hexachordally based interpretation of signatures, I should acknowledge a likely application of the theory. This is signaled by the lack of low *B*-flats in *Fuions de ci* and other pieces like it. Clearly, the low *B*-flat is needed, yet it is not signed in

any of the sources. Since there is no evidence promoting octave transference of accidentals, it is generally assumed that the lack of the sign cannot be explained by presence of high *b*-flats. Hexachordal arguments would suggest that low *B*-flat is generated by solmizing *E*-flat as *fa*. This situation is illustrated by the Parisian Anonymous of 1375; see Ellsworth, ed. and trans., *The Berkeley Manuscript*, 56–9. It is not uncommon to discover this pattern – of *E*-flat signature only in a tenor with implication for solmized *B*-flat – in fourteenth-century chansons.

than *c* to *c*-sharp.[59] We should pause to note how this approach differs from that which I have put forward in Chapter 2: that the composer chooses not on the basis of hexachords but according to his interest in cadential hierarchies. I argue that the choice of *E*-flat would reflect the decision to make a weaker and unstable cadence; the choice has nothing to do with a transposition of the hexachordal system caused by a *b*-flat signature. Bent and Hughes find the distinction between musica recta and musica ficta to be of great importance, while I would argue (see the Introduction) that it is of very limited importance. The reader is thus provided with two contradictory ways of thinking about inflections. The fundamental differences in underlying conception generate different musical texts, and accidentals in these musical texts are understood in very different ways.

Based on scrutiny of the theoretical record, Karol Berger has argued against the idea that signatures transpose hexachords in such a way that musica ficta pitches become musica recta pitches, making their use more likely.[60] Based on a survey of manuscript evidence, I am inclined to agree with him. Consider the implications of the theory for *Fuions de ci*. The *b*-flat signature in the cantus should make the choice of *e*-flat more likely; yet there is no obvious place to apply unnotated *e*-flat in this voice, and, as we have seen, *e*-natural is an important leading tone. And the *E*-flat signature in the tenor should make *a*-flat likely. But of the five *a*'s in the tenor, most cannot be sung with the flat, and the others seem unlikely to have been sung that way. This is true throughout the repertory: as a rule, *E*-flat signatures in the tenor do *not* generate implied *a*-flats – or at least that is what my own sense of the musical logic at work in this repertory suggests. For the theory to hold true, one would expect it to be supported by implied *a*-flats with some consistency. Moreover, manuscript collation does not yield an array of variants that can be used to support the theory. There are no variants from the sources for *Fuions de ci*, for example, that one could interpret along the lines of hexachordally implied accidentals made manifest; *Modena A* adds sharps, not flats.

I would argue that one must work primarily through variants in order to uncover the workings of this and, indeed, any unnotated tradition. This is a point that bears emphasis, for it is relevant far beyond this piece and this theoretical problem. In the past, it has been argued that manuscript evidence and theoretical evidence represent alternative lines of inquiry for uncovering unnotated practices; ideally, the two lines should be integrated,

---

[59] Bent, "Musica Recta and Musica Ficta," 99, and Hughes, *Manuscript Accidentals*, 52.

[60] Berger, *Musica ficta*, 64–5 and 83–4.

but they need not be integrated at a preliminary stage of research. But, as I have argued, theorists from this period do not clearly relate what they recommend to unnotated performance practice. They may in fact be talking about compositional conventions at a rudimentary level, which would make their testimony of secondary importance. If this is so, then the only way to advance research on implied but unnotated accidentals is by placing manuscript evidence at the center of the inquiry; the difficulties in advancing to firm conclusions along this line of inquiry do not negate the importance of the method.

Taking Lewis Lockwood's work as a point of departure, Berger has sketched one way to proceed. He divides accidentals into two categories, as a means by which to gain greater control over variants. "Conventional accidentals" are those involving situations that are, presumably, part of a commonly understood performance practice. "Unconventional accidentals," on the other hand, would not be applied unless notated.[61] The notation of conventional accidentals might routinely vary from source to source, since the inflection does not need to be notated; some scribes make the inflection explicit, while others drop the accidental because it is obvious. Our sense of what the conventions were comes, in part, from theorists, so to work with this model does not mean that one dismisses theory. What is most important, though, is that theory be tested through manuscript evidence. Collation becomes the most important tool. The manuscript is the primary witness to practice, even though it will always be difficult to sort through all the possible explanations for any given variant – error and deterioration, active scribal editing, and implied practice made explicit.

The variants we have for *Fuions de ci* do not support a hexachordal analysis, but they are certainly not capricious. They are clearly conventional in one sense – though it is a broader sense than Berger has in mind. It may be useful to adapt these categories of conventional and unconventional inflections by breaking them off from imagined performance practices. Conventional inflections would be those that found their way into the basic precepts of music theory; unconventional inflections did not. It is easy to see the cadential logic that lies behind *Modena A*'s sharps, but it is a bit of a stretch to imagine that these inflections would have been obvious to any skilled performer working with the uninflected versions of the piece transmitted by *Chantilly 564* and the *Reina Codex*. *f*-sharp in measure 16, for example, does follow the expansion from sixth to octave in cantus and tenor; but the expansion occurs on a weak part of the measure, and the

61　Berger, *Musica ficta*, 162–88; Lockwood, "A Sample Problem of *Musica Ficta:* Willaert's *Pater Noster*," 161–82.

contratenor undermines the event. *b*-natural in measures 26–8 is even more aggressive, for it enters against *E*-flat, creating an augmented fifth. *b*-natural in measure 40 emphasizes the arrival on *C/G/c*, and since contratenor and tenor immediately move to a cadence on *B*-flat/*b*-flat, the harmonic shift from one arrival to the next makes a strong effect. The inflections are supported by cadential logic, but they would seem more likely to represent the study and adjustment of an editor than they represent the explicit documentation of what singers routinely brought to uninflected parts.

By highlighting secondary cadences on *G* and *C*, the editor at work in *Modena A* makes the piece more discursive than it is in the clean hierarchy of the uninflected reading. It is possible that his emendations represent nothing more than an attempt to uniformly apply the propinquity convention. Then again, his ambition may have been to make the piece more discursive and unsettled by strengthening the secondary cadences. In any event, there is some indication of a redactional pattern for *Modena A*, which often carries more accidentals than other sources carry.[62] The manuscript has been associated with the composer Matteo da Perugia, and it is tempting to imagine the strong editorial hand of a composer at work.[63]

A fine performance of *Fuions de ci* has been recorded by the Hilliard Ensemble, whose rendition carries on the history of inflecting this piece.[64]

---

[62] Perhaps fourteen of the twenty-three chansons preserved both in *Modena A* and at least one other surviving source show variants that are significant in this regard. Using the numbering provided in Ursula Günther's inventory of *Modena A* – "Das Manuskript Modena, Biblioteca Estense, [a] M. 5, 24 (*olim* lat. 568=*Mod*)," *Musica Disciplina* 24 (1970), 52–67 – see the following songs: nos. 18, 24, 26, 34, 35, 44, 47, 48, 51, 54, 57, 59, 65, and 68. That leaves nine from the twenty-three that have concordances. Of these, four are by Machaut; for these, *Modena A* is largely in step with the other peripheral sources. Thus, if we regard the songs by Machaut as a special case, a high percentage of the songs show inflections in *Modena A* that are not found elsewhere. For good examples, see Matheus de Sancto Johanne's *Sans vous ne puis* (f. 15v., ed. Greene in PMFC 18: 133), Senleches's *En ce gracïeux temps* (f. 25v, ed. Greene in PMFC 21: 9), Ciconia's *Sus un fontayne en remirant* (ff. 26v–27, ed. Margaret Bent and Anne Hallmark in PMFC 24: 170), *Amour doi je servir* (ff. 30v., ed. Greene in PMFC 20: 82), and *Je la remiray* (f. 34, ed. Greene, in PMFC 21: 88). Another issue for *Modena A* is location, for many accidentals have been placed in the margins or squeezed in where no room was left for them. This is true not just for unique accidentals but for many that agree with those in other sources, as well (agree even down to details of horizontal pre-placement, often). Thus, one has the impression of editing "by a later hand"; yet the editing sometimes follows what appear to be received readings while, other times, it veers off independently.

[63] *Modena A*'s copy of Grenon's *Je ne requier* (f. 45v; Greene, ed., PMFC 20: 44) includes a contratenor contributed by Matteo, and the contratenor is fairly well inflected. Just as Matteo added an inflected contratenor to a received song, he may also have added accidentals here and there to others. For a recent review of Matteo's possible connections to *Modena A* and of his interest in adding contratenors, see Anne Stone, "Writing Rhythm in Late Medieval Italy: Notation and Musical Style in the Manuscript Modena, Biblioteca Estense, Alpha. M. 5. 24" (Ph.D. diss., Harvard University, 1994), 26–51.

[64] *Recording to Accompany Music of the Middle Ages: an Anthology for Performance and Study*, by David Fenwick Wilson (New York: Schirmer, 1990); recorded December 6 and 7, 1989, London.

The performers have chosen *Modena A*'s inflections over the cleaner, less discursive version. And to *Modena A* the performers add an inflection not indicated by any manuscript: for the *ouvert* ending of part 1, the chord *D/F/a* is altered so that the contratenor sings *F*-sharp. It is interesting to analyze this choice, which shows modern-day performers enjoying the same freedoms that fourteenth-century performers and editors obviously enjoyed. It is not unusual to find, in *Chantilly 564* and *Oxford 213*, "raised thirds" in *ouvert* position.[65] Yet there is no theoretical basis for this adjustment, particularly when it is used in the context that the Hilliard Ensemble is working with. It is not a propinquity inflection, since the major third, *D/F*-sharp, does not expand to a perfect fifth. In fact, the inflection runs counter to the voice leading, for the *F*-sharp is left dangling when the contratenor sings *B*-flat at the return to the beginning of part 1. The cross relation with *F* is very strong, given the importance of this pitch in the piece, both as fifth above *B*-flat and as a main melodic and cadential pitch. We must not conflate this kind of event with the High Renaissance practice of raising the third for a final chord.[66] In the fourteenth century, a minor third is transformed into a major third in order to bring harmonic direction into focus. In the High Renaissance, major thirds sound more "pleasant" than minor thirds; it is a matter of decoration rather than harmonic syntax.

Just as *Modena A*'s sharps enhance the discursive nature of the piece, so does this inflection have an unsettling effect. The Hilliard Ensemble's *F*-sharp may be taken as a small stroke in the reception-history of *Fuions de ci*. One imagines the performers having been attracted to the harmonic dislocation between *D/F*-sharp/*a* and *B*-flat/*b*-flat/*b*-flat; given the simplicity of the harmonic relations Senleches works with (according to the analysis given above), his interests may have been quite different. He may well have

---

[65] Machaut's *Honte, paour, doubtance* (Schrade, ed., PMFC 3: 106) receives the same inflection in the same chord in the same *ouvert* position in *Florence P 26* (f. 76); here the inflection is less abrupt, since this voice (the tenor) moves directly to *G* upon the return. *Florence P 26* provides the same *F*-sharp for the midpoint cadence of *Se vous n'estes* (Schrade, ed., PMFC 3: 146). *Chantilly 564*'s reading of Petrus Fabri's *Laus detur multipharia* (f. 16v, Greene, ed., PMFC 18: 25) has *F*-sharp in the triplum for the *ouvert* ending at measure 29. *Chantilly 564*'s reading of Cuvelier's *Se Galaas* (f. 38, Greene, ed., PMFC 19: 13) has a strong dislocation in the contratenor, from *c*-sharp in *ouvert* position to *f* at the return of part 1. And the example that is closest to *Fuions de ci* may be *Chantilly 564*'s transmission of Trebor's

Passerose de beaute (Greene, ed., PMFC 19: 50). The piece resembles *Fuions de ci* in its use of the same signature format with *B*-flat final, in locating the *ouvert* cadence on *D*, and in the important use of *e*-natural in the cantus. The contratenor has *F*-sharp signed above *D* in the tenor for the *ouvert* cadence, and it moves to *F* at the repeat of part 1. For commentary on this ballade, including difficulties in placement of accidentals, see Ursula Günther, "Datierbare Balladen des Späten 14. Jahrhunderts, I," *Musica Disciplina* 15 (1961), 49–51; commentary on *Fuions de ci* on pp. 43–5.

[66] The practice is described by Aaron, Lanfranco, Vanneo, and Vicentino; see Berger, *Musica ficta*, 138–9. Surely changes in tuning have something to do with the transition in status of the third.

liked the continuity that *F*-natural provides by linking the three main sonorities of the piece, those built on *B*-flat, *D*, and *F*. If the Hilliard Ensemble's *F*-sharp is a stroke of beauty, it may be beauty that is conditioned by the reputation of the late fourteenth century for more inscrutability and instability than was actually the case.

Sharps versus Flats

Since compositional practice can be so idiosyncratic and transmission so unreliable, it is not easy to generalize about how accidentals are used. Generalization is all the more difficult when dealing with a large repertory that lacks a coherent identity. Yet within the chronological frame that *Oxford 213* provides, it is possible to detect, however dimly or inconsistently, some patterns of use. There is some evidence of an earlier favoring of sharps, then a later favoring of flats. The transition is hardly universal, and there are significant exceptions. Nevertheless, the evidence is strong enough to warrant exposure and reflection on its possible meaning, particularly as that might be construed in the context of an important style change that marks the history of the chanson during the decades after 1400.

One indication for a changing preference is a statistical shift that emerges through comparison between songs in fascicle 7 of *Oxford 213*, an early layer, and songs in fascicles 4 and 1, the most recent layer. Fascicle 7 has a high concentration of older songs, and it may well preserve the oldest music in the manuscript. Four of its twenty songs are attributed to Baude Cordier (*d.* before 1398?), and one is an ars subtilior essay (*De tous les biens*, f. 107v) that may have been copied into the *Trémoïlle Manuscript* by 1376.[67] Four of the songs we have associated with *Medée fu* through prominent use of sharped-fourth are here. At the other end of the manuscript's chronological spectrum, fascicles 4 (with 41 chansons) and 1 (which has but two chansons and which was the last to be copied) preserve some of the most recent music in the manuscript. Here is a bald count of internally signed accidentals:[68]

---

[67] On the *Trémoïlle Manuscript*, see Margaret Bent, "A Note on the Dating of the Trémoïlle Manuscript," in *Beyond the Moon: Festschrift Luther Dittmer*, ed. Bryan Gillingham and Paul Merkley, Wissenschaftliche Abhandlungen 53 (Ottawa: Institute of Mediaeval Music, 1990), 217–42. See also David Fallows's comments on this song in *The Canonici Codex: a Facsimile of Oxford Bodleian Library, MS. Canon. Misc. 213*.

[68] By "sharps," here, I mean all hard *b*'s, and by "flats" I mean all soft *b*'s. The counts that follow do not include signature-accidentals, except when the signature is temporary. Nor do they include high "*ff*-flat," which signals not an inflection but a pedantic clarification: the Guidonian gamut goes only up to *ee*; hence, *ff* is literally "beyond the hand," and the flat indicates the status of the pitch as *fa* in solmization beyond the normal range.

Fascicle 7: 20 chansons; 31 flats; 76 sharps.

Fascicles 4 and 1[69]: 43 chansons; 97 flats; 54 sharps.

Songs in fascicle 7 carry more than twice as many sharps as flats; those in fascicles 4 and 1 have nearly twice as many flats as sharps. The same trend comes through even more dramatically when we compare songs by Baude Cordier with those by Du Fay, two leading representatives of the older and younger generations, respectively. Seven songs by Baude Cordier have been copied into *Oxford 213*. One has no internally signed accidentals, but the other six have 27 sharps and only five flats. Du Fay is well represented in a number of fascicles, but his presence is especially strong in fascicles 4 and 1, where ten songs are attributed to him. Of these, two have no internally signed accidentals, while in the remaining eight there are 25 internally signed flats and three sharps. At least in this small sampling of songs by two leading composers, the evidence for a changing preference in notated accidentals is imposing.

Yet one would not want to put too much weight on a bald inventory that is, after all, rather selective. And it must be acknowledged that these tallies by fascicle do reflect the strong presence of Du Fay in fascicles 4 and 1. But no matter how selective the inventory is, this dramatic turn must tell us something. Obviously, any composer could, at any time, notate as many of one accidental as the other. Guillaume Legrant's brief virelai *Ma chiere mestresse*, copied into fascicle 6, has ten sharps and ten flats. More interesting than statistical consistency, perhaps, would be the possibility of relating this pattern to broader stylistic issues. It may never be possible to completely remove the suspicion that the notational evidence has been tainted by inconsistently documented performance practices. But the more thoroughly we are able to integrate, in coherent interpretation, the analysis with other parameters, the more convincingly the notated trends may appear to demonstrate a change in composers' sense of how to use inflections.

Another way to approach the matter is by comparing the distribution and function of two commonly used melodic figures, one featuring sharps and the other flats (see Ex. 3.10). These figures turn up in many cantus lines, though it is rare to find both in the same song or even the same groups of songs. They bear a superficial resemblance to one another. In each case, an inflected pitch falls after the first beat of the measure (that is, the breve); this inflected pitch is emphasized by virtue of its longer duration.

The sharped figure is used by several older composers, including

---

[69] Including Du Fay's *Quel fronte signorille* and *Dona i ardenti*.

Example 3.10a and 3.10b

Solage,[70] Velut,[71] Malbecque,[72] and Lebertoul,[73] in precisely this form or with slight variation (in augmented note values, for example). It is rarely used by the younger composers in *Oxford 213*; from them, I see only three examples, each of which may be regarded as exceptional. Hugo de Lantins uses it in his single ars subtilior essay, *Je suy extent.*[74] Du Fay uses it in his *sui generis Vergene bella*, which, for a motet, is heavily inflected.[75] Arnold de Lantins uses it in *Las, pouray je mon martire celer;* this is also a special piece, upon which Arnold bestows several distinctly expressive gestures.[76] Perhaps these exceptional uses of this figure in these particular pieces had something to do with what were by then its archaic connotations; such connotations may have given the figure impact and special meaning. The flatted figure in Example 3.10b, on the other hand, is strongly associated with the younger generation. It does not occur in *Chantilly 564* at all.[77] It

---

[70] In *Chantilly 564*, see *Tres gentil cuer* (ff. 18 and 50v; Greene, ed., PMFC 18: 33), *Calextone, qui fut dame* (f. 50; PMFC 19: 102), and *Pluseurs gens voy* (f. 58; PMFC 19: 156). See also in *Chantilly 564* the anonymous *Le mont Aon* (f. 22; PMFC 18: 59), which, as we have seen, is associated with Solage in several ways, and the anonymous *Plus ne put Musique* (f. 33; PMFC 17: 122). Among anonymous songs, *J'ay grant desepoir* deserves special mention (*MS PN 6771;* PMFC 20: 151); the appoggiatura-figure is used extensively, both with and without sharps.

[71] In *Oxford 213*, see the lovely *Un pete oyselet chantant* (f. 89v; ed. Reaney, *EFCM*, II: 119), where the appoggiatura-figure occurs both with and without sharps. Reaney's edition lacks *G*-sharp at measure 29 and *F*-sharp at measure 30, both in the tenor; it adds *c*-sharp at measure 46 in the cantus (or so it appears from my photographs of the manuscript). Velut also uses the appoggiatura in *Laissiés ester vostres chans* (f. 100; *EFCM*, II: 122).

[72] In *Oxford 213*, *Quant de la belle ma parti* (f. 123v; ed. Reaney, *EFCM*, II: 98). Also in fascicle 8 of *Oxford 213* is the anonymous *Se j'ay perdu* (f. 114; *EFCM*, IV: 13).

[73] *O mortalis homo/O pastores/O vos multi* (f. 41v; *EFCM*, II: 47 – but see comments on this edition in the Introduction to this book). See also *Pleysir, soulas,* which

has been copied onto the same folio as Lebertoul's song in *Oxford 213* (*EFCM*, IV: 29). It should be noted that Velut, Malbecque and Lebertoul were all colleagues at the court of Jean, Duke of Berry, and that Solage wrote a piece for this patron.

[74] *Oxford 213*, f. 57; ed. Borren, *Pièces Polyphoniques Profanes*, 53.

[75] *Oxford 213*, f. 133v; ed. Besseler, *Guillaume Dufay Opera Omnia*, VI: 7.

[76] *Oxford 213*, f. 79v; ed. Borren, *Pièces Polyphoniques Profanes*, 25. The expressive gestures include the long notes moving simultaneously at the opening and the sonority *E/G*-sharp/*c* (mm. 30–1). Mention should be made of the occurrence of the sharped figure in *Vaylle que vaylle* by Coutreman (f. 50v; *EFCM*, II: 21); also the anonymous *Douce speranche* (f. 19; *EFCM*, IV: 64), which may be an older song that somehow found its way into fascicle 2.

[77] Note that the sharped figure is an ornamented version of the more widely used figure of a propinquity inflection held for an entire breve (for example, the sharps in *Medée fu*). Likewise, the flatted figure is one particular way to turn through *b*-flat (and, less often, *e*-flat) as the "top tone" (*Spitzenton*) in the melody. Willi Apel remarked on "the frequent notation (in *Oxford 213*) of the *b*-flat in the combination of the top-tone: a-b-flat-

occurs late in *Oxford 213*, with one example in fascicle 3 and the others in fascicle 4, particularly in songs by Binchois,[78] Hugo de Lantins[79] and Du Fay.[80]

This point about distribution of the two figures should be related to the mensurations through which they manifest themselves. In Example 3.10, the sharped figure is in major prolation with imperfect tempus and the flatted figure in minor prolation with perfect tempus. Now we can see why the chronological distribution of the two figures is not surprising: these two mensurations follow a pattern of use that shows the same tendencies in chronological distribution. It is true that composers working *c.* 1400, like composers working *c.* 1430, are free to use either mensuration – just as they are free to use either flats or sharps. But they tend to choose major prolation with imperfect tempus *c.* 1400, and they tend to choose minor prolation with perfect tempus *c.* 1430. Major prolation with imperfect tempus eventually becomes a novelty (for example, *L'homme armé*). Heinrich Besseler analyzed this change based on statistical comparison between older fascicles (5 and 6) and younger fascicles (4) of *Oxford 213*.[81] In fascicles 5 and 6, Besseler found 80 per cent use of major prolation, imperfect tempus, while in fascicle 4 he found 66 per cent use of minor prolation,

a"; "The Partial Signatures in the Sources up to 1450," *Acta Musicologica* 10 (1938), 13. My impression is that this is not because this manuscript makes explicit an inflection that is implicit in other sources; rather, it is because this gesture is so common in fascicles 3 and 4. Apel raised the question whether this notational pattern makes it likely that when the flat is absent, then *b*-natural is implied in this source; it is a provocative idea, since most modern editors assume that the flat should always be applied, regardless of notational patterns. Apel's question points towards the kind of inquiry that needs to be pursued by those working on implied performance practices. If implied inflections are made explicit, then what about other inflections that go unnotated in the same piece? Is it possible to rank inflections on a scale of most conventional to least conventional, thereby coordinating the notational patterns with these probabilities of inflecting? If an "automatic" inflection is notated, does that mean that the notation of accidentals generally is more complete in that source (or in that piece), and that "less automatic" inflections that are not notated are meant to remain uninflected?

[78] *Toutes mes joyes* (f. 61; ed. Rehm, *Die Chansons von Gilles Binchois*, 39), *Amours et souvenir* (f. 72; ed. Rehm, *ibid.*, 7), *Rendre me vieng* (f. 76v; ed. by Rehm, *ibid.*, 33),

Mesdisans (f. 77v; ed. Rehm, *ibid.*, 51 – the figure occurs in measure 12 of the modern edition, assuming that the flat signed for the previous measure still holds), *Ay, douloureux* (f. 78v; ed. Rehm, *ibid.*, 8), and *Amours merchi* (f. 44; ed. Rehm, *ibid.*, 44, m. 14 – assuming that the flat placed in the previous measure, in both manuscripts, is *b*-flat, meant to inflect the figure in measure 13, an assumption that runs counter to that discussed by Dennis Slavin, "In Support of 'Heresy,'" *Early Music* 19 [1991], 179–90; I shall develop this point in more detail in a future study).

[79] *Ce j'eusse fait ce que je pence* (f. 46v; ed. Borren, *Pièces Polyphoniques Profanes*, 46).

[80] *Las, que feray* (f. 72; ed. Besseler, *Guillaume Dufay Opera Omnia*, VI: 85), *Je donne a tous les amoureux* (f. 77; ed. Besseler, *ibid.*, 71 – *bb*-flat is given in the key signature, generating the figure in measure 2), *Navré je sui d'un dart penetratif* (f. 78v; ed. Besseler, *ibid.*, 55 – the figure occurs in measure 7 of the edition, where the flat is incorrectly transcribed as *ee*-flat; instead, the flat should be read as "*ff*-fa"), *Ce jour le doibt* (f. 79; ed. Besseler, *ibid.*, 34).

[81] *Bourdon und Fauxbourdon* (revised edn, 1974), Chapter 7 and especially Table on p. 111.

perfect tempus; he also cited *Escorial A* as manifesting the new trend even more dramatically, with 91 per cent use of minor prolation, perfect tempus.

Besseler was not a scholar to shy away from speculation, and the imaginative spark in his analysis of this situation is characteristic of his boldest work. Upon the foundation of these statistics, he constructed a provocative interpretation of stylistic change during the first four decades of the century. He associated minor prolation, perfect tempus with a new, more flowing melodic profile that often breaks free of the measure – *Strohmrhythmus* is his term for the new style. The dotted rhythm of Example 3.10b is an important part of the new "cantabile" sensitivity. Besseler imagined the transition between the two favored mensurations as having been accomplished through the use of tempus perfectum diminutum. It is fair to say, I think, that even though these ideas about melody are among the best known of Besseler's many important interpretations for this period, the interpretation has not been widely accepted as the epoch-defining one that he clearly had in mind. Nevertheless, the analysis is of great interest in the present context, since the change in mensural preference appears to complement the transition from sharp preference to flat preference that we have seen evidence for in our tallies from *Oxford 213*. Perhaps this loose correlation between mensuration and accidentals is not simply coincidental. The change in the former may not generate a melodic idiom that is new to the degree Besseler imagined, and the change in the latter does not uniformly characterize the entire repertory. Yet an underlying change in emphasis may well have conditioned both tendencies, which developed as general trends.

The melodic figures in Example 3.10 provide a way to focus the inquiry, since they are wedded to the two mensurations in question. As I have said already, the resemblance between the two figures is only superficial. Typically, the harmonic contexts are very different. The syncopated figure with sharp is invariably tied to dissonance on the downbeat, as in the example; the minim (or semibreve, in the case of augmented note values) is an appoggiatura. The sharped pitch is the consonant note of the measure, and it is usually a propinquity inflection. Three parameters work together: both the rhythmic tension of the syncopation and dissonance of the appoggiatura intensify the harmonic tension of the propinquity inflection. The flatted figure is organized quite differently. The first note is always consonant. The tenor often moves in parallel sixths with the cantus, or, sometimes, the cantus turns 5–6–5 or 3–4–3 above a static tenor; in both cases, the measure is mainly consonant, and the flat may be described as a decoration.[82]

Thus, the two figures generate different effects. We may try to project some meaning onto the chronological distribution of these effects. It is clear that the older songs in *Oxford 213* are more loaded with rhythmic tension, relative to the more recent songs. Ars subtilior is only the most glaring manifestation of this tendency. In the more modern song idiom, emphasis is placed on a more relaxed – more *lyrical*, one wants to say – melodic flow, one more lightly animated by harmonic and rhythmic stress. This is the general point that we may draw from Besseler, and in doing so we may recall that the rhythmic profile for the flatted figure in Example 3.10b, ♩♩♪, is so much a part of the modern style of the 1430s. The sharped figure and the flatted figure are formulaic manifestations of two different stylistic sensibilities. The gentle stress of the dotted figure fits well with the new, relatively relaxed rhythmic flow, and it stands in contrast to the more aggressive syncopation of the sharped figure.

With these thoughts in mind, let us turn back to the tallies from *Oxford 213*. Harmonic tension may be the key to interpreting the changing preference from sharps to flats. I have argued elsewhere in this book that by working with a distribution of flats and sharps in propinquity inflections, composers hierarchically distinguish cadences from one another. Sharps yield a stronger sense of closure; flats yield a special *ouvert* status. As a result, sharps are used far more often than flats in propinquity inflections. It is not surprising, then, that the formula in Example 3.10a, a concise evocation of musical tension derived from syncopation, from dissonance and from harmonic propinquity, features sharps rather than flats. The turn through *b* flat (and occasionally *e*-flat) in the other figure is part of a new lyrical impulse that may welcome flats more than it welcomes sharps. This association of flats with lyricism calls to mind Machaut's *Rose, lis* (Chapter 2), and it is an association that blossoms fully in Du Fay's practice (as we shall see in Chapter 4). Du Fay belongs firmly to the lineage of composers who enjoy the expressive potential of "beautiful" inflections, and his inclinations in the 1430s lead him to favor flats over sharps for this purpose. Baude Cordier, on the other hand, is more consistently in step

---

[82] A few instances in which the flat serves as a propinquity inflection (and, not coincidentally, also causes dissonance in the measure) bridge the two figures. This happens in Binchois' *Mesdisans*, for example (*Oxford 213*, f. 77v; ed. Rehm, *Die Chansons von Gilles Binchois*, 51); the inflection prepares a forthcoming cadence (*ouvert*, as one would expect) on *a*. Hugo de Lantins does the same thing in *Ce j'eusse fait ce que je pence* (*Oxford 213*, f. 46; ed. Borren, *Pièces Polyphoniques Profanes*, 46).

Example 3.11 Binchois' *Amoreux suy*, m. 19 (after Rehm, ed., *Die Chansons von Gilles Binchois*, 5)

with well-established practices of the ars nova, including the regular use of sharps and harmonic tension to maintain forward drive (see Ex. 3.8a, above).

Binchois may have been slightly older than Du Fay – or so one might assume from his better representation in early sources. Let us keep this possibility in mind as we reflect upon accidentals in his songs preserved by *Oxford 213*. By one possible count, the manuscript includes a total of 28 songs by this composer. Five of these appear in the early layers. Given Besseler's observations about mensuration, it is not surprising to discover that all five move in major prolation, imperfect tempus. And given our previous tallies for accidentals, it is not surprising that *Oxford 213* gives 32 sharps and only five flats for these five songs.[83] By his choice of mensuration, Binchois is in step with normative practice for the older fascicles, and it is possible to read the preference for sharps in the same way. The count is shaped mainly by *Amoreux suy* (eleven sharps and no flats), *Je loe amours* (five sharps and one flat), and *Tant plus ayme* (eleven sharps and two flats).

It is particularly noteworthy, I think, that sharps are abundant in the cantus parts of *Amoreux suy* (six sharps) and *Tant plus ayme* (seven).[84] And with this observation we arrive at the final turn in this selective comparison

[83] These counts follow the same guidelines as before: by "sharps" I mean any hard *b* and by "flats" I mean any soft *b* (excepting high "*ff*-flats"); signature-accidentals are excluded, unless they are temporary. The five songs are *Je me recommande* (f. 81v), *Amoreux suy* (f. 82), *Adieu m'amour et ma maistresse* (f. 86v), *Je loe amours* (f. 88), and *Tant plus ayme* (f. 125v). For a tentative attempt to organize Binchois' songs chronologically, see Dennis Slavin, "Questions of Authority in Some Songs by Binchois," 22–61; see also Reinhard Strohm, *The Rise of European Music*, 184 and 188–9. It should be noted that the correspondence between location by fascicle and

chronology is easily broken, since songs could be copied into an earlier fascicle at a later date. Graeme Boone suggests, for example, that *Je me recommande humblement* and *Adieu m'amour et ma maistresse* were both entered into fascicle 5 at the time that the much later fascicle 3 was copied; "Dufay's Early Chansons," 57.

[84] Ed. Rehm, *Die Chansons von Gilles Binchois*, 5 and 38. The following adjustments to these editions seem likely to me: for *Amoreux suy*, cantus should have *g*-sharp rather than *f*-sharp in measures 8 and 26; for *Tant plus ayme*, cantus should have *f*-sharp in measure 29.

Example 3.12 Binchois' *Tant plus ayme*, m. 19 (after Rehm, ed.,
Die Chansons von Gilles Binchois, 38)

of sharps and flats. The restriction of analysis to accidentals in cantus lines
only will open up possibilities for interpretation. This restriction would
follow the assumption that an accidental in the cantus has a special status;
the inflection takes its place in the design of the dominating melody. By
focusing on cantus lines we will be in a better position to weave together, in
a coherent interpretation, three ingredients: (1) shifting preference from
sharps to flats; (2) the special importance of inflections in a cantus line; and
(3) a shift towards a more relaxed melodic idiom, one associated with
changing mensural preference from major prolation, imperfect tempus to
minor prolation, perfect tempus.

The abundance of sharps in the cantus lines of *Amoreux suy* and *Tant
plus ayme* stands out especially when compared with the lack of sharps in
cantus lines for the 23 songs by Binchois in more recent fascicles of *Oxford
213*. For in this larger group, only one song has as many as three sharps in
the cantus; only two songs have two sharps, while the others have one or
none. The contrast makes it likely that *Amoreux suy* and *Tant plus ayme*
each occupy an early position in Binchois' oeuvre, and that this early position is reflected both in the choice of mensuration and in the frequency and
prominence of sharps. *Amoreux suy* uses (twice) an abbreviated form of the
sharped figure (see Ex. 3.11). And true chromaticism occurs in the cantus
of *Tant plus ayme*, recalling *Medée fu* and several other songs in the early
layers of *Oxford 213* (see Ex. 3.12). Binchois' *Triste plaisir* (Ex. 3.13),
copied into fascicle 3, another recent layer, shows that the impact of
inflections need not be determined quantitatively. *Oxford 213* reports but a
single sharp; yet that one sharp is enough to generate considerable tension,
of a kind that would have been understood by older composers going back
to Machaut. *f*-sharp in measure 8, held for a complete breve, stands in a
cross relation to *F*-natural in the tenor from measure 5, and it forms an

Example 3.13 Binchois' *Tristre plaisir*, mm. 1–14 (after Rehm, ed., *Die Chansons von Gilles Binchois*, 40)

indirect diminished fourth with *b*-flat in the cantus of measure 6. With this *f*-sharp, cantus and tenor form a major sixth that should, by textbook theory and by the context of this song, resolve directly to *G/g*. But there is no immediate resolution. Instead, the line leaps away; unpredicted arrivals on *c* in measure 10 and *f* in measure 14 follow in turn. The cantus has a lyric role that Binchois crafts with his customary skill, and it also has a role in generating harmonic tension.

Example 3.14 Binchois' *Amours et souvenir*, mm. 1–10 (after Rehm, ed., *Die Chansons von Gilles Binchois*, 7)

In the modern songs from fascicle 4 that move in minor prolation with perfect tempus, Binchois continues to use a few prominent sharps in cantus lines. In two songs, sharps inflect a repeated-semibreve figure (Example 3.14).[85] Here, in *Amours et souvenir*, is the characteristically elegant flow of minor prolation, perfect tempus. The turn through the repeated *f*-sharp is a sudden one, and when *f*-natural follows (presumably it is *f*-natural in measures 9 and 10) we may recall the sense of dislocation caused by cross relations and sudden turns in *Tristre plaisir*. This repeated-semibreve figure is every bit as characteristic of the modern melodic idiom as the dotted figure of measure 2 is. Binchois and Du Fay both use repeated semibreves fre-

[85] The same repeated figure on *f*-sharp is heard again in the final phrase of *Amours et souvenir*; Binchois uses it again in *Ay douloureux* (m. 40). Modern editions by Rehm, ed., *Die Chansons von Gilles Binchois*, 7 and 8. The repeated figure on *f*-sharp occurs also in the anonymous *Adieu, ma tresbelle maistresse* (*Escorial A*, f. 26v; ed. Walter Kemp, *Anonymous Pieces in the Chansonnier El Escorial, Biblioteca del Monasterio, Cod. V. III. 24*, Corpus Mensurabilis Musicae 77 [Neuhausen-Stuttgart: American Institute of Musicology, 1980], 16, m. 17). Kemp has argued that this (and other anonymous songs in *Escorial A*) is by Binchois; see *Burgundian Court Song in the Time of Binchois: the Anonymous Chansons of El Escorial, MS V. III. 24* (Oxford: Oxford University Press, 1990).

quently. But it is revealing, I think, that Du Fay never inflects a pitch that is repeated in this way.[86] Binchois does that several times, and this small difference between the two composers betrays a larger point.

For among Du Fay's songs in *Oxford 213* that move in minor prolation, perfect tempus, it is rare to discover any sharps at all in cantus lines. A few exceptions do not trouble our sense of a general trend in Du Fay's practice.[87] On the other hand, in seven songs that move in major prolation, imperfect tempus, Du Fay is in step with Binchois and an older generation when he makes good use of sharps in the cantus.[88] The evidence of fascicle 4 suggests that Binchois carries this practice into the modern idiom, though he uses it there far less frequently. In contrast, Du Fay turns away from it, finding flats more suited to his new-found lyric sensitivity.[89] If

---

[86] One song associated with Du Fay does have a sharp on a repeated-semibreve figure: *Je languis en piteux martire* is attributed to Du Fay in *MS Trento, Museo Provinciale d'Arte, Castello del Buonconsiglio 92*, but Margaret Bent has persuasively argued against the attribution. Since the inflection seems foreign to Du Fay's sense of line, the sharp may be taken as further evidence in support of her argument. See "The Songs of Dufay: Some Questions of Form and Authenticity," *Early Music* 8 (1980), 458–9. Modern edition of *Je languis en piteux martire* in Besseler, ed., *Guillaume Dufay Opera Omnia*, VI: 33. There is one case of repeated minims with sharped pitch, however, in Du Fay's oeuvre; see Besseler's edition of *J'ay mis mon cuer et ma pensee*, ed. Besseler, *ibid.*, 28, m. 14. David Fallows reports that a concordant source omits the sharp: *The Songs of Guillaume Dufay: Critical Commentary to the Revision of Corpus Mensurabilis Musicae, ser. 1, vol. VI* (Neuhausen-Stuttgart, American Institute of Musicology, 1994), 66.

[87] Twenty-one songs by Du Fay in *Oxford 213* move in minor prolation, perfect tempus. Sharps are signed in the cantus lines of only three: *Vergene belle, He compaignons*, and *Pouray je avoir*. As already mentioned, *Vergene belle* is exceptional in a number of respects. It and *He compaignons* both move, presumably, in diminished values in what would be represented as φ; this is the mensuration Besseler has identified as transitional between favored use of major prolation with imperfect tempus and favored use of minor prolation with perfect tempus. Datings for these two pieces suggested by Alejandro Enrique Planchart would support this: Planchart suggests *c.* 1423 or slightly later for *He compaignons*; see "Guillaume Du Fay's Benefices and his Relationship to the Court of Burgundy," *Early Music*

History 8 (1988), 124–6. He suggests *c.* 1426–8 for *Vergene belle*; "What's in a Name? Reflections on Some Works of Guillaume Du Fay," *Early Music* 16 (1988), 170. *He compaignons*, in any event, is a "double-cantus," motet-like song, so it is exceptional. *Pouray je avoir* belongs squarely in the midst of Du Fay's mature use of minor prolation with tempus perfectum, and *Oxford 213* does carry a sharp in the cantus, thus challenging the pattern of sharps being inappropriate in this voice in this group of songs; see the modern edition by Besseler, *Guillaume Dufay Opera Omnia*, VI: 54, m. 14. It is worth noting, however, that the sharp is lacking in *MS Escorial A*. The line moves from the *c*-sharp up to *f* (with an intervening rest); it is not an impossible leap, but perhaps, given the tendency to avoid sharps, it is unlikely. Yet, a third source, *MS Paris 6771*, agrees with *Oxford 213* at measure 14; furthermore, it carries an additional *c*-sharp for the cantus at measure 21.

[88] The seven songs are *J'ay mis mon cuer, Resvelliés vous, Je me complains, Par droit je puis, Helas, ma dame, Mon chier amy*, and *Ma belle dame souverainne*.

[89] Among later songs by Du Fay, *Helas mon dueil* (ed. Besseler, *Guillaume Dufay Opera Omnia*, VI: 42), which unfolds in its first phrase through a bold diminished fourth in the cantus, is the text-illustrating exception to this general rule; the piece is discussed by David Fallows, *Dufay*, 155–6; and also by Norbert J. Schneider, "Die verminderte Quarte als Melodieintervall: Eine musikalische Konstante von Dufay bis Schönberg," *Schweizerische Musikzeitung* 120 (1980), 205–6. Hugo de Lantins had earlier used a similar opening gesture (with indirect diminished fourth) in his chromatically charged *Prendre couvint de tout en gré* (*Oxford 213*, f. 36; ed. Borren, *Pièces Polyphoniques Profanes*, 39). And much

Binchois was, indeed, slightly older than Du Fay, then this would account for the difference. Or it may be that Du Fay was more or less isolated in his tendency to use sharps more sparingly (and often not at all) in his mature songs.

*

By way of summary, the manuscript documentation of accidentals from the period between Machaut and Du Fay leads to the following lines of analysis:

(1) If Machaut's musical legacy did enjoy the late-century presence that is usually assigned to it, then we may imagine various references to his use of accidentals. Among other things, Machaut may have been directly responsible for subtle developments in cadential hierarchies based on manipulating propinquity applications.

(2) Rarely does late-fourteenth-century practice go beyond Machaut. A few glaring exceptions may be thought of as "musica ficta essays," radical demonstrations of the discursive style. Other songs feature a high concentration of accidentals in only isolated phrases or sections (and in both cases, there is an analogy to make with ars subtilior rhythms).

(3) A main development in the late decades of the century is the tendency towards expansive phrases, and this is occasionally coordinated with a design featuring prominent use of a few carefully chosen inflections. *Medée fu* features prominent *g*-sharp in the cantus as a point of high tension in a piece that is stably built around *D*. Other composers work with prominent, dislocating sharps in the first phrase. When given prominence in this context of expansivity, the inflections loom large; exceptionally, in cases such as *Medée fu*, their implications may play out over longer stretches of time. Not uncommonly in ars nova practice, propinquity inflections drive a piece forwards. In the exceptional case this sense of forward drive is integrated with large-scale design. In this way, accidentals play a role in developing the late-century aesthetic of the *grande ballade*.

(4) The principle of harmonic tension from sharps as a source of forward drive surfaces regularly in the older layers of *Oxford 213*, not only

later, Busnoys (or Mureau or Compère) will feature a rare sharp to similarly etch out a distinctive profile for the opening of *Je ne fais plus* (ed. Howard Brown, *A Florentine Chansonnier from the Time of Lorenzo the Magnificent* [Chicago: University of Chicago Press, 1983], "Music Volume," 109; on the attribution, see "Text Volume," 229). In each of these songs, flats and sharps are juxtaposed as a way to highlight the first four syllables of the poem, thereby marking the poetic caesura. The events give each song a distinct identity. These would represent specific manifestations of the general principle that we have seen much earlier – chromatic tension in the first phrase, as if to launch the piece. Whether they were aware of it or not, these composers place themselves, with these gestures, in a tradition that surely goes back to Machaut.

in ballades but also in the lighter rondeaux of Baude Cordier; in the next generation, Binchois and Du Fay follow this practice. Harmonically tense sharps are rarer in the most recent fascicles of the manuscript. There, we more often discover cantus lines that shun participation in the generation of harmonic tension. In his most modern songs transmitted by this manuscript, those moving in minor prolation with perfect tempus, Du Fay rarely features sharps in cantus lines. Following Besseler, we may read the situation in this way: the modern idiom represents a move towards relaxed lyricism, and Du Fay finds it more felicitous to use flats in this context.

The decision to end this survey with Du Fay has not been made arbitrarily. It is true that it often seems a little silly to argue about firsts and lasts in late medieval music; the only way to work with that line of analysis confidently is when some writer of the period speaks to it, and this rarely happens. Yet a case can be made that Du Fay's interest in discursive accidentals was not continued by the leading composers who followed him. Perhaps this is only an illusion caused by lack of sources; that is definitely a problem for the 1440s and 1450s. In any event, Okeghem and Busnoys, the leading chanson composers of the next generations, appear not to have been very interested in accidentals. They mainly compose in a diatonic pitch field, with little or no signed musica ficta, and even b-flats are rare. Du Fay's later songs (*Vostre bruit, Par le regard, Franc cuer gentile*, for example) often follow the diatonic trend, and this may indicate influence from the younger composers; there are clear signs in other areas that Du Fay was so influenced. Nevertheless, he did not completely abandon discursive accidentals. The most famous use of all comes from very late in his life, in the troped *Ave regina celorum* (copied 1464–5), a plea to the Blessed Virgin Mary to intercede on behalf of "your dying Du Fay."[1]

---

[1] And, as in the phrase given in Example 4.1, on behalf of "your suppliant Du Fay." Modern editions of this and all pieces by Du Fay cited in this chapter by Heinrich Besseler, *Guillaume Dufay Opera Omnia*, Corpus Mensurabilis Musicae 1 (n.p.: American Institute of Musicology, 1951–66). On the copying date of *Ave regina celorum*, see, most recently, Alejandro Enrique Planchart, "Notes on Guillaume Du Fay's Last Works," *Journal of Musicology* 13 (1995), especially 55–60. Planchart elegantly constructs a psychological profile of Du Fay during his last decade. For Example 4.1, I have used the plainchant and not the trope as text underlay in the contratenor bassus, as indicated by the only surviving source, *MS San Pietro B 80*, f. 26v. The contratenor bassus does not get troped text until the very end of the piece. It is possible that this voice and the tenor were meant to carry only the chant text, which would indicate a conception of the texture similar to that of the old-style isorhythmic motet. Also, several accidentals are most likely missing from the sole source for this motet. This we know by comparison with Du Fay's Mass by this title, which quotes the motet in the second Agnus Dei. Four additional accidentals given in sources for the Mass seem likely for this passage: f-sharp for measure 89, cantus; F-sharp for measure 90, contratenor altus; b-flat for measure 91, contratenor altus; and e-flat for measure 94, cantus. Each of these inflections seems stylistic to me. E-flat for the contratenor bassus at measure 90 is surely demanded by necessity and perhaps implied by the continuing duration of the flat in measure 89; with the emended reading, E-flat would also be demanded by necessity in measure 94, contratenor bassus. The most famous textual problem in this passage would be measure 95, cantus, where one wonders if e-flat from the (emended) previous measure still holds; I would assume that it does. The passages from the motet and the Mass are given in comparative example by Rob Wegman, "*Miserere supplicanti Dufay:* the Creation and Transmission of Guillaume Dufay's *Missa Ave regina celorum*," *Journal of Musicology* 13 (1995), 33: Wegman's example 1c includes, apparently by mistake, the F-sharps in question; there is no sign of them in the facsimile edition of *MS San Pietro B 80* available as vol. 23 of Renaissance Music in Facsimile, ed. Christopher Reynolds (New York: Garland, 1986).

Example 4.1 Du Fay, *Ave regina celorum*, mm. 86–96 (Tenor *tacet*; after Besseler, ed., *Guillaume Dufay Opera Omnia*, V: 127)

Four textual tropes personalize the Marian antiphon text, and all voices of the motet paraphrase the antiphon's melody, at least to some degree. Two of the textual tropes (including the passage given as Ex. 4.1) are set chromatically. Both passages begin with the word "miserere," and Du Fay responds with discursive flats. This chromatic technique is one that Du Fay had worked out some 40 years earlier in chansons. In this sense, and in the more general sense of being dominated by a lyric top voice (a common feature established well before this time), the motet incorporates techniques from the chanson. The decision to use expressive flats may also have been inspired by the paraphrased plainchant, for it is possible that the version of this antiphon known to Du Fay carried *b*-flat and *b*-natural adjacent to one another; his polyphonic paraphrase of the chant seems to imply this, in any event. The idea of Du Fay taking a chromatic lead from the cross relation of the chant brings to mind a point made in Chapter 1: alternation between *b*-flat and *b*-natural in chant may have been one inspiration for discursive inflections in the chanson. By mixing paraphrased plainchant with the melodic lyricism of courtly love, the motet may be read as a universal statement. In terms of polyphonic texture it also represents a stylistic synthesis, for it blends old elements (polytextuality, true tenor foundation) with new (the pacing and integration of the voices). It is as if Du Fay offers up to Mary his entire life's work.

Chromaticism provides the central expressive device. In emphasizing discursive accidentals at this late date, Du Fay is slightly out of step with the times, which have witnessed, over the previous decades, the trend towards favoring a uniform pitch field. During the early part of his career, however, he was very much in step with his times, and we may review a few aspects of his chromatic technique during this formative period.

Helas, ma dame

In Chapter 3, we considered the idea of the "musica ficta essay," a category that stands analogously to "ars subtilior essay." Du Fay carries both of these traditions into the 1420s. If *Resvelliés vous* is Du Fay's ars subtilior essay, *Helas, ma dame* (Ex. 4.2) is his nearly contemporary musica ficta essay.[2] *Oxford 213*, the only surviving source for *Helas, ma dame*, reports 21 accidentals in the span of the 31-breve rondeau refrain. Not only does the piece demonstrate the extreme of Du Fay's chromatic practice; it is also valuable for the opportunity it provides to reflect on the evolution of harmony, an opportunity that has been previously recognized by Heinrich Besseler and by Carl Dahlhaus.

As I have argued, we may think of harmonic syntax as two-sided. On the one hand, the basic components of the syntax – alternation of sonority type, contrary motion, and propinquity – are recognized and practiced to a degree that encourages the notion of a paradigm. On the other hand, the syntax yields various points of flexibility. *Helas, ma dame* represents an experiment with harmonic syntax bold enough to recall Machaut. Musica ficta essays in the early fascicles of *Oxford 213* may have provided antecedents to *Helas, ma dame*, but there are no surviving descendants. Perhaps there is a historiographic point here. Fifty years earlier, Machaut would

---

[2] *Oxford 213*, f. 33v. David Fallows reports that the key signature for the contratenor was added by a later hand: *The Songs of Guillaume Dufay*, 139. The poem given in Example 4.2 follows Fallows, 139, as does the emendation suggested there for the contratenor at measure 14 (changing the source's *F* to *G*).

Example 4.2 Du Fay, *Helas, ma dame*, Oxford 213, f. 33v

Example 4.2 (*cont.*)

have understood this kind of writing; fifty years later, Tinctoris might have ridiculed it.[3] Though chromatically experimental, the harmonic logic here is traditional, contrary to Besseler, who thought that the song behaves tonally.[4] The obvious anachronism of Besseler's analysis speaks well of musicological progress, for he was, unquestionably, a leading interpreter of music from this period. Besseler was particularly interested in the low-lying contratenor, which he saw as "bearing" the harmony (*Harmonieträger*). The contratenor does move, at times, like a tonal bass line, but it has been sufficiently stressed by Carl Dahlhaus and others that the voice must have been added to a self-sufficient cantus–tenor pair; the

[3] Since, in 1477, Tinctoris claims that no music worth hearing was written more than forty years earlier, the song falls before his date for the advent of good music. The passage is from the Introduction to Tinctoris's treatise on counterpoint. As translated by Albert Seay: "And, if I may refer to what I have heard and seen, I have held in my hands at one time or another many old songs of unknown authorship which are called *apocrypha* that are so inept and stupidly composed that they offended

our ears rather than pleased them. In addition, it is a matter of great surprise that there is no composition written over forty years ago which is thought by the learned as worthy of performance." *Johannes Tinctoris: the Art of Counterpoint (Liber de Arte Contrapuncti*, ed. and trans. Albert Seay, Musicological Studies and Documents 5 (n.p: American Institute of Musicology, 1961), 14.

[4] *Bourdon und Fauxbourdon*, 40–3.

contratenor follows, it does not control. Traditional harmonic syntax operates, and tonal syntax is far in the future.

At several turns in this song, E-natural alternates with E-flat, B-natural with B-flat. C is the main pitch at the beginning and at the end. Thinking in terms of the root progressions of tonality, Besseler parsed the music as "dominant tonality with freedom of thirds" (*dominantische Tonalität mit Terzfreiheit*). This gets the matter exactly wrong, for it puts the imaginary function of root progressions ahead of the aspects of the fourteenth-century harmonic paradigm that still operate. The altered degrees contradict the harmonic functions that Besseler would like to hear, and the superficial resemblance to root motion is misleading. The analogy between harmonic function in this repertory and that in common-practice tonality does not depend on tendency tones, but when the tendency tones are manipulated, the manipulation works against the analogy.

Helas, ma dame demonstrates also the continuing importance, even now, in Du Fay's mature songs of the mid-1420s, of thirds as markers of harmonic tension. Much later in the century, Tinctoris will recommend thirds for decorating sonorities; that way of thinking represents a completely different assessment of the interval.[5] Dahlhaus has effectively critiqued many sides of the discourse surrounding harmony in late medieval polyphony, but his analysis of *Helas, ma dame* is based on a fundamental error, one that stems from incorrect assumptions about cadential formulas and the role of thirds.

> In *Helas, ma dame* . . . the next-to-last and last sonorities of the Phrygian clausula relate to each other directly (mm. 9–10, 19–20, and 26–27). In lines 2, 4, and 6 of the chanson they form not half cadences, but endings that stand with equal right alongside those on G of lines 3 and 5 [mm. 14–15, 22–3], and those on C of lines 1 and 7 [mm. 4–5, 30–1]. The clausulas on C, G, and D form an association without a central focus: an association in which the difference between the G-mode of the vocal middle section and the C-mode of the instrumental opening and closing sections – perplexing to a tonal way of hearing – implies no contradiction.[6]

We may overlook the references to "G-mode" and "C-mode" (which stem from the untenable conviction that "chromatic alterations are contrapuntal means that have no effect on the mode," p. 197). The more imposing

---

[5] "If there be any third, either perfect or imperfect, either superior or inferior, it is in itself of the highest smoothness, adaptable in the most consonant way to all notes . . ." *The Art of Counterpoint*, ed. and trans. Seay, 25.
[6] *Studies on the Origin of Harmonic Tonality*, trans. Robert O. Gjerdingen (Princeton: Princeton University Press, 1990), 84–9, quotation on p. 89. The suggestion of instrumental performance on what are viewed today – nearly unanimously, it would seem – as opening and closing melismas is, in any event, irrelevant to the argument (though Besseler magnified this point).

Example 4.3 Analysis of phrases in *Helas, ma dame*

4 + 1 measure stasis (m. 5)

4 + 1 measure tension (m. 10)

4 + 1 measure stasis (m. 15)

4 + 1 measure tension (m. 20)

2 + 1 measure stasis (m. 22)

3 + 1 measure tension (m. 27)

3 + 1 measure stasis (m. 31)

issue arises from Dahlhaus's treatment of all cadences as equal. Leave open, for the moment, the question of whether the *mi*-clausulas (preferable to "Phrygian clausulas") are indeed equal, in a hierarchical sense, to the *ut*-clausulas. For Dahlhaus's analysis collapses on an even more basic point. The main cadences are at measures 5 (on *C*), 15 (on *G*), and 31 (on *C*); these arrivals feature perfect intervals only. Cadences at measures 10, 22, and 27 are built on *D*, and each one features *F*-sharp, the third above *D*. The presence of thirds unequivocally marks these arrivals as secondary, in a hierarchical sense; they are indeed half-cadences. Here is the harmonic language of the ars nova, the language that Du Fay and Binchois continue to use in the 1420s (especially in major prolation with imperfect tempus). These are not "sweet" thirds; they are harmonically tense.

Since it is clear from the thirds that the cadences at measures 10, 22, and 27 occupy a secondary rank in a cadential hierarchy, we may assume that the use, in the same cadences, of the "lowered-second" *E*-flat instead of the "raised-seventh" *C*-sharp contributes to this rank, as well. Lowered-second at the penultimate sonority and imperfect third at the point of arrival work together to define open cadences. There can be no better demonstration of continuity from ars nova harmonic practice into Du Fay's songs of the 1420s.[7]

A pre-cadential appoggiatura figure also threads together the big three arrivals of measures 5, 15, and 31.[8] And the midpoint cadence at measure 15 occurs very near the temporal midpoint of the 31-measure plan. Furthermore, in the layout of phrases (Ex. 4.3), Du Fay works with additional symmetries of harmony and time.

[7] Undoubtedly, the harmonic functions associated with lowered seconds and tense thirds carry on. See the discussion below of Okeghem's *Baisiés moy*, in which precisely these two inflections are the only two accidentals signed in the entire piece.

[8] Howard M. Brown has made a similar observation concerning cadences linked to one another via melodic motif in his study "A Ballade for Mathieu de Foix: Style and Structure in a Composition by Trebor," 82–3.

Example 4.4

This analysis follows the organization of the text (thinking of a melisma as a kind of textual entity). Harmonically, there is systematic alternation between arrivals marked by stasis and those marked by tension. Temporally, phrase lengths are identical through the first four phrases, with variation towards the end of the refrain. Perhaps there is one additional touch of symmetry: the two main cadences on *C* each feature *bb*-natural as leading tone, but the midpoint cadence to *G* lacks a raised leading tone. Given the nuanced use of propinquity inflections in this song, it is possible that *f*-sharp is not there (m. 14) because the composer wishes the arrival on *G* at the midpoint to be relatively weaker than the outer arrivals on *C*.[9]

Having sorted out the main outline of the plan, we are in a position to assess the steady chromaticism of the internal phrases. One is struck immediately by the absence of accidentals in the first phrase (mm. 1–5) and by the presence of *f*-sharp, *bb*-flat, and *e*-flat in the second (mm. 6–10). Surely the main point is movement from a passage that is musically stable to one that is unstable. Phrase 1 could not be more firmly centered on *C*. By the end of phrase 2, measure 10 points unquestionably towards *G*, but this moment of clarity follows considerable harmonic instability. In phrase 2, *F*-sharp and *bb*-flat both serve to turn the sense of direction away from *C* and towards *G*. The role of *f*-sharp is clear. The role of *bb*-flat is clear, too, once we recognize the technique of "pre-cadential lowered thirds," a structural device common to many songs by Du Fay, his contemporaries, and his predecessors (see below). This pre-cadential lowered third serves to establish direction away from *C* and towards *G*, in complement to *f*-sharp.

Example 4.4 contains the pitch collection of phrase 2, reduced to a single octave. Obviously, this collection of pitches has nothing to do with Guido's hexachord or any hexachord. In addition to their directional implications,

[9] It is possible, on the other hand, that *f*-sharp from measure 10 remains in force through measure 14. And it is also possible, of course, to assume, as Besseler did, that the inflection is not signed because it is tacitly understood; but that assumption might be buried by the density of notated inflections in this song. These thoughts on cadential hierarchies follow from the argument developed in Chapter 2 for Machaut's music. For observations on cadential hierarchies in Binchois' songs, as mapped out by virtue of voice leading, see Dennis Slavin, "Some Distinctive Features of Songs by Binchois: Cadential Voice Leading and the Articulation of Form," *Journal of Musicology* 10 (1992), 342–61.

these pitches serve to generate a potent array of indirect (both vertical and horizontal) augmented and diminished intervals – *f*-sharp versus *bb*-flat, *a* versus *e*-flat, *e*-flat versus *f*-sharp, *c* versus *f*-sharp. The cantus is stripped down to a series of austere turns; emphasis is placed not on lyrical quality of line but on these cross relations and the harmonic shifts. Accidentals are used motivically when the cantus turns first around *a*-*b*-flat-*a* (mm. 7–9) and then, in transposition, around *d*-*e*-flat-*d* (mm. 16–18). The motif is melodically expressive, perhaps, but the main point would seem to be the augmented and diminished intervals that are achieved – both vertically, with reference to tenor and contratenor, and within the line itself. Put another way, the expressive half steps in the cantus would be much less effective without this harmonic context.

The unsettled passages clear out alternately on the perfect consonances (mm. 15 and 31) and on the directional thirds (mm. 10, 20, and 27) to produce the foremost moments of harmonic clarity. Measures 6–15 lean towards *G*. In measures 16–18, *b*-natural and *e*-flat clearly serve to turn the piece back towards *C*; the transposition of the half-step motif highlights the analogy in harmonic function with the turn towards *G* in measures 6–8. Alongside these signposts are ambiguous moves. For example, it is surely notable that the contratenor contributes *C* in measure 11. It will not do to simply rank this resolution as one choice among equal possibilities, as one among several contrapuntal resolutions allowed by the discant treatises. In context, the resolution is both irregular, since resolution to *G* is clearly implied at measure 10, and structural, since *C* was so strongly established in the first phrase. The contratenor makes a similar contribution in measure 27, where the drop to *b*-natural predicts in a whisper the final turn to *C*. Thus, the contratenor, low lying or not, is traditional in its role of supplementing the harmonic organization of the cantus–tenor pair, though it is also clear how a clever composer may find a way for the contra-tenor to make an independent contribution (*b*-natural in m. 27).

Alas, no more than the poetic refrain survives. There must have been more text; performed as a complete rondeau, the piece would take on the weightiness that Du Fay clearly had in mind for it. Performed with the repetitions of rondeau form (with instruments, perhaps, being used today to provide an account of the poetic sections that have not survived), the dynamics of the design would be both clarified, through increasing familiarity with the goals of phrases, and enriched, through the varied combinations of phrases. Encouraged by Martin le Franc's famous (though indirect and possibly meaningless) association of Du Fay and Johannes

Cesaris, Besseler proposed that Cesaris's *Bonté bialté* influenced Du Fay's chromatic practice.[10] Stylistically, a more likely precedent for *Helas, ma dame* would be the anonymous *Arriere tost*; here is a similarly unornamented melodic flow, marked by many easy turns through quick successions of flats (including *D*-flat) and sharps (including *g*-sharp). The comparison with Du Fay makes clear his superior sense of concentrated and formally controlled expression. An even more attractive possibility as a model for Du Fay would be the lovely *Confort d'amours*, which also has an austere cantus and which makes good use of augmented and diminished intervals in a rich texture.[11]

It may be important that Du Fay wrote both an ars subtilior essay and a musica ficta essay, while Binchois, apparently, did not. One wonders about professional reasons beyond patronage and beyond the purity of artistic inspiration for writing such pieces. Du Fay does not hesitate, throughout his career, to overwhelm a piece of music with compositional skill. This tendency must reflect his status as a *musicus*, someone educated in all areas of musical knowledge; perhaps it is designed to advertise that status. From an early age, he received a specialized book-education that few of his fellow composers could claim.[12] Binchois' training, in contrast, may have been more courtly and less ecclesiastical.[13] That Du Fay (along with Dunstaple) is the leading composer of isorhythmic motets for his time, while Binchois penned a single surviving example, may also indicate different backgrounds. At the other end of the spectrum, opposite from Du Fay, stand gentlemen-composers like Briquet, who is represented in *Oxford 213* by a single, simple rondeau.[14] It would be unsympathetic to think of *Resvelliés vous* and *Helas, ma dame* as tokens – certainly Du Fay was inspired by any compositional challenge. It may not be inappropriate, however, to think of them as emblems of status in a diverse musical world.

---

[10] Besseler's remarks are in *Bourdon und Fauxbourdon*, 53–4, and article "Cesaris" in *Die Musik in Geschichte und Gegenwart* (1952), II: cols. 987–8. Modern editions of all surviving pieces attributed to Cesaris in *EFCM*, vol. I.

[11] *Arriere tost* is transmitted by *Oxford 213*, f. 43v; Reaney, ed., *EFCM*, IV: 56; *Confort d'amours* in *Oxford 213*, f. 115v; *EFCM*, IV: 18.

[12] See, for example, Alejandro Enrique Planchart, "The Early Career of Guillaume Du Fay," *Journal of the American Musicological Society* 46 (1993), especially 351.

[13] See the discussion of Binchois' biography by Strohm, *The Rise of European Music*, 190–1.

[14] *Ma seul amour* is transmitted by *Oxford 213*, f. 96v. On Briquet and music for Philip the Bold's *Cour d'amour* during the early years of the fifteenth century, see Craig Wright, *Music at the Court of Burgundy, 1364–1419: a Documentary History*, Musicological Studies 27 (Henryville: Institute of Mediaeval Music, 1979), 134–7. As for Du Fay's strong representation in isorhythmic motets and Binchois' weaker representation, patterns of survival for sources also account for the difference, most likely: Du Fay wrote for Italian occasions, and Binchois for Burgundian ones, and Italian sources far outnumber northern ones for the first half of the fifteenth century.

Terzfreiheit

Terzfreiheit was Besseler's term for the alternating use of major third and minor third in a single melody.[15] It is useful, I think, to distinguish between two slightly differing usages. Pre-cadential lowered thirds may represent an initial stage that was then expanded into a more purely melodic practice. The pre-cadential practice occurs regularly in the older fascicles of *Oxford 213*.[16] Later, especially in Du Fay's songs that move in tempus perfectum, a more purely melodic *Terzfreiheit* leaves a distinctive imprint on lyric melody. With spectacular results, Du Fay then transfers melodic *Terzfreiheit* to motets like *Nuper rosarum* and, at the end of his life, *Ave regina celorum*. The technique is one of great importance, so it fittingly concludes our survey of discursive inflections. Although there are ample precedents for Du Fay's practice, he does not seem to have inspired any followers, and again one has the impression of him standing at the end of a tradition. Here and elsewhere, this composer does not easily fill the familiar historiographic role so often assigned to him of path-breaker for a musical Renaissance.

Heavy chromaticism in *Helas, ma dame* obscures the simplicity of pre-cadential lowered thirds. More typically, the gesture is isolated, as in this final cadence of *Quel fronte signorille* (Ex. 4.5).[17] *C* is emphasized much more strongly than *G* in this song, and if not for the final cadence it would unquestionably be perceived as the main pitch; put differently, *c* is the main pitch and the piece ends unexpectedly away from it. The lowered third may be interpreted in light of that analysis: *b*-natural, as leading tone to *c*, yields to *b*-flat before the final cadence on *g*. If the flat were not there, *b*-natural would be left hanging as a would-be leading tone.[18] When Du Fay expanded *Quel fronte signorille* to make *Craindre vous vueil*, he added a phrase at the end that brings the rondeau to a conclusion on *c*. This expansion points to the severe limitations of modal analysis based on

[15] *Bourdon und Fauxbourdon*, 41–4.

[16] To cite a few examples: Loqueville – presumably one of Du Fay's teachers at Cambrai – uses *b*-flat before cadences on *G* in several songs from fascicle 6 of *Oxford 213* (*Je vous pri, Puis que je suy amoureux*, and *Pour mesdisans*; all edited by Reaney, *EFCM*, III). There is an extended pre-cadential use of *b*-flat in *Dame que j'ay loingtamp servie* (*Oxford 213*, f. 62v; Reaney, ed., *EFCM*, IV: 34). The gesture is used, extraordinarily, on *A*-flat (with ending on *F*) in Vide's *Il m'est si greif* (*Oxford 213*,

f. 77; ed. Marix, *Les musiciens de la cour de Bourgogne*, 21); and, even more extraordinarily, on *D*-flat (with ending on *B*-flat) in *Je vueil vivre* (*Oxford 213*, f. 124v; Reaney, ed. *EFCM*, IV: 25 – the flat is placed low, but I think that Reaney has interpreted it correctly).

[17] *Oxford 213*, f. 73.

[18] The concept of "leading tone" is relevant to this music only in the restricted sense that we might think of inflections as having tendency, as I have suggested in Chapter 1.

Example 4.5 *Quel fronte signorille,* closing measures (after *Guillaume Dufay Opera Omnia,* VI: 11)

final.[19] Pre-cadential lowered thirds cannot be read modally, either, and one must read the technique in terms of its impact on the cadence. A related gesture is the much rarer pre-cadential lowered seventh, which Binchois and Du Fay each use.[20]

When the lowered third is signed in one voice and the raised seventh, functioning as leading tone, is signed in another (or, when both are signed in the same voice, one after the other), then an augmented or diminished interval is implied, generating pre-cadential tension. In *C'est bien raison*

[19] For discussion of the chronological priority of the two songs, with references to additional literature, see Fallows, *The Songs of Guillaume Dufay:* 44–6. Pirrotta argues that the final cadence of *Quel fronte signorille* is "disturbing and unsatisfactory," and that the piece should end on an abbreviated return at measure 4; see "On Text Forms from Ciconia to Dufay," in *Aspects of Medieval and Renaissance Music: a Birthday Offering to Gustave Reese,* ed. Jan LaRue (New York: Norton, 1966), 679–82. To legitimize the more regular ending, one would want to cite similar examples of unexpected finals, such as Machaut's *Biauté qui toutes autres pere* and, closer to the point, Du Fay's *Je me complains, Vostre bruit,* and *Par le regard.* I discuss these songs (and the suggestion by Howard Brown that they should be negotiated in a way similar to that suggested by Pirrotta for *Quel fronte signorille*) in "Genre, Style and Compositional Technique," Chapter 2, especially 104–8. Jacques Vide's *Espoir m'est venu conforter* plays with the same idea (*Oxford 213,* f. 49v; ed. Marix, *Les musiciens de la cour de Bourgogne,* 20). The piece ends on *a/aa* and the final cadence is preceded by *b*-flat. Clearly, it is not an early example of Phrygian mode (which will not be

favored until mid-century). Rather, the ending is away from the main pitch, *d,* which marks the midpoint of the rondeau and marks the first cadence (in m. 2) – significantly, the phrase begins on *a.* An alternative is to view endings like this as being located on the *confinal* of the mode; this is discussed by Howard Brown, among others; see "A Rondeau with a One-line Refrain Can Be Sung," *Ars Lyrica* 3 (1986), 31–2. Of that argument, one would have to ask how even more radical endings, like that of *De plus en plus* (see Introduction), can be modally accommodated, and whether the analysis does not depend on one of the many escape hatches built into the late medieval modal system – depend on them to the degree that the analytical model is stripped of its rigor.

[20] In Binchois' *Adieu, adieu mon joieulx souvenir,* the contratenor has *B*-flat before a weak arrival on *C* in the final line; Rehm, ed., *Die Chansons von Gilles Binchois,* 1. In Binchois' *Je ne pouroye,* the contratenor contributes *E*-flat before a weak arrival on *F* in the final line; ed. *ibid.,* 19. And in Du Fay's *Las, que feray,* the contratenor does precisely the same thing. The lowered seventh makes the raised seventh fresher at the final cadence.

Example 4.6 Du Fay's *C'est bien raison*, mm. 16–19 (after *Guillaume Dufay Opera Omnia*, VI: 31)

(Ex. 4.6), for example, *aa*-natural (presumably; there is doubt since *aa*-flat is signed three breves earlier) is followed by *aa*-flat in the cantus; then, to prepare the cadence, *a*-flat in the tenor is followed by *b*-natural in the contratenor and *e*-natural in the cantus. The chromatic mix has the effect of intensifying the sense that the voices move in contrary directions. It is as if the accidentals produce a centripetal force; the implied augmented intervals repel the voices out, away from each other, before blending together in the arrival on a perfect sonority. Augmented intervals function centripetally, diminished intervals centrifugally. Even though they are only implied, these pre-cadential augmented and diminished intervals may be heard as a specific manifestation of the general principle, often promoted in late medieval theory going back at least to Anonymous 2, that dissonances make consonances sweeter.[21]

The typical format for conflicting signatures, with one "extra" flat in the tenor, generates a polyphonic version of pre-cadential lowered thirds. We have observed in Chapter 3 how the extra flat in a tenor may function as lowered second that generates *mi*-cadences. It may also function as lowered third (*b*-flat in a cadence to *G*, *e*-flat in a cadence to *C*) which is given added weight by virtue of the cross relation between tenor and cantus (as happens in a single voice in *Quel fronte signorille*). In *Belle veulliés moy retenir*, for example, the signature in the tenor of *b*-flat and *E*-flat causes lowered-third cadences on *G* and *C*, along with *mi*-cadences on *D*.[22] Exceptionally, neither flat is used in the signature for the cantus; as a result, *b*-natural in

[21] Cited by Richard Crocker, "Discant, Counterpoint and Harmony," *Journal of the American Musicological Society* 15 (1962), 4.

[22] *Oxford 213*, f. 50v. Hans Schoop observes the interesting fact of four propinquity sharps having been scratched out of the contratenor's part; *Entstehung und Verwendung der Handschrift Oxford Bodleian Library, Canonici misc. 213*, 108.

the cantus leads to strong cadences on *c*, and *e*-natural leads to strong cadences on *f*. The cadential functions are neatly distributed, and the cross relations invigorate the various tendency tones (Ex. 4.7). One often discovers Du Fay using a variety of cadential types, and here we see how the conflicting signature format gives him a good start in that direction, even before putting a note on the page. Once again we have come upon the idea that notated evidence (including the *lack* of accidentals) may be regarded as not only complete but also structural.

The tension of the cross relation drives the piece forward. This is the general principle that probably accounts for pre-cadential lowered thirds, and it may partly explain Du Fay's interest in conflicting signatures. We may take as one measure of skill, I think, a composer's ability to highlight the respective functions of pitches that stand in cross-relationship with one another, while, at the same time, he is able to keep them apart.[23] In supplying editorial inflections that he assumed were implied through performance practices of the period, Besseler often eliminated cross relations. A few of Du Fay's carefully chosen flats in the second part of *Ne je ne dors*, for example, caused Besseler to imagine 27 implied flats in the space of twelve measures. Besseler was bothered, in this song, by a diminished-fourth leap in the cantus (mm. 21–2), and by a pre-cadential diminished fifth between cantus and tenor (m. 15). I would keep them both, and I would even keep the brief crunches of *aa*-flat versus *aa*-natural (m. 23) and *aa*-natural versus *a*-flat (m. 26) – they occur on weak beats, and they resolve in contrary motion by step, as one assumes they should.[24] Tinctoris describes and gives in musical example exactly this situation. By doing so, he makes its legitimacy crystal clear, even though he would probably prefer that it be avoided.[25]

---

[23] For a splendid earlier example see Baude Cordier's *Se cuer d'amant*, recently edited by Reinhard Strohm, *The Rise of European Music*, 142. Unquestionably, the skillful use of conflict between *bb*-natural in the cantus and *b*-flat in tenor and contratenor goes a long way towards keeping the polyphonic flow fresh; this is important, given the repetitive melody (as analyzed by Strohm). The composer takes care that the two versions of *b* are used according to their respective functions and kept apart. *b*-flat is used in the tenor in two and only two ways: it moves cadentially towards *a* (as lowered second) and towards *G* (as lowered third). *bb*-natural is used freely in the cantus and for a cadence on *cc* in measure 6.

[24] This agrees largely with David Fallows, *The Songs of Guillaume Dufay*, 209–10. I would note, however, that Fallows bases his analysis in part on his discovery that

Besseler missed an accidental in the source. I would say (as I did in my dissertation, "Genre, Style and Compositional Technique," 121 and n. 70) that Besseler's emendations are unnecessary even without the missed accidental. In some cases, Fallows is more willing to go along with some of Besseler's recommendations that seem to me excessive. See, for example, his discussion of the last phrase of *Or pleust a dieu* (*The Songs of Guillaume Dufay*, 167–8); I see no need for *e*-flats and *aa*-flats in the cantus. My response to Fallows's thoughtful hesitance regarding *Mille bonjours je vous presente* (*The Songs of Guillaume Dufay*, 174–6) would be similar.

[25] The passage is quoted and discussed by Urquhart, "Cross-Relations by Franco-Flemish Composers after Josquin," 29–31.

Example 4.7 Two-voiced, contrapuntal framework for cadences in *Belle veulliés moy retenir*

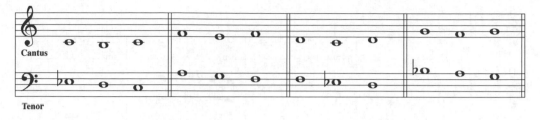

An attitude of purification can be detected in Besseler's editing. He wants to see and hear a Du Fay who anticipates later refinements in counterpoint – and, ultimately, in tonality. He is constructing a Renaissance Du Fay, and imagined traditions of performance practice help him to do it. With Du Fay, perhaps more than any other composer, the textual problem of unnotated inflections mixes not only with musical analysis but with historiography. The impact of the musicological tradition that Besseler represents (which goes back at least to Riemann) should not be underestimated.[26] Du Fay is awkwardly pushed into a vision of the musical Renaissance, which does not easily define itself at this early date. Perhaps the effort to impose modal analysis on his music may be read in the same way, if we think of that effort as a search for complete syntactic control over pitch relations. It is a revealing comment on modern historiography: the urge to capture Du Fay as a tonal composer is, in part, a different manifestation of the urge to capture him as a modal composer. Both projects, at heart, seek to impose far-reaching systems of rational control on his music, and it is easy enough to relate this control to the concept of a musical Renaissance.

*

In Chapter 3, we observed some correlation between changing mensural preferences (as noted by Besseler) and a less consistent though still noteworthy change in preference for sharps versus flats. I suggested that for Du Fay, especially, there is a movement towards a more relaxed melodic idiom, and that this fresh trend may explain his interest in flats and avoidance of sharps, especially in the cantus. It is not only that he uses flats more often as he explores the expressive possibilities of minor prolation with perfect tempus; he also expands the range of technical application, beyond what he

---

[26] I do not wish to imply that Du Fay did not make his counterpoint with care. For some sensitive observations, see Bonnie Blackburn, "On Compositional Process in the Fifteenth Century," *Journal of the American Musicological Society* 40 (1987), 210–84.

Example 4.8 Du Fay's *Or pleust a dieu qu'a son plaisir*, mm. 1–6 (after *Guillaume Dufay Opera Omnia*, VI: 78)

has received. As I have said, there is ample precedent, in the earlier layers of *Oxford 213*, for the pre-cadential lowered thirds that Du Fay likes to use. There are also a few songs by other composers that may have predated his expansion of this practice in the direction of a more purely melodic *Terzfreiheit*. Nevertheless, the clarity and systematic consistency associated with Du Fay's use of this technique is found in the work of no other chanson composer.

Straightforward pre-cadential lowered thirds occur in a handful of Du Fay's songs that move in major prolation with imperfect tempus (for example, *J'atendray, Je ne suy plus, L'alta belleza tua*); the gesture continues to appear in minor prolation, perfect tempus songs (for example, *Se la face ay pale, Quel fronte signorille*). But the more expansive, melodic use of *Terzfreiheit* occurs only in perfect tempus. Its absence from minor prolation with imperfect tempus suggests that it is part of the same lyric impulse that gives rise to the new mensural preference and (as we have seen in Chapter 3) to fewer sharps, especially in the cantus. From three directions, we may construe Du Fay's more melodic practice as an expansion upon the

Example 4.9 Du Fay's *Ma belle dame, je vous pri,* mm. 25–31 (after *Guillaume Dufay Opera Omnia*, VI: 53)

older, pre-cadential practice. First, the lowered third is moved ahead, to the front of the phrase. For example, consider the first phrase of *Or pleust a Dieu* (Ex. 4.8), which stands as a textbook example of melodic design. The design highlights the inflection, which no longer serves a purely cadential function. By the 1430s, Du Fay has become an unrivaled master of melodic detail, and *Terzfreiheit* is part of his craft.

In *Ma belle dame, je vous pri* (Ex. 4.9) the lowered third occurs in the cantus at the beginning of the final melisma, well before the pre-cadential A-flat in the tenor. This may be how the technique developed historically: composers expanded the pre-cadential gesture by placing the lowered third earlier in the phrase, yielding a technique of greater expressive potential.[27] This event also occurs at the end of the song, and this is the second sense in which Du Fay's mature practice may be read as an expansion of the pre-cadential practice: just as a pre-cadential lowered third marks the end of a phrase, so does Du Fay often use the more melodically weighty inflection towards the end of a piece. He does this in *Ma belle dame, je vous pri, Je prens congié de vous, Navré je sui, Estrinez moy, C'est bien raison* (at the end of each of the two parts of the ballade) and the later *Ne je ne dors.*[28] We have

[27] A similar procedure is followed by Malbecque in *Adieu vous di* (*Oxford 213*, f. 21; Reaney, ed., *EFCM*, II: 100). *b*-flat is used as lowered second, predicting an *ouvert* cadence on *a* for part 1 of the ballade; in part 2, *b*-flat is introduced twice in the superius as lowered third before the final cadence on *G*. Other pieces that recall Du Fay's expanded practice include the lovely *Les mesdisans ont fait raport* (*EFCM*, II: 70) by Johannes Le Grant; Coutreman's *Vaylle que vaylle* (*Oxford 213*, f. 50v; *EFCM*, II: 21); Vide's *Puisque je n'ay plus de maystresse* (*Oxford*

213, f. 49v; ed. Marix, *Les musiciens de la cour de Bourgogne*, 24); Bartholomeus Bruolo's *Entrepris suis par grant lyesse* (*Oxford 213* f. 39v; *EFCM*, V: 70); Hugo de Lantins' *Plaindre m'estuet* (*Oxford 213*, f. 46v; ed. Borren, *Pièces Polyphoniques Profanes de Provenance Liégoises*, 48).

[28] As Karol Berger observes, Besseler transcribed incorrectly *Oxford 213*'s high "*ff*-flat" as *ee*-flat for the cantus of *Navré je sui*; *Musica ficta*, 244, n. 34; see Berger's extensive discussion of this piece on pp. 177–88.

seen similar designs before: in trouvère songs from *MS O* there was some use of accidentals towards the end of the stanza; and Machaut occasionally comes upon the technique of using accidentals in the second part of a rondeau or ballade. Coincidentally, different composers come upon similar designs.

Thirdly, we may read Du Fay as expanding upon older practice in cases where the lowered third brings along additional flats. This happens in *Navré je sui*, *Estrinez moy*, and *Ne je ne dors* – and in the troped *Ave regina celorum* (Ex. 4.1), where *ee*-flat brings along *a*-flat. All of these tendencies show Du Fay using formal control to maximize the effect of his flats. He skillfully controls both local nuance and large-scale design. Even at the extreme range of intense chromaticism (*Helas, ma dame*), the overall context is one of absolute stability. Which is not to say that chromaticism is a purely formal matter, just that it is formally controlled. It is undoubtedly true that Du Fay's chromaticism is bound to the ethos of courtly love. The surprising step is his apotheosis of that ethos, accomplished by transferring chromatic beauty associated with the chanson to Marian motets such as *Nuper rosarum* and the troped *Ave regina celorum*, where lyric flats stand at the center of a stylistic fusion of tremendous, unforeseen power.[29]

Mid-century developments

In the mid-1470s, while the aging Du Fay was preparing for his death and making arrangements to have the troped *Ave regina celorum* sung at the moment of that death, Johannes Tinctoris was writing or about to write a

[29] *Nuper rosarum flores* may be the most written-about piece of medieval music ever. See, most recently – and, on the numerology of the motet, most convincingly – Craig Wright, "Dufay's *Nuper rosarum flores*, King Solomon's Temple, and the Veneration of the Virgin," *Journal of the American Musicological Society* 47 (1994), 395–441. For general remarks on accidentals in the motet and on the transference of chanson techniques to Marian motets, see my "Du Fay's Use of Musica Ficta in Three Motets," forthcoming. I should note here (as I note in the article) that the generic associations of using accidentals in particular ways in chansons but not motets change in the early fifteenth century, when motets begin to take on features of the chanson. Hence, the defense given in the Introduction to this book for isolating one genre, the chanson, for study of accidentals, begins to break down at this point. Du Fay's *Terzfreiheit* occurs mainly with *C*-pieces and *G*-pieces. Rarely does it occur in *F*-pieces (certainly because of the remoteness of *a*-flat); and never does it occur in *D*-pieces (certainly because sharps carry the implication of a propinquity inflection); see my "Genre, Style and Compositional Technique" (especially pp. 108–38) for discussion of these points as well as other associations between accidentals and "tonal types." Du Fay probably transposes the cantus firmus down a fifth in the lower tenor of *Nuper rosarum flores* in order to have *G* as the main pitch (rather than *D*); the transposition allows him to use *Terzfreiheit*, a customary technique for *G*-pieces (but not *D*-pieces). For additional discussion of the influence of the chanson on the motet, see Julie Cumming, "The Aesthetics of the Medieval Motet and Cantilena," *Historical Performance: the Journal of Early Music America* 7 (1994), 71–84.

treatise on modality, *Liber de natura et proprietate tonorum* (1476).[30] There is a bit of poetry in the near coincidence of these events. Tinctoris is about to say something new. Earlier we have considered Johannes de Grocheio (*c.* 1300), who suggests that modality does not govern polyphonic music and vernacular monophony. Then there is the half-hearted summary of how to analyze polyphony modally from the Parisian Anonymous of 1375. A century later, Tinctoris's presentation of this topic shows more serious-ness of purpose, and it cannot be merely by chance that Tinctoris makes his case following a marked decrease in notated accidentals. Tinctoris dedi-cates his modal treatise to Okeghem and Busnoys, whose chansons exem-plify this trend, rather than to the recently deceased Du Fay, whom he surely knew from his years at Cambrai.[31] I do not intend, in these conclud-ing pages, to take up the legitimate controversies regarding details of the relationship between modal theory and compositional practice. My purpose is a limited and general one: the decrease in notated accidentals is a tendency that may be read as a modal phenomenon. Or, put differently: it is a phenomenon that makes modal theory possible. Furthermore, this turn in practice makes Du Fay's chromatically inflected music look much less modal by comparison. Tinctoris's interest in mode would seem to be at odds with Du Fay's chromatic practice, at odds with the discursive flats the composer favors at the end of his life, when he uses them in *Ave regina celorum* to gain the good graces of the Blessed Virgin Mary.

Tinctoris is our foremost witness to musical thought in the second half of the fifteenth century. In *Liber de natura et proprietate tonorum*, he spells out in fine detail his conception of "species" modality. It is a traditional view, novel only in its explicit insistence that the theory applies not only to plainchant, to which it had been applied in the past, but also to polyphony. Distinct patterns of half steps and whole steps define the various species of fourths, fifths, and octaves. The four main modes, *protus*, *deuterus*, *tritus*, and *tetrardus*, are distinguished from one another by their use of different combinations of these different species. *Protus* mode, in its authentic arrangement, for example, uses the "first type of fifth" (whole tone, semi-tone, whole tone, whole tone) and the "first type of fourth" (whole tone, semitone, whole tone), the latter above the former. Tinctoris may well have derived species modality directly from Marchetto of Padua, just as he and

---

[30] Ed. Albert Seay, *Liber de natura et proprietate tonorum*, Corpus Scriptorum de musica 22 (n.p.: American Institute of Musicology, 1975), I: 65–104. Translated edition by Albert Seay as *Concerning the Nature and Propriety of Tones* (Colorado Springs: Colorado College Music Press, 1976).

[31] Planchart suggests that Tinctoris's visit to Cambrai in 1460 was specifically for the purpose of studying with Du Fay: "The Early Career of Guillaume Du Fay," 367–8, n. 100.

others got a variety of theory from Marchetto.[32] But Marchetto had never mentioned or in any way implied that modal theory has anything to do with polyphonic music. That Tinctoris is so committed to the idea would seem to reflect the diatonic trends of the mid-fifteenth century.

Tinctoris is literal-minded about the procedure for identifying intervallic species and determining mode. For this reason, his approach is at odds with Du Fay's discursive accidentals; it would be absurd to apply it to *Helas, ma dame*, for example. Now, it is true that Du Fay likes a melody with firm boundaries, and that these boundaries often yield melodic contours that mark strong fourths, fifths, and octaves. This tendency may be taken as a guide for making melodies that does not necessarily have anything to do with modal theory. So often with Du Fay, the definition of a main pitch is over-determined, by various harmonic and melodic means. Almost inevitably, these means include outlining fifth and octave above the main pitch (or pitches). Then, having achieved this stable definition of the main pitch, the markers of expression lie in other, less predictable qualities of line. Du Fay's discursive accidentals do not indicate a complicated modality; rather, they indicate, at best, a hollow modality – or, if one thinks that Grocheio's opinion still stands, the irrelevance of modality to polyphony and to secular songs. As I have suggested in the Introduction to this book, it is possible to take this point in the direction of saying that chromaticism gains expressive strength by virtue of *departing from* a diatonic pitch field which may be quantified through modal theory. That is quite different from saying that the expressive devices are somehow subservient to modal control.[33]

---

[32] Powers, "Mode," 392–5.

[33] This points towards the problem with Leo Treitler's "Tone System in the Secular Works of Guillaume Dufay," *Journal of the American Musicological Society* 18 (1965), 131–69. Here is a key series of thoughts (pp. 133–4): "The tonal coherence of melodies depends on their construction of phrases that are made on one or the other member of a single pentachord-tetrachord pair. That coherence is not upset by the appearance of a phrase belonging to some other pentachord or tetrachord, as long as no ultimate ambiguities arise regarding the prevailing species. This doctrine appears, then, as a workable criterion for the determination of mode and, in general, as a genuine analytical tool. From the point of view of the composer it means that the choice of a tone system determines a great deal about the construction of the melody." In response, one must say that it is not the prevailing species but the prevailing *pitch* that commonly yields coherence; often enough, the melodies do not systematically define consistent fifths and fourths. Also, that there may be no one-dimensional coherence at all, either because more than one pitch is emphasized (see note 19, above) or because no species "prevails" (as with *Terzfreiheit*). For further comments on Treitler's approach, see my "Genre, Style and Compositional Technique," 78–84. A contemporary voice supporting my point of view is Johannes Gallicus, who states in *Ritus canendi* (between 1458 and 1464) that secular songs (*cantus seculares et lascivos*) are not subject to the traditional rules of plainchant, including those rules related to the modal species of fourths and fifths; Albert Seay, ed., *Johannes Gallicus: Ritus Canendi (Pars Secunda)* (Colorado Springs: Colorado College Music Press, 1981), 41.

Having said all of this, it is ironic indeed to discover that the only poly-phonic song Tinctoris names in his modal treatise may have been com-posed by Du Fay; moreover, the song may not have been modal at all in its original cast. Tinctoris labels the cantus of *Le Serviteur* as first "irregular" mode. By "irregular," he means that the mode has been transposed from its normal location, which, in this case, means that the piece is *protus* mode, transposed down a whole step ("*C*-Dorian"). The song is probably by Du Fay, though only one of the fourteen surviving sources – a huge number – gives an attribution. Since it was transmitted anonymously so often, it is possible that Tinctoris did not know who wrote it.[34]

Besseler doubted the attribution, and he thought that the composer must have been younger than Du Fay. He edited the song according to *MS Oporto 714*, which has uniform signatures of *B*-flat and *E*-flat in all three voices. *MS Wolfenbüttel 287*, however, transmits the piece with signatures of *B*-flat only. *E*-flats are then signed internally, but only for measures 5 (tenor), 24 (contratenor), 25 (tenor), and 26 (cantus); in other words, this version features *Terzfreiheit*.[35] The prominent *e*-flats in the imitative figure of measures 25–6 make a striking effect, contrasting with previous *e*-natu-rals. In this reading the piece sounds more like Du Fay and less like the work of a younger composer. (Some sources carry *a*-flat towards the end, extend-ing the resemblance to Du Fay's practice.) It is not difficult to imagine late fifteenth-century scribes having trouble with the more "difficult" chro-matic reading, for they would not have had much experience with *Terzfreiheit*. Combining the advice of *difficilior lectio potior* with the various stylistic fingerprints that support an attribution to Du Fay, we are led to the likely priority of this very unmodal reading. In citing the song, Tinctoris must have been thinking of the uniform reading, which is very much *C*-Dorian and much less interesting, though more in step with the times by 1476.

*

[34] Peter Reidemeister argued that the chanson is by Du Fay; he compared it with *Par le regard*; see *Die Chanson-Handschrift 78 C 28 des Berliner Kupferstichkabinetts* (Munich: E. Katzbichler 1973), 62ff. For a full critical report on the sources and further information on the attribution, see David Fallows, *The Songs of Guillaume Dufay*, 259–65.

[35] *MS MC 871* transmits the piece similarly to *Wolfenbüttel*, but it has signatures of two flats for tenor and contratenor – according to the edition of the piece by Isabel Pope and Masakata Kanazawa, *The Musical Manuscript Montecassino 871* (Oxford: Clarendon Press,

1978), 333–5. The superius in this source has no signed *E*-flats, even in measure 26. *MS Dijon 517* appears to have an *E*-flat signature for the contratenor only; in the facsimile edition of the manuscript the flat is faint on system 1, clear on system 2, and apparently absent on system 3; *Dijon Bibliothèque Publique Manuscript 517*, intro. Dragan Plamenac, Publications of Medieval Musical Manuscripts 12 (Brooklyn, n.d.). Like *Wolfenbüttel*, *Dijon 517* has *E*-flat signed in the superius at measure 26, *E*-flat signed in the tenor at measures 5 and 25, and *E*-flat signed in the contratenor at measure 24.

Tinctoris dedicates his modal treatise to "the most famous and most celebrated teachers of the art of music, Sir Johannes Okeghem, first chaplain of
the Most Christian King of France, and Master Antoine Busnois, singer for
the most illustrious Duke of Burgundy."[36] Perhaps this is nothing more
than name dropping, but it is tantalizing to speculate that Tinctoris may be
telling us something about how these composers thought about their own
music, however overly systematic and pedantic his own rendering of those
thoughts may have been. There are precious few accidentals signed in chansons by Okeghem and Busnoys. Given the many escape hatches built into
the modal system, it would seem that virtually any music from the late
Middle Ages that is predominantly notated within the pitch field of the
Guidonian gamut is capable of being analyzed modally. That is possible for
lightly chromatic music, too, but the overwhelmingly diatonic notation of
songs by Okeghem and Busnoys makes modal analysis easy.[37]

    It is rare to find more than one or two internal accidentals in Okeghem's
songs, and those that we do find rarely cause much of an event. *Fors seulement l'actente* (Ex. 4.10) has a surprising *e*-flat in the first phrase. One must
wonder whether the inflection is authorial – it is so exceptional that the
question must be raised, yet it is so lovely that one would rather not linger
on that question. If Okeghem put it there, then he has taken care to maximize its effect: it stands in cross relation to *e*-natural in the cantus, one
measure earlier, and it outlines an indirect diminished fifth with the
opening *a*.[38] Less problematically, *Baisiés moy* has *e*-flat just before the
ouvert arrival at the midpoint on *D/f*-sharp (recalling, with both
inflections, the harmonic logic analyzed in Du Fay's *Helas, ma dame*).[39]
There is an attractive movement through *E*-flat in *La despourveue*.[40]

    Peter Urquhart has cleared up an uncharacteristic passage in Busnoys' *Je
ne puis vivre ainsi tousjours*. A non-authorial revision of the piece introduced troubling inflections that caused several modern-day editors to
imagine a large-scale "modulation" through all three voices; the authorial

[36] *Concerning the Nature and Propriety of Tones*, 1.

[37] See, for example, Leeman Perkins's analysis of
chansons in *The Mellon Chansonnier* (New Haven: Yale
University Press, 1979), II: 24–50. As I have already
implied, my purpose here is not to argue in favor of
modal analysis at a close level of detail; rather, my
purpose is more general than that. The controversies
surrounding modal analysis even during the High
Renaissance are well known; one can gain a sense of the
complexities surrounding the topic from Harold Powers,
"Mode," *The New Grove Dictionary of Music and*

Musicians, XII: especially 397–419.

[38] Edition by Richard Wexler with Dragan Plamenac,
Johannes Ockeghem: Collected Works (Boston: American
Musicological Society, 1992), III: 62. Wexler reports in
the critical notes (p. lxv) that the flat is absent from four
of the seven sources. Only two of the seven sources give
an attribution to Okeghem, while the others give no
attribution.

[39] *Ibid.* 60.

[40] *Ibid.* 70.

Example 4.10 Okeghem's *Fors seulement*, mm. 1–10 (after Wexler and Plamenac, eds., *Johannes Ockeghem: Collected Works*, III: 62)

version of the phrase is uninflected.[41] Some 70 songs are attributed to Busnoys (fourteen with conflicting attributions to another composer). Overwhelmingly, Busnoys tends to write without accidentals. I have already mentioned (in Chapter 3) *Je ne fais plus*, which has forceful chromaticism before the poetic caesura after the fourth syllable; since there are conflicting attributions and since the inflection is uncharacteristic of Busnoys, perhaps the balance shifts towards one of the rivals. One motet deserves mention here, since it shows late and exceptional use of a gesture we have seen before. A setting by Busnoys of the antiphon *Regina celi letare* has, in its first phrase, a jarring *f*-sharp after a stable beginning on *f*, which is

[41] Urquhart, "Three Sample Problems of Editorial Accidentals in Chansons by Busnoys and Ockeghem," forthcoming. I thank Professor Urquhart for sending me a copy of this article before its publication. The authoritative version – by standards of certainty that one must get used to in fifteenth-century studies, Urquhart's argument is persuasive enough to justify this description, I think – is edited by Eugénie Droz and Geneviève Thibault, *Trois Chansonniers Français du XVe Siècle* (Paris: Imprimé par F. Paillart, 1927), 64. The revised version is edited by Leeman Perkins, *The Mellon Chansonnier*, I: 65. Two songs by Busnoys show use of pre-cadential lowered sevenths: see *Je ne demande autre de gré* and *Je ne demande lialté*, both ed. Brown, *A Florentine Chansonnier from the Time of Lorenzo the Magnificent*, 306 and 118.

the stable reference for the paraphrased chant and for the motet as a whole. The event recalls Solage's *Corps feminin* and, less precisely though perhaps more directly, Du Fay's *Resvelliés vous*.[42] Busnoys must have written this piece at least 30 years after Du Fay composed his ballade. But Busnoys is a composer who shows exceptional awareness of older music (especially, it would seem, of Du Fay's music), so a direct influence would not seem to be out of the question.[43] Composers may well have kept copies of their compositions with them all of their lives – Du Fay is likely to have been such a composer. Inevitably, they would have made the portfolio available to students and fellow composers. Tinctoris may have thought that no music composed more than 40 years before 1475 was worth hearing, but there is no reason to project that attitude onto Busnoys.

*

Michael Baxandall has described Alberti's idea of composition (*compositio*; the concept was derived from rhetoric) as "a systematic harmonization of every element in a picture towards one desired effect."[44] That does not seem like a bad way to think about modality – if what we wish to make out of modality is a source of syntactic control. It is possible that the diatonic trends of the mid-fifteenth century were thought of in this way. Are the effects of discursive accidentals analogous to multiple perspective? If that is pushing the analogy too hard, then it is perhaps easier to imagine how accidentals might have been felt as getting in the way of complete, rational control of the pitch field. By "rational," I mean, first, hierarchical ordering around a single main pitch; second, a stable and uniform pitch field. Theorists of all times and places have been interested in systems, and composers do not necessarily share that interest. Yet modality and the diatonic trends seem to go hand in hand. Modality grows stronger in music theory, and eventually the cry becomes rather shrill: "even if you under-

[42] Edition of *Regina celi letare* by Richard Taruskin, *Antoine Busnoys: the Latin-texted Works* (New York: Broude, 1990), II: 168.

[43] On Busnoys's exceptional late use of the techniques associated with isorhythm – a tradition that would have been represented to him mainly by Du Fay, one imagines – see my "Vestiges of the Isorhythmic Tradition in Mass and Motet, c. 1450–1475," *Journal of the American Musicological Society* 44 (1991), 1–56. Building upon Alejandro Planchart's suggestion that Du Fay may be the author of Mass Proper cycles from the 1440s, Anna Maria Busse Berger has credited Du Fay with a redefinition of the mensuration sign "O2"; *Mensuration*

and Proportion Signs: Origins and Evolution (Oxford: Oxford University Press, 1993), 22–3. If the attribution is accepted, then it implies an even greater connection between Du Fay and Busnoys, for whom O2 is, exceptionally, a favored sign.

[44] Michael Baxandall, *Painting and Experience in Fifteenth Century Italy: a Primer in the Social History of Pictorial Style* (Oxford: Clarendon Press, 1972), 135. See also Baxandall, *Giotto and the Orators: Humanist Observers of Painting in Italy and the Discovery of Pictorial Composition, 1350–1450* (Oxford: Clarendon Press, 1972), 130–9.

stood consonances and dissonances, . . . and you did not understand the modes, and, consequently, their cadences, you would be like a blind man, who just goes around and has no guide and at last finds that he has lost the way."[45] Without proper attention to modes, polyphony will sound like a "horrible chaos of mixed-up consonances."[46]

Helas, ma dame may, indeed, have represented modal chaos, at least in retrospect; and so might the chromatic redactions in *Trouvère MS O*, the chromatic experiments by Machaut, and a variety of music by late four-teenth-century composers. By 1500, there is greater awareness in poly-phonic music not only of modality but also of hexachords; there is, as well, gradual movement towards a more systematic sense of intervallic decorum. Earlier, and especially in chansons, we discover accidentals used to *disrupt* these very standards. Accidentals are the primary tool for dis-turbing a stable pitch field, for suddenly redirecting the polyphonic flow, for generating jagged and difficult leaps of line, for imparting harmonic tension. As the High Renaissance approaches, the situation changes. The concepts are not new; what is new is that they are held up as pre-eminent values for polyphony. What is striking about the earlier period is not the strict adherence to "irregular" qualities caused by discursive accidentals but, rather, the continuing possibility, explored by the leading composers, of writing songs that feature them to one degree or another.

Against the modal vehemence of the High Renaissance, virtually all that we have from earlier writers is the whispered, anecdotal aside that musica ficta is a source of beauty, particularly in chansons. But, of course, we have something far more valuable than opinions – we have a fairly large body of inflected songs, many of them compelling on artistic grounds that we can work to locate historically. The songs are often fitfully transmitted, making textual criticism difficult, and they are even harder to interpret. Yet their lyric beauty comes through, bridging the gap of so many centuries and of such different sets of musical values, to help define one of the great tradi-tions in the history of European music.

---

[45] ". . . perche, ancora c'havesti cognitione delle consonantie, et dissonantie . . ., et poi non havesti cognitione delli Tuoni, et conseguentemente delle lor cadenze, saresti à modo d'un cieco, che pur và, et non hà guida, e nel fine si truova giù di strada. . ." From *Ragionamento di musica* by Pietro Pontio (Parma 1588), quoted and translated in Bernhard Meier, *The Modes of Classical Vocal Polyphony*, trans. Ellen S. Beebe (New York: Broude, 1988), 25–6, n. 5.

[46] Seth Calvisius, *Melopoiia* (Erfurt, 1592), quoted and translated in Meier, *The Modes of Classical Vocal Polyphony*, 26, n. 6.

Works cited

1 Music theory treatises cited

Anonymous (cited in this book as "Parisian Anonymous of 1375"). *Tractatus de contrapuncto*. Ed. and trans. Oliver B. Ellsworth as *The Berkeley Manuscript: University of California Music Library, MS. 744 (olim Philipps 4450)*. Greek and Latin Music Theory 2. Lincoln, Nebr., and London: University of Nebraska Press, 1984.

Anonymous ("Anonymous 2"). *Tractatus de discantu*. Ed. and trans. Albert Seay as *Anonymous II: Tractatus de Discantu (Treatise Concerning Discant)*. Critical Texts with Translations 1. Colorado Springs: Colorado College Music Press, 1978.

Anonymous ("Anonymous of St. Emmeram"). *De Musica Mensurata: the Anonymous of St. Emmeram*. Ed. and trans. Jeremy Yudkin. Bloomington: Indiana University Press, 1990.

Anonymous ("Anonymous 4"). *De mensuris et discantu*. Ed. Fritz Reckow as *Der Musiktraktat des Anonymus 4*. 2 vols. Beihefte zum Archiv für Musikwissenschaft 4–5. Wiesbaden: Franz Steiner, 1967.

Anonymous ("Anonymous 11"). *Tractatus de musica plana et mensurabili*. Ed. and trans. Richard Wingell, "Anonymous XI (CS III): an Edition, Translation, and Commentary." Ph.D. diss., University of Southern California, 1973.

Anonymous. *Sequitur de synemenis*. Ed. and trans. Jan Herlinger, *Prosdocimo de' Beldomandi: Brevis Summula Proportionum Quantum ad Musicam Pertinet*. Lincoln, Nebr.: University of Nebraska Press, 1987.

Bartolomeo Ramis de Pareia. *Musica practica*. Ed. Johannes Wolf, Publikationen der Internationalen Musikgesellschaft 2. Leipzig: Breitkopf und Härtel, 1901. Trans. edition by Clement A. Miller, Musicological Studies and Documents 44. Neuhausen-Stuttgart: American Institute of Musicology, 1993.

Boethius, Anicius Manlius Severinus. *De institutione musica*. Trans. edition by Calvin M. Bower as *Fundamentals of Music*. Ed. Claude V. Palisca. New Haven: Yale University Press, 1989.

Hothby, John. *La caliopea legale*. Ed. Edmond de Coussemaker in *Histoire de l'harmonie au moyen âge*. Paris: Librairie Archéologique de Victor Didron, 1852.

Jacques de Liège. *Speculum musicae*. Ed. R. Bragard, Corpus Scriptorum de Musica 3. 7 vols. N.p.: American Institute of Musicology, 1955–73.

Jehan de Murs. *Ars contrapuncti secundum Johannem de Muris*. Ed. Edmond de Coussemaker, Scriptorum de Musica Medii Aevi: Nova Series a Gerbertina Altera 3. Paris: A. Durand, 1869.

Jerome de Moravia. *Tractatus de musica*. Ed. S. M. Cserba, Freiburger Studien zur Musikwissenschaft 2. Regensburg: Friedrich Pustet, 1935.

Johannes de Garlandia. *De mensurabili musica: Kritische Edition mit Kommentar und Interpretation der Notationslehre*. Ed. Erich Reimer, Beihefte zum Archiv für Musikwissenschaft 10–11. Wiesbaden: Franz Steiner, 1972. Trans. edition by Stanley Birnbaum as *Concerning Measured Music*. Colorado College Music Press Translations 9. Colorado Springs: Colorado College Music Press, 1978.

Johannes de Grocheio. *De musica*. Facsimile in Ernst Rohloff, ed., *Die*

Quellenhandschriften zum Musiktraktat des Johannes de Grocheio. Leipzig:
Deutscher Verlag für Musik, 1972. Ed. and trans. Albert Seay as *Johannes de
Grocheo: Concerning Music (De Musica).* Colorado College Music Press
Translations 1. Colorado Springs: Colorado College Music Press, 1967; 2nd edn,
1973.

Johannes Gallicus. *Ritus canendi.* Ed. Albert Seay. Colorado College Music Press Critical
Texts 14. Colorado Springs: Colorado College Music Press, 1981.

Marchetto da Padua. *Lucidarium in arte musice plane.* Ed. and trans. Jan W. Herlinger.
Chicago: University of Chicago Press, 1985.

Pomerium. Ed. G. Vecchi. Corpus Scriptorum de Musica 6. N.p.: American Institute of
Musicology, 1961.

Petrus Frater dictus Palma Ociosa. *Compendium de discantu mensurabili.* In Johannes
Wolf, ed., "Ein Beitrag zur Diskantlehre des 14. Jahrhunderts." *Sammelbände der
Internationalen Musikgesellschaft* 15 (1913–14), 504–34.

Philippus de Caserta. *Regule contrapuncti.* In Nigel Wilkins, ed., "Some Notes on
Philipoctus de Caserta (*c.* 1360?-*c.* 1435)." *Nottingham Mediaeval Studies* 8 (1964),
82–99.

Prosdocimo de' Beldomandi. *Contrapunctus.* Ed. and trans. Jan W. Herlinger, Greek and
Latin Music Theory 1. Lincoln and London: University of Nebraska Press, 1984.

Tinctoris, Johannes. *Liber de arte contrapuncti.* Ed. Albert Seay, Corpus Scriptorum de
musica 22, II: 11–157. N.p.: American Institute of Musicology, 1975. Ed. and trans.
Albert Seay as *The Art of Counterpoint.* N.p.: American Institute of Musicology,
1961.

Liber de natura et proprietate tonorum. Ed. Albert Seay, Corpus Scriptorum de musica
22, I: 65–104. N.p.: American Institute of Musicology, 1975. Ed. and trans. Albert
Seay as *Johannes Tinctoris: Concerning the Nature and Propriety of Tones.* Colorado
College Music Press Translations 2. Colorado Springs: Colorado College Music
Press, 1976.

Ugolino of Orvieto. *Declaratio musicae disciplinae.* Ed. A. Seay, Corpus Scriptorum de
Musica 7. 3 vols. N.p.: American Institute of Musicology, 1964. Section on musica
ficta ed. and trans. in Andrew Hughes, *Manuscript Accidentals: Ficta in Focus
1350–1450.* Musicological Studies and Documents 27. Rome: American Institute of
Musicology, 1972.

Vitry, Philippe de. *Ars nova.* Ed. G. Reaney, A. Gilles, and J. Maillard. Corpus Scriptorum
de Musica 8. N.p.: American Institute of Musicology, 1964.

Walter of Odington. *De speculatione musice.* Ed. Edmond de Coussemaker, *Scriptorum de
Musica Medii Aevi: Nova Series a Gerbertina Altera,* I: 182–250. Paris: Durand,
1864.

Zarlino, Gioseffo. *Le istitutioni harmoniche: Facsimile of the 1558 Venice Edition.* New York:
Broude, 1965.

2 Literature and editions of music

Allaire, Gaston. "Debunking the Myth of Musica Ficta." *Tijdschrift van de Koninklijke
Vereniging voor Nederlandse Muziekgeschiedenis* 45 (1995), 110–26.

The Theory of Hexachords, Solmization and the Modal System: a Practical Application.
Musicological Studies and Documents 24. N.p.: American Institute of Musicology,
1972.

Apel, Willi. "The Partial Signatures in the Sources up to 1450." *Acta Musicologica* 10 (1938), 1–13.

Apel, Willi. ed. *French Secular Compositions of the Fourteenth Century.* Corpus Mensurabilis Musicae 53. Stuttgart: American Institute of Musicology, 1970–2.

Arlt, Wulf. "Aspekte der Chronologie und des Stilwandels im französischen Lied des 14. Jahrhunderts." In *Aktuelle Fragen der Musikbezogenen Mittelalterforschung: Texte zu einem Basler Kolloquium des Jahres 1975,* Forum Musicologicum: Basler Beiträge zur Musikgeschichte 3 (Wintertur: Amadeus 1982), 193–280.

Aubry, Pierre, with A. Jeanroy, eds. *Le Chansonnier de l'Arsenal (Trouvères du XIIe-XIIIe Siècle): Reproduction Phototypique du Manuscrit 5198 de la Bibliothèque de l'Arsenal.* Paris: Geuthner, 1909.

Beck, Jean Baptiste, ed. *Le Chansonnier Cangé: Manuscrit français no. 846 de la Bibliothèque Nationale de Paris.* Corpus Cantilenarum Medii Aevi 1, 2 vols. Paris: University of Pennsylvania Press, 1927 [facsimile and modern edition].

Bent, Margaret. "A Contemporary Perception of Early Fifteenth-Century Style: Bologna Q 15 as a Document of Scribal Editorial Initiative." *Musica Disciplina* 41 (1987), 183–201.

"Diatonic *Ficta.*" *Early Music History* 4 (1984), 1–48.

"The Machaut Manuscripts *Vg, B* and *E.*" *Musica Disciplina* 37 (1983), 53–82.

"Musica Recta and Musica Ficta." *Musica Disciplina* 27 (1972), 73–100.

"A Note on the Dating of the Trémoïlle Manuscript." In *Beyond the Moon: Festschrift Luther Dittmer,* ed. Bryan Gillingham and Paul Merkley, 217–42. Wissenschaftliche Abhandlungen 53. Ottawa: Institute of Mediaeval Music, 1990.

"The Songs of Dufay: Some Questions of Form and Authenticity." *Early Music* 8 (1980), 454–9.

Bent, Margaret, Lewis Lockwood, Robert Donington, and Stanley Boorman. "Musica Ficta." In *The New Grove Dictionary of Music and Musicians,* ed. Stanley Sadie, XII: 802–11. London: Macmillan, 1980.

Berger, Christian. *Hexachord, Mensur und Textstruktur: Studien zum Französischen Lied des 14. Jahrhunderts.* Beihefte zum Archiv für Musikwissenschaft 35. Stuttgart: Franz Steiner, 1992.

Berger, Karol. "Musica Ficta." In *Performance Practice: Music Before 1600,* ed. Howard Mayer Brown and Stanley Sadie, 107–25. New York: Norton, 1989.

Musica ficta: Theories of Accidental Inflections in Vocal Polyphony from Marchetto da Padova to Gioseffo Zarlino. Cambridge: Cambridge University Press, 1987.

Besseler, Heinrich. *Bourdon und Fauxbourdon: Studien zur Ursprung der Niederländischen Musik.* Revised second edition by Peter Gülke. Leipzig: Breitkopf, 1974.

"Cesaris." In *Die Musik in Geschichte und Gegenwart,* ed. Friedrich Blume, II: cols 987–8. Basel: Bärenreiter, 1952.

Besseler, Heinrich, ed. *Guillaume Dufay Opera Omnia.* Corpus Mensurabilis Musicae 1. 6 vols. N.p.: American Institute of Musicology, 1951–66.

Blackburn, Bonnie J. "On Compositional Process in the Fifteenth Century." *Journal of the American Musicological Society* 40 (1987), 210–84.

Boone, Graeme M. "Dufay's Early Chansons: Chronology and Style in the Manuscript Oxford, Bodleian Library, Canonici misc. 213." Ph. D. diss., Harvard University, 1987.

Borren, Charles van den, ed. *Pièces Polyphoniques Profanes de Provenance Liégoises (XVe siècle).* Flores Musicales Belgicae. Brussels: Editions de la Libraire Encyclopédique, 1950.

Brahney, Kathleen J., ed. *The Lyrics of Thibaut de Champagne.* Garland Library of Medieval Literature, ser. A, vol. 41. New York and London: Garland, 1989.

Brothers, Thomas. "Genre, Style and Compositional Technique in French Music of the Fifteenth Century." Ph.D. diss., University of California, Berkeley, 1991.

"Musica Ficta and Harmony in Machaut's Songs." Forthcoming in *Journal of Musicology.*

"Sharps in *Medée fu:* Questions of Style and Analysis." Forthcoming in *Studi Musicali.*

"Vestiges of the Isorhythmic Tradition in Mass and Motet, *c.* 1450–1475." *Journal of the American Musicological Society* 44 (1991), 1–56.

Brown, Howard M. "A Ballade for Mathieu de Foix: Style and Structure in a Composition by Trebor." *Musica Disciplina* 41 (1987), 75–108.

"A Rondeau with a One-line Refrain Can Be Sung." *Ars Lyrica* 3 (1986), 23–35.

Burstyn, Shai. "The 'Arabian Influence' Thesis Revisited." *Current Musicology* 45–7 (1990), 119–46.

Chailley, Jacques. "Les Premiers Troubadours et les *versus* de L'École d'Aquitaine." *Romania* 76 (1955), 212–39.

Corrigan, Vincent. "Modal Rhythm and the Interpretation of *Trouvére* Song." In *The Cultural Milieu of the Troubadours and Trouvères,* ed. Nancy van Deusen, 125–32. Musicological Studies 62/I. Ottawa: Institute of Mediaeval Music, 1994.

Crawford, David. "Performance and the Laborde Chansonnier: Authenticity of Multiplicities: Musica Ficta." *College Music Symposium* 10 (1970), 107–11.

Crocker, Richard. "Discant, Counterpoint and Harmony." *Journal of the American Musicological Society* 15 (1962), 1–21.

A History of Musical Style. New York: Dover, 1966.

Cumming, Julie. "The Aesthetics of the Medieval Motet and Cantilena." *Historical Performance: the Journal of Early Music America* 7 (1994), 71–84.

Dahlhaus, Carl. "Relationes Harmonicae." *Archiv für Musikwissenschaft* 32 (1975), 208–27.

Studies on the Origin of Harmonic Tonality. Transl. Robert O. Gjerdingen. Princeton: Princeton University Press, 1990.

"Tonsystem und Kontrapunkt um 1500." *Jahrbuch des Staatlichen Instituts für Musikforschung Preussischer Kulturbesitz* 2 (1969), 7–18.

"'Zentrale' und 'Periphere' Züge in der Dissonanztechnik Machauts." *Aktuelle Fragen der Musikbezogenen Mittelalterforschung.* Forum Musicologicum: Basler Beiträge zur Musikgeschichte 3 (Wintertur: Amadeus 1982), 281–306.

Dömling, Wolfgang. *Die Mehrstimmigen Balladen, Rondeaux und Virelais von Guillaume de Machaut: Untersuchungen zum Musikalischen Satz.* Münchner Veröffentlichungen zur Musikgeschichte 16. Tutzing: Hans Schneider, 1970.

Earp, Lawrence. *Guillaume de Machaut: a Guide to Research.* New York: Garland, 1995.

"Lyrics for Reading and Lyrics for Singing in Late Medieval France: the Development of the Dance Lyric from Adam de la Halle to Guillaume de Machaut." In R. Baltzer, et al., ed., *The Union of Words and Music in Medieval Poetry,* 101–31. Austin: University of Texas, 1991.

"Machaut's Role in the Production of Manuscripts of His Works." *Journal of the American Musicological Society* 42 (1989), 461–503.

Review of *Machaut's Mass: an Introduction* and *Compositional Techniques in the Four-*

Part Isorhythmic Motets of Philippe de Vitry and His Contemporaries, both by Daniel
  Leech-Wilkinson. *Journal of the Amercan Musicological Society* 46 (1993), 295–305.
"Scribal Practice, Manuscript Production and the Transmission of Music in Late
  Medieval France: the Manuscripts of Guillaume de Machaut." Ph.D. diss.,
  Princeton University, 1983.
Ellsworth, Oliver B. "The Origin of the Coniuncta: a Reappraisal." *Journal of Music Theory*
  17 (1973), 86–109.
Ellsworth, Oliver B., ed. and trans. *The Berkeley Manuscript: University of California Music
  Library, MS. 744 (olim Philipps 4450)*. Greek and Latin Music Theory 2. Lincoln,
  Nebr., and London: University of Nebraska Press, 1984.
Ensemble Project Ars Nova. *Ars Magis Subtiliter: Secular Music of the Chantilly Codex*.
  New Albion Records, Inc. NA 021 CD DDD. Recorded at Wellesley, Mass., July
  20–22, 1987.
Everist, Mark. *French Motets in the Thirteenth Century*. Cambridge: Cambridge University
  Press, 1994.
Polyphonic Music in Thirteenth-Century France: Aspects of Sources and Distribution.
  New York: Garland, 1989.
"Song Manuscripts of the Middle Ages." Unpublished paper.
Fallows, David. *Dufay*. London: Dent, 1987.
"L'origine du Manuscrit 1328 de Cambrai." *Revue de Musicologie* 62 (1976), 275–80.
"Robertus de Anglia and the Oporto Song Collection." In *Source Materials and the
  Interpretation of Music: a Memorial Volume to Thurston Dart*, ed. Ian D. Bent,
  114–15. London: Stainer and Bell, 1982.
*The Songs of Guillaume Dufay: Critical Commentary to the Revision of Corpus
  Mensurabilis Musicae, ser. 1, vol. VI*. Neuhausen-Stuttgart: American Institute of
  Musicology, 1994.
"Sources, MS, section III, 4: Secular Monophony." In *New Grove Dictionary of Music
  and Musicians*, ed. Stanley Sadie, XVII: 634–49. London: Macmillan, 1980.
Fallows, David, ed. *The Canonici Codex: a Facsimile of Oxford Bodleian Library, MS.
  Canon. Misc. 213*. Chicago: University of Chicago Press, 1995.
Fuller, Sarah. "Guillaume de Machaut: *De toutes flours*." In *Models of Musical Analysis:
  Music Before 1600*, ed. Mark Everist, 41–65. Cambridge, Mass.: Basil Blackwell Ltd.,
  1992.
"Modal Discourse and Fourteenth-Century French Song." Paper read at the 1995
  National Meeting of the American Musicological Society, New York City.
"On Sonority in Fourteenth-Century Polyphony: Some Preliminary Reflections."
  Journal of Music Theory 30 (1986), 35–70.
"Tendencies and Resolutions: the Directed Progression in *Ars Nova* Music." *Journal of
  Music Theory* 36 (1992), 229–58.
Gallo, Ernest. *The Poetria Nova and its Sources in Early Rhetorical Doctrine*. Paris: Mouton,
  1971.
Gallo, F. Alberto. "Alcune Fonti Poco Note di Musica Teorica e Pratica." In *L'ars Nova
  Italiana del Trecento: Convegni di Studi 1961–1967*, ed. Gallo, 49–76. Certaldo:
  Centro di Studi sull'Ars Nova Italiana del Trecento, 1968.
"Beziehungen zwischen grammatischer, rhetorischer und musikalischer Terminologie
  im Mittelalter." D. Heartz and B. Wade, eds., *International Musicological Society,
  Report of the Twelfth Congress Berkeley 1977*, 789. Kassel: Bärenreiter, 1981.

Gaunt, Simon. *Troubadours and Irony.* Cambridge: Cambridge University Press, 1989.

Geoffrey de Vinsauf. *Poetria Nova.* In *The Poetria Nova and its Sources in Early Rhetorical Doctrine,* ed. and trans. Ernest Gallo (Paris: Mouton, 1971).

Gombosi, Otto. Review of *French Secular Music of the Fourteenth Century,* ed. Willi Apel. *The Musical Quarterly* 36 (1950), 607.

Greene, Gordon, ed. *French Secular Music: Ballades and Canons.* Polyphonic Music of the Fourteenth Century 20. Monaco: L'Oiseau-Lyre, 1982.

French Secular Music: Manuscript Chantilly, Musée Condé 564. 2 vols. Polyphonic Music of the Fourteenth Century 18–19. Monaco: L'Oiseau-Lyre, 1981–2.

French Secular Music: Rondeaux and Miscellaneous Pieces. Polyphonic Music of the Fourteenth Century 22. Monaco: L'Oiseau-Lyre, 1989.

French Secular Music: Virelais. Polyphonic Music of the Fourteenth Century 21. Monaco: L'Oiseau-Lyre, 1987.

Günther, Ursula. "Datierbare Balladen des Späten 14. Jahrhunderts, I." *Musica Disciplina* 15 (1961), 39–61.

"Das Ende der Ars Nova." *Die Musikforschung* 16 (1963), 105–20.

"Das Manuskript Modena, Biblioteca Estense, alpha M. 5, 24 (*olim* lat. 568=*Mod*)." *Musica Disciplina* 24 (1970), 17–67.

"Unusual Phenomena in the Transmission of Late 14th Century Polyphonic Music." *Musica Disciplina* 38 (1984), 87–109.

Gutiérrez-Denhoff, Martella, ed. *Der Wolfenbüttel Chansonnier: Untersuchungen zu Repertoire und Überlieferung einer Musikhandschrift des 15. Jahrhunderts und ihres Umkreises.* Wiesbaden: Harrassowitz, 1985.

Der Wolfenbütteler Chansonnier: Herzog August Bibliothek, Wolfenbüttel, Codex Guelf. 287 Extrav. Musikalische Denkmäler 10. Mainz: Schott, 1988.

Hamm, Charles E. *A Chronology of the Works of Guillaume Dufay Based on a Study of Mensural Practice.* Princeton: Princeton University Press, 1964.

general editor. *Census-Catalogue of Manuscript Sources of Polyphonic Music, 1500–1550.* 5 vols. Neuhausen-Stuttgart: American Institute of Musicology, 1979.

Harden, Bettie Jean. "Sharps, Flats and Scribes: 'Musica Ficta' in the Machaut Manuscripts." Ph.D. diss., Cornell University, 1983.

Hasselman, Margaret. "The French Chanson in the Fourteenth Century." Ph.D. diss., University of California, Berkeley, 1970.

Herlinger, Jan W. "Marchetto's Division of the Whole Tone." *Journal of the American Musicological Society* 24 (1981), 193–216.

Herlinger, Jan W., ed. *The Lucidarium of Marchetto of Padua: a Critical Edition, Translation, and Commentary.* Chicago: University of Chicago Press, 1985.

Higgins, Paula. "Music and Musicians at the Sainte-Chapelle of the Bourges Palace, 1405–1515." In *Trasmissione e recezione delle forme di cultura musicale. Atti del XIV Congresso della Società Internazionale di Musicologia,* vol. III, ed. Angelo Pompilio, et. al., 689–701. Turin: Edt, 1990.

Hilliard Ensemble, directed by Paul Hillier. *Recording to Accompany Music of the Middle Ages.* New York: Schirmer Books, 1990.

Hirshberg, Jehoash. "Hexachordal and Modal Structure in Machaut's Polyphonic Chansons." In *Studies in Musicology in Honor of Otto E. Albrecht,* ed. John Walter Hill, 19–42. Kassel: Bärenreiter, 1980.

"The Music of the Late Fourteenth Century: a Study in Musical Style." Ph.D. diss., University of Pennsylvania, 1971.

Hoppin, Richard. *Medieval Music.* New York: Norton, 1978.

Hoppin, Richard, ed. *Anthology of Medieval Music.* New York: Norton, 1978.

Hughes, Andrew. *Manuscript Accidentals: Ficta in Focus 1350–1450.* Musicological Studies and Documents 27. Rome: American Institute of Musicology, 1972.

Hult, David F. *Self-fulfilling Prophecies: Readership and Authority in the First Roman de la Rose.* Cambridge: Cambridge University Press, 1986.

Huot, Sylvia Jean. *From Song to Book: the Poetics of Writing in Old French Lyric and Lyrical Narrative Poetry.* Ithaca: Cornell University Press, 1987.

Karp, Theodore. "Borrowed Material in Trouvère Music." *Acta Musicologica* 34 (1962), 87–101.

"The Trouvère MS Tradition." *Twenty-fifth Anniversary Festschrift (1937–1962): The Department of Music, Queens College of the City University of New York,* ed. Albert Mell, 25–52 (U.S.A: Q. C. Press, 1964).

Kay, Sarah. *Subjectivity in Troubadour Poetry.* Cambridge: Cambridge University Press, 1990.

Kelly, Douglas. *Medieval Imagination: Rhetoric and the Poetry of Courtly Love.* Madison: University of Wisconsin Press, 1978.

Kemp, Walter. *Burgundian Court Song in the Time of Binchois: the Anonymous Chansons of El Escorial, MS V. III. 24.* Oxford: Oxford University Press, 1990.

Kemp, Walter, ed. *Anonymous Pieces in the Chansonnier El Escorial, Biblioteca del Monasterio, cod. V. III. 24.* Corpus Mensurabilis Musicae 77. N.p.: American Institute of Musicology, 1980.

Kenney, Edward J. "Textual Criticism." In *New Encyclopaedia Britannica: Macropaedia,* XVIII: 194. Fifteenth edition. Chicago: Benton, 1981.

Kottick, Edward L. "Flats, Modality, and Musica Ficta in Some Early Renaissance Chansons." *Journal of Music Theory* 12 (1968), 264–80.

Labaree, Robert R. "'Finding' Troubadour Song: Melodic Variability and Melodic Idiom in Three Monophonic Traditions." Ph.D. diss., Wesleyan University, 1989.

Leech-Wilkinson, Daniel. *Machaut's Mass: an Introduction.* Oxford: Clarendon Press, 1990.

"Machaut's *Rose, lis* and the Problem of Early Music Analysis." *Music Analysis* 3 (1984), 9–28.

"*Le Voir Dit* and *La Messe de Nostre Dame:* Aspects of Genre and Style in Late Works of Machaut." *Plainsong and Medieval Music* 2 (1993), 43–73.

Lefferts, Peter M. "Signature-Systems and Tonal Types in the Fourteenth-Century French Chanson." *Plainsong and Medieval Music* 4 (1995), 117–48.

"*Subtilitas* in the Tonal Language of *Fumeux fume.*" *Early Music* 16 (1988), 176–84.

Lerch, Irmgard. *Fragmente aus Cambrai: Ein Beitrag zur Rekonstruktion einer Handschrift mit Spätmittelalterlicher Polyphonie.* Göttinger Musikwissenschaftliche Arbeiten 11. Kassel: Bärenreiter, 1987.

Levitan, Joseph. "Adrian Willaert's Famous Duo *Quidnam ebrietas:* a Composition which Closes Apparently with the Interval of a Seventh." *Tijdschrift van de Vereniging voor Nederlandse Muziekgeschiedenis* 15 (1939), 166–223.

Lockwood, Lewis. "A Sample Problem of *Musica Ficta:* Willaert's *Pater Noster.*" In *Studies in Music History: Essays for Oliver Strunk*, ed. H. S. Powers, 161–82. Princeton: Princeton University Press, 1968.

Lorris, Guillaume de, and Jean de Meun. *The Romance of the Rose*. Trans. Charles Dahlberg. Princeton: Princeton University Press, 1971.

Lowinsky, Edward E. "Foreword." In *Musica Nova*. Monuments of Renaissance Music 1, ed. H. Colin Slim, 5–21. Chicago and London: The University of Chicago Press, 1964.

"The Function of Conflicting Signatures in Early Polyphonic Music." *The Musical Quarterly* 31 (1945), 227–60.

Secret Chromatic Art in the Netherlands Motet. New York: Columbia University Press, 1946.

Ludwig, Friedrich, ed. *Guillaume de Machaut: Musikalische Werke*. 2 vols. Leipzig: Breitkopf und Härtel, 1926–9.

Mahrt, William. "Grammatical and Rhetorical Aspects of Troubadour Melodies." In *The Cultural Milieu of the Troubadours and Trouvères*, ed. Nancy van Deusen, 116–24. Ottawa: Institute of Mediaeval Music, 1994.

Marix, Jeanne, ed. *Les musiciens de la cour de Bourgogne au XVe siècle*. Paris: Droz, 1937.

McGee, Timothy. *The Sound of Medieval Song: Ornamentation and Vocal Style According to the Treatises*. Forthcoming.

Meier, Bernhard. *The Modes of Classical Vocal Polyphony*. Trans. Ellen S. Beebe. New York: Broude, 1988.

Michels, Ulrich. *Die Musiktraktate des Johannes de Muris*. Beihefte zum Archiv für Musikwissenschaft. Wiesbaden: Franz Steiner, 1970.

Nádas, John, and Agostino Ziino, eds. *The Lucca Codex: Codice Mancini Lucca, Archivio di Stato, MS 184, Perugia, Biblioteca Comunale Augusta, MS3065*. Lucca: Libreria Musicale Italiana, 1990.

Page, Christopher. *Discarding Images: Reflections on Music and Culture in Medieval France*. Oxford: Oxford University Press, 1993.

"The English *A Cappella* Heresy." In Tess Knighton and David Fallows, eds., *Companion to Medieval and Renaissance Music*, 23–9. London: Dent, 1992.

"Johannes de Grocheio on Secular Music: a Corrected Text and New Translation." *Plainsong and Medieval Music* 2 (1993), 17–42.

The Summa Musice: a Thirteenth-Century Manual for Singers. Cambridge: Cambridge University Press, 1991.

"A Treatise on Musicians from ?*c.* 1400: the *Tractatulus de differentiis et gradibus cantorum* by Arnulf de St. Ghislain." *Journal of the Royal Music Association* 117 (1992), 1–21.

Voices and Instruments of the Middle Ages: Instrumental Practice and Songs in France, 1100–1300. Berkeley and Los Angeles: University of California Press, 1986.

Parker, Ian. "Notes on the Chansonnier St. Germain des Prés." *Music and Letters* 60 (1979), 261–80.

Patterson, Lee. *Negotiating the Past: the Historical Understanding of Medieval Literature*. Madison: University of Wisconsin Press, 1987.

Perkins, Leeman with Howard Garey, eds. *The Mellon Chansonnier*. 2 vols. New Haven: Yale University Press, 1979.

Pirrotta, Nino. "On Text Forms from Ciconia to Dufay." In *Aspects of Medieval and*

Renaissance Music: a Birthday Offering to Gustave Reese, ed. Jan LaRue, 673–82. New York: Norton, 1966.

Planchart, Alejandro Enrique. "The Early Career of Guillaume Du Fay." *Journal of the American Musicological Society* 46 (1993), 341–68.

"Guillaume Du Fay's Benefices and his Relationship to the Court of Burgundy." *Early Music History* 8 (1988), 117–71.

"Notes on Guillaume Du Fay's Last Works." *Journal of Musicology* 13 (1995), 55–72.

"What's in a Name? Reflections on Some Works of Guillaume Du Fay." *Early Music* 16 (1988), 165–75.

Plumley, Yolanda. *The Grammar of 14th Century Melody: Tonal Organization and Compositional Process in the Chansons of Guillaume de Machaut and the Ars Subtilior.* New York: Garland, 1996.

Pope, Isabel, and Masakata Kanazawa, eds. *The Musical Manuscript Montecassino 871: a Neapolitan Repertory of Sacred and Secular Music of the Late Fifteenth Century.* Oxford: Clarendon Press, 1978.

Powers, Harold S. "Language Models and Musical Analysis." *Ethnomusicology* 24 (1980), 1–60.

"Mode." In *The New Grove Dictionary of Music and Musicians*, ed. Stanley Sadie, XII: 377–450. London: Macmillan, 1980.

Reaney, Gilbert. "Modes in the Fourteenth Century, in particular in the Music of Guillaume de Machaut." In *Organicae Voces: Festschrift Joseph Smits van Waesberghe*, 137–43. Amsterdam: 1963.

Reaney, Gilbert, ed. *Early Fifteenth-Century Music.* 7 vols. Corpus Mensurabilis Musicae 11. Rome and Stuttgart: American Institute of Musicology, 1955–83.

Reese, Gustave. *Music in the Renaissance.* New York: Norton, 1959.

Rehm, Wolfgang, ed. *Die Chansons von Gilles Binchois.* Musikalische Denkmaler 2. Mainz: Schott, 1957.

Codex Escorial: Chansonnier (Manuscript EscA). Documenta Musicologica 1, no. 2. Kassel: Bärenreiter, 1958.

Reidemeister, Peter. *Die Chanson-Handschrift 78 C 28 des Berliner Kupferstichkabinetts.* Munich: E. Katzbichler, 1973.

Riemann, Hugo. *History of Music Theory, Books I and II: Polyphonic Theory to the Sixteenth Century.* Ed. and trans. by Raymond H. Haggh. Lincoln, Nebr.: University of Nebraska Press, 1962.

Verloren gegangene Selbstverständlichkeiten in der Musik des 15.–16. Jahrhunderts: Die Musica Ficta; eine Ehrettung. Musikalisches Magazin 17. Langensalza: H. Bayer, 1907.

Robertson, D. W. *A Preface to Chaucer: Studies in Medieval Perspectives.* Princeton: Princeton University Press, 1962.

Rohloff, Ernst. *Die Quellenhandschriften zum Musiktraktat des Johannes de Grocheio.* Leipzig: Deutscher Verlag für Musik, 1972.

Sachs, Klaus-Jürgen. *Der Contrapunctus im 14. und 15. Jahrhundert: Untersuchungen zum Terminus, zur Lehre und zu den Quellen.* Beihefte zum Archiv für Musikwissenschaft 13. Wiesbaden: Franz Steiner, 1974.

"Die Contrapunctus-Lehre im 14. und 15. Jahrhundert." In *Die Mittelalterliche Lehre von der Mehrstimmigkeit.* Geschichte der Musiktheorie 5, ed. Frieder Zaminer, 199–208. Darmstadt: Wissenschaftliche Buchgesellschaft, 1984.

Schneider, Norbert J. "Die verminderte Quarte als Melodieintervall: Eine musikalische Konstante von Dufay bis Schönberg." *Schweizerische Musikzeitung* 120 (1980), 205–12.

Schoop, Hans. *Entstehung und Verwendung der Handschrift Oxford Bodleian Library, Canonici misc. 213.* Publikationen der Schweizerischen Musikforschenden Gesellschaft 2, vol. XXIV. Berne and Stuttgart: Paul Haupt, 1971.

Schrade, Leo, ed. *The Works of Guillaume de Machaut: Second Part.* Polyphonic Music of the Fourteenth Century 3. Monaco: L'Oiseau-Lyre, 1956.

Schubert, Johann. *Die Handschrift Paris, Bibl. Nat. Fr. 1591: Kritische Untersuchung der Trouvèrehandschrift R.* Frankfurt, 1963.

Seay, Albert. "The 15th-Century *Coniuncta*: a Preliminary Study." In *Aspects of Medieval and Renaissance Music: a Birthday Offering to Gustave Reese,* ed. Jan La Rue, 723–37. New York: Norton, 1966.

Slavin, Dennis. "'Binchois' Songs, the Binchois Fragment, and the Two Layers of Escorial A." Ph.D. diss., Princeton University, 1988.

"Questions of Authority in Some Songs by Binchois." *Journal of the Royal Musical Association* 117 (1992), 22–61.

"Some Distinctive Features of Songs by Binchois: Cadential Voice Leading and the Articulation of Form." *Journal of Musicology* 10 (1992), 342–61.

Snyder, John. "Non-Diatonic Tones in Plainsong: Theinred of Dover Versus Guido d'Arezzo." In *La Musique et le Rite Sacre et Profane,* ed. Marc Honegger and Paul Prevost, II: 49–6. Strasbourg: Assn. des publications près les Universités de Strasbourg, 1986.

Spanke, Hans. *Eine Altfranzösische Liedersammlung: der Anonyme Teil der Liederhandschriften KNPX.* Romanische Bibliothek 22. Halle: Max Niemeyer, 1925.

G. Raynauds Bibliographie des altfranzösischen Liedes. Rev. edn Hans Spanke. Leiden: E. J. Brill, 1955.

Steiger, Adrian V. "Das Berner Chansonnier-Fragment: Beobachtungen zur Handschrift und zum Repertoire." *Schweizer Jahrbuch für Musikwissenschaft* 11 (1991), 43–66.

Stevens, John. "Medieval Song." In *The New Oxford History of Music: the Early Middle Ages to 1300,* ed. Richard Crocker, 357–451. Oxford: Oxford University Press, 1990.

Words and Music in the Middle Ages: Song, Narrative, Dance and Drama, 1050–1350. Cambridge Studies in Music. Cambridge: Cambridge University Press, 1986.

Stone, Anne. "What is subtler about the ars subtilior?" Forthcoming.

"Writing Rhythm in Late Medieval Italy: Notation and Musical Style in the Manuscript Modena, Biblioteca Estense, Alpha. M. 5. 24." Ph.D. dissertation, Harvard University, 1994.

Strohm, Reinhard. *The Rise of European Music, 1380–1500.* Cambridge: Cambridge University Press, 1993.

Taruskin, Richard, ed. *Antoine Busnoys: the Latin-Texted Works.* 2 vols. New York: Broude, 1990.

Treitler, Leo. "Medieval Lyric." In *Models of Musical Analysis: Music Before 1600,* ed. Mark Everist, 1–19. Oxford: Blackwell, 1992.

"Music and Language in Medieval Song." In *The Medieval Lyric,* ed. Howell Chickering and Margaret Switten, 12–27. Mount Holyoke College, 1988.

"Tone System in the Secular Works of Guillaume Dufay." *Journal of the American Musicological Society* 18 (1965), 131–69.

Urquhart, Peter. "Cross-Relations by Franco-Flemish Composers after Josquin." *Tijdschrift van de Vereniging voor Nederlandse Muziekgeschiedenis* 43 (1993), 3–41.

"Three Sample Problems of Editorial Accidentals in Chansons by Busnoys and Ockeghem." Forthcoming.

Warren, Charles W. "Punctus Organi and Cantus Coronatus in the Music of Dufay." In *Papers read at the Dufay Quincentenary Conference, Brooklyn College, December 6–7, 1974*, ed. Allan W. Atlas, 128–43. Brooklyn: Brooklyn College, 1976.

Wegman, Robert C. "*Miserere supplicanti Dufay:* the Creation and Transmission of Guillaume Dufay's *Missa Ave regina celorum.*" *Journal of Musicology* 13 (1995), 18–54.

Werf, Hendrik van der. *The Chansons of the Troubadours and Trouvères: a Study of the Melodies and their Relations to the Poems.* Utrecht: A. Oosthoek's Uitgeversmaatschappij, 1972.

The Extant Troubadour Melodies: Transcriptions and Essays for Performers and Scholars. With Gerald A. Bond, text editor. Rochester: Van der Werf, 1984.

Werf, Hendrik van der, ed. *Trouvères-Melodien.* 2 vols. Monumenta Monodica Medii Aevi, vols. 11 and 12. Kassel: Bärenreiter, 1977 and 1979.

The Lyrics and Melodies of Gace Brulé. Text ed. and trans. by Samuel N. Rosenberg and Samuel Danon. Garland Library of Medieval Literature, series A, vol. 39. New York and London: Garland, 1985.

Werf, Hendrik van der and Wolf Frobenius. "Cantus Coronatus." In *Handwörterbuch der Musikalischen Terminologie.* Ed. Hans Eggebrecht. Wiesbaden: Fritz Steiner, 1983.

Wexler, Richard, with Dragan Plamenac, eds. *Johannes Ockeghem Collected Works: Volume III, Motets and Chansons.* Boston: American Institute of Musicology, 1992.

Wilkins, Nigel. "Some Notes on Philipoctus de Caserta (*c.* 1360?–*c.* 1435)." *Nottingham Mediaeval Studies* 8 (1964), 82–99.

Wilkins, Nigel, ed. *The Lyric Works of Adam de la Hale.* Corpus Mensurabilis Musicae 44. Dallas: American Institute of Musicology, 1967.

Wolf, Johannes. *Geschichte der Mensural-Notation von 1250–1460.* Leipzig: Breitkopf und Härtel, 1904. Reprint, Hildesheim: Breitkopf und Härtel, 1965.

Wright, Craig. "Dufay's *Nuper rosarum flores,* King Solomon's Temple, and the Veneration of the Virgin." *Journal of the American Musicological Society* 47 (1994), 395–441.

Music at the Court of Burgundy 1364–1419: a Documentary History. Brooklyn: Institute of Mediaeval Music, 1979.

"Tapissier and Cordier: New Documents and Conjectures." *The Musical Quarterly* 59 (1973), 177–89.

Yudkin, Jeremy. *Music in Medieval Europe.* Englewood Cliffs: Prentice Hall, 1989.

Zumthor, Paul. "De la circularité du chant." *Poétique* 2 (Paris: Seuil, 1970), 129–40.

Translated by R. Carter as "On the Circularity of Song." In *French Literary Theory Today: a Reader,* ed. Tzvetan Todorov. 179–91 (Cambridge: Cambridge University Press, 1982).

Manuscript sigla

Cambrai 1328	Cambrai, Bibliothèque Municipale, MS B. 1328
Chantilly 564	Manuscript Chantilly, Musée Condé 564
Dijon 517	Dijon, Bibliothèque de la Ville, MS 517

Escorial A	Escorial, Real Monasterio de San Lorenzo del Escorial, Biblioteca y Archivo de Música, MS V. III. 24
Faenza 117	Faenza, Biblioteca comunale, Cod. 117
Florence 2211	Florence, Biblioteca laurenziana, MS Archivio capitolare di San Lorenzo 2211
Florence P 26	Florence, Biblioteca Nazionale Centrale, MS Panciatichiano 26
Machaut MS A	Paris, Bibliothèque Nationale, MS f. fr. 1584
Machaut MS B	Paris, Bibliothèque Nationale, MS f. fr. 1585
Machaut MS C	Paris, Bibliothèque Nationale, MS f. fr. 1586
Machaut MS E	Paris, Bibliothèque Nationale, MS f. fr. 9221
Machaut MS F–G	Paris, Bibliothèque Nationale, MSS f. fr. 22545–22546
Machaut MS Vg	New York, Wildenstein Galleries, MS without shelfmark
MC 871	Montecassino, Badia, Codex 871 N
Modena A	Modena, Biblioteca Estense e universitaria, MS α. M.5.24
NL Uu 37	Utrecht, Bibliotheek der Rijksuniversiteit, MS 6 E 37/1, II (*olim* 1846)
Oporto 714	Oporto, Biblioteca Publica Municipale, MS 714
Oxford 213	Oxford, Bodleian Library, MS Canonici Misc. 213
PN 568	Paris, Bibliothèque Nationale, MS it. 568
PN 6771	Paris, Bibliothèque Nationale, MS n. a. f. 6771 (the "Reina Codex")
PN 23190	Paris, Bibliothèque Nationale, MS n. a. f. 23190 (the "Trémoïlle manuscript")
Reina Codex	See *PN 6771*
Strasbourg 222	Strasbourg, Bibliothèque Municipale, MS 222 C.22 (no longer extant)
Trémoïlle	See *PN 23190*
Trent 92	Trent, Museo Provinciale d'Arte, Castello del Buonconsiglio, MS 92
Troubadour MS W	Paris, Bibliothèque Nationale, f. fr. 844
Trouvère MS a	Rome, Vatican, MS Reg. lat. 1490
Trouvère MS K	Paris, Bibliothèque de l'Arsenal, 5198
Trouvère MS M	Paris, Bibliothèque Nationale, MS f. fr. 844
Trouvère MS O	Paris, Bibliothèque Nationale, MS f. fr. 846
Trouvère MS R	Paris, Bibliothèque Nationale, MS f. fr. 1591
Trouvère MS U	Paris, Bibliothèque Nationale, MS f. fr. 20050
Trouvère MS X	Paris, Bibliothèque Nationale, MS f. fr. 1050
Trouvère MS V	Paris, Bibliothèque Nationale, MS f. fr. 24406
Wolfenbüttel 287	Wolfenbüttel, Landesbibliothek, MS extrav. 287

Index